Crime in America

Some Existing and Emerging Issues

Jay S. Albanese
Niagara University

Robert D. Pursley
State University of New York
College at Buffalo

REGENTS/PRENTICE HALL
Englewood Cliffs, NJ 07632

Library of Congress Cataloging-in-Publication Data

Albanese, Jay S.
Crime in America : some existing and emerging issues / by Jay S. Albanese and Robert D. Pursley.
p. cm.
Includes bibiographical references and index.
ISBN 0-13-191446-4
1. Crime—United States. I. Pursley, Robert D. II. Title.
HV6789.A365 1993
364.973—dc20 92-9904
CIP

Acquisition Editor: Robin Baliszewski
Production Editors: Fred Dahl and Rose Kernan
Copy Editor: Rose Kernan
Designers: Fred Dahl and Rose Kernan
Prepress Buyer: Ilene Levy
Manufacturing Buyer: Ed O'Dougherty
Cover Designer: Marianne Frasco
Cover Photo: Frank Romero, 1984, "The Closing of Whittier Blvd.," oil on canvas, 6 × 10′.
Cartoon Artwork: From Original Drawings by William E. Phelps
Captions: Jay S. Albanese

A Division of Simon & Schuster
Englewood Cliffs, New Jersey 07632

Printed in the United States of America
10 9 8 7 6 5 4 3 2 1

ISBN 0-13-191446-4

Prentice-Hall International (UK) Limited, London
Prentice-Hall of Australia Pty. Limited, Sydney
Prentice-Hall Canada Inc., Toronto
Prentice-Hall Hispanoamericana, S.A., Mexico
Prentice-Hall of India Private Limited, New Delhi
Prentice-Hall of Japan, Inc., Tokyo
Simon & Schuster Asia Pte. Ltd, Singapore
Editora Prentice-Hall do Brasil, Ltda., Rio de Janeiro

Crime in America

Contents

CHAPTER 6

Developing Problems for the Administration of Justice? Aspect of AIDS and the Perinatal Drug Issue, 167

Section III Issues Affecting the Social Order, 197

CHAPTER 7

The Rebirth of Youth Gangs, 200

CHAPTER 8

Crimes Involving the Family, 225

Preface

As the curtain descends on the twentieth century, it would appear that our nation stands in a peculiar position. With the forseeable end of the Cold War and the Soviet menace we find ourselves poised on a new threshold—a time for America to pause from its international preoccupation and look inward. What we see is alarming. In many ways, America now appears more threatened from within than from without. Perhaps, Pogo, the cartoon character, says it best, "I have seen the enemy and they is us." Pogo may be providing us with a uniquely apocalyptic view of America and American society. One thing is certain: It doesn't take extraordinary insight to realize that serious domestic issues face the United States. What may be a little less obvious—but even more disconcerting to thoughtful observers of the American scene—is the realization that our nation may be weary to the task; in no mood to stiffen their sinews and summon up their blood. America's complex and daunting challenges may continue to metastasize until they overwhelm us or seriously weaken this great nation.

A major challenge is the seriousness of the nation's crime problem. Stripped of all its esoteric trappings and theory, crime is a unique barometer of the most basic character of a society and the people who comprise it. Scholars talk about crime as an expression of social change. While true, such insights provide little more than observation borne of human experience. Rapid social change and its effects can be seen by what has occurred in Europe's eastern bloc countries. After the dissolution of Soviet control, crime problems throughout the region increased dramatically. There can be no doubt that American society is also changing rapidly. With this has come some ominous overtones. Changes can be seen in the composition of the population, in a growing sense of alienation fueled by observable social and economic displacement with its inevitable backlash. It can be seen in the rising threat from focused yet often motiveless rage and violence such as the highly publicized acts of "wilding" in which violence becomes "fun" or an escape for bored and hedonistic-driven youth. One must also ponder the loss of moral conviction and ethical standards among all social strata. Couple this with population shifts, changes in technology and the crime-enhancing opportunities this will provide, and the threat of a permanently established underclass in our society—a Hobbe's world where life is always poor, nasty, brutish, and often short. Together, these are the ingredients providing both the impetus and the opportunities for new crimes and changes in existing crime.

And like society itself, many aspects of crime are changing and growing in their complexity. The growing internationalization of certain forms of crime is but one important example of change and the complexity this poses. Although America will continue to struggle with conventional and traditional predatory and property crimes, it confronts new forms of crime and variations on long-existing crimes; a situation that presents crime control challenges that are unprecedented in our history.

This book sets out to examine particular crimes which are either currently major issues or pose the potential for being important future concerns for our nation and the administration of justice. A bit of crystal ball gazing went into the selection of crimes to be examined. Some were obvious, others were chosen because they are developing important significance. Such forms of criminality as narcotics, new variations on juvenile gang violence, computer crimes, and white-collar offenses are examples of crime problems which our nation, its legal system, and the administrative machinery of justice is currently grappling. On the other hand, environmental crimes, the evolving nature of organized crime, terrorism (especially the domestic variety), family offenses, governmental corruption, bias crime, perinatal drug addiction, and an ominous aspect of AIDS need to be explored as forms of criminal activity—events and circumstances while less established as existing "crime problems" must be addressed for they certainly promise future significance.

The premise is a simple one: these forms of "crimes" will be important in the future because the issues and causes which underlie them show no promise of disappearing. We are not suddenly going to stamp-out corruption involving public officials, eradicate drug dependency, solve the AIDS problem or the growing social polarization in our country that seems to be increasing expressed in acts of sporadic violence directed at racial or ethnic groups and which threaten to grow into acts of domestic terrorism. There is also little hope at this time that our nation will solve the seemingly intractable social ills which contribute to the ravaging of families and neighborhoods and spawn ever-increasing violence among segments of our population. It also suggests that as long as these issues are not resolved and they continue to fester (or even worse, grow) as social problems, it is likely that the criminal law and the criminal-legal system will be increasingly called upon to deal with them. If this is the case, there are implications here that warrant an examination of these issues as criminal events.

Although it offers a few directions for needed change, this book poses no comprehensive answers to these complex existing and developing crime problems. While it is a chronicle of change, the authors realize their limitations as providers of solutions. What needs to be done, however, is to bring to the reader an appreciation for the complexity of the crimes examined and to provide an important and broad examination of the problems and issues they pose. However, in some cases even these are still undefined. But there must be a beginning. Perhaps as the sixteenth century philosopher and mathematician Descartes says, upon the knowledge of the problem rests any beginning of its solution. Let us hope his words prove to be prophetic for America and its people.

Acknowledgments

We are indebted to a number of people for their help and encouragement. The people from Prentice Hall must rank at the top of our list. Cathy Colucci supported the idea for this book from the beginning. Robin Baliszewski was our senior editor who was always patient, insightful, and available to iron out any wrinkles. We are also indebted to Rose Kernan and the production people at Inkwell Publishing Services who were able to get the book in print with amazing rapidity and with a minimum of last minute problems for the authors.

We want to thank those who reviewed the manuscript and offered some very positive and constructive assistance. Robert E. Bagley, John A. Conley, James A. Embree, Bette D. Fox, Joseph W. Lipchitz, Roslyn Myraskin, and Carl E. Russell each made thoughtful comments.

Finally, we wish to express our appreciation to our wives, Leslie and Nancy. They offered encouragement when required, criticism when justified, motivation when our efforts lagged, and love always. It is to them we dedicate this book.

About the Authors

JAY S. ALBANESE is Professor and Chair of the Department of Political Science and Criminal Justice at Niagara University. He received the B.A. degree from Niagara University and M.A. and Ph.D. from Rutgers University. He was the first Ph.D. graduate from the School of Criminal Justice at Rutgers. He is author of seven books, including *Organized Crime in America* and *Dealing with Delinquency*. Dr. Albanese was recipient of the Teaching Excellence and Campus Leadership Award from the Sears Foundation in 1990. He was a Visiting Professor at the School of Criminology at Simon Fraser University in British Columbia, Canada, and is a Past President of the Northeastern Association of Criminal Justice Sciences.

ROBERT D. PURSLEY is Professor in the Department of Criminal Justice at the State University of New York College at Buffalo. He holds a doctorate from the University of Georgia. His other books include *Managing Government Organizations* and *Introduction to Criminal Justice*. He has held previous faculty positions at Michigan State University and the University of Arkansas at Little Rock. He has served as the National Chairman of the Section on Criminal Justice Administration of the American Society of Public Administration.

Crime in America

SECTION I

ISSUES AFFECTING THE ECONOMIC ORDER

What distinguishes emerging crime problems of the future from those of the past is their complexity. The crime problem today is distinguished by crimes that involve more organization, technology, and fraud than ever before. Indeed, ''strong-arm'' robberies, and the other so-called ''street crimes'', are decreasing as part of a significant aging of the population, combined with a radical change in the opportunities available to commit crimes. Fewer people are carrying cash, fewer juveniles and young adults are around to steal it, desired products are taking new forms, and technology is making crime a more organized business. In fact, crime is becoming a growth industry. Unfortunately, it does not appear that the increasing average age of citizens makes them significantly less crime-prone than are younger citizens, but it *does* appear that that today's offender uses more guile, organization, and technology, while using less force, violence, and stealth.

This section of the book examines white collar crime, computer crime, and changes in organized crime to demonstrate how criminal activity is shifting from simple burglaries, larcenies, and drug sales, to more creative ways to violate the law. Methods that include complex fraudulent schemes, misuse of technology, and organized criminal cartels are becoming more common and also more devastating in their impact.

The objective of most (although not all) white collar, computer, and organized crimes is financial gain. Virtually all offenses of this nature have substantial economic impact. As these chapters will show, organized crimes in business, government, and illicit cartels cost many times the loss from conventional street crimes each year. The public is waking up to this fact, especially in a time of business recession, government debt, and a gloomy economic outlook for individuals.

Each chapter in this section provides precise definitions of the generic (and sometimes unclear) terms of white collar, computer. and organized crime. A unique typology of these offenses has also been included. The extent of these crimes, and how they are addressed by the criminal justice system, is examined for each of these categories of crime, as is the outlook for the future of these offenses and the criminal justice response.

Significant new information is included in these chapters that has not appeared elsewhere in any form. An ''ethical alternative'' for explaining and preventing white collar and computer crime is presented. A new typology of these crimes is introduced. The relation between technology and criminal opportunity for computer crime is examined in an innovative way. The prospects for reducing organized crime in the future based on shrinking illicit markets is explained, as is the tenuous relation among ethnicity, violence, and organized crime. In addition, shifts in organized crime activities are noted and predicted for the future based on the successful prosecutions of the last decade.

The reader should come away with a better understanding of white collar, computer, and organized crime, as well as insight into different ways to manage, adjudicate, and prevent these offenses in the future. Some ideas have already shown promise for the future, but many have not even been tried. The lessons of history, and the limits of our imagination, are all that stand between a future empty with despair about crime and one filled with hope for its reduction.

CHAPTER 1

The White Collar Crime Epidemic

CONTENTS

White collar crimes characterize the 1990s much in the same way street crimes characterized the 1960s. White collar crime has been increasing in volume, public concern, and in the legal response. Consider some noteworthy cases of recent years:

- Savings and Loan banks failed at an alarming rate during the late 1980s and early 1990s, many of which were due to fraud on the part of management. In what may be the largest fraud in U.S. history, the estimated bail-out cost is $500 billion.
- Toxic dumping at the Love Canal site in Niagara Falls resulted in evacuation of 1,300 families and a clean-up costing $250 million, initiating national outrage over waste disposal.
- Radiation leaks at Three Mile Island nuclear power plant provoked public concern over perceived negligence and the safety of nuclear power, when millions of dollars of damage resulted, compounded by fear of long-term effects of exposure to radiation.
- Vietnam veterans filed a class action suit alleging that exposure to a chemical defoliant during combat resulted in injury and death years later, resulting in an outcry over the long-term effects of exposure to hazardous materials.
- Ford Motor Company became one of the first companies ever to be prosecuted for criminal homicide for building the Ford Pinto, allegedly knowing there was a structural defect that caused the car to explode when hit at low speeds, provoking concern over corporate responsibility for product safety.
- Drexel, Burnham, Lambert, Inc., a Wall Street brokerage firm, plead guilty to securities fraud and was fined $650 million. Michael Milken, head of the company's junk-bond department, was sentenced to 10 years in prison.
- G.D. Searle stopped manufacture of IUD birth control devices due to 775 lawsuits arising from pelvic infections caused by the device.
- Exxon was fined $2 billion for overcharging for oil and gas during the energy crisis of the 1970s.
- Three executives of a silver-recovery plant were sentenced to 25 years in prison for the poisoning death of an employee due to improper safety measures.
- ''Insider trading'' scandals, where stocks were traded illegally based on information not available to the public, resulted in several fines of $25 million. Ivan Boeksy was sentenced to three years in prison and a $300 million fine.

These cases are examples of only a few of the major cases of the last two decades that, due to their size, scope, injury, and financial impact, pushed white collar crime into the public consciousness.

Given existing conditions, and social and economic trends already underway, white collar crime will undoubtedly grow in significance in the coming years. As will be discussed later in this chapter, white collar criminals are somewhat older than traditional criminals, due to the need for special opportunities to commit various kinds of frauds. Demographic trends in North America indicate that the median age of the population is increasing from the early 30s in 1990 to nearly 42 by the year 2050.[1] Combine this age factor with the growing number of corporate mergers which place more economic power (and the means of exploitation) in the hands of fewer individuals facing less competition. Add a nationwide recession, higher unemployment rates, and a relaxed regulatory environment in recent years, and the seeds of a white collar crime epidemic have been sown.

White collar crime is not an issue faced by a handful of states, but a crisis requiring action on the federal level. An outline of the scope of the problem, its causes, the government response, and potential long-term remedies are the focus of this chapter.

This chapter explains the definitions and illustrates the various types of white collar crimes. Their extent and causes are examined, as well as the criminal justice system response in the investigation and prosecution of these offenses. The outlook for the future also is assessed, considering the possible alternatives to reduce the incidence of these crimes in the years to come. This chapter also features some new arguments, that include:

- an "ethical" approach to understanding the causes of white collar crime; and
- how private citizens may become a significant law enforcement resource in the future.

It will be demonstrated that white collar crime is more varied, amorphous, and difficult to prevent than one might expect at first glance.

What is White Collar Crime?

It is easy to distinguish a mugging from embezzlement, but what about the difference between simple theft versus fraud? Or an injury resulting from a defective product versus an assault? The distinctions between white collar crimes and the so-called "street" crimes (i.e., homicide, rape, robbery, assault, burglary, larceny, arson) are not always clear. These two categories of offenses are not distinguishable by the harm caused to the victim, because frauds or unsafe products can cause much more injury and harm than any number of street crimes. They are also difficult to discern by the level of violence involved. Many street crimes, such as larceny and burglary, involve no personal confrontation, but conspiracy, extortion, or food and drug manufacturing violations can involve threats, injury, and even death. These facts have not been lost on the public, which has rated white collar crime as increasingly more serious than it has in past opinion surveys.[2] The distinctions between white collar crime and more traditional forms of crime, therefore, do not always lie in the nature of the victim, or violence, or injury. Instead, white collar crime is most distinguishable by *the manner in which it is carried out,* given the opportunities for commission. Such opportunity is often determined by one's position in society for, as we will see later, one cannot embezzle funds without first holding a position of financial trust, nor can one commit regulatory offenses without a requisite position in business or industry. As a result, it can be seen that *access* to financial or governmental resources provides the *opportunity* to commit white collar offenses, so they are distinguishable from conventional crimes in how they are accomplished.

Street crimes can be characterized by the use of force or stealth. *Force and/or stealth* is required for homicide, rape, robbery, assault, burglary, larceny, or arson. Alternatively, white collar crimes are characterized by planning and deceit. *Planning and deceit* are required to carry out a successful conspiracy, fraud, extortion, embezzlement,

"Wait a minute! Stop wasting the taxpayer's money. I'm not a *real* criminal."

forgery, or regulatory offense. White collar crimes can be defined, therefore, as *planned or organized* illegal acts of deceit. These acts can be committed by an individual, a group, or organization, and they are often carried out as a knowing, illegal departure from legitimate business activity. The objective can be personal enrichment or to advance the legitimate goals of an organization illegally. In addition, the victim can be a consumer, a business, a political entity, or the public welfare in general. To summarize, white collar crime can be defined as follows:

> A planned or organized illegal act of deceit committed by an individual or organization, usually conducted as a deviation from legitimate business or governmental activity, for personal or corporate gain.

The deviation from legitimate business can take place in three ways: nonfeasance, misfeasance, and malfeasance. *Nonfeasance* involves failing to perform a required act, such as not filing a tax return or acquiring a necessary permit. *Misfeasance* is failure to perform a required action properly, such as filing compliance reports inaccurately or altering information in a stockholders' report. *Malfeasance* is engaging in an act that is illegal by its nature, such as fraud and other forms of theft. Unlike street crimes, which often result from unplanned or random acts, white collar crimes require planning. The manifestations of white collar crime include several different types of offenses which can be classified into three distinct categories: organized crimes of fraud (i.e., embezzlement, extortion, forgery, fraud), regulatory offenses (i.e., administrative, environmental, labor, manufacturing, unfair competition violations), and offenses against public administration (i.e., bribery, obstruction of justice, official misconduct, and perjury). Each of these offenses will be explained in more detail later.

Although white collar crimes can be grouped according to their criminal intention (i.e., theft, obstruction or misuse of government procedures, or health, safety, and welfare violations in business and industry), *all* white collar crimes are distinguished by their *organization. Conspiracy* characterizes white collar crime, as it does all organized forms of criminal behavior (such as organized crime). A conspiracy is an agreement between two or more people to commit a criminal act, or to achieve a lawful objective in an illegal manner. The essence of conspiracy, therefore, is the planning of a crime. Like all crimes, conspiracy requires a specific act and a particular state of mind for liability. The act requirement is fulfilled by the *agreement* to commit the illegal act. The state of mind requirement is less clear, but court decisions over the years suggest that more than the agreement itself is necessary for liability. There must be some evidence that demonstrates the intention to carry out the illegal act planned. This has led to a series of court cases that attempt to make clear how conspiracy is to be applied in practice.

Perhaps the best way to see how the law of conspiracy applies to white collar crime in practice is to examine an actual case. The case of *U.S. v. Beech-Nut Nutrition Corp.*, 871 F.2d 1181 (2nd Cir. 1989), involved an alleged conspiracy to sell adulterated apple juice.

A Vice-President of Beech-Nut was told by his Director of Research that the company's purchase of apple juice concentrate from an outside supplier was adulterated (containing syrups and substances other than apples). The Director of Research conducted tests that demonstrated the supposed apple juice concentrate was largely sugar syrup. The Vice-President took no action. The company's plant manager in San Jose, California notified the Vice-President later that year that the apple concentrate he had received was "almost pure corn syrup." He recommended that Beech-Nut demand its money back, but the Vice-President instructed the manager to use that syrup in the company's mixed juices which were labelled "100 percent pure juice." Several other employees informed the Vice-President of problems with the apple juice during the next few years, except that these employees were criticized for not being "team players," and the scientists were called "Chicken Little." One of them was threatened with dismissal.

Nearly four years after the original detection of adulterated juice concentrate, a detective, hired by the Processed Apple Institute, visited the Vice-President at the Beech-Nut manufacturing facility in Canajoharie, New York and told him that the company was about to be sued for its use of adulterated concentrate. This prompted the Vice-President immediately to sever Beech-Nut's contract with the supplier and return whatever concentrate he could.

Unfortunately, Beech-Nut had an existing inventory worth millions of dollars. To avoid seizure of these products by New York State officials, the President of Beech-Nut had the juice transported to a warehouse in Secaucus, New Jersey during the night. The President offered unprecedented huge discounts to distributors to buy the juice, so that it would not be seized by the state or by Food and Drug Administration officals, which would result in a large economic loss to the company.

Ultimately, Beech-Nut negotiated with the government a national recall of only apple juice, excluding products in stores and mixed juice products. By the time of the recall, the President of Beech-Nut knew that nearly all the adulterated apple juice had been sold.

The President and Vice-President of Beech-Nut eventually were indicted and convicted, along with the suppliers of the tainted concentrate, for conspiracy to violate Food and Drug laws and 429 counts of introducing adulterated and misbranded apple juice into interstate commerce.

The Vice-President argued on appeal that there was no agreement between him and the suppliers of the concentrate. Therefore, the elements of conspiracy were not present. The U.S. Court of Appeals examined the law of conspiracy as it applied to this case. It found that a defendant is part of a conspiracy if there is "some indication that [he] knew of and intended to further the illegal venture," or that he "encouraged the illegal use of the goods or had a stake in such use." The Court found the evidence "ample to permit the . . . jury to infer that the Vice-President and the concentrate suppliers were participants in a single scheme of passing off bogus substances as pure 100 percent fruit juice."[3] Therefore, it can be seen that a formal agreement is not necessary for the crime of conspiracy.

In another conspiracy case, a physician in South Carolina ordered extremely large quantities of morphine from a supplier in Buffalo, who encouraged such sales through deep quantity discounts. The U.S. Supreme Court held that a tacit (unspoken) agreement is sufficient for the crime of conspiracy when the company *should have known* what was occurring with its morphine marketing, even if it did not.[4] As a result, a reasonableness standard is applied in cases like these. A *reasonable person* (i.e., the drug manufacturer) should have known in this situation that their marketing methods created a substantial risk that their drugs would be dispensed illegally, which is what the physician ultimately did. In fact, the Courts have recognized that "conspiracies are rarely evidenced by explicit agreements, and must almost always be proven by inferences that may be fairly drawn from the behavior of the alleged conspirators."[5]

Although no formal agreement is required among the conspirators, an overt act (legal or illegal) is required in furtherance of the conspiracy as evidence of intention to commit the planned offense.[6] The overt act might include taking steps to sell apple juice known to be adulterated, or otherwise acting on the conspiratorial agreement. It is also necessary for conspirators to agree voluntarily to violate the law, so you may not be convicted of engaging in a conspiracy against your will.[7] Once you voluntarily engage in the conspiracy, however, it is not possible to withdraw and escape legal liability, unless you can show evidence that you took action to defeat or disavow the purpose of the conspiracy.[8]

Although conspiracy is characteristic of white collar crime, one can also conspire to commit a murder or burglary, for example, but this type of conspiracy is less common because these street crimes typically involve little advance planning. Most conspiracy cases in recent years have involved illicit drug manufacture, importation, and sales. Conspiracy law also has been applied, though, to groups that blockade entrance to abortion clinics in violation of the law, for example, and to those who alter automobile odometers.[9] Several of the drug cases will be considered in Chapter 3 on organized crime.

The Extent of White Collar Crime

It is ironic that while we keep precise measures of street crimes in the United States, there is no accurate count of white collar crimes. This occurs despite the fact that the average robbery nets under $400 dollars, while the IRS estimates $1.2 *billion* is unreported on corporate tax returns each year. The largest robbery in history involved only $5 million, compared to Exxon's oil price-fixing scam noted previously which defrauded consumers of $1 billion, 200 times the amount of the largest robbery on record. In addition, approximately 20,000 people are victims of criminal homicide in the United States each year, but many times that number are killed and injured due to faulty products, pollution, and unsafe working conditions.[10] Perceptions of the seriousness of white collar crimes among the general public have been found to be generally commensurate with street crimes.[11] Therefore, it is not through a lack of public concern that more extensive data on white collar crimes are not collected.

Only limited data are available on the extent of embezzlements, forgery, and fraud in the *Uniform Crime Report* (UCR). The UCR counts crimes reported to the police for eight conventional ''street'' crimes and the number of people arrested for 19 other offenses. Arrests are a poor measure of crime because they reflect police and citizen reporting activity more than criminal activity. Nevertheless, it is not unreasonable to expect a high correlation between offenses known to the police and arrests for white collar crimes. One is not likely to report the crimes of embezzlement, forgery, or fraud until you realize you have been victimized; and once you know, you often have a good idea who victimized you.

What we do know is that arrest rates for white collar crimes have climbed during the last two decades. Arrest rates for fraud have increased 272 percent, for forgery and counterfeiting 35 percent, and embezzlement 15 percent.[12] These data indicate that either police have become more active in pursuing white collar crimes, citizens are reporting them more often, or there has been a genuine increase in the incidence of these offenses. It is likely that all three are occurring and that each has contributed to the rise in arrests for these offenses.

The large increase in arrests for fraud is especially notable when it is compared to arrest rates for conventional crimes of violence and against property over the same period. During the last two decades, arrest rates for violent crimes (i.e., criminal homicide, rape, robbery, and aggravated assault) have increased 53 percent and arrest rates for conventional property crimes (i.e., burglary, larceny, auto theft, and arson) have increased 28 percent. These increases pale in comparison to the 272 percent increase in the rate of fraud arrests.

Law enforcement agencies shows similar activity in forgery and counterfeiting cases. During the last 15 years, there has been a 21 percent increase in the number of counterfeit U.S. currency notes seized by the U.S. Secret Service. There also has been a 20 percent increase in the number of counterfeiting plant operations suppressed.[13]

Similarly, embezzlement and bank fraud investigations have kept the Federal Bureau of Investigation (FBI) active in recent years, given the predicament of hundreds of failing Savings and Loan banks. The FBI completed nearly 12,000 investigations of suspected embezzlement and fraud from federally insured banks, credit unions, and savings and loans in a single year, up 14 percent from a year earlier.[14]

Violations of regulatory offenses are not counted annually, so it is difficult to compare their incidence to those of the white collar crimes of theft. There is evidence to suggest, however, that these corporate offenses occur at high rates. A survey of 70 large corporations by Edwin Sutherland, more than 40 years ago, found that each had at least one violation in its history with an average of 14 violations per corporation.[15] A similar survey by Clinard and Yeager 15 years ago counted regulatory violations during a single year. They found more than 60 percent of the 582 largest U.S. corporations surveyed had at least one enforcement action initiated against them. Ninety (90) percent of corporations in the automobile, drug, and oil refining industries violated the law at least once. In addition, there was an average of more than four actions completed against each corporation that violated the law at least once.[16] Still another investigation of the 50 largest corporations in Canada over a 21-year period found every one to have committed at least one violation with an average of three violations per company.[17] These three investigations suggest that corporate entities violate the law at least as often as individuals.

Given rising arrest rates for embezzlement, forgery, and fraud over the last two decades, it is likely that this high level of activity in the detection and enforcement of white collar crime laws will continue in the future. Shifting demographics, combined with information regarding the age groups most commonly arrested for these white collar crimes, portend higher arrest rates in the future. Table 1.1 presents the age distribution for those arrested for embezzlement, forgery and fraud, compared to those arrested for conventional property crimes.

As Table 1.1 indicates, white collar crimes appear to be committed by persons older than those arrested for conventional street crimes. For example, 43 percent of arrests for the property crimes of burglary, larceny, auto theft, and arson are of person under age 20. This is more than twice the rate for embezzlement or forgery arrests, and more than four times the rate for fraud arrests.

Significantly, it can be seen that between 35 and 47 percent of all arrests for embezzlement (36 percent), forgery (35 percent), and fraud (47 percent) are of persons 30

TABLE 1.1 ARRESTS FOR WHITE COLLAR CRIMES BY AGE OF SUSPECT
(Compared to Arrest Rates for Conventional Crimes)

	Embezzlement	*Forgery*	*Fraud*	*Street Crimes*
Under 20 yrs	19%	19%	10%	43%
20–29	45	47	44	31
30–39	24	26	31	17
40+	12	9	16	9

Compiled from the U.S. Department of Justice, *Crime in the United States*, Washington, D.C.: U.S. Government Printing Office, 1989. (Figures rounded to nearest whole number.)

years and older, whereas only 26 percent of arrests for conventional property crimes are in this age group. As one might guess, the planning and deceit required for white collar crimes, as well as the necessary opportunities for their commission, make them best suited for older offenders.

If one combines this information with the fact that the median age in the population is rising, it is likely that arrests for these white collar crimes will continue to escalate. Population projections by the U.S. Bureau of the Census predict a declining number of young people in the population (due to low birth and immigration rates) and an increasing proportion of older people (due to the aging "baby boom" generation and low mortality rates). In 1990, 10 percent of the U.S. population was under 25 years of age; this will drop to nine percent by the year 2000, and rise only slightly by 2010. On the other hand, 25 percent of the population was between 35 and 54 years of age in 1990, and this group should increase in size to 40 percent of the population by 2000 and stay close to that size through the year 2010.[18]

Economic changes as well may be predictive of future changes in white collar crime. More industries, such as automobile manufacturing, oil, home appliances, computers, entertainment, and many others, are increasingly dominated by fewer companies, as small companies are acquired by larger ones. This ultimately results in a less competitive environment and creates opportunities for price-fixing, bid-rigging, and other monopolistic practices illegal in a free enterprise economy.[19] Another aspect of the economy with implications for the future is the phenomenal growth of the service sector. Fewer companies are engaged in manufacturing, while many more are offering services such as "900" telephone services, physical fitness, counseling, legal services, among many others. One only has to watch television for a single day to witness the commercials that have grown in length from 30 seconds to 30 minutes or more to convince the public it needs services it had heretofore lived without. Many of these service companies are new, small and survive only through "800" and "900" telephone lines and credit-card numbers. The ephemeral nature of some of these companies, combined with the lack of regulation of many of these businesses, leaves room for fraudulent conduct. The dramatic increase in the population group that accounts for a significant proportion of arrests for white collar crimes, the declining competition in major industries due to mergers and acquisitions, and the unchecked growth of a sprawling service economy, suggest this high level of concern and activity in white collar crime will continue into the next century.

The Causes of White Collar Crime

When a white collar crime occurs, or a suspect is arrested, for a large fraud, illegal toxic dumping, or other serious offense, people want to know, "How could somebody do that?" Why do individuals find it necessary to engage in crime to enrich themselves, their company, or to gain some other advantage? Most people respond by saying, "Greed!" But greed explains nothing. There are many greedy people who do not break the law, and what makes a person greedy anyway? Such "explanations" do nothing more than provide a rationalization to the observer without giving the problem more serious thought.

Serious efforts to explain crime, historically, are of two types. One type of explanation emphasizes rational decison making. According to this view, people freely choose to violate the law, because it brings them pleasure (usually financial gain or advantage) and the prospect of pain (i.e., apprehension) is low. This "pain-pleasure" principle runs through much of the criminological literature and is known as the "classical" school of thought.[20]

The other type of explanation places more emphasis on factors that influence the offender to act in a certain way. Whether illicit behavior is learned from others, or promoted by economic conditions, these explanations generally look outside the individual for the causes of crime.[21] According to these theories, crime will be reduced only through mitigating the influences that promote criminal behavior. This is known as "positivism" in criminology. Neither of these explanations has proven entirely satisfactory in explaining white collar crime, and an alternative approach is proposed here.

The Positive Approach

The term "white collar crime" was invented by sociologist Edwin Sutherland who wrote a book of the same name in 1949. He used this term in response to what he saw was criminology's focus on poverty and poor economic opportunities as the primary cause of crime up to that time. It was Sutherland's belief that a great deal of crime is committed by those who are not poor and do not suffer economic deprivation. The exclusion of this group from the study of criminology was, to Sutherland, a "bias . . . quite as certain as it would be if the scholars selected only red-haired criminals for study and reached the conclusion that redness of hair was the cause of crime."[22] Instead, Sutherland argued that crime was democratically distributed among *both* the wealthy and the poor. He claimed that crimes are learned in the same way as you learn anything else: by association with those who approve of such illicit behavior and by isolation from those who perceive it unfavorably. Sutherland argued that white collar (and street) crimes occur "if and only if, the weight of favorable definitions (to crime) exceeds the weight of the unfavorable definitions."[23]

An example provided by Sutherland of this theory of "differential association" was an interview with a shoe salesman who recounted a lecture given him by the shoestore manager.

> My job is to move out shoes, and I hire you to assist in this. I am perfectly glad to fit a person with a pair of shoes if we have his size, but I am willing to misfit him if it is necessary in order to sell him a pair of shoes. I expect you to do the same. If you do not like this, someone else can have your job. While you are working for me, I expect you to have no scruples about how you sell shoes.[24]

Through this example, Sutherland hoped to illustrate how otherwise conforming individuals "learned" to bend or break the rules. He used several other examples to show how employees in several other professions were "pressured" to ignore law violations, or to go along with past practice, even if it was unlawful. This pressure has also been manifested in several notable cases, such as B.F. Goodrich's cover-up of a defective aircraft brake it had designed and a price-fixing conspiracy among electrical equipment manufacturers.[25]

While it is true that association with those who view illicit behavior as "OK," can *influence* a person's behavior, it clearly does not *determine* it. In the same way, a person's isolation from others who might frown on a questionable activity may lead him or her in a certain direction, but it does not *cause* that behavior. What Sutherland's theory shortchanges is individual volition. Even in the face of pressure, a person must *decide* to go along the easiest route or to make his or her own path. Sutherland's explanation offers an example, therefore, of how learning principles can *influence* someone's behavior to violate the law, but it does not follow that learning is either *necessary or sufficient* to explain an individual instance of white collar crime.

Another explanation of white collar and organized crimes was offered by Dwight Smith, who argues that organized crimes result from "the same fundamental considerations that govern [legitimate] entrepreneurship."[26] Smith suggests that the only difference between a legitimate banker and a loanshark, for example, is the (often arbitrary) interest rate charged. All organizations, legal and illegal, strive to survive and to make a profit. The "task environment" of these organizations puts pressure on them through inevitable problems with suppliers, customers, regulators, or competitors. Uncertainties posed by these influences can result in criminal activities, if these challenges cannot be met legally (while also insuring survival and profit of the organization).

Like Sutherland, Smith cites *influences* that can result in *pressure* toward illegal activities. These same pressures, however, can cause businesses to redouble their efforts, change markets or products, or to engage in other non-criminal alternatives. Therefore, Smith's theory of enterprise offers *possible* factors that could influence the decision to commit a crime, but these factors do not make the decision to violate the law.

Another attempt to explain criminal behavior in the positive tradition is "neutralization" theory, originally posited by Sykes and Matza.[27] According to this view, the harm caused by criminal acts is neutralized in the minds of the perpetrators prior to their commission. Denial of the extent of injury caused, responsibility for the harm, and higher justification for the act are examples of techniques of neutralization. There is empirical evidence that demonstrates that white collar criminals use these techniques to "justify" illegal acts to themselves in many cases.[28] Nevertheless, such a theory explains *how* these crimes are committed, rather than *why* they exist. Techniques of neutralization, like differential association, an organization's "task environment" and other positive theories are useful in explaining the *process* of criminal activity, but they do not explain its *origin* satisfactorily.

The Classical View

A recent attempt to explain white collar crime in the classical tradition was proposed by Hirschi and Gottfredson. They argue, as Sutherland did, that white collar crimes can be explained in the same manner as conventional crimes. Their theory of criminality finds crime to result from "the tendency of individuals to pursue short-term gratification in the most direct way with little consideration for the long-term consequences of their acts."[29] Indicators of this tendency, they argue, "include impulsivity, aggression, activity level, and lack of concern for the opinion of others." As a result, "people high on this tendency are relatively unable or unwilling to delay gratification."[30]

Unlike other explanations of crime, which give too much emphasis to the affect of various external influences on behavior, Hirschi and Gottfredson argue that the tendencies they identify "do not lead ineluctably to crime." Instead, crimes require "physical opportunity and immunity from immediate punishment" in addition to the tendencies they identify. This explanation of crime is based on the "assumption that human behavior is motivated by the self-interested pursuit of pleasure and avoidance of pain."[31]

Unfortunately, Hirschi and Gottfredson's "tendencies" characterize not only criminals but many non-criminals as well, including most juveniles and professional athletes (i.e., they are also impulsive, active, and aggressive). Most problematic, however, is their notion of a criminal "tendency" toward short-term gratification with little regard for consequences. There exist many examples of white collar offenders who acted in what they believed to be the long-term interests of their company or the public,[32] and the fact that most individuals do not violate the law, even when given the opportunity, indicates that a remarkable number of people choose to exercise their free-will in a non-criminal direction. This occurs despite the fact that the object desired has value and that the odds of apprehension are low. Furthermore, it is not clear where these "tendencies," identified by Hirschi and Gottfredson, come from and, if they do exist, why they are not manifested by most people who face criminal opportunities.

An Ethical Alternative

Whether one chooses to place most emphasis on learning, pressures in the business environment, or on criminal tendencies, is not there a failure of an individual to choose the proper course of conduct at the root of all crime? Positivists claim that by improving bad or "deviance-producing" external influences, crime can be reduced. These conditions undoubtedly play some role but, as shown above, they provide the background, rather than the reason, for the criminal decision. Classicists also come to the wrong conclusion. If criminal behavior is the result of mere pain-pleasure decisions, a way to control it effectively would be to increase the certainty of apprehension. Dramatic increases in the number of laws, law enforcement officials, and a loosening of procedural constraints in recent years, however, has had no apparent affect on the incidence of serious crime.

The alternative proposed here lies in recognition of three facts:

1. External factors play a role in influencing some people to engage in crime, although these factors obviously do not *cause* the crime by themselves;
2. A freely willed decision lies at the base of virtually all criminal behavior, although there is no ''tendency'' to engage in crime, controlled by the possibility of apprehension;
3. The prevention of crime lies in reducing contributory external factors to the extent possible, *and* by altering the perceived ''pleasure'' derived from law violation.

As shown above, some attempts to explain white collar crimes lay the blame at bad influences, a bad environment, or criminal tendencies. Clearly, these factors are static attributes of an individual or his or her environment. Biographical attributes cannot cause crime. They may help one to justify (or blame) a bad decision, but they do not make the decision for the actor.

The answer lies in discovering how to help people to make non-criminal choices. The most effective way is also the most obvious: ''Where do people learn to make ethical decisions?'' People are rarely taught how to make proper decisions. How should one act, when faced with conflicting demands? Is there always a proper or correct way to make a decision? In the arena of white collar crime, there exists a growing number of examples of business and professional decisions that violate the law.[33] The principles of ethical decision-making are not taught to most people, as the educational process assumes that knowledge of facts implies knowledge of what to do with them. Given the pressures of the marketplace, ''pro-criminal'' definitions within industry, and the wide availability of techniques of neutralization, how is it that many choose to conduct business honestly and fairly, while others are not able to resist the pressures to ''succeed'' at all costs? What is the process by which people choose to deny themselves an immediate gain for a higher principle? Most people have no education or experience in *prioritizing* values when they are placed in difficult situations. Instead, people do what often becomes second-nature in the business community: operate quickly, efficiently, and always in the best interests of the company. Therefore, shortcuts are chosen, safety is secondary, and the law is ignored, when it comes between profit and self-interest.

The method by which ethical principles are taught and internalized can vary, but it is not an overstatement to say that most people have little knowledge of ethics, and are incapable, generally, to think through a business decision in an ethical context. The ability to distinguish higher principles from immediate rewards, and the welfare of society from corporate well-being, for example, is a skill rarely transmitted through contemporary business education, professional certification processes, or corporate training. Incentives must be offered to spur a greater national commitment toward ethical decision making in business and government. As James Coleman has observed, "any effort to deal with the problem of white collar crime on this level must be aimed at changing the 'ethical climate' within the corporations and the government."[34]

It can be said that positivists lay too much blame for crime on the doorstep of social and economic conditions, whereas the classicists give too much credence to the impact of threatened penalties. Inculcation of ethical principles, alternatively, would redirect the positivists' focus on external conditions to individual responsibility for decisions to commit crimes. In a similar way, it would redirect the classical focus on punishment to the "pleasure" portion of the pain-pleasure principle. When one internalizes ethical principles, criminal conduct is prevented when pleasure is no longer derived from crime, due to the understanding and value placed on the crime's wrongfulness and impact.

If everyone received training in ethical decision making, it does not mean, of course, that people would no longer commit crimes. It would mean, however, that people could be held liable for their bad decisions without the continual recriminations and debate over "who" or "what" was responsible for their behavior. Individuals would be held responsible for their own poor decisions with the knowledge that they did in fact know better. This approach is distinguished from the positivist approach in its focus on individual responsibility for personal decisions, rather than on external influences. It is distinct from classical approaches in that it focuses not on the certainty of apprehension or on punishment, but rather on the "pleasure" portion of the pain-pleasure principle. That is to say, crime would be avoided more often due to its failure to bring pleasure (by applying the principles of ethics), rather than due to the fear of pain through apprehension and punishment.

White collar crimes are especially amenable to this approach because they involve planning, rationality, and status. Unlike street crimes, which are more random, and committed more often by uneducated people, white collar criminals are easier to reach. Attempts to inculcate ethical principles find a more receptive audience among those who contemplate their actions, consider the consequences, and have a degree of social status by the nature of their employment. As will be discussed later, attempts to reduce white collar crime through the threat of criminal penalties has had limited success, and dramatic changes in the business environment to reduce the "pressures" toward criminal behavior are unlikely in the forseeable future. Therefore, the ethical approach is an alternative that may be pursued in the future.

White Collar Crime and the Criminal Justice System

When one reads any criminal code, it is unlikely that the phrase "white collar crime" will appear. This is because white collar crime has become a colloquial term to describe a number of specific types of crimes. In this section, the precise offenses that comprise "white collar crime" will be defined, using examples drawn from recent court cases, and the criminal justice response to these offenses will be assessed.

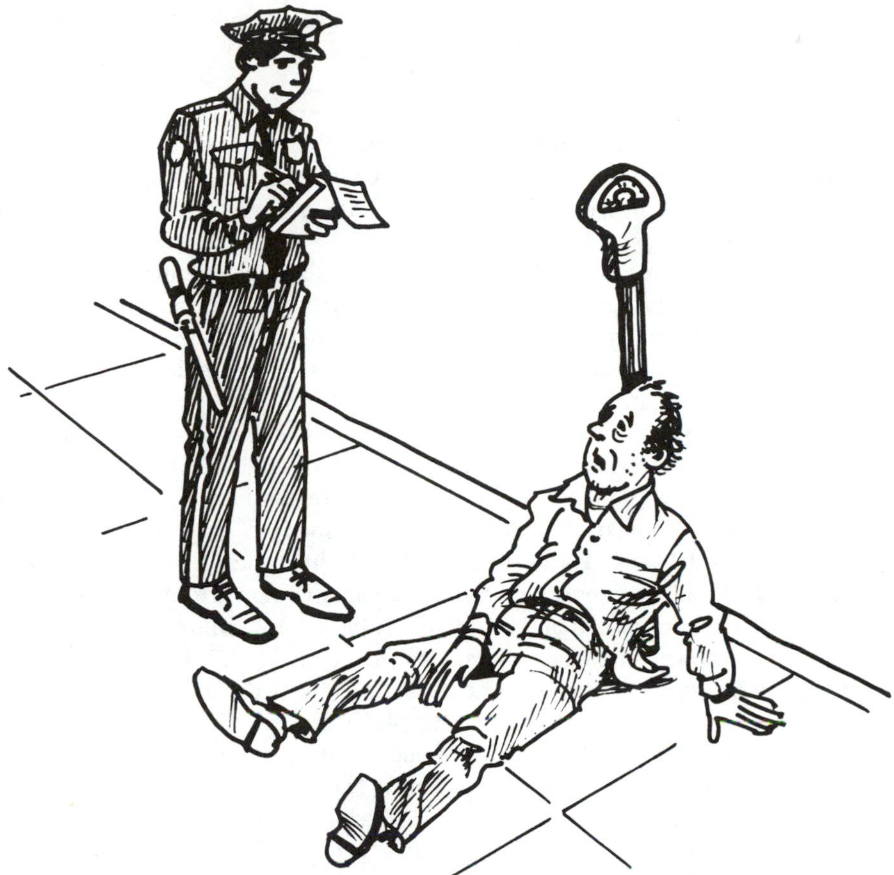

"Yes, officer. It was *more* serious than a mugging. It was a mail-order scam, followed by a 900-number telephone scam, that was followed by the savings and loan scam. I guess I *have* been mugged!"

White Collar Crime in Criminal Law

As noted earlier, white collar crime consists of three general types of offenses: organized crimes of fraud (embezzlement, extortion, forgery, fraud), offenses against public administration (bribery, obstruction of justice, official misconduct, perjury), and regulatory offenses (administrative, environmental, labor, manufacturing, unfair trade practices). The definition, and examples, of each of these offenses follows.

Crimes of Fraud

White collar crimes of fraud are distinguished in their attempt to obtain money or property under false pretenses. There are four ways to use some degree of planning and deceit or fraud to achieve this objective. The crimes of embezzlement, extortion, forgery, and fraud constitute the four white collar crimes where theft is the objective.

Embezzlement. Embezzlement is stealing property entrusted to you. Funds taken without permission by bank tellers, cashiers, or salespersons are examples of this violation of financial trust. Embezzlement can be defined, therefore, as the purposeful misappropriation of property entrusted to one's care, custody, or control to which you are not entitled.

The misappropriation of property required for embezzlement must be made without the consent of the owner and with the specific intention to defraud the owner. Because the property must belong to another, a person cannot embezzle property he or she owns jointly.[35] An actual case from the recent savings and loan crisis illustrates how the law of embezzlement applies in practice.

Harold Ticktin was President of the Manning Savings and Loan Corporation in Chicago. During the early 1980s, the net worth of the bank (funds on reserve) began to decline below the minimum required by federal regulations. Faced with the prospect of a forced merger or takeover, Ticktin engaged in a variety of maneuvers to manipulate the net worth of the bank. For example, he bought interest in five Texas oil wells for $2.25 million and sold the interests on credit to another company for $4.5 million. Ticktin used this transaction to record an immediate profit of $2.2 million, although the purchasing company was only eight days old and had assets of $1,000. In addition, the oil interests were purchased with a written understanding that if the oil wells did not produce, the purchaser did not have to pay the bank $4.5 million.

In another transaction, Ticktin bought and sold condominiums. He purchased 123 condominiums and 19 mortgages in Forest Park, Illinois for $3.4 million. He simultaneously sold them in multiple units to 10 purchasers, paying the realtors a commission of $10,000 per unit. Ticktin set the price and financed 100 percent of the sales, loaning 80 percent to each purchaser, and allowing a second mortgage to each purchaser for the remaining 20 percent. The appraisals of the units "were rife with inaccuracies and misrepresentations," and they were overpriced. The bank actually lent more than 100 percent of the market value of the property. In the midst of these transactions, Ticktin received bonuses for his "fantastic" and "exemplary" work in keeping the bank solvent, even though the bank was not solvent, and the board of directors of the bank was "dominated by Ticktin's family."

Ticktin was convicted of embezzlement for these, and other, loans he made, but he appealed, arguing that he should not be convicted for simply making loans without collateral. He felt he had made bad business decisions, not criminal acts. The U.S. Court of Appeals held that "an unsecured or undersecured loan can be misapplication of funds if made with intent to defraud or injure the bank." The Court found "ample evidence for the jury to believe . . . that Ticktin embarked on a series of fraudulent schemes to keep Manning Savings and Loan artificially alive" and concluded that "Ticktin was able to receive the bonuses because of his pattern of fraudulent conduct." As a result, there was "sufficient evidence for the jury to find that by accepting the bonuses Ticktin converted [the bank's] funds to himself with the intent to defraud or injure Manning Savings and

Loan''.[36] Even though Ticktin's bonuses were authorized by the bank, he was still held liable for embezzlement due to his intent to defraud or injure the bank.

Other embezzlement cases have made it clear that the crime is complete once the misuse of funds occurs. A defendant's repayment of the funds taken is not a defense to the crime, nor is the defendant's intention to return the money.[37] The offense of embezzlement holds great importance due to the increasing complexity of society where many people now hold the property of others without owning it. The nature of banking, lending, renting, and investing are sure to create additional opportunities for embezzlement in the future.

Extortion. Like embezzlement, extortion is a crime of theft involving a unique method. Extortion is obtaining property from another, using future threats of physical injury, property damage, or exposure to ridicule, criminal charges, or abuse of public office. The threat of *future* intimidation of some kind distinguishes extortion from robbery which involves the *immediate* threat of force. Extortion can characterize certain kinds of either white collar and organized crime, depending on the precise circumstances. Examples of extortion in an organized crime context are presented in Chapter 3.

Originally, extortion was limited to those holding public office, but most states now have laws that include private individuals as well. ''Blackmail'' is often used as a synonym for extortion. Extortion requires the intent to commit the crime, together with an overt act towards its completion, although it is not necessary for the threatened action to be carried out to be held liable.

A case illustrating the elements of extortion is *United States v. Campo,* 774 F.2d 566 (2nd Cir. 1985). Campo was a patrolman in the New York City Police Department, assigned to the Chelsea section of Manhattan's West Side. The Funhouse Disco had opened in this area, catering to a young crowd. It was open only on weekends until 6 to 8 A.M. The disco attracted ''large and often unruly crowds,'' so a number of bouncers were employed. Many cars parked illegally near the disco. In addition, a number of assaults took place in the area. Officer Campo and his partner were summoned by one of the bouncers, Angelo, who told them ''he would appreciate their giving the block as much attention as they could because of recurring fights and double parking.''

Campo and his partner spent as much time as they could near the disco, except when they answered calls for service elsewhere in the precinct. Toward the end of the shift one morning at 8 A.M., Angelo again waived the police car over, thanked the officers for staying around, and dropped $50 through the window of the patrol car. The officers discussed whether to keep the money. They finally decided to split it between them.

After this incident, Campo and his partner worked the same shift about 10 times, with a total take of $250 each. The officers ''habitually spent a large portion of such shifts near the Funhouse,'' and Campo's partner testified that they ''anticipated getting paid by Angelo.'' Near the end of each shift, they returned to the Funhouse as it was closing and Angelo would pay them. On one night, the officers were kept busy by other calls and Angelo declined to pay them at the end of the shift because they had not been visible outside the disco. Otherwise, the officers were paid each time they spent considerable time near the Funhouse. An officer who took payments from Angelo on other nights discussed with Campo how late the Funhouse was staying open into Sunday morning, and the payoff was then raised to $75 on that shift.

Campo was convicted of extortion for receiving benefits as a public official. He appealed on grounds that there was no proof that he *induced* the payments. Without such an inducement, the crime is bribery (discussed further in Chapter 5), rather than the more serious offense of extortion. The U.S. Court of Appeals affirmed Campo's conviction, finding sufficient evidence of inducement. The Court found that Campo returned to the Funhouse at the end of each shift, which a jury could find "the sole purpose of returning was to get the money from Angelo." Such "repeated, deliberate seeking of payment constitutes a request, demand, or solicitation" beyond the mere acceptance of benefits. This was found "more than sufficient" to prove Campo induced the payments. In addition, Campo knew that if he did not spend adequate time near the disco, he would not be paid. The Court found this a *quid pro quo,* which was "also sufficient to prove inducement".[38]

It can be seen that harm need not be threatened for extortion. Rather, any form of intimidation suffices. In this case, it can be inferred from the officers' conduct that there was an unspoken promise that the disco would be "protected" and not summoned or fined for parking, noise, or curfew violations. In addition, Campo and his partner solicited a benefit for abusing their roles as police officers. This is the essense of extortion; it is an attempt to benefit from a threatened future act or from abuse of a public office.

Forgery. Forgery is a crime of theft that requires making false legal documents or altering existing documents with intent to defraud. It can be distinguished from *uttering,* which is the *passing* of forged documents. As a result, forgery and uttering are separate crimes. A specific type of forgery is *counterfeiting,* which is the forging of U.S. currency.

Forgery is a felony in most states, regardless of the nature or value of the document forged. The heavy reliance upon checks, stocks, bonds, leases, licenses, and credit cards in today's society make forgery a growing legal problem.

An interesting court case involved falsified odometer readings on cars. Al Davis' wholesale automobile dealership in Manheim, Pennsylvania regularly sent Federal Express packages containing certificates of title to Buddy's Auto Sales in Chesapeake, Virginia. The owners of Buddy's Auto sales would then apply for Virginia certificates of title for those cars in the name of *their* dealership at the mileage listed on the titles, which already had been altered.

The "washed" Virginia titles were then returned to Davis, who paid $100 per title for this service. Davis distributed these "washed" titles back to area dealers, charging them each a fee for the "title washing service." Eventually, these cars with rolled-back odometers and falsified titles were sold to unknowing customers.

Davis, and others, were caught and convicted of counterfeiting automobile titles. They appealed on grounds that "although the 'washed' certificates may contain incorrect information, they were not 'falsely made' '' because they were validly issued by the Commonwealth of Virginia. Therefore, they argued, the titles were ''genuine documents'' that happened to contain ''a false statement of fact,'' and this is not sufficient for the crime of forgery.[39]

The U.S. Court of Appeals affirmed the convictions, holding that mileage is a ''material part'' of a certificate of title. Documents validly issued, but containing false information, are ''falsely made'' under law. The fact that the title was valid, except for the mileage, ''does not vitiate the fraud that is foisted on the unsuspecting customer'' when the falsely made document is used as the basis for a sale.[40]

Forgery requires only some part of the document be forged. Therefore, a person who forges an entire document incurs the same liability as someone who forges only the signature. It is only necessary that the falsification invalidate the entire document, and that the document have legal significance, regardless of economic value (whether it be a title, check, passport, or diploma).

Fraud. The last white collar crime involving theft is fraud. The essence of fraud is larceny by trick; that is, possession of property obtained through deception. There are many kinds of fraud including false advertising, bankruptcy fraud, and criminal impersonation. The object of frauds is always the same: to obtain property through false representations.

In *United States v. Zalman,* 870 F.2d 1047 (6th Cir. 1989), the U.S. Court of Appeals reviewed the conviction of an attorney who arranged bogus marriages. Bruce Zalman, an attorney in Louisville, charged between $1,000 and $1,500 to arrange fictitious marriages for Iranians so they could gain permanent resident status in the United States after their temporary student visas expired.

In one instance, Zalman arranged a delusive marriage between an Iranian student and one of his divorce clients. Zalman rehearsed the ''couple'' regarding a course of conduct necessary to mislead officials of the Immigration and Naturalization Service (INS). This advice included misleading information on INS application forms, how to respond to INS inquiries, and how to project the appearance of a valid marriage, such as moving the wife's belongings into the husband's residence and appearing publicly together to promote the ''charade'' of a valid marriage. The wife then filed for divorce after six months, once the Iranian's permanent residency status was obtained. The wife was compensated $1,000 for her time and trouble.

Zalman was convicted of several counts of arranging these fraudulent marriages because they involved making false statements to a government agency (the INS). The convictions were upheld because Zalman and his clients' conduct required commission of a fraud on the U.S. government through false and misleading statements. The mens rea requirement was satisfied by the specific intention to obtain property of value (i.e., marriage to a U.S. citizen solely to obtain permanent residency status).

As this case illustrates, most fraud cases involve either false representations or concealment of relevant facts. To incur liability, it is necessary that the representation or concealment be intentional, and not just mistaken.

Crimes Against Public Administration

The second category of white collar crimes can be called "crimes against public administration," inasmuch as they are most often committed by those who have some connection with the government (e.g., employees, elected officials, or witnesses in an official proceeding). The four crimes in this category include: bribery, official misconduct, obstruction of justice, and perjury. The elements of these crimes are discussed only briefly here as numerous examples are provided in Chapter 5 on public integrity offenses.

Bribery occurs when one voluntarily solicits or accepts any benefit in exchange for influencing an official act. Unlike most offenses, both the briber and receiver are liable under bribery law. Obstruction of justice takes place when one intentionally impairs a lawful government procedure by means of intimidation or through any independent unlawful act. Examples would include the failure to respond to a subpoena, jury tampering, destruction of evidence, or any attempt to impair, prevent, or interfere with a legal government procedure where there is a legal duty to cooperate.[41] Official misconduct occurs where a public servant knowingly performs an unauthorized official act, or fails to perform a legal duty, with intent to receive a benefit or injure or deprive another. The nature of the misconduct can vary, but it must be known to be unauthorized. In a New York State case, a court clerk agreed to issue a pistol permit only if the applicant's friend would have sex with him.[42] Most cases of this type involve a public official attempting to misuse his or her office for personal advantage. Perjury is intentional false swearing under oath at an official proceeding. As long as the false testimony is intentional and material to the proceeding, a person is liable for the crime of perjury.

Regulatory Offenses

The third, and final, category of white collar crimes is regulatory offenses. These are laws designed to insure fairness and safety in the conduct of business of politics. They are usually applied to corporations and can be grouped into five categories: administrative violations, environmental violations, labor violations, manufacturing violations, and unfair trade practices.

Regulatory offenses are enforced by particular regulatory agencies assigned responsibility for overseeing specific facets of commerce and government. Alleged violations are usually heard in administrative hearings, and only repeated or severe violations generally result in criminal cases. Nevertheless, most regulatory violations can incur criminal penalties, making them part of the criminal law.

Administrative violations involve failure to comply with regulatory agency requirments or court orders. For example, the Federal Election Campaign Act requires those candidates running for federal office to disclose the source and amounts of contributions to their campaigns to insure fairness and to prevent undue influence in the election process. The regulatory agency responsible for enforcement is the Federal Election Commission.

Likewise, the Securities and Exchange Commission (SEC) is responsible for overseeing the activities of all companies that sell stock. Recent cases involving "insider trading" were first detected by the SEC. A notable case was that of Dennis Levine, an investment banker with Drexel, Burnham, Lambert, Inc. Levine made $12.6 million by trading stock and investing money, using tips about the performance of companies not yet available to the public. This use of "inside information" unfairly denied other investors equal opportunity to invest based on public information. Levine was forced to pay back most of the $12 million by the SEC. Also, he was sentenced to two years in prison for the related crimes of fraud and perjury that evolved from this scheme.[43] Administrative violations, therefore, almost always involve failure to submit compliance reports, acquire requisite permits, or to keep proper records of transactions.

Environmental violations include the manufacture, transportation, or disposal of waste outside legal standards. The Resource Conservation and Recovery Act, for example, places restrictions on the generation and disposal of hazardous waste into the land, air, or water. The Environmental Protection Agency is responsible for issuing the precise levels permitted and for enforcing the standards set. The Nuclear Regulatory Commission performs the same function for radioactive production and waste. Recent concern over illegal toxic dumping has focused attention on the enforcement of environmental laws.

The use of Agent Orange in Vietnam during the 1960s and 1970s became a major environmental case in the 1980s. Agent Orange, a defoliant, was sprayed over the jungles in Southeast Asia during the Vietnam War, so the enemy could be seen. This defoliant, a herbicide, contains dioxin, which has been linked to cancer. More than 250,000 Vietnam veterans and families filed claims against the government and the chemical companies that made Agent Orange, claiming that their exposure in Vietnam caused caused cancer, skin problems, and birth defects. After a decade of legal manuevering, the U.S. Supreme Court approved a $180 million settlement between the veterans and the chemical companies. Unfortunately, death benefits from this fund total only $3,400, and those with 100 percent disabilities receive $741 per year for 10 years.[44] Environmental violations are discussed further in Chapter 6.

Labor violations are those that involve discriminatory practices, unsafe exposure, or unfair treatment of employees. Firings without cause, refusing employment on the basis of race or sex, and wage and hour violations are examples. The Equal Employment Opportunity Commission enforces the regulations affecting hiring and firing procedures. The Occupational Safety and Health Administration (OSHA) regulates workplace safety.

An example of a labor violation is provided by Union Carbide Corporation which was fined $1.37 million by OSHA for 221 health and safety violations in its West Virginia plant. The U.S. Secretary of Labor remarked, "We found employees without respirators being asked to detect the presence of deadly gas by sniffing the air after alarms indicated a leak."[45]

Manufacturing violations involve the production of unsafe products. This would include electric shock hazards, fire hazards, inadequate labeling, contaminated products, among others. The Beech-Nut apple juice case, presented earlier, is an example of a manufacturing violation as well as a violation of conspiracy law. As a result, Beech-Nut could be punished for both conspiracy and a series of manufacturing violations. The Federal Hazardous Substances Act and Flammable Fabrics Act are examples of laws establishing rules for the manufacture of certain types of products.

Recently, Cordis Corporation in Miami pleaded guilty to charges it concealed defects in the thousands of heart pacemakers it manufactured. The company was fined, notified doctors who implanted the devices, and four former executives were indicted.[46] The Food and Drug Administration, Consumer Product Safety Commission, and National Highway Safety Administration are a few of the agenices that enforce manufacturing violation provisions.

Unfair trade practices are those that prevent fair competition in the marketplace. Monopolization, price discrimination, price fixing, and bid rigging are some examples. The Sherman Anti-trust Trust Act made it illegal for businesses to monopolize a product market for this violates the principles of a free market on which the economy is based.

Exxon Corporation was ordered to pay the largest fine in U.S. history (more than $2 billion) in 1985 for overpricing Texas crude oil during the energy crisis of the 1970s. Exxon overcharged customers by nearly $1 billion by selling "old" oil as if it were "new" oil, priced at $5 to $6 more per barrel.[47] In a similar vein, General Electric Corporation was charged with 108 counts of overbilling the U.S. government on a nuclear warhead contract. The company plead guilty and was fined $1.04 million for altering work records and submitting time cards for work not done.[48] The Department of Justice Anti-trust Division, Federal Trade Commission, and Interstate Commerce Commission are agencies that oversee commerce to prevent unfair trade practices.

There are large numbers of possible violations for each type of regulatory offense and they change as laws are revised in response to the latest toxic waste, food poisoning, unsafe product, and workplace injury disaster. An example is the case of *Hon v. Stroh Brewery Co.*, 835 F.2d 510 (3rd Cir. 1987) where a widow brought suit against a brewer alleging that her husband's consumption of beer caused his death. Her husband, William Hon, died from pancreatitus at age 26.

In the six years preceding his death, Hon's alcohol consumption consisted largely of Old Milwaukee Beer manufactured by Stroh's Brewery. He drank two to three cans per night, an average of four nights per week. Medical evidence suggested that Hon's drinking caused his pancreatitus and, ultimately, his death. Mrs. Hon also presented evidence that Stroh's commercials "attempted to cultivate a belief among the consuming public that moderate consumption of its product is safe."[49] The Court found "no case holding a brewer strictly liable for the failure to warn" about the dangers of its product. The standard to decide such cases is whether a reasonable person "knew or should have known" that the amount of beer he drank was potentially lethal. The trial court held that Strohs was under no duty to warn its customers of the risks of prolonged consumption of beer according to this "reasonable person" standard. The Court of Appeals vacated the judgment on procedural grounds for a rehearing.

The Strohs case is an example of an alleged manufacturing violation for inadequate labeling, which the courts did not support as "reasonable." There are many more possible manufacturing violations than any other type of regulatory offense due to the plethora of regulations in this area. Problems of enforcement, however, are considerable and they are discussed in the next section.

Investigation Avenues

The prevention of white collar crime can be approached in two ways: short-term and long-term strategies. *Short-term strategies* are those which involve the detection and prosecution of existing white collar offenders in the hope that interruption of criminal activity will reduce its incidence in society. *Long-term strategies* are those that involve policy decisions that promote a less criminogenic environment.

The enforcement of white collar offenses differs from traditional crimes. For most street crimes, persons or property are victimized and the police are called to investigate. This *reactive* role characterizes most policework. In the case of white collar crimes, however, it is common for the victim of a fraud, embezzlement, forgery, conspiracy, or regulatory offense not to know that he or she has been a victim until well after the act. Therefore, it is necessary for police to adopt a *proactive* approach in these cases to attempt to uncover law violations from suspicious circumstances alone.

The largest problem with proactive policework is that it often results in dead-ends. Most investigations of "suspicious" business or government activity will be unfounded. This makes white collar investigations frustrating, and the planned nature of the offenses makes them difficult to detect as well.

Many methods can be used to detect white collar crimes with or without the knowledge of the suspect. These involve either examinations of financial or personal history, or surveillance of current activities. Investigative techniques include examination of bank and credit records, tax returns, criminal records, Dunn & Bradstreet reports (information regarding business ownership and net worth), inside informants, and "mail covers" where the addresses from which a suspect receives mail is recorded. Methods requiring warrants or other official authorization include search warrants, electronic surveillance, undercover surveillance, and subpoenas to force the appearance of a reluctant witness or document.

Examination of personal and financial records have been fruitful avenues of investigation in many cases. A bank teller in Nyack, New York, responsible for depositing parking-meter coins, was arrested on charges she kept $250 to $300 weekly.[50] The charges were based on an analysis of her bank, credit, and spending history begun when annual parking-meter deposits declined noticeably. Another woman, nicknamed "Robin-HUD," was indicted for stealing $5.5 million in Housing and Urban Development funds. She was later convicted and sentenced to 46 months in prison. Lax financial controls allowed her to divert the proceeds from government-foreclosed properties for personal use.

During 1989, there were 140 HUD-related convictions arising from the mismanagement scandal in that Department during the Reagan Administration.[51] Virtually all of the criminal cases emanating from the savings and loan scandal also developed evidence through a review of bank deposits, credit and expenditure records, or changes in net worth. In each of these cases, suspicious shortfalls in cash were investigated through financial analysis of those having access to it.

Physical and electronic surveillance also have proven useful in white collar crime investigations. Two men were convicted in Los Angeles of running a travel scam where they would call people offering free trips to Hawaii. Using this technique, they were able to obtain credit card numbers from 3,000 victims. They then used the numbers to bill $1 million in unauthorized charges.[52] They had 400 workers on four shifts, using 90 phone lines, to carry out this fraud.

A woman, known as ''Coupon Connie,'' was sentenced to more than two years in prison for conspiracy and fraud when she participated in a scheme to distribute more than 600,000 bogus copies of manufacturers' rebate coupons from 47 different companies.[53] In both these cases, surveillance was used to determine the suspects' role in the purported scheme and formed the basis for the ultimate charge.

It can be seen from this small sampling of cases that white collar crime prosecutions often result from tips or complaints from people outside investigative agencies. The investigators then determine whether there is a basis for a criminal case through further investigation. An examination of all criminal prosecutions of collusive trade agreements by the U.S. Department of Justice over a 25-year period found that most cases originated from complainants and informants outside the agency.[54] The importance of such tips led the U.S. General Accounting Office, the investigative arm of Congress, to establish a 24-hour hotline in 1979 to allow citizens to report anonymously suspicions of fraud within the government. In its first nine years, the hotline received more than 94,000 calls, nearly 14,000 of which resulted in further review for investigation and possible prosecution.[55] A New York State hotline for reporting environmental offenses began in 1989 and receives about 200 calls monthly.[56] The importance of public input to begin the investigative process is significant, therefore, and necessary to begin most proactive investigations.[57] Several states have recognized the need for more public input, and have passed laws to reward or compensate those whose tips result in criminal cases.

Prosecution Issues and Outcomes

The prosecution of white collar crimes differs from that of street crimes. Nearly all street crimes are prosecuted in criminal court, whereas many white collar crimes are not. The reason for this is that white collar crimes are often detected by regulatory agencies who usually hold administrative hearings or bring a case in civil court. This is because the role of these agencies is to insure compliance rather than to prosecute. Prosecution is reserved for the most severe or repeat violators. Recommendations for criminal prosecution must be made by a regulatory agency to the U.S. Department of Justice or its counterpart on the state level for that is the only agency that can bring a criminal case. The result of this process is that most street crimes, once proven, bring probation or prison sentences. White collar crimes, however, are often prosecuted civilly, resulting in fines and compensation. Many of the examples used in this chapter illustrate that white collar crimes can be devastating in their impact, and offenders sometimes do go to jail, but many white collar crimes are resolved through administrative fines, thereby avoiding possible criminal convictions.

In order to determine the precise differences in outcomes of white collar versus conventional crime prosecutions, the U.S. Bureau of Justice Statistics compiled the prosecution results for three white collar crimes as compared to traditional violent crimes, property crimes, and public order offenses in eight states (California, Minnesota, Nebraska, New York, Ohio, Pennsylvania, Utah, and Virginia) and the Virgin Islands. These jurisdictions account for more than a third of the nation's population and an equal proportion of its serious crimes. The crimes counted were typical of each category:

- white collar crimes (embezzlement, forgery, fraud);
- violent crimes (homicide, kidnapping, rape, robbery, and assault);
- property crimes (burglary, larceny, arson, stolen property); and
- public order offenses (commercialized vice, drug offenses, disorderly conduct, weapons offenses).

Of the nearly 459,000 felony arrests examined, only six percent were for white collar crimes; most of these were forgery (54 percent) and fraud (38 percent). A comparison of the outcomes of these arrests is presented in Table 1.2.

Contrary to the opinion of many, white collar offenders appear to be prosecuted and convicted at least as often as suspects for conventional crimes. Of course, this may be due to the fact that only the most serious white collar crimes land in criminal court, while the remaining cases are handled civilly through fines and compensation. White collar offenders are sentenced to jail terms slightly less often than violent and property offenders, but slightly more often than those convicted of offenses against the public order. As one might expect, violent offenders are sentenced to more than one year in prison twice as often as are white collar offenders, and property offenders are sentenced about one-third more often. Public order offenders were sentenced to long prison terms at the same rate as white collar offenders.

Interestingly, this investigation found that between 86 and 89 percent of those arrested for violent, property, and public order crimes were males, but only 61 percent of those arrested for the white collar crimes were male.[58] This suggests that white collar crime may be more attractive to female offenders than conventional crimes. Undoubtedly, the opportunities for commission and the absence of a need for violence in most white collar crimes play a role in the difference in sex-arrest ratios.[59]

The future of white collar crime investigation and prosecution should look to obtain citizen input more widely in discovering law violations. Unlike the reactive nature of traditional policework, white collar enforcement must develop cases based on incomplete facts. States must work to encourage and reward responsible citizen reports of alleged wrongdoing, and they must see to it that employees are not penalized for reporting unsafe conditions in the workplace. Enforcement techniques like this should be aimed at the goal "to make ethical behavior more rewarding than criminal behavior."[60] Government efforts, thus far, in protecting whistle-blowers from retaliation have been lackluster.[61]

TABLE 1.2 PROSECUTION OUTCOMES OF FELONY ARRESTS

	White Collar Crimes	*Violent Crimes*	*Property Crimes*	*Public Order Offenses*
Arrest Prosecuted	88%	82%	86%	81%
Conviction Result	74	66	76	67
Incarceration	60	67	65	55
Over One-Year Prison	18	39	26	18

Source: Don Manson, *Tracking Offenders: White Collar Crime* (Washington, D.C.: Bureau of Justice Statistics, 1986).

There currently exists a large number of regulatory agencies, rules, and enforcers. During the last two decades the number of rules has increased dramatically, although investigative staffs are often inadequate and have declined in some areas, while some agencies have been co-opted and rendered ineffective by the industries they regulate.[62] Investigators and attorneys for the Consumer Product Safety Commission, for example, declined by 35 percent during the 1980s.[63]

Although additional investigative resources are always needed, it is not always clear how they are best utilized. It is paramount that the certainty of apprehension is as high as possible for it serves to reinforce the underlying moral principles. *Perceptions* of certainty are just as valid and highly publicized cases do a great deal to transmit the fear of apprehension. There are arguable limits, however, in both constitutional and financial terms as to how much authority and resources should be devoted to white collar crimes.

What is now missing is a will to bring to bear the existing apparatus more effectively. In recent years, the regulation of white collar crime has been subject to the view or whim of the incumbent administration about the "true need and role" for such a regulatory system. This has led to a passive enforcement effort for many white collar crimes.[64] The savings and loan debacle, the HUD misappropriation prosecutions, and on-going cases of illegal hazardous waste disposal are a few examples that illustrate the need for vigilant enforcement. As Frank and Lombness suggest, regulatory agencies must have a "sense of accountability" in building "a professional identification with the public's interest" rather than with political considerations.[65] White collar crime investigations should occur apart from the political leanings of the day. The costs in both financial and human terms demand it.

The Future of White Collar Crime

The investigation and prosecution of white collar crime will never eliminate it. They can interrupt it, reduce it, and delay it, but only a removal of the causes of such behavior will ultimately prevent it. In fact, Mary McIntosh found that increasingly sophisticated law enforcement has resulted in a parallel increase in the complexity of the nature of many scams that now occur. She found that crimes must involve enough organization to insure a reasonable probability of success. And as law enforcement methods become more sophisiticated over time, criminals must also become more sophisticated to maintain acceptable levels of success.[66] Prosecution, therefore, may change the method of commission of white collar crimes, their target, or their complexity, but it is not sufficient to prevent these crimes entirely. After all, criminal sanctions do not teach moral boundaries as much as they reinforce ethical principles to those already possessing them.

Penalty Changes

Increases in penalties are always suggested in response to instances of white collar crimes, but some kinds of penalties appear to work better than others. Gary Green has argued for ''occupational disqualification'' upon conviction for certain offenses.[67] There is no way to estimate reliability how much impact such a strategy would have on future offenses committed by new offenders, however, or by those who continue in the occupation in an unlawful capacity. Braithwaite has argued for ''enforced self-regulation,'' where companies would write their own rules to be approved by the regulatory agency.[68] The number and kinds of rules would be limitless, though, and the approval process difficult to carry out objectively. Increased regulatory costs would undoubtedly result as well, due to the particularized nature of each company's rules and approval status.

Fisse and Braithwaite examined the impact of negative publicity in 17 different well-known cases of corporate crimes. Although this negative publicity had little adverse financial effect on the companies, they found that every company made procedural changes designed to prevent future occurrences. These changes apparently were the result of the moral approbation expressed toward the corporations, manifested by a decline in employee morale, media attacks, unpleasant cross-examination by investigators, and a perceived loss of prestige in their communities. Based on the perceptions of the management, therefore, ''financial impacts were not a strong deterrent, while non-financial impacts (lowered prestige, morale, job distraction, and humiliation by investigators) were acutely felt.''[69] Therefore, it appears that negative publicity may do more to prevent white collar crime in the long term than some other alternatives. Unfortunately, this does not often take place. There are many documented cases where people have been victimized due to a failure to publicize reports and judgments about defective products and court settlements with injured parties.[70] Once responsibility is determined in such cases, it should be mandatory that potential users (victims) be warned of the danger.

We can reduce the pressures in the business environment that create opportunities for white collar crime through greater stability in the balance created among suppliers, customers, regulators, and competitors so that businesses can survive and make a profit with as little struggle as possible. Or we can minimize the significance of associations with those who see law violations as justifiable through prosecution and by incentives for whistle-blowers.

Likewise, corporations can be held more accountable for their actions. Expansion of strict liability offenses and punishments, which permit criminal penalties for unintentional violations in hazardous industries, is a method by which corporate actors and individuals can be held to a high standard of informed, ethical conduct. This is especially important in businesses or government agencies that have a direct impact on public health or welfare. Also, conspiracy laws can be more stringently applied to individuals and corporations. In many states, conspiracy is punished less severely than the crime which is the object of the conspiracy; so conspiracy to defraud, for example, is punished less severely than fraud itself. The organization and plan to commit a crime, together with the act needed in furtherance of the conspiracy, should result in very similar punishment, whether or not the planned crime was ever carried out. In this way, illegal decisions would be punished severely regardless of whether or not they actually were able to cause the intended harm.

Changing the Ethical Tone

Nevertheless, there always will be pressures "pushing" an individual or a corporation in an illicit direction. These might be resisted more effectively if business, law, and public administration education more widely included and emphasized ethical decision making in their curricula. As Green has suggested, "Moral education that discourages illegal behavior must be continuous. Inculcation must start early in life and be reiterated constantly, because early moral socialization can be mitigated by subsequent pro-criminal associations."[71] Marshall Clinard interviewed 64 retired middle managers from *Fortune 500* companies and found that top management in a company also is critical because it "sets the corporate ethical tone."[72]

An example of the existing indifferent attitude toward unethical behavior is provided by an investigation of alleged ethical misconduct on the part of federal employees. Federal agencies must refer such cases to the Department of Justice when their Offices of Inspector General find that violations of criminal law may have occurred. In a sample of 10 agencies over two years, the U.S. General Accounting Office found that 124 allegations of criminal ethical violations were referred to the Department of Justice. Only two of the 124 cases were prosecuted.[73] Clearly, a more sincere effort is needed to promote ethical decision making if white collar crime is to be more effectively controlled.

NOTES

[1]Bennett, Georgette. *Crime-Warps: The Future of Crime in America,* Revised ed. (New York: Anchor Books, 1989), p. 3.

[2]Cullen, Francis T., Maakestad, William J., and Cavender, Gray. *Corporate Crime Under Attack: The Ford Pinto Case and Beyond* (Cincinnati: Anderson Publishing Co., 1987), pp. 42–45.

[3]*United States v. Zambrano,* 776 F.2d 1091 (2nd Cir. 1989) at 1193.

[4]*Direct Sales Co. v. United States,* 63 S.Ct. 1265 (1943).

[5]*DeLong Equipment v. Washington Mills Abrasive Co.*, 887 F.2d 1499 (11th Cir. 1989) and *H.L. Moore Drug Exchange v. Eli Lilly & Co.*, 662 F.2d 935 (*cert. denied* 1982).

[6]*United States v. Hernandez,* 876 F.2d 774 (9th Cir. 1989).

[7]*United States v. Roper,* 874 F.2d 782 (11th Cir. 1989).

[8]*United States v. West,* 877 F.2d 281 (4th Cir. 1989).

[9]*New York State National Organization for Women v. Terry,* 886 F.2d 1339 (2nd Cir. 1989) and *Attorney General of Maryland v. Dickson,* 717 F. Supp. 1090 (1989).

[10]Pepinsky, Harold E. and Jesilow, Paul. *Myths That Cause Crime,* 2nd ed. (Cabin John, MD: Seven Locks Press, 1985), ch. 4.

[11]Cullen, Francis T., Maakestad, William J., and Cavender, Gray. *Corporate Crime Under Attack,* (Cincinnati: Anderson Publishing, 1987), chs. 1 and 2.

[12]U.S. Department of Justice, *Crime in the United States* (Washington, D.C.: U.S. Government Printing Office, Issued Annually).

[13]Jamieson, Katherine and Flanagan, Timothy. *Sourcebook of Criminal Justice Statstics—1988* (Washington, D.C.: U.S. Government Printing Office, 1989).

[14]Flanagan, Timothy and Jamieson, Katherine. *Sourcebook of Criminal Justice Statistics—1987* (Washington, D.C.: U.S. Government Printing Office, 1988) and Jamieson and Flanagan, *Sourcebook.*

[15]Sutherland, Edwin. *White Collar Crime* (New York: Dryden Press, 1949).

[16]Clinard, Marshall B. and Yeager, Peter C. *Corporate Crime* (New York: The Free Press, 1980).

[17]Goff, Colin and Reasons, Charles. *Corporate Crime in Canada* (Toronto: Prentice Hall of Canada, 1978).

[18]U.S. Bureau of the Census, *Statistical Abstract of the United States* (Washington, D.C.: U.S. Government Printing Office, 1989).

[19]See, for example, Geis, Gilbert. "The Heavy Electrical Equipment Antitrust Cases of 1961," in Clinard, M.B. and Quinney, R., eds. *Criminal Behavior Systems: A Typology* (New York: Holt, Rinehart and Winston, 1967), pp. 140–51.

[20]Beccaria, Cesare. *On Crimes and Punishments* (1764) trans. Henry Paolucci (Indianapolis: Bobbs-Merrill Educational Publishing, 1963).

[21]Sutherland, Edwin. *White Collar Crime;* Merton, Robert K. "Social Structure and Anomie," *American Sociological Review,* Vol. 3 (October, 1938), pp. 672–82.

[22]Sutherland, Edwin. *White Collar Crime* (New York: The Dryden Press, 1949), p. 9.

[23]Sutherland, *White Collar Crime,* p. 234.

[24]Ibid at 238.

[25]Vandivier, Kermit. "Why Should My Conscience Bother Me?," and Geis, Gilbert. "The Heavy Electrical Equipment Antitrust Cases of 1961," in *Corporate and Governmental Deviance,* 3rd ed., Ermann, M. David and Lundman, Richard J. (eds.) (New York: Oxford University Press, 1987), pp. 103–44.

[26]Smith, Dwight C. "Organized Crime and Entrepreneurship," *International Journal of Criminology and Penology,* 6 (1978), p. 164. See also Smith, Dwight C. "Paragons, Pariahs, and Pirates: A Spectrum-Based Theory of Enterprise," *Crime & Delinquency,* Vol. 26 (July, 1980).

[27]Sykes, Gresham and Matza, David. "Techniques of Neutralization: A Theory of Delinquency," *American Sociological Review* Vol. 22 (1957), pp. 667–70.

[28]For a review, see Green, Gary S. *Occupational Crime* (Chicago: Nelson-Hall, 1990), pp. 81–82.

[29]Hirschi, Travis and Gottfredson, Michael. "Causes of White-Collar Crime," *Criminology,* Vol. 25, No. 4 (November, 1989), pp. 959.

[30]Ibid.

[31]Ibid.

[32]For examples, see Albanese, Jay S. *Organizational Offenders* (Niagara Falls, NY: Apocalypse Publishing Co., 1987).

[33]See Coleman, James William. *The Criminal Elite* 2nd ed. (New York: St. Martin's Press, 1989); Frank, Nancy and Lombness, Michael. *Controlling Corporate Illegality: The Regulatory Justice System* (Cincinnati: Anderson Publishing, 1988).

[34]Coleman, James William. *The Criminal Elite: The Sociology of White Collar Crime,* 2nd ed. (New York: St. Martin's Press, 1989), p. 249.

[35]*United States v. Taylor,* 867 F.2d 700 (D.C. Cir. 1989).

[36]*United States v. Bailey,* 859 F.2d 1265 (7th Cir. 1988).

[37]*United States v. Coin,* 753 F.2d 1511 (9th Cir. 1989) and *United States v. Burton,* 871 F.2d 1566 (11th Cir. 1989).

[38]*United States v. Campo,* 774 F.2d 566 (2nd Cir. 1985) at 569.

[39]*United States v. Davis,* 888 F.2d 284 (3rd Cir. 1989).

[40]Ibid at 285.

[41]For a review of the Watergate case as an example of obstruction of justice, see Albanese, *Organizational Offenders,* pp. 38–42.

[42]*People v. Dunbar,* 58 A.D. 2d 329, 396 N.Y.S. 2d 720 (1977).

[43]Poulson, David. "Inside Trader Starts Serving Time Today," *USA Today,* April 6, 1987, p. 1B.

[44]Beissert, Wayne. "Court OKs $180M in Orange Case," *USA Today,* July 1, 1988, p. 3 and Marshall, Steve. "Agent Orange Reprise," *USA Today,* May 10, 1989, p. 3.

[45]Mattox Berry, Cheryl. "Carbide Safety Hit at Home," *USA Today,* April 2, 1986, p. 1.

[46]"Faulty Pacemakers," *USA Today,* September 1, 1988, p. 3.

[47]Reilly, John. "Exxon Fined $2B for Overcharges," *USA Today,* July 2, 1985, p. 1.

[48]"GE Fined $1.04 Million for Defense Fraud," *USA Today,* May 14, 1985, p. 1.

[49]*Hon v. Stroh Brewery Co.*, 835 F.2d 510 (3rd Cir. 1987) at 512.

[50]"Nyack," *USA Today,* June 15, 1990.

[51]Stone, Andrea. "'Robin HUD' is Indicted in Scandal," *USA Today,* November 22, 1989, p. 3.

[52]"$1M Travel Scam in L.A.," *USA Today,* September 2, 1987, p. 3.

[53]Bearak, Barry. ‘‘Fake-Rebate Case Heads for Court,’’ *The Buffalo News*, October 30, 1989, p. C1.

[54]Scott, Donald W. ‘‘Policing Corporate Collusion,’’ *Criminology*, Vol. 27, No. 3 (August, 1989), pp. 559–87.

[55]U.S. Comptroller General, *Fraud Hotline: 9-Year GAO Fraud Hotline Summary* (Washington, D.C.: U.S. General Accounting Office, 1988).

[56]‘‘Newburgh,’’ *USA Today*, January 2, 1990.

[57]Kusic, Jane Y. *White-Collar Crime 101 Prevention Handbook* (Vienna, VA: White-Collar Crime 101, 1989).

[58]Manson, Don. *Tracking Offenders: White-Collar Crime* (Washington, D.C.: U.S. Bureau of Justice Statistics, 1986).

[59]Albanese, Jay S. ‘‘Women and the Newest Profession: Females as White Collar Criminals,’’ in C. Culliver, ed. *Female Criminality: The State of the Art* (New York: Garland Publishing, 1992).

[60]Coleman, *The Criminal Elite*, p. 249.

[61]U.S. Comptroller General, *Whistle-blower Complainants Rarely Qualify for Office of the Special Counsel Protection* (Washington, D.C.: U.S. General Accounting Office, 1985) and ‘‘Debate: Law Must Protect the Whistle-blower,’’ *USA Today*, March 21, 1989, p. 8.

[62]Coleman, *The Criminal Elite*, p. 250 and Frank, Nancy and Lombness, Michael. *Controlling Corporate Illegality: The Regulatory Justice System* (Cincinnati: Anderson Publishing Co., 1988), ch. 6.

[63]U.S. Comptroller General, *Consumer Product Safety Commission: Personnel Resources and Other Matters* (Washington, D.C.: U.S. General Accounting Office, 1988).

[64]Cullen, Francis T., Maakestad, William J. and Cavender, Gray. *Corporate Crime Under Attack: The Ford Pinto Case and Beyond* (Cincinnati: Anderson Publishing Co., 1987), p. 322 and Pepinsky and Jesilow, *Myths That Cause Crime*, pp. 73–75.

[65]Frank and Lombness, *Controlling Corporate Illegality*, p. 133.

[66]McIntosh, Mary. *The Organization of Crime* (London: Macmillan, 1975).

[67]Green, Gary S. *Occupational Crime* (Chicago: Nelson-Hall, 1990), p. 245.

[68]Braithwaite, John. ‘‘Enforced Self-Regulation: A New Strategy for Corporate Crime Control,’’ MICHIGAN LAW REVIEW, Vol. 80 (1982), pp. 1466–507.

[69]Fisse, Brent and Braithwaite, John. *The Impact of Publicity on Corporate Offenders* (Albany, NY: State University of New York Press, 1985). See also Braithwaite, John. ‘‘Criminological Theory and Organizational Crime,’’ *Justice Quarterly*, Vol. 6, No. 3 (September, 1989), pp. 323–58.

[70]Reynolds, Barbara. ‘‘ ‘If Only We Had Known,’ Say Victims of Secrecy,’’ *USA Today*, April 23, 1990, p. 7.

[71]Green, *Occupational Crime*, p. 230.

[72]Clinard, Marshall B. *Corporate Ethics and Crime: The Role of Middle Management* (Beverly Hills, CA: Sage Publications, 1980), p. 145.

[73]U.S. Comptroller General, *Ethics Enforcement: Results of Conflict of Interest Investigations* (Washington, D.C.: U.S. General Accounting Office, 1988).

CHAPTER 2

New Ways to Steal and Vandalize: Computer Crime

CONTENTS

- The Organization of Theft
  - Computers: A New Way to Commit An Old Crime
  - Types of Computer Crime
- The Extent of Computer Crime
- Computer Crime and Criminal Justice
  - Computer Crime Laws
  - Enforcement Issues
  - Protecting Computerized Information
- The Future of Computer Crime
  - Electronic Fund Transfer
  - Demographic Trends
  - Technology and Criminal Opportunity
  - Computer Standards and Ethics

Perhaps the oldest form of criminal behavior is theft. From biblical times forward, the crime of theft has been reported to be one of the most common forms of deviant behavior. Although theft is criminalized in every society on Earth, it remains quite popular. In the United States, crimes of theft outnumber crimes of violence by a ratio of 10 to 1. In Canada, the ratio is similar. In fact, the universality of theft as the crime of choice is evident in all societies of all types.[1] That theft is common, and has remained so throughout history, attests to its popularity as a form of crime.

An exceptional change in this history, however, has been shifts in its forms and methods. Chapter 1 investigated recent and expected future changes in the *forms* of theft associated with the rise of white collar crime (i.e., frauds). This chapter examines changes in the *methods* by which these thefts occur. It will establish a basis for understanding the types of computer crime, review cases that illustrate these variations, offer an explanation for the growth of computer crime, and examine alternative methods for its control.

The Organization of Theft

The most common form of theft, historically, has been larceny by stealth. That is to say, most thefts over the centuries have involved stealing by secretive or furtive means. Of course, theft requires that property be taken without consent of the owner. Therefore, it has been important that the owner be unaware of the larceny as it occurs.

Property owners, over the years, have taken great precautions to protect their property. Public police did not exist in England and the United States until the 19th century.[2] Prior to that, citizens were responsible for their own property, and they either armed themselves, hired bodyguards, or fashioned "safes" as places to store their valuables. Later during the 1800s, banks became a central repository of valuable private property, when government currency and jewels came to be the primary indicators of wealth and the means for exchange.

The evolution of bank safes offers an interesting example of the manifestations of theft that change over time. As Donald Cressey has observed, patterns of theft from banks were strongly related to the available opportunities.[3] During the early 20th century, safes were locked with a key. Thieves learned how to pick the locks, so the combination lock was invented. Criminals found a way to pry the entire combination spindle from the safe, so sturdier locks were manufactured. In an apparent response to this move, safe-burglars drilled holes in the safe and inserted explosives to open it. Metals were then alloyed to make them difficult to violate. Some criminals obtained nitroglycerine which could be inserted into tiny crevices or used oxyacetylene torches to open safes. Safes soon appeared with perfectly fitted doors that could not be pried, drilled, melted, or inserted with explosives. Some criminals turned to kidnapping bankers, forcing them to open the safes. The time lock was then invented to prevent such actions. In a variation on this technique, some burglars began to cart away the entire safe to be opened later, so safes were enlarged and made too heavy to move. In addition, night depositories were invented to provide businessmen an alternative to keeping cash in their smaller store safes. Safes were later invented that would release gas when disturbed, so criminals went equipped with gas masks.

This "progression" in the organization of thefts from bank safes illustrates an important factor in the history of theft. It appears that there is a relationship between the "technology" of criminals and the "counter-technology" of enforcement. If changes in the nature of bank safe thefts is generalizable to other forms of theft (and the computer is today's safe), it may be true that the more sophisticated the detection technology (e.g., harder metals, time locks, and the like), the more sophisticated criminals must become to maintain acceptable levels of success (e.g., explosives, banker kidnappings, and so on).

British sociologist Mary McIntosh was the first to employ this idea to explain the "technology of crime."[4] That is to say, the economy and social conditions, in general, provide the opportunities for theft, but it is improvements in crime detection that force criminals to become more organized in order to remain successful. As McIntosh explains, "Criminals and their opponents are thus engaged in an all-out war which has a tendency to escalate as each side improves its techniques to outwit the other."[5] Occasionally, criminals must be prepared for violence when there is a direct confrontation with the victim, but the planning and organization are designed to minimize this risk. As a result, the primary goal of most thieves is sufficient organization to reduce the possibility of apprehension and, thereby, increase the chances for success.

If McIntosh's explanation of theft is correct, it is likely that rapid changes in technology generate opportunities for theft that are exploited by criminals for financial gain. Only after they experience some success does the government or private industry take steps to reduce the opportunities for theft. This improvement in the detection technology must then be matched, or surpassed, by the criminal element if they are to avoid apprehension.

This is an intriguing notion, which suggests that laws and law enforcement will always lag behind the innovative techniques of criminals in exploiting technological change. It also makes intuitive sense when one considers that improved street lighting, for example, is often added *after* a number of robberies have taken place in a neighborhood. The same can be said for steering-column locks on automobiles, burglar alarms in stores, cameras in banks, and secure safes at all-night convenience stores. It appears that the detection technology, historically, has been reactionary. Only *after* existing crime prevention measures have been successfully exploited (many times) are improvements made in the detection technology to reduce or, at least change, criminal opportunities.

Computers: A New Way to Commit An Old Crime

The advent and growing popularity of computers has provided the latest opportunity resource for criminal misuse. The proliferation of smaller, more powerful computers combined with the changing nature of American business will contribute greatly to an increasing rate of computer crime. The computer literacy of the nation is growing rapidly as "user-friendly" computer hardware and software make them easier to use. Much in the same way as hand-held calculators made the use of the slide-rule obsolete, the growing ease of computer usage will do the same to calculators. This high-level of computer literacy is promoted by the development of more powerful computers in smaller packages. "Notebook" size computers, weighing in at about six pounds, can perform as many tasks as room-size computers did 10 years ago. This has led to the adoption of small computers by many American businesses, including very small businesses which are springing up at a rapid rate. The result is more computer-literate users, having access to more computers and their data, offering innumerable possibilities for data manipulation, vandalism, and theft. The cases described in this chapter illustrate how this trend has already begun.

In the same way that the invention of the automobile during the early 20th century has been said to have doubled the number of offenses in the criminal codes of most countries, the invention of the computer is likely to have the same impact in the 21st century. Automobiles provided opportunities for misuse through untrained operators, manufacturing shortcuts, numerous rules for road usage, complex registration requirements, repair frauds, storage (parking) problems, as well as theft. It is likely that computers will have a similar impact as the technology becomes more sophisticated and more popular. Codified offenses are now being added to eliminate opportunities for misuse such as untrained operators, manufacturing shortcuts, numerous rules for allowable usage, complex registration requirements, repair frauds, information storage problems, and theft. Similar to the invention of the automobile, therefore, the invention of the computer will provide abundant opportunities for misuse and theft.[6]

Types of Computer Crime

Computers are most often used to steal, but they can be used to commit other crimes as well. There are several different types of computer crime which can be grouped into two distinct categories. There are crimes where computers are used as the *instrument* of the offense and crimes where computers are the *object* of the offense. Computers are used as an instrument in crimes of theft, such as embezzlement, fraud, or larceny by computer. Computers can also be instruments of crime when they are used for purposes of extortion or harassment. The recent spread of computer "viruses," where hidden programs threaten or simply bother users, are examples.

Computers can be the object of a crime when the intention is to cause damage to computer hardware (machines) or software (programs). Data destruction, simple theft, or vandalism of computers or programs are examples. Likewise, computers can be the object of crime when the intention is to alter data stored there. Attempts to alter financial statements, credit histories, or college grades are examples of this type of computer crime. Table 2.1 illustrates the two categories of computer crime and the two types of crime within each category.

TABLE 2.1 TYPES OF COMPUTER CRIME

Computer as Instrument	*Computer as Object*
1. Theft by computer	1. Damage to software/hardware
2. Harassment/extortion	2. Data alteration

Legal challenges to laws that prohibit these activities illustrate how the law has struggled to keep up with the application of new computer technology to criminal purposes.

The most common form of computer crime is theft by computer. For example, a woman in New Jersey was sentenced to six to 10 years in prison for her role in a scheme

"Oh no! I think I've caught a virus. Do you think these things are contagious?"

where bogus Blue Cross insurance claims were processed through a special "override" computer terminal designed to rush checks in emergency cases.[7] In this case, the computer was used as an instrument to carry out thefts in the form of fraud and embezzlement.

A former executive at Squibb and Sons, Inc., one of the largest pharmaceutical firms in the United States, pleaded guilty to fraud in a scheme to steal more than $1 million of merchandise from the company. In one instance, this executive arranged to have $8,000 worth of merchandise shipped from a Massachusetts distribution center through a computer order. Moments later, he arranged to have the computer "kill" the invoice without leaving a trace. The goods were eventually sold to a middleman who distributed them at a discount to drug stores.[8]

Stanley Mark Rifkin stole $10.2 million from a California bank in less than an hour using a computer to transfer the money by wire to a New York bank and later to Zurich to buy diamonds.[9] Kevin Mitnick was charged with four counts of fraud for using a friend's office computer to break into the computer system at Digital Equipment Corporation and copying software which cost $1 million to develop. He was also charged with electronically entering the Leeds University computer system in England and transferring his telephone charges to a non-existent MCI long-distance account.[10] Three members of the "Legion of Doom" in their early 20s plead guilty to fraud and conspiracy for bilking Bell South and credit firms by invading their computers.[11] Computer hackers apparently stole $12 million in telehpone charges from NASA over two years, using long-distance credit card numbers.[12] These are examples of a trend toward using computers as a "burglar's tool," where computers are the instrument used to conduct a theft.[13]

There also have been cases where computers themselves have been stolen. In Fremont, California police reported more than $5 million in computer chips were stolen in 1990. One 486 microprocessor silicon chip, the so-called "brains" of a personal computer, has a street value of more than $1,000, according to police.[14] Therefore, larceny *of* computers is growing together with larceny *by* computers. As computers continue to shrink in size, such theft is likely to increase in the future.

The second type of instrumental computer crime is use of a computer to harass or extort a victim. Perhaps the most notorious case of this type is that of Donald Burleson who placed a "virus" into the computer systems at the USPA & Co. brokerage after he was fired. The virus erased 168,000 sales commission records.[15] A number of other viruses have been planted in computer programs, and some have been relatively innocuous, flashing "Peace" or other messages on thousands of computer screens.[16] The potential for damage, realized in the Burleson case, has sparked progress in computer security technology.

Robert Morris, a 23-year old graduate student, released a virus program that copied itself over and over again, bringing more than 6,000 university, research, and military computers to a standstill, although no information was taken or lost.[17] A 19-year old college student in Los Angeles was arrested for using his home computer to break into a Defense Department international communications system.[18] A group of 13- to 17-year old computer users in Milwaukee, called the "414s," unlawfully obtained access to the computer at New York's Memorial Sloan-Kettering Cancer Center and erased a file. They also gained access to unclassified material at the Los Alamos nuclear weapons laboratory in New Mexico.[19] The Union Trust Bank in Connecticut was held liable under the Electronic Fund Transfer Act for not disclosing to a customer the circumstances under which it would provide information about a customer's account to her employer.[20] In each of these cases, the computer was used as an instrument to harass, invade privacy, or extort a victim.

The other general category of computer crime includes offenses where the computer is the object of the criminal act. One kind of crime of this type is damage to hardware or software. The damage can be physical or competitive. For example, Microsoft Corporation, working with U.S. Marshals, seized more than $1 million in counterfeit software in Los Angeles involving a ring of 10 businesses.[21]

There have been a number of cases where companies claim damages for losses suffered due to "stolen" or altered computers or programs they had designed. These cases often allege a theft of ideas or "trade secrets." Trade secrets can include inventions, client and inventory lists, pricing and marketing strategies, research and development data, or other non-public information.[22] Determination of what constitutes a trade secret is established by law only through litigation.

A case that illustrates these principles occurred in Minnesota where a computer software company filed suit against several employees who had formed a software company of their own. This new company solicited several of their former employer's clients, attempting to sell them software nearly identical to that of their employer. The

Court of Appeals of Minnesota affirmed that the software was a trade secret and was wrongfully misappropriated.[23] The Court held that reasonable efforts had been made to maintain the secrecy of the program through written warnings of proprietary ownership and copyright protection. Therefore, the company was entitled to monetary damages for compensation for losses suffered and an injunction against the employees' activities to prevent future harm.

Another type of computer crime, where the computer is the object, involves data alteration for an unlawful purpose. An example is provided by Eddie Lee Alston, a Washington, D.C. car dealer, who was involved in a scheme where he would pay an accomplice to delete unfavorable credit information from computerized files and add favorable, but false, credit information for people who had difficulty obtaining loans. The altered credit records were then sent to banks for approval, allowing these people to secure car loans.[24] This case of data alteration occurred prior to passage of a federal computer crime law, so Alston was charged with mail fraud for sending the altered credit applications to banks. His conviction was reversed, however, because the mailings occurred *after* each applicant had taken possession of a car and *prior* to the actual fraud taking place (i.e., a bank loan secured on false pretenses). Therefore, mail fraud did not apply in this case because the mailings themselves did not obtain the loan, nor did they conceal his fraudulent representations in the loan applications. This case illustrates how computer crime laws became necessary to prosecute computer-based schemes regardless of whether or not they had reached their ultimate objective.

TRW Information Services, the largest credit bureau in the United States with information on 90 million Americans, has admitted that computer "hackers" were able to get into its system and view information, but they were unable to change any of it.[25] A computer systems manager at Lawrence Berkeley Laboratory in California realized an unauthorized user was looking at his computer files, so he set up a phony "star wars" computer file the hacker could not resist. The suspect was eventually tracked through 40 defense installations around the world to Hanover, West Germany, where three people have been charged with selling secrets to the Soviet Union.[26] In each of these cases, unauthorized attempts were made to alter data stored in computer files. Indeed, the analogy between computer hackers, and the damage and viruses attributed to some of them and the organic "parasites" in the human body, is not far-fetched.[27] In recent years, several telephone networks have mysteriously "crashed." Other "crashes" have included computers at a nuclear power plant and an airline reservations system.[28] Distinguishing accidental errors from criminal conspiracies is not always simple. The difficulty in detecting and diagnosing these intrusions is discussed in the next section.

The Extent of Computer Crimes

A growing number of computer crimes of all types are now occurring, posing problems for the law and law enforcement technology. A survey of 3,500 computer security professionals by the National Center for Computer Crime Data estimated the annual loss from computer abuse to be more than $555 million nationwide. The average computer installation experiences losses of $109,000, 365 person hours, and 26 hours of computer time as a result of this abuse. Telephone services were found to be the most common service theft, followed by computer services.[29] Employees, and those presumed to be employees, account for nearly two-thirds of suspected cases of computer crime.[30] Some estimates have placed the number as high as 90 percent.[31]

A study by Ernst & Whinney estimated the annual loss from computer crime at $3 to $5 billion annually.[32] In addition, there are more than 300,000 computer viruses that have been recorded, although there is disagreement about their true extent and seriousness.[33] A sample of more than 2,700 automatic teller machine (ATM) incidents which resulted in accountholder complaints found that 45 percent involved a potential fraud. Wire transfers among banks and businesses can also result in losses. A survey for the National Institute of Justice found losses to have occurred in 56 percent of reported incidents.[34]

Losses from automatic teller machines (ATM) passed the $100 million mark for the first time in 1983, and they continue to increase. ATM losses now triple the losses resulting from robberies.[35] It is clear that as computers come to be used by more citizens through ATMs, credit cards, home banking, bank transfers, and business transactions, the opportunities for their fraudulent operation will increase proportionately. A survey of 1,200 security managers found that nearly 20 percent of the companies had detected a computer crime within the last five years, and that the rate of these crimes was directly related to the number of employees using computers.[36]

Computer Crime and Criminal Justice

Forty-nine states and the federal government now have laws that deal specifically with computer crime. Virtually all of these laws were passed during the decade of the 1980s. Canada also added a computer crime law of its own in 1985. These laws were necessary due to loopholes in existing larceny statutes.

Traditionally, larceny statutes required "taking of property" that had "value," whereas fraud required misrepresentation to a "person." Likewise, vandalism could only be charged where there was "damage" to property. For alleged computer crimes, these requirements could not always be met.

The application of larceny statutes to computer crimes is not clear. For example, an electronic signal or sequence can be generated to alter an account (no "property" is actually "taken"). If only a copy of existing information is taken from a computer, does it have inherent "value?" In the case of fraud, a computer is not a person under the law, so how can unlawful entry and deception of a computer be construed as "misrepresentation to a person"? If a computer virus reeks havoc in a computer system, but then erases itself without causing any damage, is this sufficient harm for a prosecution under vandalism laws? New statutes were necessary, therefore, to correct these loopholes.[37] Because many of the laws against crime by computer are so recent, their impact is difficult to determine over the long term.[38] Nevertheless, a review of the beginnings of some of these laws illustrates how laws and law enforcement lag behind changes in technology that create new opportunities for crime.

Computer Crime Laws

The first federal computer crime law was passed in 1984, entitled the Counterfeit Access Device and Computer Fraud and Abuse Act.[39] The law was directed primarily at unauthorized access to computers and made it a felony to obtain classified information that could threaten the national security. The U.S. Secret Service was empowered under this law to investigate credit card offenses. It also became a misdemeanor to obtain protected credit or financial information from a computer without authorization, or to alter, destroy, or disclose such information. This last provision was criticized because whistle-blowers who disclosed unclassified, but embarrassing, information about their agency could be prosecuted under this law.

Congress passed the Computer Fraud and Abuse Act of 1986[40] and excluded authorized federal employees from possible prosecution as whistle-blowers. The 1986 law also broadened its scope to include "card issuers," as well as financial institutions, as a source of unauthorized financial information. The law was amended again in 1989 to broaden its application by substituting "institution" for bank, and by dropping reference to the Federal Savings and Loan Insurance Corporation which was abolished after the savings and loan scandal.[41] In addition, the Computer Security Act of 1987 was passed in response to the discovery that only five of 25 federal computer systems surveyed by the U.S. General Accounting Office contained minimum security safeguards. The Act was designed to improve and coordinate security and privacy in federal computer systems.[42] Other nations are also developing computer security laws, and several African nations have sponsored "Guidelines on Data Protection," set forth by the United Nations.[43]

The impact of these sometimes minor changes in the law can mean a great deal in investigations and prosecutions. In one case, an Air Force employee altered computer contracts "only to show a lack of security safeguards," and not to defraud the government. The statute, however, only required proof of computer usage for any unauthorized purpose, so the prosecution was permitted.[44] A student in Virginia used a university computer without authorization, totaling more than $5,000 worth of computer time. He also took computer printouts. The Virginia Supreme Court disallowed the prosecution under the state's larceny statute because computer usage and printouts had no ascertainable monetary value required for a larceny conviction.[45] A year later, the Virginia legislature passed a computer-crime law stipulating that computer time is property with value.

Additional legal changes are needed, however, to punish wrongdoers more effectively. In about a third of state computer crime statutes, the punishment depends on the amount of the damage or loss incurred. The problem is that computer losses are not always easy to assess. In the case of Burleson's computer virus that wiped out 168,000 computer records, it is difficult to put a price on what it would cost to replace those records in their original form. Other states take perhaps a more equitable approach by basing the penalty on the seriousness of the invasion, rather than on the extent of damage caused. Victims are then empowered in all states to pursue civil damages to compensate for their loss.[46]

Enforcement Issues

Computer crime statutes have no impact by themselves, of course, without a significant enforcement effort.[47] Several aspects of computer crimes work against this goal. First, like other white collar crimes, computer abuses are not always known to the victim and, if they are, they often are not reported to authorities. This is because offenders are often employees, and victims often businesses or government agencies which fear the impact of public disclosure of employee fraud that could adversely affect public confidence in the institution.[48] In fact, the size of the computer theft or damage caused may be inversely related to the likelihood it will be reported or prosecuted, due to the ''embarrassment'' factor. Just prior to leaving a small business in Arizona, a disgruntled employee changed all the computer passwords affecting W-2 tax statements. Later, the former employee demanded a ransom for the changed passwords. Despite this attempt at extortion, the company did not press charges.[49]

Another reason why the enforcement effort has not been greater is that many computer crimes are technically complicated. As a result, they require computer expertise on the part of the investigator. Few investigators have such expertise, and businesses often cannot afford to assign an employee with the requisite knowledge to assist the police in a protracted investigation.[50] There are two detectives who investigate computer crime in the Philadelphia Police Department, for example, neither of whom ''has had any formal training in the investigation of computer-related offenses.''[51] Most departments have no computer-crime investigators at all. A recent survey found only 15 training programs in the United States for the use of computers in computer-crime investigations.[52]

The investigations that do occur are time-consuming with estimates ranging from four to 12 months to complete.[53] This is illustrated by a case investigated by the Jefferson County Sheriff's Department in Colorado. An 18-year old was suspected of defrauding investors of $1 million. The Sheriff's Department had to analyze over 80 computer disks, producing 11 notebooks of evidence. In cases involving telephone systems and electronic bulletin boards, a great deal of time must be spent on electronic surveillance to gather evidence of wrongdoing. In a suspected child pornography case, the suspect was identified simultaneously by Philadelphia Police and an Oklahoma trooper through their monitoring of an electronic bulletin board in their respective jurisdictions.[54]

A third reason for few prosecutions is the fact that detection of possible computer misuse is often made by fellow employees or auditors who are sometimes reluctant to inform management of their suspicions. This occurs for many reasons including the fact that they see such reporting as outside their job role, the offense as not serious, or a general disdain for being an ''informant.'' When management *is* informed, however, it is still no guarantee that a complaint will be filed. A department store employee in Philadelphia used the cash register, which was tied into the store's computer system, to clear

Constructing a Computer Crime Statute

Deciding to pass a law against computer crime is only the first step. Construction of the statute itself can be difficult. The experience in New York State is instructive. After making a decision to add a computer crime statute in the mid-1980s, it became apparent that computer crime is more than a single offense. The state legislature ultimately passed laws addressing five different aspects of computer crime: unauthorized use, trespass, tampering, duplication, and possession. The terms are defined as follows:

- *Unauthorized Use:* Knowing use without permission when the computer is equipped with a coding system to prevent such use.
- *Computer Trespass:* Knowingly gain access to computer material with intent to commit a felony.
- *Computer Tampering:* Intentional altering or destruction of computer programs or data without lawful right to do so.
- *Unlawful Duplication:* Intentionally copy, reproduce, or duplicate in any form computer programs or data in furtherance of a felony or when it wrongfully deprives the owner in an amount exceeding $2,500.
- *Criminal Possession:* Knowing possession of any unlawfully duplicated computer program or data with intent to benefit someone other than its owner.

In New York State, unauthorized use of a computer is a misdemeanor. The other four types of computer crime can be punished as felonies with a maxmimum sentence of four years imprisonment.

It is a defense in most states to charges of unauthorized use or trespass that the defendant had a *reasonable belief* that he or she had authorization to use the computer. Likewise, it is a defense to charges of computer tampering that the defendant reasonably believed he or she had the right to alter or destroy data or a program. A conviction for unlawful duplication of computer material also cannot stand when the defendant reasonably believed he or she had the right or permission to copy the program or data. The reasonableness of the belief, of course, is an issue ultimately to be determined by a judge or jury.

Like most states, the New York State's laws focus on the two major categories of computer crimes. Prohibiting the use of *computers as objects* of data or programming damage, alteration, or destruction is accomplished through unauthorized use, unlawful duplication, and criminal possession statutes. The use of the *computer as an instrument* to commit such crimes as larceny, harassment, or extortion is covered through computer trespass and tampering statutes. These "instrumental" crimes can also result in punishment under traditional larceny and extortion statutes as well. In this way, the *method of commission* of these crimes is punished under computer crime laws, as are the crimes themselves.

her own charge account and those of her friends as well.[55] The store chose not to prosecute, illustrating the difficulty of deterring computer crimes through prosecution.

A final reason why these crimes are not prosecuted more often is simply because they are new, and most law enforcement and prosecution officials have little experience with them. Future attorneys obtain little advance training in computer crime, as only a third of all U.S. law schools offer a course on computer law.[56] Once these officials are more widely trained and gather greater experience with these laws, more prosecutions will undoubtedly occur. The advent of dedicated computer crime units within several large law enforcement agencies is already having an effect on the reporting of computer crimes and in successful prosecutions, although investigations are slow and the evidence trail sometimes difficult to follow.[57]

Protecting Computerized Information

In addition to apprehending and adjudicating those charged with crimes, the criminal justice system maintains a huge repository of information about the people and cases it handles—most of it on computer. This information is used in subsequent police and court inquiries and for a number of indirectly related tasks, such as employment background investigations. How secure is this information from unauthorized inquiries?

A large amount of information is gathered about *all* individuals as well, based on information derived from magazine subscription services, business and employee information, census data, and other sources. To what degree are we protected from exploitation by those who might use this information unscrupulously?

Unfortunately, technology (as noted previously) is proceeding faster than our ability to recognize abuses. Electronic (or ''E'') mail permits information to be sent from one computer screen to another instantly through telephone lines. Privacy is not assured, however, as an employee at Epson America found, when she sent an electronic message to a fellow employee, calling the boss a ''boneheaded tyrant.'' Her messages were monitored without her knowledge and she was fired for insubordination.[58] Polygraph testing of job applicants for many types of private sector employment was banned by the federal government in 1989. It has been alleged that some companies now rely on credit checks to assess the trustworthiness of an applicant.[59]

The simple return of a ''lead card'' from a magazine insert results in information that is often rented or sold among companies. It has been discovered that ''qualified'' leads (who express interest when called by telemarketers) sell for between $5 and $50 per name.[60]

The concept of privacy under the Fourth Amendment to the U.S. Constitution lies at the center of the debate regarding computerized information. The Fourth Amendment protects ''persons, houses, papers, and effects'' from unwarranted government intrusion, but it says nothing about intrusions by the private sector into the lives of private citizens, or of how (or whether) computerized information fits into these protected classes of property. It was not until 1967 that the U.S. Supreme Court held that under the Fourth Amendment *conversations* are protected in the same way as are persons and places for purposes of wiretapping.[61] Therefore, police need a warrant to eavesdrop on the conversations of citizens due to a constitutionally protected "legimitate expectation of privacy." No such protection yet exists for exchanges of computer information (most of it carried out over telephone lines). Until such protection is guaranteed, exchanges and monitoring of computerized information can occur without regard for the privacy of those involved.

There are a growing number of instances where the privacy of those "captured" in computerized information, and those who transmit it, are alternately abused or ignored. For example, the U.S. Secret Service held surprise raids in 14 cities in 1990, seizing 14 computers and thousands of floppy disks. They suspected a group of young computer users with trafficking in stolen credit card and telephone numbers. A year later, there were still no indictments. Subscribers to the Prodigy information system, owned by Sears and IBM, posted computer messages protesting a rate hike. Prodigy then banned such messages and severed relations with those who continued to protest through private messages and advertisers. Lotus Development announced a joint venture to sell a computer file system that would allegedly contain information on the shopping habits of 120 million U.S. households. Lotus received 30,000 requests from individuals to remove their names from the data base resulting in the cancellation of the project. When Caller ID was first proposed (a system that displays the telephone number of incoming calls), it was seen by many as an unwarranted invasion of privacy. Several states have since passed laws mandating a "blocking" option for those who do not wish to have their numbers known.[62] In each of these cases, it appears as if computerized information is in the public domain, and its wide dissemination is prevented only through public protest. Clearly, a more reliable mechanism is required to protect privacy, such as new laws and constitutional interpretation. Law professor Lawrence Tribe has gone so far as to recommend a new Amendment to the U.S. Constitution to protect computerized information.[63]

Protection of criminal justice information, such as arrest, conviction, and other court records from unauthorized access is also not yet accomplished effectively. A General Accounting Office investigation into the computer centers of the Internal Revenue Service found them "vulnerable to prolonged disruptions caused by accident, fire, natural disaster, or sabotage because the agency does not have adequate contingency plans." It was also found the IRS "has not assessed the risks to which its centers are exposed."[64] The privacy of criminal history records has been the subject of an ongoing debate that attempts to balance the public's right to know with the individual's right to privacy. Generally speaking, the courts have given increasing credence to the rights of the public over the right of individual privacy in recent years, although there exist some decisions on both sides.[65] What is needed is national policy on proper security and disclosure procedures of criminal justice information from intelligence and investigative data to conviction records. This would eliminate the confusion of the existing patchwork of often conflicting state laws and court decisions, and it would provide a foundation on which to base a dissemination policy for such information.

"The other worms said this was an ideal environment."

The Future of Computer Crime

The incredible number of computers in circulation, combined with their increasing efficiency and capacity, may produce an impact for law and law enforcement greater than that created by the invention of the automobile. There is now more than one computer for every 50 people in the United States, and these computers are frequently employed to provide direct access to cash or merchandise. The vast majority of government computers (85 percent) are used for payrolls.[66] Likewise, *electronic fund transfer* (EFT) systems have great potential for abuse due to their ready access to cash or credit and accessibility to the general public.[67] The potential for escalation in computer misuse is apparent.

There are four important dimensions of computer crime for the future:

1. electronic fund transfer;
2. demographic trends;
3. changes in criminal opportunity; and
4. computer standards and ethics.

Each of these dimensions provides an opportunity for both crime and for prevention. The direction the future will take depends on decisions made in each of these areas.

Electronic Fund Tranfer

EFT systems allow for financial transactions via remote terminals. *Automatic teller machines* (ATM), home banking, and financial transactions among banks and businesses are the most common types of EFT systems now in operation. The opportunities for theft from EFT systems are many, although they generally require more organization than have larcenies in the past. Because the computer system has been given programmed authority to provide access to cash, it is necessary to deceive the computer in order to commit larceny or fraud. Laws are required to address frauds such as unauthorized use of access devices (e.g., identification numbers), insider manipulation (e.g., stolen ID numbers, removal of "holds" on a bad account), and frauds by legitimate card holders (e.g., disclaiming knowledge of withdrawals, and merchant collusion). As one financial expert observes, "From eight to 10 people in any bank know the PIN of anybody in that bank. It's not possible to send out a form letter notifying me of my PIN without a programmer, supervisor, mail clerk or secretary knowing what it is if they want to." Furthermore, it has been found that more than half of bank customers wrote their PIN number on the card itself or kept it in their wallets.[68] Dramatic increases in the ATM banking, home banking, and credit cards will result in corresponding increases in opportunities for theft.

Demographic Trends

Demographic characteristics and crime trends lend support to the view that computer crimes will occur more often in the future. In the United States, for example, arrests for forgery and fraud are up dramatically during the last 25 years. In Canada, frauds reported to the police in recent years have increased as well.[69] When one compares these trends in frauds to trends in larceny by stealth, a shift is apparent.

The aging North American population has crept to a median age of 33, up from 26 during the 1960s. This trend is due largely to declining birth and immigration rates since the "baby boom" generation and a concommitant increase in life expectancy. Therefore, the speed and agility required for street crimes of theft and violence are not present to the extent they once were. The rise in crimes of fraud during the last 25 years suggests that perhaps offenders are merely changing the *nature* of their thefts, rather than terminating their criminal activities. This is supported by the fact that most offenders arrested for crimes of fraud are better educated and between 25 and 44 years of age, whereas as two-thirds of those arrested for larceny are 24 or younger.

Many employers now utilize computers for orders, inventory, sales records, employee data, among other purposes. These computers are often microcomputers with little or no security measures for data or programs. If employees need passwords for access, they are often widely circulated (officially or unofficially) within the company. This shift toward everyday use of computers in business and government has required the development of "user friendly" or "integrated" software that permits access for employees without computer skills. Software like this, where only a few programs perform many different tasks, also provides access to many different types of information to all users. An employee responsible for mailing lists, for example, may also gain access to sales and employee records. This situation has made it easier for employees (of all ages) to misuse the trust placed in them by their employers. When one combines this with the fact that employees change employers more frequently now than ever before, the security threat to computerized information is great.

Technology and Criminal Opportunity

The opportunities for computer frauds are increasing dramatically, and they will continue to do so. In the United States, the first interstate ATM network was begun only in 1983, and it is predicted that home banking will account for the bulk of all retail bank transactions by the turn of the century.[70] This large increase in opportunities for fraud has not been overlooked by the criminal element. Losses from credit card fraud have increased 50 percent in five years. The opportunities will continue to grow as access devices (ID numbers and credit cards) multiply, together with the access available to legitimate cardholders and through insider manipulation.[71]

The growing popularity of cellular phones provides another opportunity for computer misconduct. In New York City, for example, 18 people were arrested and charged with stealing *electronic serial numbers* (ESN) and programming them into their own cellular phones. Any calls made with these phones were then charged to innocent third parties. There have been similar cases of computer theft and manipulation in California and Florida as well, some involving the transactions of drug dealers.[72] Cases like these suggest a relationship among computer technology, opportunity, and fraud.

The enforcement technology has improved in recent years in an effort to reduce computer fraud, but new, better-organized scams continue. As credit cards have become popular during the last 20 years, fewer citizens carry large amounts of cash and fewer purchases are made with cash. This has resulted in theft of credit cards. Banks issuing credit cards began to publish regular listings of valid cards so merchants could make sure a card was not stolen or cancelled. Criminals then used stolen cards as many times as possible, immediately after they were stolen, to avoid detection by the published list. Banks responded with magnetic tape readers in stores that communicated with the bank's computer at the point of sale to determine whether a card was valid. Some thieves decided to take an alternate approach. They would go through store trash bins and retrieve used carbons from credit card purhases which contain both the owner's account number and signature. These would be used in forging a duplicate card that would not show up as stolen on the bank computer.

Recently, banks have added three-dimensional holograms to credit cards to make them more difficult to forge, and they also have introduced carbonless receipts. Now that many purchases can be made at home with a credit card via telephone or interactive cable systems, banks intend to issue credit cards without a visible account number in the near future to make theft of credit cards a less attractive criminal opportunity. *Smartcards* have also been developed in response to credit card frauds. These cards are imbedded with a programmable microprocessor that eliminates the need for checking with a central computer to approve purchases, and they can be programmed to make it extremely difficult for unauthorized users to access.[73]

Computer Standards and Ethics

Standards of acceptable computer conduct must also be established to correspond with the incredible increase in computer literacy. Codes of ethics to guide users, as well as minimum security standards to guide computer centers, are necessary to provide guidelines for behavior that support legal prohibitions. The Computer System Security and Privacy Advisory Board was established within the U.S. Department of Commerce in 1988 as a joint business/government initiative to identify issues and offer advice regarding computer security and privacy.[74] Likewise, a Computer Standards Program has been established in the National Institute of Standards and Technology to develop "standards and guidelines" for the operation, security, and privacy of federal computer systems.[75] Each federal agency with a computer system must now have a "security and privacy" plan to be submitted to the National Institute of Standards and National Security Agency for advice and comment.[76] Nevertheless, a recent survey of 214 private-sector executives in charge of computer security found that only 64 percent have a formal security plan in place.[77]

Codes of ethics for computer operators also are required to encourage professional sanctions for computer misconduct, as an adjunct to possible criminal penalties. The large number of computer crimes committed by employees with computer access may make the threat of professional suspensions or expulsion a deterrent, especially given the low certainty of involvement by the criminal justice system.

If a company has 15 trucks, for example, delivering five types of doughnuts from 10 bakeries to 150 stores, there are 112,500 ways to get the doughnuts to the stores. Only one method is most efficient. It can be calculated by a computer, whereas the other 112,499 ways are less efficient, and can be added to the innumerable ways to misuse this system to steal, misdirect, or frustrate the process.[78] A recent survey of 3,500 computer security professionals ranked the establishment of corporate ethical norms for computer use as the most important component of a computer security strategy, second only to top management commitment to security.[79] Following the discovery of the computer virus released by Robert Morris, the National Science Foundation Division of Networking and Communications Research and Infrastructure unanimously supported a statement of ethics regarding use of national network resources.[80] The National Institute of Justice, in cooperation with the U.S. Department of Education, is currently sponsoring initiatives to promote ethics and the responsible use of technology in schools and business.[81] Violations of ethical standards should be enforced with professional suspensions, funding ineligibility, and other penalties commensurate with the nature of the transgression. Some have argued that computer criminals should be prevented from working with computers after conviction.[82]

It appears that the enforcement technology always will lag behind the criminal technology. Whether it is the technology of bank thefts or credit card fraud, criminals historically have exploited opportunities for theft in a manner that exceeds the existing law enforcement technology. Whether efforts to prevent computer frauds in the 21st century effectively limit criminal opportunities, also providing quick reactions to changes in the criminal technology, remains to be seen.[83] If history is to be a guide, however, the risk of apprehension must be significantly increased beyond current levels, and the available opportunities more effectively circumscribed. Computer crime also can be prevented through the development of legally enforced access and operation standards and ethics that increase apprehension risks and decrease opportunities for unauthorized access.

NOTES

[1]See Archer, Dane and Gartner, Rosemary. *Violence and Crime in Cross-National Perspective* (New Haven: Yale University Press, 1984).

[2]Rubinstein, Jonathan. *City Police* (New York: Ballantine, 1974).

[3]Cressey, Donald R. *Criminal Organization* (New York: Harper & Row, 1972).

[4]McIntosh, Mary. *The Organization of Crime* (London: Macmillan, 1975).

[5]Ibid at p. 44.

[6]Parker, Donn B. *Fighting Computer Crime* (New York: Charles Scriner's Sons, 1983); Bologna, Jack. *Computer Crime: Wave of the Future* (San Francisco: Assets Protection, 1981).

[7]"Woman Jailed for Computerized Bilk," *The Star-Ledger* (Newark), October 22, 1977.

[8]Rudolph, Robert. "Ex-Drug Firm Computer Exec Admits Million-Dollar Product Bilk," *The Star-Ledger* (Newark), April 30, 1980, p. 32.

[9]Schuyten, Peter J. "Computers and Criminals," *The New York Times*, September 27, 1979, p. D2.

[10]Rebello, Kathy. " 'Senstive Kid' Faces Fraud Trial," *USA Today*, February 28, 1989, p. 1B.

[11]Howlett, Debbie. "Computer Fraud: A Big Bite Crime," *USA Today*, July 7, 1990; "Hackers Guilty," *USA Today*, July 10, 1990.

[12]"Computer Security a Mess, Report Says," *USA Today*, December 6, 1990, p. 3.

[13]Ball, M. "To Catch a Thief," *Security Management*, Vol. 32, No. 3 (March, 1988), p. 72; Hyman, "Computer Crime Easy As A-B-C," *Niagara Gazette*, September 4, 1983, p. 5C.

[14]"Computer Chips Go Underground," *USA Today*, July 8, 1991, p. 4B.

[15]Lewyn, Mark. "Computer Verdict Sets 'Precedent'," *USA Today*, September 21, 1988, p. 1.

[16]Elmer-DeWitt, Philip. "Invasion of the Data Snathers!" *Time*, September 26, 1988, pp. 62–67; Lewyn, Mark. "First 'Computer Virus' Trial Starts Today," *USA Today*, September 6, 1988.

[17]Rebello, Kathy and Werstein, Leslie. "Brilliance Has Its Roots in Family Life," *USA Today*, November 10, 1988, p. 1B; Eisenberg, Ted et al., "The Cornell Commission On Morris and the Worm," *Communications of the ACM*, Vol. 32, No. 6 (June, 1989), pp. 706–09; Kates, William. "Cornell Student Convicted in Computer Case," *Buffalo News*, January 23, 1990, p. 3.

[18]Meddis, Sam. "Lawmakers: Pull Plug on Hackers," *USA Today*, November 4, 1983, p. 3.

[19]O'Driscoll, Patrick. "At 17, A Pro at Testifying on Computers," *USA Today*, September 26, 1983, p. 2.

[20]*Spain v. Union Trust*, 674 F. Supp. 1496 (1987).

[21]"Bogus Software," *USA Today*, August 30, 1991, p. 1D.

[22]Friedman, Jon and Meddis, Sam. "White Collar Crime Cuts Into Companies' Profits," *USA Today*, August 30, 1984, p. 1B.

[23]*Aries Information Systems, Inc. v. Pacific Management Systems Corporation*, 366 N.W.2d 366 (1985).

[24]*United States v. Alston*, 609 F.2d 531 (*cert. denied* 1980).

[25]Benedetto, Richard and Kenny, Timothy. "Computer Crooks Spy on Our Credit," *USA Today*, June 22, 1984, p. 1.

[26]Stoll, Clifford. *The Cuckoo's Egg: Inside the World of Computer Espionage* (New York: Doubleday, 1989).

[27]Morrison, Perry R. "Computer Parasites," *The Futurist,* (March–April, 1986), pp. 36–38.

[28]Schneidawind, John. "Software Flaws Take a Costly Toll," *USA Today,* August 29, 1991, p. 1B.

[29]Bloombecker, J.J. "Short-Circuiting Computer Crime," *Datamation* (October 1, 1989), p. 71.

[30]O'Donoghue, Joseph. *Mercy College Report on Computer Crime in the Forbes 500 Corporations,* 1986.

[31]Hafner, Katie. "Morris Code," *New Republic,* (February 19, 1990), pp. 15–16.

[32]Conly, Catherine H. and McEwen, J. Thomas. "Computer Crime," *NIJ Reports,* 218 (January–February, 1990), p. 2.

[33]McAfee, John. "Computer 'Infections' Are Invisible, Deadly," *USA Today,* September 22, 1988, p. 11; "Computer Virus Attacks," *CJ the Americas,* Vol. 3, No. 6 (December–January, 1991), p. 21.

[34]Tien, James M., Rich, Thomas F., Cahn, Michael F., and Kaplan, Carol G. *Electronic Fund Transfer Fraud* (Washington D.C.: Bureau of Justice Statistics, 1985.)

[35]Meddis, Sam. "Automatic Teller Fraud: $100 Million," *USA Today,* March 11, 1985, p. 1.

[36]Zalud, W. "Security and Data Processing Cooperate to Attack Computer Crime," *Security,* Vol. 24, No. 10 (October, 1987), pp. 52–58; "How Business Battles Computer Crime," *Security,* Vol. 23, No. 10 (October, 1986), pp. 54–60.

[37]Nugent, Hugh. *State Computer Crime Statutes* (Washington, D.C.: National Institute of Justice, 1991); American Bar Association Section of Criminal Justice, Task Force on Computer Crime, *Report on Computer Crime* (Washington, D.C.: American Bar Association, 1984); Thornton, Mary. "Computer Crime: Age of Electronic Convenience Spawning Inventive Thieves," *Washington Post,* May 20, 1984, p. 1A; Lyons, Richard D. "This is the Era of Digital Depredations," *The New York Times,* July 3, 1977; O'Driscoll, Patrick. "New Laws Cope with Technology," *USA Today,* September 26, 1983, p. 1B.

[38]Freidland, Lois. "Getting a Lock on Computer Crime," *State Legislatures* (September, 1984).

[39]18 U.S.C.A. sec. 1030.

[40]P.L. 99-474. 100 Stat. 1213.

[41]P.L. 101-73, 103 Stat. 502.

[42]U.S. House of Representatives, Science Space and Technology Committee, *Report No. 100-153,* (to accompany H.R. 145), June 11, 1987; see also U.S. Comptroller General, *Computer Security: Contingency Plans and Risk Analyses Needed for IRS Computer Centers* (Washington, D.C.: U.S. General Accounting Office, 1986); Sherizen, S. *Federal Computers and Telecommunications—Security and Reliability Considerations and Computer Crime Legislative Options* (Washington, D.C.: U.S. Office of Technology Assessment, 1985).

[43]Madsen, Wayne. "African Nations Emphasizing Security," *Datamation,* May 1, 1990, p. 104.

[44]*Sawyer v. Dept. of Air Force,* 31 M.S.P.R. 193 (1986).

[45]*Lund v. Commonwealth of Virginia,* 232 S.E.2d 745 (1977).

[46]McEwen, J. Thomas. *Dedicated Computer Crime Units* (Washington, D.C.: National Institute of Justice, 1989), p. 75.

[47]Schjolberg, Stein and Parker, Donn B. "Computer Crime," in *Encyclopedia of Crime and Justice,* ed. Kadish, S.H. (New York: The Free Press, 1983), Vol. 1; Whiteside, Thomas. *Computer Capers* (New York: Mentor Books, 1979).

[48]Sanger, David E. "New Breed of Workers: Computer Watchdogs," *The New York Times,* October 16, 1983, p. 7.

[49]Conly, Catherine H. *Organizing for Computer Crime Investigation and Prosecution* (Washington, D.C.: National Institute of Justice, 1989); Conser, J.A., Carsone, L.P., and Snyder, R. "Investigating Computer-Related Crimes Involving Small Computer Systems," in *Critical Issues in Criminal Investigation,* 2nd ed., ed. Palmiotto, Michael J. (Cincinnati: Anderson Publishing, 1988), pp. 35-58.

[50]Conly, Organizing for Computer Crime Investigation and Prosecution, p. 10.

[51]Conly, *Organizing for Computer Crime,* p. 18.

[52]Conly, *Organizing for Computer Crime,* Appendix H.

[53]Conly and McEwen, "Computer Crime," p. 7; Gemignani, M.C. "What is Computer Crime and Why Should We Care?" *University at Arkansas at Little Rock Law Journal,* Vol. 10, no. 1, (1987–88), pp. 55–67.

[54]Conly, *Organizing for Computer Crime,* pp. 11, 19.

[55]Conly, *Organizing for Computer Crime,* p. 7.

[56]Conly, *Organizing for Computer Crime,* Appendix D.

[57]McEwen, J. Thomas. *Dedicated Computer Crime Units,* ch. 2; Schwartz, John. "The Hacker Dragnet," *Newsweek,* (April 30, 1990), p. 50.

[58]Maney, Kevin. "Computers Do More of the Talking," *USA Today,* June 26, 1991, p. 1B.

[59]Mauro, Tony and Lawlor, Julia. "More Bosses Set Rules for After Hours," *USA Today,* May 13, 1991, p. 1.

[60]"Telefraud: They've Got Your Number," *Consumer Reports,* (May, 1987), pp. 289–93.

[61]Albanese, Jay S. *Justice, Privacy, and Crime Control* (Lanham, MD: University Press of America, 1984), ch. 1.

[62]Elmer-Dewitt, Philip. "Cyberpunks and the Constitution," *Time,* April 8, 1991, p. 81.

[63]Ibid.

[64]U.S. Comptroller General, *Computer Security: Contingency Plans and Risk Analyses Needed for IRS Computer Centers* (Washington, D.C.: U.S. General Accounting Office, 1986), p. 7.

[65]Search Group, Inc., *Privacy and Security of Criminal History Information: Privacy and the Media* (Washington, D.C.: Bureau of Justice Statistics, 1979); Search Group, Inc., *Criminal*

Justice Information Policy: Intelligence and Investigative Records (Washington, D.C.: U.S. Government Printing Office, 1985).

[66]Bennett, Georgette. *Crime-Warps: The Future of Crime in America* rev. ed. (Garden City: Anchor Books, 1989), p. 110.

[67]EDP Fraud Review Task Force, *Report on the Study of EDP-Related Fraud in the Banking and Insurance Industries* (New York: American Institute of Certified Public Accountants, 1984).

[68]Berger, Lisa. ''Banking by Computer: Is Your Money Safe?'' *Parade,* September 17, 1978, p. 24.

[69]Canadian Centre for Justice Statistics, *Canadian Crime Statistics* and U.S. Department of Justice, *Crime in the United States* (Washington, D.C.: U.S. Government Printing Office, Issued Annually).

[70]Bequai, August. ''The Rise of Cashless Crimes,'' *USA Today Magazine,* January, 1986.

[71]Tien, James M., Fosque, George L., Cahn, Michael F., and Colton, Kent W. *Electronic Fund Tranfer and Crime* (Washington, D.C.: Bureau of Justice Statistics, 1984).

[72]McEwen, *Dedicated Computer Crime Units,* p. 86.

[73]Wishik, Debra. ''A Plastic Computer for Your Wallet,'' *USA Today,* December 5, 1983, p. 1B.

[74]P.L. 100-418, 102 Stat. 1433.

[75]Ibid.

[76]P.L. 100-235, 101 Stat. 1728.

[77]Dooley, A. ''Crime Time,'' *Computerworld: Focus on Integration,* June 5, 1989, pp. 30–32.

[78]*USA Today,* August 8, 1988; U.S. President's Council on Integrity and Efficiency Prevention Committee, *Computers: Crimes, Clues and Controls—A Management Guide* (Washington, D.C.: National Institute of Justice, 1986).

[79]Bloombecker, ''Short-Circuiting Computer Crime,'' *Datamation,* p. 72.

[80]Farber, David J. ''NSF Poses Code of Networking Ethics,'' *Communications of the ACM,* Vol. 32, No. 6 (June, 1989), p. 688.

[81]McEwen, J. Thomas. ''Computer Ethics,'' *National Institute of Justice Reports,* January–February, 1991, pp. 8–11.

[82]Rosenblatt, Kenneth. ''Deterring Computer Crime,'' *Technology Review,* (February–March, 1990), pp. 34–40.

[83]Browne, Malcolm. ''Locking Out the Hackers,'' *Discover,* (November, 1983); Tafoya, William L. ''Law Enforcement Beyond the Year 2000,'' *The Futurist,* (September–October, 1986).

CHAPTER 3

Evolving Nature of Organized Crime

CONTENTS

Organized crime is a fascinating form of criminal behavior, but it is also the most mythologized. Everyone seems to know it when they see it, but they have trouble explaining exactly what it is to others. The "Mafia," the "mob," the "syndicate," are common descriptive terms, as are "gangland" crimes, and "racketeers"; but it is not clear to most people *what* these organizations, or their crimes, are, how they differ from "unorganized" crime, and whether they comprise a small or large part of all criminal activity.

In recent years, popular images of organized crime have been blurred. Nontraditional organized crime appears to be changing. At one time, investigation and prosecution of organized crime concentrated almost exclusively on the so-called "Mafia" or "Cosa Nostra." Now, increasing attention has been focused on Chinese, Asian, and Jamaican gangs as forms of organized crime. The full implications of this are not clear. Is the Mafia, as some law enforcement officials contend, so severely crippled after many successful prosecutions that its demise is imminent? Does the rise of other organized criminal groups signal the emergence of a new form of organized crime even more formidable than its predecessor? Or are these new forms of organized crime merely a reflection of new criminal career opportunities brought about by growing illegal markets in drugs, weapons, and other products, resulting in more attention from law enforcement and the media? In the final analysis, it is law enforcement which defines and creates the perceptions of organized crime for the public and the media. Therefore, shifts in law enforcement strategy and priorities can generate changes in public perceptions that are misleading. As a result, questions remain. Is Italian organized crime becoming a thing of the past, or is its form merely changing? Are new organized crime groups creating new illicit markets or only taking over existing territory from established groups? Is organized crime becoming more violent or are a few sensational cases misleading us?

Questions regarding the linkage between organized crime and street crime, the groups that are on the rise and those that are declining, and how organized crime makes a distinct impact on the criminal justice system are the focus of this chapter. A history of major events that have formed the public image of organized crime as "Mafia" and "Cosa Nostra" will be provided, followed by a discussion of the evolving nature of organized crime after many significant prosecutions of the last decade. The problems and prospects for the control of organized crime through law, investigation, and prosecution will be evaluated and alternative methods for breaking the continuing cycle of organized crime in the future will be assessed.

What is Organized Crime?

The fundamental definition of organized crime has remained controversial for many years. There are different definitions offered in nearly every serious book published on the subject. Frank Hagan analyzed these various definitions and found 11 different attributes of organized crime identified by 13 different authors.[1] Only 5 of these attributes were identified by most of the authors. They are:

1. an organized hierarchy;
2. making a rational profit through crime;
3. use of force or threats;
4. corruption of public officials; and
5. high public demand for their services.

Therefore, a definition of *organized crime,* based on a consensus of writers in the field would read:

> Organized crime is a continuing criminal enterprise that works rationally to profit from illicit activities that often are in great public demand. Its continuing existence is maintained through the use of force, threats, and/or corruption of public officials.[2]

The immediate question posed by such a definition is how "organized" must crimes be in order to be considered part of "organized crime?" Are prostitutes included? Drug dealers? Pickpocket gangs? In all of these cases the answer is "yes," because each is a "*continuing*" enterprise to make money from crime. On the other hand, a group that organizes to commit a one-time bank robbery, or a "typical" thief, would not be considered part of organized crime because there is no continuing criminal enterprise.

It can be seen that there are both similarities and differences between white collar and organized crime. They both require *organization* and some degree of planning in their commission, and they usually require either deceit or duress of the "victim," or of criminal justice agencies (through corruption), to insure that the criminal activity is not exposed. On the other hand, white collar crime is distinguished from organized crime in that white collar crimes generally occur during the course of otherwise legitimate business, whereas organized crimes usually result from continuing criminal enterprises that exist to profit *primarily from crime*.

Organized crime is distinguished from traditional crimes in its ability to take advantage of criminal opportunities and, indeed, *create* opportunities for crime. The formation of conspiracies to provide illicit products or services, or the development of extortion rackets to create a need for a "protection" not desired by the victim are examples of how organized crime exploits criminal opportunities. This is in stark contrast to traditional criminals who generally operate at random with minimal planning, reflection, or organization.

"I thought organized crime was supposed to be all Italians. So what are you other guys doing here?"

Traditional crimes that capture the public consciousness are often manifestations of organized crime activity. Street muggings, assaults, or murders that result from drug deals are the result of organized crime inasmuch as they are the outcome of an organized illicit market in drugs. Growing concern about the rise in the number of murders nationwide in recent years is not due to the fact that Americans are more violent than they used to be. Instead, there are more organized crime groups and gangs involved in illicit enterprises that compete for customers and are desperate to evade law enforcement. In legitimate business, disputes among competitors over territory, monopolies, or pricing policies are resolved in the courts. Illegitimate enterprises, involving such products as prostitution, gambling, loansharking, drugs, and stolen property, have no lawful way to resolve these disputes. As a result, disagreements are often resolved through threats or intimidation. Apparent street crimes, therefore, can be the result of a peculiar form of "dispute resolution" between organized crime groups. The differences between organized crime and "low-level" street crimes, therefore, are not always large.

An Episodic History of Organized Crime

The history of organized crime in North America is an episodic one. Unlike white collar crimes, where actions can be traced to legally established businesses or employees on a payroll, organized crime lacks these easy reference points. Much of the popular history of organized crime, then, has been written through police investigations and journalistic attention to specific crimes and groups in different cities at different times. This has been further complicated by the fact that, when popular accounts of supposedly "major" events in organized crime are subsequently investigated through an examination of historical records, events are found to be less important than they were perceived to be at the time. The significance of such events as the killing of David Hennessey, the Kefauver hearings, the Apalachin Incident, and the Valachi hearings is questionable when they are examined objectively, leading to questions about the true nature of organized crime.

The ''Mafia'' became synonymous with organized crime in North America beginning with an ambiguous event more than a century ago. The Superintendent of Police in New Orleans, David Hennessey, was shot by unknown assailants in 1890. On his deathbed, he was said to have uttered either ''Sicilians have done for me,'' or ''Dagoes.'' This statement provoked the arrest of 17 Italian immigrants who were called part of a Sicilian Assassination League. None of the suspects were ever convicted due to a lack of evidence connecting them with the shooting, but an angry mob of townspeople broke into the jail and killed 11 of the defendants.

A number of separate historical investigations into this murder have been conducted in both the United States and Canada. They concluded that the shooting resulted from a business rivalry between two Italian families and that the police chief showed partiality toward one, provoking his killing.[3] There was no evidence that a Sicilian Assassination League ever existed, but the popular belief in an Italian-based crime ''organization'' persisted, despite the absence of evidence to support such a belief. It is likely that the Italians drew such a high degree of unpopular attention due to their status as the newest immigrant group in the United States. As will be explained later, America has a history of blaming all kinds of problems (especially crime) on the last ethnic group to arrive.

In 1950, U.S. Senator Estes Kefauver, chair of the Special Senate Committee to Investigate Organized Crime, conducted 12 months of televised public hearings in major cities across the United States. A number of police officials and criminal offenders testified, the police claiming there existed a ''Mafia,'' the offenders claiming there did not. No objective evidence was ever presented one way or the other. Despite the lack of evidence, however, Kefauver was not deterred from concluding there exists ''a sinister criminal organization known as the Mafia operating throughout the country with ties in other nations. . . .''[4] Once again, subsequent reviews of the Kefauver Committee found its conclusions to be ''overblown and unfounded'' and that no ''real evidence'' was presented to support its findings.[5] Nevertheless, the public accepted the Committee's conclusions, and as historian William Moore argues, ''popular myths and misunderstandings grew stronger.''[6] No one doubted, of course, that organized crime existed; the real issue was how large (and how organized) the problem actually was. Was it confined to major metropolitan areas and best handled locally, or should it be treated as a national problem using federal resources?

An event in 1957 firmly linked the ''Mafia'' with organized crime in the public's mind and began a series of investigations and new laws that forever changed the criminal justice response to this form of criminal activity. Sixty-five Italians were arrested at the home of Joseph Barbara in Apalachin, New York at what was later considered a ''meeting of the mob.'' A great deal of publicity ensued, including a page one story in *The New York Times* and several official investigations including New York State's formation of a Temporary State Commission of Investigation. No convictions ever resulted because no prearrest surveillance was conducted at the home or of the participants. In fact, the actual purpose of this alleged meeting was never actually known as the arrestees all refused to testify. Despite this lack of evidence, the New York State Commission's final report called this incident a meeting of "major racketeers."[7] The U.S. Court of Appeals remarked in overturning several subsequent convictions for contempt (for refusing to testify before the Commission) that "a prosecution framed on such a doubtful basis should never have been allowed to proceed so far." Nevertheless, the Apalachin investigation was filled with "pervasive innuendo" and was given "unusual and disturbing publicity."[8]

In Joseph Bonanno's 1983 autobiography, he claimed the Apalachin Incident in 1957 was a meeting of leaders or organized crime groups in the New York area to discuss the implications of the recent murder of Albert Anastasia.[9] This account may or may not be accurate because Joseph Bonanno did not attend the meeting, nor was it ever made clear that a meeting actually took place. The true significance of the incident lies in the fact that it gave credibility, at least for some, to the notion that organized crime was highly organized and, therefore, posed a more serious threat than was once believed.

It was not until the early 1960s that an inside member of an organized crime group would testify about its true nature. In 1963, Joseph Valachi became the first "insider" to testify before Congress about his role and the extent of organized crime. A confessed "soldier," Valachi claimed that his organization was called "La Cosa Nostra," and that he had never heard of the "Mafia." Ironically, law enforcement officials had not heard of "La Cosa Nostra" (LCN) prior to Valachi. Valachi said there was a national gangland Castellammarese War which occurred in 1930 and 1931 during which up to 60 killings occurred, culminating in the organization called La Cosa Nostra. Valachi's testimony as a government witness became the cornerstone of government policy, and his version of organized crime in America was repeated as fact in two subsequent Presidential Commissions on Organized Crime. Several subsequent historical investigations have confirmed only four or five deaths that could possibly be related to organized crime during this period, however, and no evidence of a national gangland war.[10] Nevertheless, the impact of Valachi's testimony on public and government attitudes was apparent: organized crime was now seen as a problem of national significance. Valachi was introduced by U.S. Attorney General Robert F. Kennedy when he testified. Kennedy made clear his intention:

> One major purpose in my appearing here is to seek the help of Congress in the form of additional legislation—the authority to provide immunity to witnesses in racketeering investigations; and reform and revision of the wiretapping law.[11]

Federal legislation, enabling a massive government effort to combat organized crime, was to be a direct result of impact of Valachi's testimony.

It is clear from the examples of Hennessey, Kefauver, Apalachin, and Valachi that major "events" in the history of organized crime are not always as significant as they were portrayed at the time. Nevertheless, the public perception of "gangland wars" and "meetings of the mob" were developed largely through these events and have been supported over the years through journalistic accounts of organized crime and Hollywood portrayals that blur fact with fiction. Most people do not realize, for example, that the book and movie, *The Godfather,* is a work of fiction. Whether or not the beginnings of federal law and policy were based on actual or overblown events, however, public and governmental perceptions were established through these episodes. And once established, these opinions became the foundation for public policy. The impact of this new organized crime law and policy on the criminal justice system will be discussed next, following an assessment of how organized crime appears to have changed since the days of Valachi.

The Prosecutions of the Last Decade

If one uses convictions (rather than mere allegations) as a general indicator of serious organized crime activity, one quickly discovers that the past decade was perhaps the most significant in the history of organized crime. There were more prosecutions and convictions during the last 10 years than during any other period in the history of the United States. These convictions resulted in severe sentences in many cases and have changed the face of organized crime.

Beginning in the 1980s and continuing into the 1990s, there was a significant organized crime prosecution effort across the United States. The target of these prosecutions, in most cases, was "traditional" organized crime "families" that were alleged to control large illegal gambling, loansharking, and drug markets in a number of major cities. These prosecutions are summarized in Table 3.1 It is clear that a large number of significant prosecutions have taken place, resulting in long prison sentences (averaging 25 years), although the list presented here is just a sample of more notable convictions. There were more than 1,000 mafia-related convictions during the last decade alone.[12] The various charges of conspiracy, extortion, and racketeering involved gambling, loansharking, narcotics distribution, car theft, garbage collection contracts, tax evasion, bribery, construction contracts, labor bribery, the moving industry, hijacking, and murder.[13] It should be kept in mind that most of these trials had multiple defendants (averaging five per trial). Therefore, a significant number of organized criminals have been imprisoned during the last decade and more are under indictment. This impact is compounded by the fact that the average age of these defendants was over 60. Given their advanced age, long prison terms, and the substantial fines and forfeitures ordered in a number of cases, it is likely that organized crime in these cities will exist under new leadership and perhaps be run by entirely different groups in the future.

Evolving Nature of Organized Crime

Given the massive prosecution effort of the last decade, changes have already taken place in the "organization" of organized crime. Emerging trends also have begun to appear that forecast what can be expected in the future. Specific conclusions and projections can be made about changes in the nature, activities, and control of organized crime.

In the midst of the prosecution effort against "traditional" Italian organized crime suspects, there has been a noticeable effort to recognize the significance of other orga-

TABLE 3.1 SIGNIFICANT MOB CONVICTIONS OF THE LAST DECADE

Defendant	*Charge*	*Alleged Role*	*Sentence*
Gennaro Langella	Perjury	NYC Columbo Group	10 yrs.
Michael Franzese	Conspiracy	Son of Columbo Head	10 yrs.
Joseph Lombardo	Casino Control	Chicago OC Figure	16 yrs.
Gennaro Anguilo	Racketeering	New England Group	45 yrs.
Francesco Anguilo	Racketeering	New England Group	45 yrs.
Donato Anguilo	Racketeering	New England Group	45 yrs.
Michele Anguilo	Racketeering	New England Group	45 yrs.
Samuel Granito	Racketeering	New England Group	45 yrs.
Anthony Gaggi	Conspiracy	NYC Gambino Group	5 yrs.
Anthony Columbo	Racketeering	NYC Columbo Group	14 yrs.
Joseph Columbo	Racketeering	NYC Columbo Group	5 yrs.
Vincent Columbo	Racketeering	NYC Columbo Group	5 yrs.
Joseph Bonanno	Contempt	Bonanno Group	14 mos.
Carmine Persico	Racketeering	NYC Columbo Group	39 yrs.
Alphonse Persico	Racketeering	NYC Columbo Group	12 yrs.
Gennaro Langella	Racketeering	NYC Columbo Group	65 yrs.
Paul Vario	Extortion	NYC Lucchesi Group	6 yrs.
Paul Castellano	Racketeering	NYC Gambino Leader	Murdered
Anthony Salerno	Racketeering	NYC Genovese Leader	100 yrs.
Anthony Corallo	Racketeering	NYC Lucchesi Leader	100 yrs.
Carmine Persico	Racketeering	NYC Columbo Leader	100 yrs.
Gennaro Langella	Racketeering	NYC Columbo Group	100 yrs.
Philip Rastelli	Racketeering	NYC Bonanno Leader	12 yrs.
Ilario Zannino	Gambling/Loan	New England Group	30 yrs.
Gaetano Badalamenti	Drug Importing	Sicilian OC Figure	45 yrs.
Salvatore Catalano	Drug Importing	Sicilian OC Figure	45 yrs.
Giuseppe Lamberti	Drug Importing	Sicilian OC Figure	35 yrs.
Salvatore Mazzurco	Drug Importing	Sicilian OC Figure	35 yrs.
Salvatore Lamberti	Drug Importing	Sicilian OC Figure	20 yrs.
Carlos Lehder	Drug Smuggling	Columbia Medellin	Life
Nicodemo Scarfo	Racketeering	Philadelphia Leader	55 yrs.
Nicodemo Scarfo	Extortion	Philadelphia Leader	14 yrs.
Nicodemo Scarfo	Murder	Philadelphia Leader	Life
Gene Gotti	Narcotics	NYC Gambino Group	10–50 yrs.

nized crime groups. For example, eight members of ''United Bamboo,'' an international Chinese gang in New York City, were sentenced to prison terms of 15 to 25 years for narcotics distribution and murder conspiracy. Tung Kuei-sen, another member of this gang, received a 25 year-to-life sentence for a murder in San Mateo, California.[14] Fok Leung Woo was arrested along with 43 others in New York City's Chinatown when 820 pounds of heroin were seized.[15] A seven-city prostitution ring was uncovered, using young Taiwanese women smuggled into the United States through Mexico.[16] In fact, there were more than 3,000 convictions of non-Mafia organized criminals in the last decade, including motorcycle gangs, Latin American, and Chinese drug traffickers.[17]

Ethnicity and Organized Crime

There has always existed a fear of immigrants in the United States. Whether that fear is based in economic competition or xenophobia, there is a history of treatment of the most recent wave of immigrants as "suspects." This fear is in evidence during virtually every period of U.S. immigration. Sociologist Daniel Bell argues that there exists a "queer ladder of social mobility" whereby new immigrant groups are only grudingly accepted into the society, causing some of these immigrants to find illegal means of supporting themselves in the interim.[18] He traces immigration, employment, and criminal suspicion patterns of Jews, Irish, and Italians as examples.

This notion of "ethnic succession" has attracted considerable attention and has influenced the characterization of organized crime in ethnic terms. Books, magazines and documentary films, such as *Black Mafia* and *Vietnamese Mafia,* illustrate this tendency.[19] In fact, more than half the final report of the 1986 President's Commission on Organized Crime, entitled *Organized Crime Today,* summarized 10 current organized groups—each described in terms of its ethnicity.[20]

The use of ethnicity to characterize various types of organized crime is both narrow and limiting, however. Organized crime is not an intra-ethnic phenomenon; it is multi-ethnic and international in scope as well. The cultivation, manufacture, and importation of narcotics, for example, requires criminal entrepreneurs in a number of different countries to interact to conduct their illicit business. In fact, the validity of Bell's notion of "ethnic succession" has been challenged in recent years, although it remains influential. Critics argue that individuals do not always leave organized crime activity while it remains profitable or when legitimate opportunities are available. This is evidenced by young people who have followed the criminal career patterns of their families, despite having legitimate opportunities for success in their own generation.[21] The fact that organized crime is often multi-ethnic is illustrated by an investigation of 2,000 criminals in the cocaine trade in New York City during the early 1900s. Historian Alan Block found the illicit drug industry was not run by a single criminal conspiracy. Although Jews appeared to dominate the trade in New York, there were also Italians, Greeks, Irish, and Blacks involved who did not always work within their own ethnic group.[22] This evidence of "interethnic co-operation" demonstrates how ethnicity does not satisfactorily explain organized crime activity.

It is somewhat troubling to note that organized crime continues to be defined in terms of a single aspect of its nature: usually its ethnicity, whether they ride motorcycles, or their race. Such an elementary level of description lacks explanatory value. Even the President's Commission on Organized Crime found it difficult to stay within its own single-attribute characterizations of organized crime groups. In its description of organized crimes of the Hell's Angels motorcycle gang, it noted "there are growing reports that members are abandoning their outlaw image, wearing business suits and driving luxury cars: in essence, becoming an outlaw motorcycle gang without motorcycles."[23] The uselessness of motorcycles as a descriptor is clear. It is time that organized crime was described in terms of the nature of the conspiracies and extortions committed as objective indicators of criminal activity, rather than overgeneralized ethnic or racial slurs to which traditional explanations fall perilously close.

Shifts in Organized Crime Activities

The success in prosecutions over the last decade will likely affect the nature of some organized crime activities. A number of the convictions in recent years were for narcotics conspiracy. A primary problem in carrying out narcotics conspiracies is that they ultimately require a street-level sale. Low-level street sellers are easily caught, and then it becomes the investigator's task to trace back the drugs from the street to the distributor, to the cutting and packaging and, finally, to the original source. These connections are most often made through prosecution deals that encourage participants to inform on their co-conspirators. The resulting high risk of detection in such street-level products and services may lead to a shift to lower-risk enterprises in the future that do not involve such a high risk of apprehension. Law enforcement officials already have noted organized crime infiltration of "new" varieties, such as credit card fraud, airline ticket counterfeiting, and illicit toxic waste disposal.[24] Arlacchi's observation comparing organized crime in Italy and America may no longer be true: "What distinguishes the contemporary Italian Mafia from American gangsterism and Mafia activity is [the] investment in the legal sector of illegally acquired capital."[25] The connection between illicit income and investment in legal enterprise may become even more common in America, as it has been for some time in Italy. It appears as if organized crime may increasingly operate at "arms-length" from high risk enterprises in the future in order to avoid street-level exposure to apprehension. Illicit methods of financing criminal enterprises may also become more sophisticated in an effort to reduce the prosecution success against organized crime activities in recent years.

There are many documented examples of how organized criminals "franchise" criminal enterprises. The President's Commission on Organized Crime identified several motorcycle gangs whose members have been found to do "contract" work for criminal organizations. It has been alleged that members of the Hell's Angels were involved in contract killings in Cleveland for a Cosa Nostra group in that city.[26] Organized crime also "franchises" criminal enterprises in which they receive a percentage of the illegal profits as "tribute" for backing the illicit enterprise, or for "protection" from police or criminal interference.[27] For example, the Commission reported that members of the Outlaws motorcycle gang used women in drug transactions "to insulate members from arrest and were put to work as masseuses, prostitutes, and as topless dancers in bars controlled by the gang."[28] This insulation from direct connections to illicit businesses will undoubtedly make apprehension more difficult and time-consuming in the future.

Violence in Organized Crime

The significant number of convictions of high-level organized crime figures in recent years will produce an entirely new leadership in the market for illicit goods and services. In the past, it has been argued that even when incarcerated, organized criminals have maintained control of their illicit enterprises through associates on the outside. This is less likely to occur now, simply due to the extraordinary length of the sentences imposed and the advanced age of many of the defendants.

It is, of course, unlikely that the imprisonment of organized crime leaders will eliminate organized crime. In fact, there is a great deal of evidence to suggest that organized crime will exist as long as there is a demand for goods and services that cannot be obtained legally. It also can be seen that incarceration of organized crime leaders produces a new, younger leadership more prone to violence. The car-bombing of Frank DeCiccio, soon after the murder of Paul Castellano during his racketeering trial, was seen as a retaliatory act by some, leading to the rise of John Gotti as a powerful crime figure in New York City.[29] Armand Dellacroce, an alleged Gambino crime group associate in New York City, disappeared before his conspiracy trial. Anthony Spilotro, an alleged overseer of Las Vegas for a Chicago crime group, was found murdered two days before his retrial on conspiracy and racketeering charges. These events portend more violence in the future as new, young leaders take control of criminal enterprises from older, indicted, imprisoned, or murdered leaders. These new leaders already have shown a propensity to use violence more often than their predecessors in order to protect themselves by ''eliminating'' perceived informants in potential prosecutions, which have been so successful in recent years.

Another reason for this increasing level of violence is the struggle for control of criminal enterprises, once the leaders are jailed or killed. Prosecutors claim that drug kingpin Rayful Edmond III had a network that controlled 30 percent of the cocaine market in Washington, D.C. He was convicted and sentenced to three life terms without parole in 1990. As Richard Rubinstein declared, ''If anything, it will get more violent,'' as new criminal entrepreneurs battle to claim Edmond's territory.[30] In 1990, 28 suspects were arrested in a scheme where cocaine was moved from Colombia through New York City to Buffalo. The drugs were moved between New York and Buffalo in cars equipped with trap doors built into interior door panels. The DEA Special Agent in Charge commented, ''I would assume in a week or so, other people will step into the void.''[31] What seems to happen in these cases are disputes, often resulting in violence, over who will manage the supply to the illicit market, once the original illicit entrepreneurs are arrested, jailed, or killed. Given the large number of successful prosecutions, continuing in recent years, it must be expected that organized criminal violence will escalate as well.

Organized Crime and the Criminal Justice System

Organized crime poses unique problems for criminal justice. There are definitional issues, problems in application of the law, and peculiar issues for law enforcement and prosecution efforts. It begins when you realize that there is something inherently more serious (and dangerous) about an *organization* that distributes a large amount of narcotics, for example, than an *individual* who does the same thing on his or her own. There should be more culpability, it seems, for those who "organize" to commit crimes, more so than for those who engage in crime on an episodic or isolated basis. This section addresses how organized crime is defined, how the law tries to address the "organization" of organized crime, and the legal tools and special problems faced by police and prosecutors.

Organized Crime and the Criminal Law

A review of the descriptions of organized crimes in state and federal law reveals that there are essentially two different types of organized crimes: the provision of illicit goods and services, and the infiltration of legitimate business. The provision of illicit services is an illegal attempt "to satisfy the public demand for money, sex, and gambling that legitimate society does not fulfill."[32] As a result, loansharking, prostitution, and illegal betting operations are the criminal response to a demand for these services that are not met by bank loans, marriage, or legal lotteries, racetracks, and casinos. The provision of illicit goods offers products the public desires but cannot obtain legally. Examples include trafficking of illegal drugs, untaxed alcohol and cigarettes, and stolen property. Many people desire illegal products, or legal products that are obtained illegally, due to a bad habit or "vice," or in order to spend less money than they care to. It can be seen that when a desired behavior is criminalized, illicit entrepreneurs emerge to service these desires for a profit.

If one examines the criminal code of any state, the words "organized crime" usually do not appear. Instead, there are offenses "characteristic" of organized crime. It is these underlying crimes that are the basis for most organized crime prosecutions. The crimes of conspiracy and extortion are the most fundamental to understanding the nature of organized crime.

Conspiracy makes it illegal to organize (or plan) to commit a crime. An actual case illustrates how the law of conspiracy applies to organized crime in the provision of illicit goods.

Provision of Illicit Goods

José Panzardi-Alvarez developed a drug importation scheme, involving the transport of marijuana from Columbia to Puerto Rico. Panzardi owned a large motorboat, the "Survive," which he decided to use for smuggling. He contacted a source to arrange a rendezvous with a Columbian ship carrying a load of marijuana. The operation had to be abandoned, however, when the Columbian ship developed engine trouble. The marijuana had to be jettisoned when the Coast Guard arrived to assist.

A few weeks later, Panzardi organized another scheme to meet a Columbian ship to transfer marijuana to his boat at a point east of St. Croix. The rendezvous was ultimately accomplished with the Columbian ship on the third try and the marijuana was loaded on the "Survive." The weight of 9,000 pounds of marijuana was so great, however, that the boat was forced to ride very low in the water, causing some swamping and damage to the marijuana. The "Survive" was finally anchored off-shore, and the marijuana was brought to shore by a small boat. It was then loaded on two vans and a truck and taken to defendant Rivera-Santiago's house for storage before distribution.

Rivera-Santiago was ultimately arrested and convicted for conspiracy to distribute narcotics. He appealed the conviction, arguing that there was insufficient evidence to link him to the larger drug importation scheme. Rivera-Santiago claimed that the use of his house for storage was insufficient to convict him as part of the complex drug importation conspiracy.[33]

Panzardi testified that he drove a truckload of marijuana to Rivera's house and unloaded it without conversation, although he knew that Rivera lived there with his wife and mother. Panzardi also told Rivera to put grillwork on the house for security reasons. This testimony was corroborated by another witness.[34]

The U.S. Court of Appeals found that "[w]hile it is true that there is no evidence Rivera was told of the scope and extent of the enterprise, he must have known that it was of some magnitude. A truckload of marijuana is not obtained without organization and planning." The Court went on to say such a truckload "is obviously not for personal use . . . Rivera must have known that storing the marijuana at his house was preliminary to distributing it for sale."[35]

This case demonstrates that the importance of the role of a conspirator in a crime does not determine his or her liability. Instead, "the fact that he participated in one step of the distribution chain, knowing that it must extend beyond his individual role, is sufficient to make him part of the enterprise. . . . "[36]

This was seen in a case in Georgia. A wife who carried money for her husband to a bus terminal and waited in a car, while he was arrested for cocaine distribution, was convicted for aiding and abetting the cocaine conspiracy.[37] In a similar way, a cocaine importation scheme between Brazil and Kennedy Airport in New York resulted in the U.S. Court of Appeals ruling, "[t]he size of a defendant's role does not determine whether that person may be convicted of conspiracy charges. Rather, what is important is whether the defendant willfully participated in the activities of the conspiracy with knowledge of its illegal ends."[38] It is clear from these examples that the crime of conspiracy is a powerful prosecution tool. It lies at the base of most organized crime prosecutions.

It is necessary, of course, that there be at least two members in any given conspiracy because under the doctrine of conspiracy one cannot conspire alone. The so-called "rule of consistency" requires that when all possible co-conspirators are tried together, and all but one is acquitted, the remaining conspirator's conviction must be reversed (because you cannot conspire by yourself).[39] The conviction of Wayne Dakin for cocaine distribution conspiracy was affirmed, however, even though a jury could not reach a verdict regarding his alleged co-conspirators, because it was not a verdict inconsistent with his own.[40] The rule of consistency does not apply when co-conspirators are tried separately or could have conspired with unindicted individuals.[41]

When conspirators deny knowledge of, or participation in, a conspiracy, the court must rely on the facts of the case to determine whether "a rational jury could reasonably infer'' such knowledge or participation.[42] This is often an issue in organized crime cases, where defendants refuse to admit their role in a conspiracy.

A case at Los Angeles International Airport found three individuals denying knowledge of a drug-importation conspiracy. The U.S. Court of Appeals had no difficulty affirming their convictions when it reviewed the facts and found that each participant knew there was four pounds of heroin in several false sided-suitcases, their driver had an itinerary of the carriers, he watched and signaled to them surreptitiously, and met them at the hotel in a taxi where they were arrested with suitcases in hand.[43]

In another narcotics trafficking case at Atlanta Airport, the Court found a conspiracy can be inferred from ''a collection of circumstances'' where airline and hotel records indicated that the co-defendants shared a hotel room on the night prior to a flight booked for them with the same itinerary, even though only one of them was found to possess cocaine at the time of the arrest.[44]

In a Minneapolis case, evidence in a defendant's house at the time of apprehension (crack cocaine, a scale, packaging material, a gun, and more than $1,200 folded in $100 bundles) was ''sufficient'' for a jury to conclude that the defendant was running a crack house as part of a conspiracy to distribute cocaine.[45]

In each of these cases, it can be seen that organized crime is characterized by conspiracy, although the role of the participants and their connection to the crime planned can vary dramatically. It is clear, however, that the law of conspiracy provides an equal degree of flexibility to insure that participants who knew, or should have known, of the implications of their role are held responsible for their conduct.

Provision of Illicit Services

An illustration of the provision of illicit services is a prostitution enterprise which operated in Kenosha County, Wisconsin and Lake County, Illinois. Two clubs in these counties were nude dancing establishments that did not serve food or alcoholic beverages. A customer entering the club was required to pay a cover charge before he was seated at a table and joined by a ''dancer.'' A waitress would then approach the table and ask the customer if he would like to purchase a drink (water or soft drink) for himself and the dancer. If the customer agreed, he purchased the drink for $40 or $50, and went with the dancer to a booth at the rear of the club. He would then be asked to buy additional bottles and, once purchased, the dancer would engage in sex acts with the customer.[46]

A third club was a massage parlor where a customer would pay a flat fee for thirty minutes in a private room with a masseuse. The masseuse would negotiate a ''tip'' with the customer, which determined the degree of sexual contact that would result. At both the dancing clubs and the massage parlor, customers could pay in cash or by credit card. The FBI uncovered this prostitution conspiracy during ''Operation Safe Bet,'' where it operated a clearinghouse for credit card transactions at nude and topless dance clubs in the region. It was found that businesses would ''launder'' this illegal income in various ways, such as through false church contributions and unrelated bank accounts, in an effort to conceal their illegal income from the IRS.

Several of the participants in this prostitution conspiracy appealed their convictions on grounds that they held bookkeeping or administrative positions with no knowledge of any criminal activity that might have been occurring. Dale Doerr's appeal on these grounds was rejected because he was identified by a masseuse at the massage parlor, as an "assistant manager," and that he had told the masseuses they had to "bring in business" and "try to make [their] quota." Another witness testified that Doerr was present during conversations where it was said that masseuses should be encouraged to have "sexual relationships" with "regular customers" in order to avoid strangers who may be undercover police officers. As the U.S. Court of Appeals concluded, "a reasonable jury could easily infer from this evidence that Dale Doerr was part of a conspiracy to facilitate prostitution."[47]

Sometimes a defendant claims he or she "withdrew" from the conspiracy prior to the commission of the crime. As a defense to a conspiracy prosecution, the only way to withdraw effectively is through the "affirmative action" of the conspirator, either by confessing to the authorities or by informing the co-conspirators that you have abandoned the conspiracy and its objectives.[48] This affirmative withdrawal must take place prior to the commission of an overt act in furtherance of the conspiracy, because the elements of the crime are completed when the overt act toward completion of the crime occurs.[49] It can be seen that the crime of conspiracy lies at the root of all organized crime, for it is the conspiratorial planning that makes these offenses "organized."

Extortion

The other offense characteristic of organized crime is extortion. Extortion is usually the result of a conspiracy to commit a particular criminal objective. It occurs when something of value is taken unlawfully, or the owner is placed under duress due to threats of future force or violence. When a business or individual is coerced to sell-out against its will, or to engage in undesirable business practices involuntarily, extortion has occurred.

An important case that illustrates the elements of extortion in organized crime is *United States v. Salerno,* 868 F.2d (2nd Cir. 1989). In this case, the "Commission" (comprised of the leaders of four New York City Cosa Nostra "families") were alleged to have engaged in an extortion and labor bribery scheme known as "The Club." The Club was a co-operative venture, involving the Commission, seven construction companies, and a labor union. Only construction companies "approved" by the Commission were permitted to obtain concrete construction contracts of more than $2 million in New York City. The Commission would approve which construction companies in the Club would get each job, and bids would be rigged so the desired company always submitted the lowest bid. The construction companies would pay the Commission two percent of the contract price, in exchange for a guarantee of "labor peace," enforced by threatened or actual labor unrest, or physical harm by associates of these organized crime groups.[50]

On appeal, the defendants argued that the evidence presented at trial was insufficient to convict them of extortion in the "Club" scheme. As the U.S. Court of Appeals explained, it is only necessary to demonstrate "an attempt to instill fear," to prove extortion, whether or not the victims were in actual fear of retaliation; the fear does not have to be of violence, but can be of economic harm as well.[51] Electronic eavesdropping into the defendants' conversations revealed that several construction companies were "made . . . [to] pay the money," the payments were actively monitored by the Commission, and one company was forced out of business due to its refusal to make payments. In addition, the reputation of the defendants as "organized crime figures . . . reinforces the conclusion that the scheme involved at least an attempt to instill fear." Finally, two construction company executives testified that the Commission used threats to enforce the kickback system.[52] This evidence was sufficient to support convictions for extortion.

The importance of demonstrating actual attempts to instill fear is fundamental to prove extortion. The convictions of two defendants charged with collecting gambling debts arising from a bookmaking operation were overturned, when the prosecution did not show "that violence was used or threatened, implicitly or explicitly" against the debtors.[53]

The federal extortion law, known as the Hobbs Act, permits conviction for extortion upon a showing of either an attempt to instill fear, *or* if property is taken "under color of official right." This is defined as any attempt by a public official to obtain money or property to which he or his office is not entitled. An example is provided by a New Mexico State official who had influence over state contracts. He told a prospective contractor that they must "pay to play," in order to receive a state contract. His actions were held to constitute extortion because his "solicitation was made on a *quid pro quo* basis and . . . the threat of economic loss was real in the mind of the [contractor]."[54]

It is clear from these actual cases that extortion is committed by organized criminals as a technique to obtain property by threat to which they are not entitled. It can also be seen that conspiracy usually lies at the foundation of extortion attempts, as it does for the provision of illicit goods and services.

Law Enforcement Issues

Given precise legal definitions, law enforcement agencies attempt to establish the elements of these crimes in the field. This is not always an easy task. Organized crime groups are remarkable for the measures they take to insulate themselves from police investigation. The planning required for conspiracy law violations is done behind closed doors and sometimes over the telephone. Victims are often reluctant to come forward, due to fear or threats. Infiltration of organized crime groups is difficult and time consuming. These are three of the most serious issues faced by investigators of organized crime: electronic surveillance, use of informants, and undercover agents.

Electronic Surveillance

An important investigative tool sought by police was the ability to use electronic surveillance evidence in court. Electronic surveillance usually takes the form of surreptitious telephone listening (wiretapping) or a hidden microphone placed in a room or car

"The public seems to admire us, but our own people keep ratting on us!"

(bugging). Federal police obtained authorization to do this in Title III of the Omnibus Crime Control and Safe Streets Act of 1968. Provided they first obtain a warrant (because conversations are protected from intrusion in the same way as persons and places under the Fourth Amendment to the Constitution),[55] police can eavesdrop on the conversations of any suspected felon and use them in court. The U.S. Supreme Court has since expanded the allowable scope of electronic eavesdropping in a series of cases during the last two decades.[56]

The utility of this powerful investigative tool has been widely debated. Twenty-one states still prohibit the use of electronic surveillance by their state and local police, although it can be used by federal investigators in all states. Proponents argue that wiretapping is an efficient way to discover criminal conspiracies as they develop.[57] The result is fewer victims and lower costs than would be the case had police discovered the crimes after the fact. Proponents also claim that the alternative is not compelling: the use of undercover agents is time consuming, dangerous, and not always feasible.

Critics of electronic surveillance point to its prohibitive cost and to unwarranted invasions of privacy.[58] The Administrative Office of the U.S. Courts reports that wiretaps and bugs costs nearly $40,000 each due to the manpower required to monitor the tap 24 hours per day, as required by law. During the last 20 years, the number of wiretaps authorized nationwide has doubled to nearly 700 per year, but the proportion of those taps revealing incriminating conversations has dropped from 49 to 19 percent of all intercepted conversations.[59] Convictions result in only about half the cases. This has raised concern that electronic surveillance is too often used on innocent people and conversations.

Use of Informants

The use of informants plays a crucial role in organized crime investigations. The typical informant in an organized crime case is a criminal who chooses to cooperate with police in exchange for a reduced charge, sentence, or immunity from prosecution. Informants can be used productively to "turn" lower-level criminals in order to apprehend the leaders.

Informants are used widely in law enforcement because there is little cost involved in terms of time or money. Oftentimes, an informant can provide information about a criminal enterprise that might take months to deduce through electronic surveillance or undercover agents. These benefits are offset to some degree by problems of reliability and credibility of criminals-turned informant.

The mob trials of the last decade, described previously, experienced some failures blamed on informants. Matthew Ianniello and Benjamin Cohen, alleged leaders of the Genovese crime group, were acquitted of major racketeering and fraud charges in New York City. Santo Trafficante's case resulted in a mistrial for his role as an alleged Florida crime leader. Nicky Scarfo was acquitted of narcotics distribution charges in Philadelphia before he was convicted of extortion and murder in other cases. John Gotti was acquitted three times of various charges of racketeering and conspiracy in the New York City area.

The reasons for these acquittals and mistrials in significant cases vary, but many of these trials relied on criminals-turned informant for evidence. It has been argued that the government's heavy reliance on former criminals as paid government witnesses is a questionable practice. Juries have been found reluctant to convict when a case is based largely on the testimony of a former criminal who usually has a documented history of criminal activity and lying.[60]

Likewise, defense attorneys attack the practice of using criminals as informants to testify against other alleged criminals. The practice is seen as self-serving; it encourages prosecutors to "work out a deal" to obtain informants and, at least indirectly, encourage informants to say what the prosecutor wants said (regardless of its veracity). As a journalist reported after one of these acquittals, "[t]he last piece of evidence requested by the jury for re-examination was a chart introduced by the defense that showed that criminal backgrounds of seven prosecution witnesses. It listed 69 crimes including murder, drug possession and sales, and kidnapping."[61] The concern of juries, of course, is that "a bought witness may tell the truth—but only if it suits his interest to do so."[62]

Undercover Agents

Undercover agents attempt to infiltrate a criminal enterprise in order to establish its size, participants, and conspiratorial aims. Undercover operations can be extremely successful, although they also have their associated costs. An FBI-run high-tech electronics store in Miami was used by drug-traffickers to purchase beepers, cellular phones, and computers. The operation lasted 17 months and resulted in 93 arrests.[63] An FBI sting in New Jersey had agents posing as fences who bought 170 stolen trucks and luxury cars worth $9 million over a two-year period. The operation netted 35 arrests.[64] The success of these operations is offset only by their length and cost.

Undercover operations are not as widely employed in law enforcement as is commonly believed. A police agency must be willing to dedicate months of time for several officers to work on a single case. This is required so the undercover officers can gain acceptance and access to the information and criminal contacts needed for prosecution.

Undercover operations have not been evaluated. As a result, little known about ''how effective undercover investigations are, what they cost (economically, psychologically, or constitutionally), or why they fail.''[65] There is evidence, however, that officers selected for undercover work are often ''inexperienced'' and have field supervision that may be ''lax.'' Interviews with undercover officers indicate that they are exposed to great danger without adequate briefing or preparation and that they often experience adjustment problems when they return to regular police duty.[66]

It is clear that electronic surveillance, informants, and undercover operatives can be useful techniques in the investigation of organized crime. Nevertheless, each has its strengths and limitations that must be evaluated on a case-by-case basis to determine its appropriateness. It is likely that the use of informants will increase in the future, however, while electronic surveillance and undercover operations will be used more sparingly. Concern about spending on all levels of government has been felt by law enforcement agencies as well. It is probable that the high costs (in manpower and financial terms) associated with wiretapping and undercover work will make them less attractive in the future. The use of informants is a much cheaper, although not problem-free, alternative.

Prosecution Issues

The most important tools in the prosecutor's organized crime repertoire are the result of two laws, both enacted in 1970: the Organized Crime Control Act and the Bank Secrecy Act. The *Organized Crime Control Act* (OCCA) provides, among other things, for witness immunity, the witness protection program, and the *Racketeer Influenced and Corrupt Organizations* (RICO) provisions. The *Bank Secrecy Act* makes it possible to trace illicitly obtained funds that are ''laundered'' through legitimate businesses.

Witness Immunity

The witness immunity provisions were included in the Organized Crime Control Act because witnesses in organized crime cases are often reluctant to testify, either because they fear reprisal or self-incrimination. OCCA permits federal prosecutors to grant witnesses immunity from prosecution in exchange for testimony. The objective is to gather evidence against leaders of organized crime groups through the testimony of lower-level figures and innocent victims who, otherwise, would not testify to what they know.

As it turns out, many of those granted immunity do not ask for it. They are granted immunity and *forced* to testify. This has drawn criticism because any kind of coerced testimony is suspect. A defendant who is granted immunity, but still refuses to testify, is held in contempt of court and can be jailed. It can be argued, therefore, that erroneous convictions can result when false testimony of an immunized witness is taken as fact by a prosecutor, judge, or jury. Proponents of witness immunity claim that this rarely happens, because immunized witnesses can be prosecuted for perjury or false statements they make. On the other hand, it is difficult to verify the testimony of an immunized witness. If there were other reliable sources for the desired information, immunity generally would not have been granted.

Witness Protection Program

The witness protection program, administered by the U.S. Marshals Service, allows the U.S. Department of Justice to relocate and establish a new identity for a witness whose life is in danger as the result of criminal proceedings. Once a witness is admitted to the program, he or she receives a new birth certificate and social security number and is relocated to an area far from the target of the testimony. Protected witnesses are also provided a subsistence allowance and other help until they can be self-supporting.

When the program first began, it was established that up to 50 witnesses would be relocated each year at a cost of under $1 million. These projections were huge underestimates. There are now nearly 5,000 witnesses in the program, together with more than 8,000 families, at an annual cost of more than $25 million.[67] The U.S. General Accounting Office conducted an evaluation of the program by comparing its benefits (i.e., convictions and prison sentences obtained) to its costs (i.e., relocation, financial assistance, and new crimes by protected witnesses). The prosecution results of cases using protected witnesses have been impressive. Seventy-five percent of the targeted defendants were convicted and 84 percent sent to prison for a median term of 4.4 years. Those defendants identified as "ringleaders" were convicted in 88 percent of the cases and were sentenced on average to more than 11 years in prison. Nearly half the cases involved narcotics or murder conspiracy and another 27 percent were "traditional" organized crime groups.

In spite of this success, the costs of the programs were found to be high. There were other problems as well. The financial cost is $25 million annually for relocation and witness support. It was also found that most witnesses entering the program were former criminals, 21 percent of whom were re-arrested within two years of entering the program. Therefore, the success of the program in convicting and incarcerating organized crime figures must be weighed against the program's financial cost and costs to society. As the General Accounting Office concluded, "program benefits do not come without costs."[68]

Racketeer Influenced and Corrupt Organizations

The RICO provisions make it unlawful to acquire, operate, or receive income from an *enterprise* through a *pattern* of *racketeering activity*. An "enterprise" has been defined as any individual or group, a "pattern" is two or more offenses within a 10-year period, and "racketeering activity" is most any felony. Persons who meet these criteria are subject to extended penalties of up to 20 years imprisonment, fines up to $25,000, forfeiture of any interest in the enterprise, treble damages, and dissolution of the enterprise itself. Table 3.2 provides a comparison between penalties under RICO versus traditional punishments.

Although the RICO provisions were designed to combat organized crime's infiltration of legitimate business, they have since been used to prosecute criminal activities in a county sheriff's department, the Philadelphia Traffic Court, a state tax bureau, the Tennessee Governor's office, the Louisiana Department of Agriculture, and a number of insider-trading cases on Wall Street. The civil penalties under RICO are being used more extensively, since the U.S. Supreme Court has permitted the law's use between corporations alleging only monetary losses in fraudulent business transactions.[69] It has been argued, however, that RICO provisions should not be applied to "garden variety frauds" where existing laws against fraud suffice. The threat of triple damages, in addition to the "racketeer" label could provoke unjust settlements.[70] Clearly, the RICO provisions are a powerful prosecution tool that can be applied to all forms of organized crime behavior.[71]

Bank Secrecy Act

The Bank Secrecy Act was enacted in 1970 as a tool to make it difficult to hide the income from illicit enterprises. The Act requires that banks file a *Currency Transaction Report* (CTR) for every deposit, withdrawal, or exchange of funds over $10,000. *A Currency or Monetary Instruments Report* (CMIR) must also be filed with the U.S. Customs Service if more than $10,000 cash enters or leaves the United States. Third, citizens holding bank accounts in foreign countries are required to declare them on their federal tax return. Criminal fines of up to $500,000 and civil penalties are incurred for violation of these provisions.

The U.S. Treasury Department is charged with enforcing the Act. An evaluation by the U.S. General Accounting Office found, however, that the Treasury Department did not "play an active role" in enforcing the Act until 1985, when the Bank of Boston pled guilty to several violations. In fact, only seven financial institutions were involved in enforcement actions in the first 15 years of the Bank Secrecy Act. This netted only $800,000 in civil penalties from 1970 to 1985.[72]

This poor enforcement record appears to be changing in recent years. In one year alone, the Treasury Department has since conducted 76 reviews, resulting in 11 enforcements, and resulting in $5.1 million in civil fines.[73] The potential of the Bank Secrecy

TABLE 3.2 COMPARISON OF PENALTIES UNDER RICO PROVISIONS VERSUS CONVENTIONAL PENALTIES

Crime	*Traditional Penalty*	*RICO Penalty**
Extortion	Maximum 7 years prison	Maximum 25 years prison
Insurance Fraud (up to $1 million)	Maximum 15 years prison	Maximum 25 years prison

*In addition to the severe criminal penalties under the RICO provisions, the government can proceed against the defendant civilly and seize any property used in the enterprise or assets gained from it. This includes cars, boats, and planes used to transport drugs, homes used to run a narcotics or illegal gambling business, and even a legitimate business used to launder illicitly obtained cash.

Source: New York State Penal Law and the NYS Organized Crime Control Act.

Act to make it difficult to move illicit profits through banks and across borders is only now being tapped. The President's Commission on Organized Crime suggested that similar laws on the state level may further intensify the enforcement effort.[74] Preventing the use of illicit profits in other legal or illegal enterprises is an effective way to remove the "profit" from organized crime activity.

The Future of Organized Crime

The last decade has been an exciting time to study organized crime. Significant prosecutions and more effective application of the law by criminal justice agencies are hopeful signs. Shifts in criminal activities, more violence, and the rise of new criminal groups are more ominous. The prospects for the future are of two types: making enforcement and prosecution more effective, and shrinking the illicit markets that spawn organized crime.

Prospects for Enforcement and Prosecution

The last decade has witnessed unprecedented success in efforts to apply the law to organized crime activities. It is likely that prosecutions will become more difficult, however, if organized crime operations become increasingly dominated by resident aliens from non-English-speaking countries. So far, prosecutions of these conspiracies have been comparatively few.

More extensive prosecutions of these non-traditional organized crime groups will occur only when the elements are overcome that made the Italian groups successful during the early part of this century: the language barrier and distrust of police within immigrant neighborhoods. Police have difficulty infiltrating organized crime operations when they do not understand the culture, have no local community support, and have no agents that speak the language. This lack of community support is often an extension of the culture brought over from the old country, where police are often corrupt and not to be trusted in many countries. This works against police recruitment in some ethnic communities and against citizens providing tips or serving as informants to develop criminal cases. This situation is aggravated by the language barrier, for police have great difficulty infiltrating new immigrant groups when there are few willing interpreters, informers, or recruits with the necessary language skills.

The significance of these cultural differences cannot be underestimated. In 1989, the U.S. General Accounting Office conducted interviews with 130 law enforcement officials nationwide, representing 34 different agencies. It was the view of these police officers that organized crime is no longer dominated by Italian-Americans. Instead, Columbian drug cartels, Jamaican posses, Chinese groups, Vietnamese gangs, and Los Angeles black street gangs are seen as a larger concern by the police officials. As the report described, "many officials told us that language differences, coupled with a shortage of skilled interpreters, and difficulty in penetrating tightly knit ethnic communities hamper police use of traditional investigative tools such as wiretaps, informants, and undercover operatives."[75]

It is also likely that police and prosecution agencies will attempt to rely more heavily on the general public to generate cases in the future. The personal issues and financial costs, described previously, of electronic surveillance, criminals-turned informant, undercover operations, and the witness protection program are high. As a result, there is a growing effort to cultivate a feeling of mutual responsibility in local communities. It began with "block watcher" and "neighborhood crime watch" programs, and it has now extended to extensive use of television and local newspapers to obtain information about unsolved criminal cases, as well as the reporting of suspicious activities in the neighborhoods. The use of non-criminal informants as a basis for criminal investigations has long been a tool of the police, and it appears we may be re-discovering it for local organized crime activities. The growing use of "fraud hotlines," and monetary incentives to report suspected illegal toxic waste disposal, are examples of how the general public can be utilized to prevent organized crime.[76]

Court interpretation of existing laws, together with the addition of several new laws, have made prosecutions easier. The Controlled Substances Act, for example, does not require the commission of an overt act to convict for conspiracy to violate this law.[77] This is an exception to traditional conspiracy law which requires proof of an overt act in furtherance of the conspiracy.[78] This has made prosecutions for drug conspiracies easier to prove.[79] Likewise, overt acts are not necessary to prove a conspiracy under the Racketeer Influenced and Corrupt Organizations provisions of the Organized Crime Control Act, making prosecutions possible that formerly were not.[80]

It does not appear that new prosecution tools are necessary in the fight against organized crime. In fact, the laws which formed the basis for the prosecution effort of the last decade were enacted in 1970. They simply were not utilized by prosecutors until the 1980s. The U.S. General Accounting Office found only 50 cases nationwide were prosecuted under the federal racketeering law from 1977 to 1980.[81] The results of the organized crime trials of the last decade indicate how underutilized existing laws were before then. The President's Organized Crime Commission found existing prosecution tools generally adequate, but admitted prosecution was not the answer to solving the problem of drug conspiracies or labor racketeering. Likewise, interviews with 130 police officials from 34 different law enforcement agencies found agreement that "federal laws are adequate to target criminal gangs involved in racketeering and other illegal activities."[82]

Laws permitting electronic surveillance, witness immunity, the witness protection program, and the racketeering law all have been available since 1970 or earlier, so there is little more to be done legislatively, except to put these investigative tools to use. The Commission concluded that longer-term prosecution success lies in a less "fragmented" approach, and greater "coordination" among government agencies, backed by a "visibly supported by a national commitment" from the public.[83] The Commission also encouraged greater emphasis on civil remedies "to bankrupt individual mobsters and to discourage union officers, employees, and public officials from accommodating organized crime."[84] Interviews with law enforcement officials around the country found a need for greater use of "multi-agency task forces" between state, federal, and local police agencies, although the interviews revealed "parochial interests and an unwillingness to share intelligence information prevent the effective use of task forces in many cases."[85]

Prospects for Shrinking Illicit Markets

A persistent argument in the debate about controlling organized crime is better regulation of the marketplace. It has been argued that the only difference between legal and illegal prostitution, gambling, and narcotics is the county you live in, whether or not you are playing in a state-sanctioned game, or whether or not you have a prescription. If our society is so concerned about gambling, drugs, and prostitution, why are they permitted under a variety of often arbitrary conditions? If the marketplace was better regulated, such as through decriminalization of consensual acts between adults (whether it was gambling, sex, or drugs), some believe that organized crime activity (that seeks to control these markets) would be reduced. There are persuasive arguments on both side of this issue. They are discussed further in the drug legalization-criminalization debate summarized in Chapter 9.

Controlling the extortionate activities of organized crime is even more difficult to address. The infiltration of legitimate business, for example, is often accomplished through threats that discourage both co-operation with the police, as well as open competition in the marketplace. Unlike the provision of illicit goods and services, the infiltration of legitimate business is clearly predatory. A predictive model has been proposed to identify the types of businesses that are at high risk of such infiltration.[86] Identified "high-risk" factors for business infiltration by organized crime include: available supply of the product, the competition, customer base, competence of the managers, government regulation of the business, and prior history of involvement of the industry in organized crime. Analysis and comparison of these factors among businesses in a given area can serve as a screening device for proactive investigations. De Franco's analysis of a planned bankruptcy, for example, found a large bank deposit from an unnamed source was used to establish credit for a struggling wholesale meat business. Large orders were then placed, using the bank deposit as collateral. Once received, the orders were sold through a fence and converted to cash. Once it became clear that no payment was forthcoming to pay for its orders, the company was forced into bankruptcy as planned, having been milked of all its assets.[87] Once a high-risk business such as this is identified, procedures can be adopted to make it difficult for a business to have "no-shows" on the payroll, or to make "payments without cause," which are common features in the extortionate infiltration of businesses.[88] Regulations could then be enforced through audits by police-accountants. The use of such a prediction model is one way for police to target investigations to "high risk" businesses in advance of specific evidence of law violation.

Unfortunately, both prosecution and increased or decreased regulation of the marketplace are flawed solutions to the organized crime problem over the long term. Prosecution is by its nature a short-term solution, imprisoning offenders who are usually replaced by others to service the demands for illicit goods and services. Decriminalization of consensual behaviors, on the other hand, may produce an increase in drug-addiction, AIDS, or other crimes.[89] Increased regulation of certain industries may produce greater resistance to government regulation in *both* the legitimate and illegitimate business community and ultimately be self-defeating. Nevertheless, both the prosecution and market regulation options have at least short-term effects on organized crime.

Prospects for Public Demand

The only effective long-term solution to the organized provision of illicit goods and services is the reduction in demand for these things. Without the demand there would be no illicit drug market, which the President's Commission on Organized Crime found to be the largest source of income for organized crime groups. The same holds true for the illicit gambling and sex markets; they are driven entirely by demand. Demand can be reduced only in the long-term through education, treatment, and more effective competition from legitimate channels for provision of these goods and services.

Education is important, because most citizens do not understand that the purchase of "hot" merchandise, for example, contributes to the existence of organized crime. Treatment is needed to reduce the customer-base for illicit narcotics and gambling. More effective competition is needed so legalized forms of gambling are better able to compete with the illegal games.

Finally, the prospects for shrinking illicit markets lie, to a large degree, with the will of the general public. Every national investigation into organized crime has observed "a lack of public and political commitment" in the fight against organized crime.[90] This is because the "consumers" of organized crime activity voluntarily engage in such acts as gambling, prostitution, narcotics, and receiving stolen property. In addition, when these activities exist on a large scale, it is impossible for them to survive without official protection.

As the Illinois Crime Survey reported back in 1929, there is a "mutuality of services" between organized crime and politics where "the politician affords protection or immunity from prosecution."[91] Chambliss found a similar relationship in his study of illegal gambling in Seattle. He discovered gambling activities were protected by corrupt police who were, in turn, protected by corrupt politicians.[92] The same was found to be true in Chester, Pennsylvania, outside Philadelphia, in an investigation conducted by the Pennsylvania Crime Commission.[93]

An investigation of suspicious arsons in Boston uncovered a similar pattern. Abandoned buildings were purchased by alleged racketeers at inflated prices with high mortgages, and commensurate insurance coverage. Buildings were then intentionally burned and paid for by a consortium of insurance companies which spread out the losses within the industry. The net effect was a tacit conspiracy in which legitimate real estate companies, banks, and insurance companies acted in conjunction with organized criminals to commit arson and fraud.[94]

As these cases make clear, both providers and consumers of the products of organized crime must be held accountable for their participation or knowing acceptance of illegal activity. A "national commitment" to the fight against organized crime is predicated on a citizenry that is unwilling to benefit from it.

NOTES

[1]Hagan, Frank E. "The Organized Crime Continuum: A Further Specification of a Conceptual Model," CRIMINAL JUSTICE REVIEW, Vol. 8 (Spring, 1983), pp. 52–57.

[2]Albanese, Jay S. *Organized Crime in America,* 2nd ed. (Cincinnati: Anderson Publishing, 1989), p. 5.

[3]Smith, Dwight C., Jr. *The Mafia Mystique* (Lanham, MD: University Press of America, 1990), pp. 27–44; Humbert S. Nelli, *The Business of Crime: Italians and Syndicate Crime in the United States* (Chicago: University of Chicago Press, 1981), ch. 2; Albini, Joseph L. *The American Mafia: Genesis of a Legend* (New York: Irvington, 1971), pp. 159–67.

[4]U.S. Senate Special Committee to Investigate Organized Crime in Interstate Commerce, *Third Interim Report,* 81st Congress (Washington, D.C.: U.S. Government Printing Office, 1951), p. 2.

[5]Moore, William H. *The Kefauver Committee and the Politics of Crime, 1950–1952* (Columbia: University of Missouri Press, 1974), p. 134; Bell, Daniel. "Crime As an American Way of Life," THE ANTIOCH REVIEW, 13 (June, 1953), p. 131.

[6]Moore, *The Kefauver Committee,* p. 134.

[7]New York State Temporary Commission of Investigation, *The Appalachin Meeting,* Summary of Activities During 1962 (New York: State Investigations Commission, 1953), p. 20.

[8]*United States v. Buffalino,* 285 F.2d 408 (1960).

[9]Bonanno, Joseph. *A Man of Honor,* New York: Pocket Books, 1984, ch. 19.

[10]Block, Alan A. History and the Study of Organized Crime. *Urban Life,* 6 (1978), pp. 455–74; Nelli, *The Business of Crime,* pp. 179–218.

[11]U.S. Congress, Senate, Committee on Government Operations, Permanent Subcommittee on Investigations. *Organized Crime and Illicit Traffic in Narcotics—Hearings Part I.* 88th Congress, 1st Session. Washington, D.C.: U.S. Government Printing Office, 1963.

[12]Magnuson, Ed. "Hitting the Mafia," *Time,* (September 29, 1986), p. 19.

[13]For more detail, see Albanese, *Organized Crime in America,* pp. 62–66.

[14]"Notes," *Criminal Organizations,* 1988, Vol. 4, No. 2, p. 10.

[15]McQueen, Mike. ''Heroin Bust a Stunner: NYC Chinatown Leader Arrested,'' *USA Today*, (February 23, 1989), p. 2.

[16]Seamonds, Jack. ''Ethnic Gangs and Organized Crime,'' *U.S. News & World Report*, January 18, 1988, pp. 29–37.

[17]Magnuson, ''Hitting the Mafia,'' p. 19.

[18]Bell, ''Crime As an American Way of Life,'' p. 144.

[19]Ianni, Francis A. J. *Black Mafia* (New York: Simon and Schuster, 1974); Seamonds, Jack. ''Ethnic Gangs & Organized Crime,'' *U.S. News & World Report*, January 18, 1988, pp. 29–37.

[20]President's Commission on Organized Crime, *The Impact: Organized Crime Today* (Washington, D.C.: U.S. Government Printing Office, 1987), pp. 33–129.

[21]Lupsha, Peter A. ''Individual Choice, Material Culture, and Organized Crime,'' *Criminology*, 19, (1981), pp. 3–24; Abadinsky, Howard. *Organized Crime*, 3rd ed. (Chicago: Nelson-Hall, 1990), pp. 56–58.

[22]Block, Alan A. ''The Snowman Cometh: Coke in Progressive New York,'' *Criminology*, Vol. 17 (May, 1979), pp. 75–99.

[23]President's Commission, *Organized Crime Today*, p. 65.

[24]Powell, Stewart, Emerson, Steven, Orr, Kelly, Collins, Dan, and Quick, Barbara. ''Busting the Mob,'' *U.S. News & World Report*, (February 3, 1986), pp. 24–31.

[25]Arlacchi, Pino. *Mafia Business: The Mafia Ethic and the Spirit of Capitalism*, London: Verso, 1986, p. 102.

[26]President's Commission, *Organized Crime Today*, p. 64.

[27]Abadinsky, Howard. ''The McDonald's-ization of the Mafia,'' in *Organized Crime in America: Concepts and Controversies*, ed. Bynum, Timothy S. (Monsey, NY: Criminal Justice Press, 1987), pp. 43–54.

[28]President's Commission, *Organized Crime Today*, pp. 67–8.

[29]Magnuson, ''Hitting the Mafia,'' p. 20.

[30]Kelley, Jack. ''Top Crack Godfather, 10 Others Convicted,'' *USA Today*, December 7, 1989, p. 3; February 14, 1990, p. 3.

[31]Anzalone, Charles. ''Smashing of Cocaine Ring Offers Chilling Lessons,'' *The Buffalo News*, January 19, 1990, p. B1.

[32]Albanese, *Organized Crime in America*, p. 7.

[33]*United States v. Rivera-Santiago*, 872 F.2d 1080 (1st Cir. 1989).

[34]Ibid. at 1081.

[35]Ibid.

[36]Ibid.

[37]*United States v. Lambert,* 887 F.2d 1568 (11th Cir. 1989).

[38]*United States v. Vanwort,* 887 F.2d 386 (2nd. Cir. 1989); see also *United States v. Ayala,* 887 F.2d 62 (5th Cir. 1989).

[39]*United States v. Patterson,* 678 F.2d 774 (9th Cir.) (*cert. denied* 1982).

[40]*United States v. Dakins,* 872 F.2d 1065 (D.C. Cir. 1989).

[41]*United States v. Sachs,* 801 F.2d 839 (6th cir. 1986); *United States v. Walker,* 871 F.2d 1298 (6th cir. 1989).

[42]*United States v. Sai Keung Wong,* 886 F.2d 258 (9th Cir. 1989).

[43]Ibid. at 257–58.

[44]*United States v. Cooper,* 873 F.2d 269 (11th Cir. 1989); see also *United States v. Robles-Pantoja,* 887 F.2d 1250 (5th Cir. 1989).

[45]*United States v. Horton,* 873 F.2d 180 (8th Cir. 1989); see also *United States v. Casamento,* 887 F.2d 1141 (2nd Cir. 1989).

[46]*United States v. Doerr,* 886 F.2d 949 (7th Cir. 1989).

[47]Ibid. at 969.

[48]*United States v. Piva,* 870 F.2d 757 (1st Cir. 1989).

[49]*United States v. Sarault,* 840 F.2d 1479 (9th Cir. 1988); *United States v. Gonzalez,* 797 F.2d 915 (10th Cir. 1986); *United States v. Herron,* 825 F.2d 50 (5th Cir. 1987).

[50]*United States v. Salerno,* 868 F.2d 529 (2nd Cir. 1989).

[51]Ibid. at 531. See also *United States v. Capo,* 817 F.2d 947 (2nd Cir. 1987).

[52]Ibid.

[53]*United States v. Zimmitti,* 850 F.2d 873 (2nd Cir. 1988).

[54]*United States v. Troutman,* 814 F.2d 1456 (10th Cir. 1987).

[55]*Berger v. United States,* 388 U.S. 41 (1967).

[56]See Albanese, Jay S. *Justice, Privacy, and Crime Control,* (Lanham, MD: University Press of America), ch. 1.

[57]National Commission for the Review of Federal and State Laws Relating to Wiretapping and Electronic Surveillance, *Electronic Surveillance Report,* (Washington, D.C.: U.S. Government Printing Office, 1976.

[58]Schlegel, Kip. "Life Imitating Art: Interpreting Information from Electronic Surveillance," in Palmiotto, M. (ed.) *Critical Issues in Criminal Investigation,* (Cinncinati: Anderson Publishing, 1984); Krajick, Kevin. "Should Police Wiretap?: States Don't Agree," *Police Magazine,* (May, 1983).

[59]Administrative Office of the United States Courts, *Report on Applications for Orders Authorizing or Approving the Intercept of Wire or Oral Communications,* (Washington, D.C.: Administrative Office of the Courts, Issued Annually).

[60]Dershowitz, Alan M. "Gotti Case Shows Flaws of Buying Witnesses," *The Buffalo News*, (March 20, 1987), p. C3.

[61]Buder, Leonard. "Gotti is Acquitted in Conspiracy Case Involving the Mob," *The New York Times*, (March 12, 1987), p. 1.

[62]Dershowitz, "Gotti Case Shows Flaws," p. C3.

[63]DeQuine, Jeanne. "High-Tech Drug Sting Zaps 93," *USA Today*, December 7, 1988, p. 3.

[64]"Car Ring Sting," *USA Today*, July 13, 1988, p. 3.

[65]Miller, George I. "Observations on Police Undercover Work," *Criminology*, (February, 1987), Vol. 25, pp. 27–46.

[66]Miller, "Observations on Police Undercover Work," p. 27; Marx, Gary T. "Who Really Gets Stung?: Some Issues Raised by the New Police Undercover Work," *Crime & Delinquency*, (April, 1982), Vol. 28, pp. 165–93; Brown, Michael F. "Criminal Informants," *Journal of Police Science and Administration*, 1985, Vol. 13, pp. 251–56.

[67]U.S. Comptroller General, *Witness Security Program: Prosecutive Results and Participant Arrest Data*, (Washington, D.C.: U.S. General Accounting office, 1984).

[68]U.S. Comptroller General, *Witness Security Program*, 1984.

[69]*Sedima v. Imrex Co*, 105 S.Ct. 3275 (1985).

[70]Ibid.

[71]Poklemba, J. and Crusco, P. "Public Enterprises and RICO: The Aftermath of *United States v. Turkette*," CRIMINAL LAW BULLETIN, (May–June, 1982), Vol. 18, pp. 197–203.

[72]U.S. Comptroller General, *Bank Secrecy Act: Treasury Can Improve Implementation of the Act*, (Washington, D.C.: U.S. General Accounting Office, 1986).

[73]Ibid.

[74]President's Commission on Organized Crime, *The Impact: Organized Crime Today*, p. 169.

[75]U.S. Comptroller General, *Non-Traditional Organized Crime*, (Washington, D.C.: U.S. General Accounting Office, 1989), p. 53.

[76]Albanese, Jay S. "Victim Compensation in Hazardous Waste Cases: Current Options and Needed Reforms," *Victimology: An International Journal*, 1986, Vol. 11; U.S. Comptroller General, *Fraud Hotline*, (Washington, D.C.: U.S. General Accounting Office, 1987).

[77]21 U.S.C. sec. 846.

[78]18 U.S.C. sec. 371.

[79]See, for example, *United States v. Pumphrey*, 831 F.2d 307 (D.C. Cir 1987); *United States v. Saviano*, 843 F.2d 1280 (10th Cir.) (*cert. denied* 1989).

[80]18 U.S.C.A. secs. 1961–68; see *United States v. Pepe*, 747 F.2d 632 (11th Cir 1984); *United States v. Torres Lopez*, 851 F.2d 520 (1st Cir.) (*cert. denied* 1989); *United States v. Anguilo*, 847 F.2d 956 (1st Cir.) (*cert. denied* 1989).

[81]U.S. Comptroller General, *Stronger Federal Effort Needed in Fight Against Organized Crime,* Washington, D.C.: U.S. General Accounting Office, 1980, p. 30.

[82]U.S. Comptroller General, *Non-Traditional Organized Crime,* p. 55.

[83]President's Commission on Organized Crime, *The Edge: Organized Crime, Business, and Labor Unions,* Interim Report, (Washington, D.C.: U.S. Government Printing Office, 1986), pp. 5–6; President's Commission, *Organized Crime and Cocaine Trafficking,* Record of Hearing IV (Washington, D.C.: U.S. Government Printing Office, 1984), p. 477.

[84]President's Commission, *The Edge,* pp. 5–6.

[85]U.S. Comptroller General, *Non-Traditional Organized Crime,* p. 58.

[86]Albanese, *Organized Crime in America,* p. 169–76.

[87]DeFranco, Edward J. *Anatomy of a Scam: A Case Study of a Planned Bankruptcy by Organized Crime* (Washington, D.C.: U.S. Government Printing Office, 1973).

[88]Ibid.

[89]Albanese, *Organized Crime in America,* pp. 176–81.

[90]President's Commission on Law Enforcement and Administration of Justice, *Task Force Report: Organized Crime,* (Washington, D.C.: U.S. Government Printing Office, 1967); President's Commission on Organized Crime, *The Edge,* p. 307; President's Commission, *America's Habit: Drug Abuse, Drug Trafficking, and Organized Crime,* Interim Report, 1986, p. 463.

[91]Landesco, John. *Organized Crime in Chicago,* Part III of the Illinois Crime Survey, (Chicago: University of Chicago Press, 1929), p. 280.

[92]Chambliss, William J. *On the Take: From Petty Crooks to Presidents,* 2nd ed., Bloomington: Indiana University Press, 1988.

[93]Pennsylvania Crime Commission, ''Racketeering in a Pennsylvania City: A Classic Case Study,'' *1989 Report,* (Conshohocken: Pennsylvania Crime Commission, 1990), p. 9–11.

[94]Brady, James. ''The Social Economy of Arson: Vandals, Gangsters, Bankers and Officials in the Making of an Urban Problem,'' in Spitzer, S. and Scull, A. eds. *Research in Law, Deviance and Social Control,* Vol. 6, (Greenwich, CT: JAI Press, 1984), pp. 199–242.

SECTION II

ISSUES AFFECTING THE POLITICAL ORDER

Crime always has a political underpinning. As Richard Quinney has said: crime is a dynamic concept incorporating:

1. process;
2. conflict;
3. power; and
4. social action.

Quinney's characterization of crime shows the essence of political policy making: the translation of social expectations into social policy. But there are strains in any such system—especially in a pluralistic society. This is particularly the case in an open society in which competing and divergent interests not only exist, they are expressed. It is the political system which must deal with these strains and translate them into public policy which is acceptable and workable. With many forms of crime there is no problem. There is general consensus that certain forms of behavior are appropriate subjects for the involvement of the criminal law and the criminal justice system. In other areas, such consensus is not so apparent.

Whether or not wide consensus exists, one fact remains: What constitutes "crime" is in its most fundamental sense a political decision. POLITICS THEN AFFECTS CRIME. In America, our elected legislative bodies formulate their public policy decisions regarding crime in a four-fold context:

1. the expressed wishes of the American public;
2. the consideration of the public necessity;

3. the legislators own biases and perceptions; and
4. the influence of special interests.

Out of this context evolve definitions of what forms of behavior are then classified as "crimes" and individuals designated as "criminals." But the process does not end here. To some extent, political considerations are also represented in what crimes receive the attention of the criminal justice community given increasingly limited resources and competing priorities. Since all forms of criminal behavior cannot be systematically identified and enforced, the political system through its expressed and implied interests—obvious as well as hidden—also identifies what crimes are then singled-out for official attention.

What has been discussed is the most obvious relationship between the political process and crime. But, crime and "politics" are a two-way street. *Crime also affects the political process.* One obvious example is that "law and order" and "crime in the streets" has infused itself into the political process by becoming a recurring issue in election campaigns and legislative efforts. There is still a third aspect of crime and a nation's political system. Certain forms of crime are, themselves, directed at the political system and government. Crimes such as treason, espionage, sedition, and political assassination are such crimes.

This section of the book looks at four crimes that mirror important aspects of these political relationships. Chapter 4 examines acts of terrorism. Criminal acts of terrorism are first and foremost political acts. They are political both in their expression and in their purposeful consequences. Although terrorists often employ a medium of criminal violence or property destruction, such consequences are intermediate to the political purposes which surround these acts. Such criminal behavior is designed to strike a blow at the existing political system, the operations of government, and its policies. This chapter examines this form of criminal behavior. It discusses both domestic and international forms of terrorism, identifies domestic terrorist organizations, their nature and extent, their ideological foundations, efforts to deal with terrorist groups and activities, and the not-so-always-obvious dangers to public dissent that could flow from a government's widening net of counterterrorism efforts.

Chapter 5 examines public integrity offenses and the growth of bias or hate crimes. These are particularly pernicious to American society. Political scientists define *politics* as "the mechanism to distribute and redistribute a nation's wealth and public services." Public integrity crimes corrupt not only the system of government, but also subvert this fundamental process. Corrupt public officials or decisions based on corruption or the abuse of political or public office for personal gain is then especially opprobrious to our system of government and to the citizens who support and rely upon government services.

Public integrity offenses are identified and classified into their major categories along with actual examples of this form of corruption. The federal government's increased efforts to uncover and prosecute corrupt government officials, the statutory authority they rely upon, and the criticism this has brought from some quarters is also explored.

Bias (hate) crime is a noisome act; a threat to our nation's political precepts that guarantees equality of rights and the assurance of protection that is not determined by a person's race, religion, or sexual inclination. Bias or hate crimes are an attack on these fundamental rights. As the incidence of hate-motivated violence has grown in recent years, the criminal justice system has begun to examine ways to deal with this form of crime. The nature of this crime is examined along with evolving statutory attempts to criminalize this express form of behavior and the problems of successful prosecution of hate-induced offenses.

Chapter 6 cautiously examines two issues which have been thrust into the political arena:

1. the growth of AIDS and the purposeful or negligent transmission of this disease to innocent sex partners; and
2. perinatal drug abuse.

Both of these issues are receiving increased attention from public policy makers and the criminal justice system. These two developing areas are included in this section because they have become political issues. They reflect very vividly the "political context" of law making, the process of statutory criminalization, and the effects upon the administration of justice. The political nature of these issues is seen by the divergent views of those who feel the criminal law must play an important role in dealing with these growing problems and those who contend that the criminal law is not an appropriately applied mechanism. These issues are explored as well as some of the developing efforts at prosecution and the use of existing criminal laws to deal with this growing social threat.

CHAPTER 4

Terrorism: Its Domestic and International Threat

CONTENTS

- **Extradtition of International Terrorists: Extending the Long Arm of the Law**
- **Issues of Enforcement**
- **The Danger of Counter-Terrorism Efforts**
- **Conclusion: The Future of Terrorism**

A great deal has been written about the subject of terrorism, especially international terrorism. Most Americans are familiar with such terroristic attacks as the Christmas, 1988 bombing and crash of Pan American's Flight 103 which crashed in Lockerbie, Scotland where 270 lives were lost. In recent years, there have been other notable terrorist successes:

- the 115 passengers and crew killed in the November, 1987 crash of Korea Air Lines Flight 858;
- the hijacking of the Italian cruise ship, the Achille Lauro; and
- the 1983 terrorist attack on the U.S. Marine compound in Beirut, Lebanon which resulted in the deaths of 241 servicemen.

While terrorist organizations operate worldwide, they have been particularly active in such global areas as the Mideast, Western Europe, portions of Asia and the subcontinent, and throughout Latin America. Such names as the Palestine Liberation Organization, the Irish Republican Army, the Red Army Faction, and the Red Brigades are known to most Americans who take even a passing interest in international affairs.

With the outbreak of the Gulf War, it was feared that terrorists would step-up their attacks on American interests. With the possible exception of Japanese invasion fears along the West Coast on the eve of WW II, unprecedented domestic security alerts went into effect at airports, military installations, and government buildings. Although experts considered the United States as a "third-level" target area, many such experts fully expected reprisals from Iraqi agents and Arab sympathizers when Saddam Hussein indicated in several speeches that he would use any means to widen the conflict.[1] All along our common borders with Canada and Mexico, beefed-up security detachments involving federal and state police were visible. Additional attention was also focused on anti-war demonstrators. Out of the Mideast turmoil came a clear message: Terrorism exists as a continuing threat to American interests and its people. Whether the successful conclusion of the war against Iraq heightens or lessens the danger is anybody's guess.

Less well-known to most Americans is the continued problem with domestic terrorist groups. In the early 1980s, the attention of the American law enforcement community focused on several police deaths at the hands of right-wing survivalist groups. There have also been sporadic bombings attributed to left-wing domestic terrorists in the United States. While these international and domestic acts of terrorism are among the most highly publicized terroristic events by the American media, they constitute only a small fraction of such acts occurring almost daily throughout the world.

This chapter examines acts of criminal terrorism. Unlike most writings on the subject, special attention will focus on acts of domestic terrorism. While it is impossible to ignore the threat of international terrorism—if for no other reason then the two are in some ways interlinked—more emphasis is placed on domestic terrorism. The reason for this emphasis is purposeful: The subject of this book is to illuminate those crime issues which have the potential to affect most directly the American people in the years ahead. In this way, it will be indigenous forms of terrorism—or at least acts of terrorism which occur on American soil—which hold the promise of having the most widespread consequence for Americans either as victims killed or injured by terroristic attacks, or indirectly as victims of successful terrorism directed at government or the economic and service infrastructure of our nation.

There is a second compelling reason to discuss domestic terrorism. Such indigenous acts of terrorism also will have a greater effect on the future administrative machinery of justice. This is not to suggest that international terrorism is unimportant, or that such acts will not have future consequences for the United States. While forms of international terrorism conducted abroad involve select components of the administration of justice (such as federal authorities), domestic terrorism, especially that of the homegrown variety, threatens to affect all levels of government—federal, state, and local—as well as involving, to a greater degree, all the components of the criminal justice system.

The United States as a Target of Terrorism

The prevailing impression given by the mass media, public officials, and experts concerned with strategies to combat terrorism is that it is a clear and present danger.[2] Marvin J. Cetron, writing in a recent issue of *The Futurist* contends that international terrorism will continue to grow into the 21st century as will acts of terrorism on American soil.[3] Cetron is not alone in making such dire predictions. Other students of terrorism also voice similar concerns.[4]

Still, such occurrences are impossible to predict. The evidence to substantiate the possible threat is less than persuasive. For one thing, such predictions run counter to recent trends. While there was a sustained increase during the 1970s in the incidence of international and domestic terrorism, the 1980s saw both international and domestic acts of terrorism fluctuate from a high incidence in the early part of the decade to relative infrequency by the late 1980s. Although the United States has the highest rates of both criminal violence and recorded crime among all industrialized nations, it has been very fortunate in escaping a major terrorist incident at home either by international or domestic terrorist groups. In fact, there has not been an international terrorist incident in the United States since 1983. Domestic terrorist groups have also been strangely quiet in the past several years. During 1990, for example, only seven acts of terrorism occurred in the United States, the Commonwealth of Puerto Rico, or the Trust Territories. What is further suprising is that we have escaped such actions in spite of the fact that we have thousands of miles of open borders, a porous program of stopping illegal immigration, a huge number of legal (and illegal) firearms in the possession of our citizenry, and the unfettered ability to travel freely.

This data makes it very difficult to reach any conclusions about long-term trends. Unless one subscribes to the questionable idea of global conspiracy theories of terrorism—that such acts are cyclical in nature and predicated on levels of international terrorism—the experts are on thin ice in predicting parallel trends between international and domestic terrorism. The reliance on adding up global or regional totals to analyze trends in either international or domestic terrorism conveys the misleading impression that trends are common to all countries or extremist movements.[5]

There is no convenient explanation for our nation's fortunate situation. Experts on terrorism seem to be equally stumped by this state of affairs. Nobody seems to know why these groups have yet to single out the United States as a location for the frequent and persistent attacks which regularly occur in other nations. While anti-American terrorism has occurred, it has been largely relegated to attacks against Americans and American interests on foreign soil. Perhaps, it is merely that foreign-based Americans

Figure 4.1. **Terrorist incidents in the United States 1980–1990.**

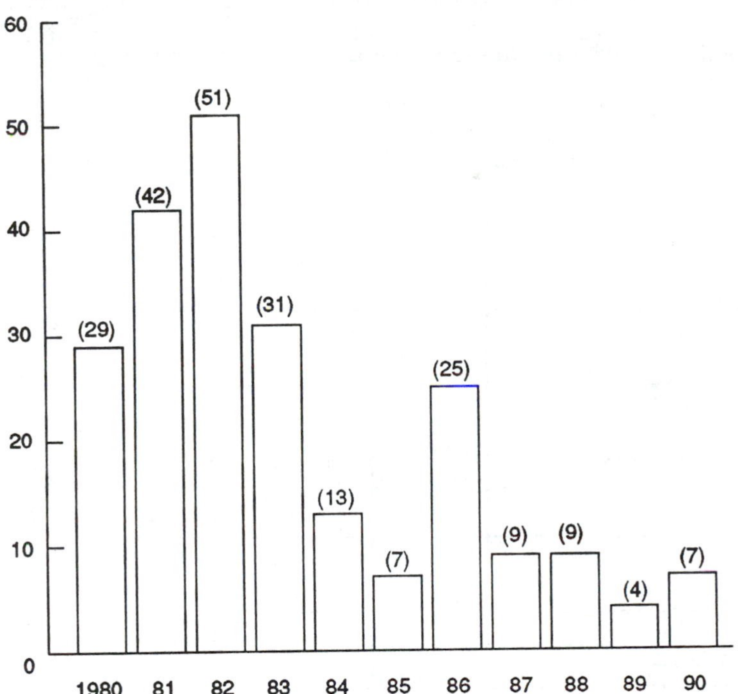

Sources: *Public Report of the Vice-President's Task Force on Combatting Terrorism* (Washington, D.C.: U.S. Government Printing Office (February 1986), p. 6; and various reports, U.S. Department of Justice, *Terrorism in the United States*, FBI.

and American interests are more vulnerable, or the support system abroad for carrying-out successful terrorist tactics and escape exists to a greater degree than in the United States.

Some law enforcement and counter-terrorist organizations ascribe the relative absence of domestic terrorism to the existence of effective deterrence and cooperative efforts among American law enforcement.[6] But this factor alone is an implausible explanation. Although successful law enforcement has probably played a role in reducing acts of domestic terrorism through effective surveillance, penetration and arrest of terrorists and terrorist organizations which has occurred since law enforcement first began such efforts against radical groups in the 1960s, who can say with any assurance what part this has played?

Still, there have been some noted anti-terrorism successes and these may have served as a deterrent. In 1990, 14 members of Yahweh (The Black Hebrew Israelites of Miami) a violent black, anti-white religious cult were arrested. The Black Liberation Army, established in 1971 by ex-convicts and embittered former members of the Black Panthers, was responsible for about 20 ambushes of police officers; by the mid-1970s, eighteen of its members were in prison and only a handful of subsequent events were attributed to the survivors.[7] In 1983 and 1984, the United Freedom Front claimed respon-

Figure 4.2. **Terrorist incidents in the United States by group 1986–1990.**

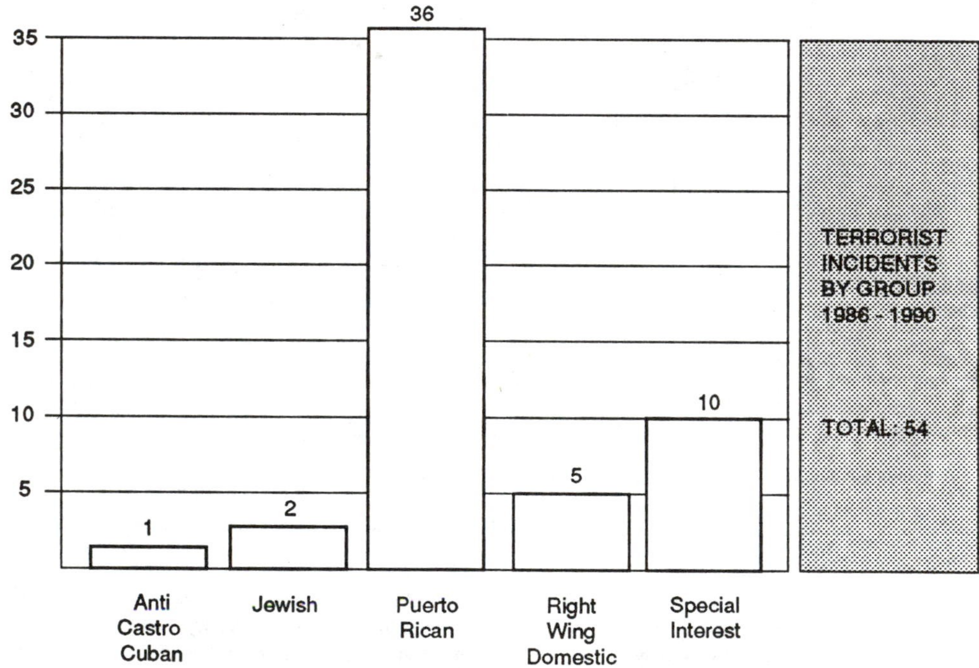

Source: U.S. Department of Justice, *Terrorism in the United States in 1990* (Washington, D.C.: Federal Bureau of Investigation, 1991), p. 12.

sibility for some 10 bombings of corporate and military targets in the New York City area. Seven of its known members were arrested in the following two years. Arrests and convictions have similarly put an end to, or substantially crippled, the terrorist actions of Puerto Rican nationalists in the continental United States, anti-Soviet terrorism by the Jewish Defense League, and the violent activities of the Aryan Nations and similar right-wing extremist groups.[8] Most recently, the 1980s saw successful law enforcement actions directed at certain domestic right-wing groups as The Covenant, the Sword, and the Arm of the Lord.

In terms of attacks by domestic terrorist groups, several other reasons are generally given for our nation's success in avoiding acts of domestic terrorism. Some experts on terrorism contend that we have largely escaped such violence not because of the effectiveness of our counter-terrorism efforts, but because the United States is not a politically polarized country. Unlike Italy, France or West Germany, where a variety of political parties represent the extremes of the ideological spectrum in national politics, the United States has traditionally been a two-party system. Another possible factor inhibiting terrorism in the United States may be our country's unparalled opportunities for economic and social mobility which provide opportunities for social and economic advancement. The United States is also a politically absorptive society. Since the turn of the century,

Figure 4.3. **Terrorist incidents in the United States by target 1986–1990.**

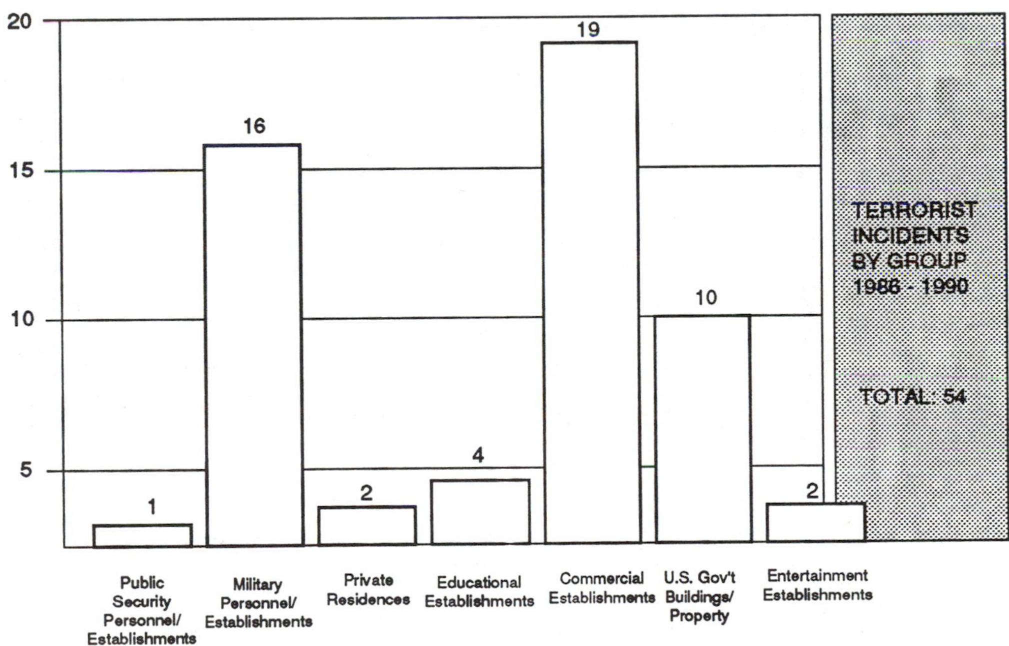

Source: U.S. Department of Justice, *Terrorism in the United States—1990* (Washington, D.C.: Federal Bureau of Investigation, (1991), p. 13.

American politics has been, to a great extent, ethnic politics. Immigrant groups have been absorbed by the existing political parties and integrated into the American political system. It may also be partly explained by the fact that while other Western nations have violent irredentist groups (e.g., the Irish in the United Kingdom, the Basques and Catalonians in Spain, and the like), there are, except for a Puerto Rican faction, none in the United States.[9] Still, while these may indeed be contributing factors, they fail to satisfactorily explain the situation.

In spite of our good fortune, the nation must remain ever-vigilant to the possibility that its relative freedom from terroristic acts could change at any time. As a major power and political leader among the world community of nations, the United States symbolizes a primary target for terroristic political expression. The safety of America from international and domestic terrorist attacks is in no way assured. Although the dissolution of the Soviet-bloc of Eastern Europe, which often provided sanctuary, training, resources, weapons, and explosives for international terrorists, is an optimistic sign of encouragement, other threatening events heighten the danger in the 1990s. The continuing problems in the Mideast and the continuing destabilization in Latin America warrant caution. Both geopolitical situations could spawn increased attacks on Americans and American inter-

Figure 4.4. **Terrorist incidents in the United States by type 1986–1990.**

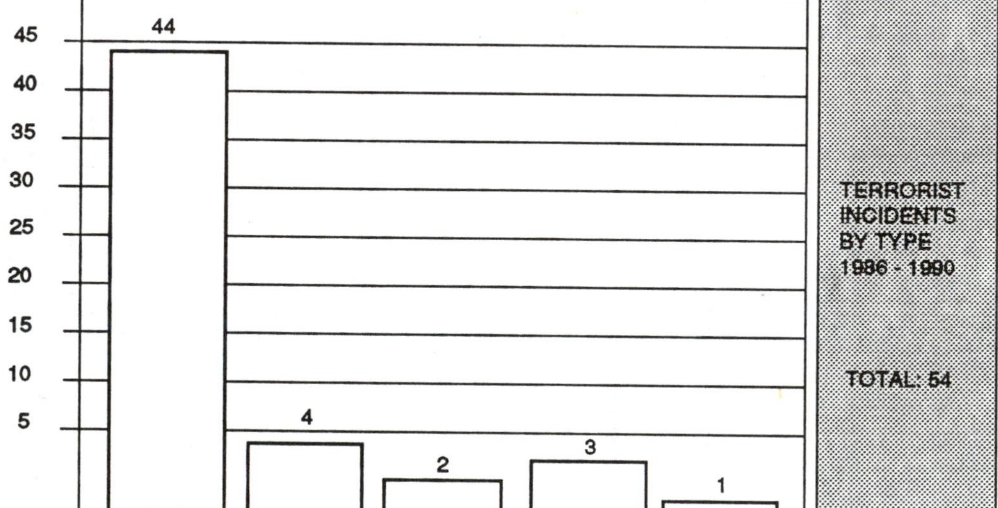

*Includes detonated and undetonated devices, tear gas, pipe and fire bombs.

Source: U.S. Department of Justice, *Terrorism in the United States—1990* (Washington, D.C.: Federal Bureau of Investigation, 1991) p. 13.

ests around the world and create additional domestic terrorist attacks as a form of reprisal to our nation's military and foreign policy efforts. Perhaps of particular concern is the haunting spectre of increasing racial and ideological polarization in American society and the possible threat this poses for increased acts of domestic terrorism by the growing disaffection of racial, economic, and political groups.

Putting Terrorism into Context

Many important questions about terrorism and terrorists themselves still go unanswered. What causes these desperate acts? What do they really accomplish beyond the obvious destruction, injury, or death which lies in their aftermath? Do terrorists act with justification? Are terrorists forced into the role of freedom fighters as claimed by members of the Palestine Liberation Organization, the Irish Republican Army, or extremist groups on both sides of the political spectrum in the United States? Or are they nothing more than cowardly, violent, psychopathic personalities whose cause is empty rhetoric used to disguise a grab for power, influence, and public opinion?

These questions lie at the center of the terrorism controversy. If terrorist motivations are base ones, then deterring terrorism may be possible by denying them the goals they seek or by a policy of swift and exacting retribution—one, incidentally, in which the criminal justice system must play an important role. At least that seems to be the conventional wisdom among some nations and world leaders. But both of these goals must be carried out simultaneously if deterrence is to occur. If terrorist goals are in fact attained, retribution after the fact runs the real risk of becoming meaningless; in fact, it may prove counterproductive and produce symbolic martyrdom. If goals are not attained, then retribution imposed (in light of unattained goals) carries a great deal more efficacy in deterring future terroristic acts.

This is generally the policy followed by the Israelis who argue that swift retaliation against terrorism and the unwillingness to accede to terroristic demands reduces such activity. Perhaps in this way, it is instructive that the Israelis make little distinction between terrorists and civilians, and confront the issue of terrorist elusiveness by randomly attacking sites thought to be strongholds of terrorists in spite of critical world opinion. The Israelis recognize that terrorists are often supported by members of the civilian populace. It was the Israeli model, and the thinking which underlies it, that was employed by the Reagan Administration when terrorist Abu Nidal's headquarters in Libya was bombed.

If, on the other hand, it is more noble motives that inspire the terrorist, than it can be argued that to eliminate terrorism, attention must be paid to its cause. The list of terrorist grievances is long and includes perceived human rights violations such as free speech and religion, self-determination, social and economic equality, enforced imprisonment and even death. It also turns on such questions as government policies, territorial rights, and the presence of foreign intervention. Many terrorists believe their actions are directly linked to the possibility of freeing the population they represent or attaining a just (or at least justified) goal. As Stepan, a character from Albert Camus' play, *The Just*

Assassin, explains, "when we kill, we're killing so as to build up a world in which there will be no more killing." Undoubtedly, some such similar logic guides many of the terrorist groups today.

Of course, it is debatable whether it is possible (or appropriate) for a government to respond to all terrorist grievances and whether such a response would, in fact, elimate such acts. It is often said, for example, that an Israeli agreement to create a Palestinian homeland would erase decades of hate and political unrest between these two groups.

There may be another consequence which is overlooked and finds expression in our own nation's history. The Ku Klux Klan, for example, largely gained power when white Southerners felt their control over the Blacks was eroding as a result of that region's defeat after the Civil War. The adoption of the Fourteenth Amendment by the federal government in 1868, which was ostensibly directed toward guaranteeing basic civil rights to freed Blacks, also provided the impetus for early Klan organizing activities. Such efforts were widely seen as antithetical to the interests of Southern whites. The recent growth of American white neo-Nazi or white supremicist groups is a backlash to their growing perception that Jews, blacks and other minorities are becoming too powerful. It must be remembered that by changing and trying to improve conditions for one disaffected and alienated group we may well create still another.

There is also significant debate over the seriousness of terrrorism. Some individuals believe that the effort and resources which are spent by major governments on the issue is wasted, arguing that terrorism is too insignificant a matter for concern. Walter Laquer is one of these critics. He says,"terrorism creates tremendous noise. It will continue to cause destruction and loss of human life. It will always attract publicity, but politically, it tends to be ineffective. Compared with other dangers out there, it is almost irrelevant."[10] It is in this sense that there is a puzzling situation that has occurred in the United States. Conventional crimes account for far more deaths, property losses, agony, and suffering to its victims than acts attributed to terroristic attacks on American citizens. But the American people and its government consider terrorism as a very important threat and one which they fear. Perhaps this is due to the escalating destructive potential of terrorism and the reality that the possibility for a major terrorist incident grows with continuing world unrest.

There is even a more important reason for our government's concern about terrorism: one that unfortunately escapes all but the most thoughtful Americans. The use of terrorism as an instrument of political action is an invasion of the state's monopoly on the use of force. It is an attack on the existing political structure itself. No political authority can long hope to survive prolonged, broad-scale, and successful terrorism without giving way to anarchy or resorting to repressive measures characteristic of totalitarian regimes.[11] This should give pause to most Americans. From this vantage point, its implications transcend other forms of traditional crimes. If considered in this way, it certainly warrants major concern as a problem which requires our nation's attention in spite of its relative infrequency.

Problems of Defining Terrorism

Although terrorism may seem pretty straightforward in meaning, the definition of terrorism is a little more complicated than most people realize.[12] This can be seen in the label of what constitutes a "terrorist." To many a terrorist is a dangerous and deadly criminal who is willing to employ the most lethal forms of violence to obtain his or her purpose. Without moral compunction they are willing to kill innocent people in furtherance of their objective. Terrorists and their supporters, however, often view such actions as those of a just and patriotic cause and those who engage in such acts as patriots. To one group then the terrorist is a malevolent and dangerous arch-criminal; to another he or she may be a "freedom-fighter" engaged in righteous struggle with an oppressor. The acts of the American colonists in their struggle against England could by today's standards be considered "terroristic acts." Many Americans would bristle at the idea that the American patriots of the Revolution be branded by modern historians as 18th century "terrorists."

Another defining characteristic of terrorism is that it represents the emergence of low-level or low-intensity conflict. Terrorism and terroristic acts serve as an available surrogate for larger armed conflict or war. This is true even of state-sponsored terroristic activities. Because such groups usually are without the necessary resources to wage conventional war on their target governments, they must resort to this substitute form of violence. In the minds of terrorists, the only recourse then is to wage a "limited war" of terrorism. Alex P. Schmid, after wrestling with the various definitions he encountered in his study of this form of violence, concluded that terrorism can best be defined by certain inclusive facts. To Schmid, terrorism is a form of combat in which random or symbolic victims are targets of violence. Through prior use of violence or the credible threat of violence, members of a group, class, or nation are put in a state of chronic fear. The target for terrorist violence is considered unusual which creates an audience beyond the target of violence. Ultimately, the purpose of terrorism is either to immobilize the target of terror in order to produce disorientation and/or compliance or to mobilize secondary targets of demand such as government or targets of attention such as public opinion.[13]

The Political Nature of Terrorism

It is important to point out that terrorism seems to have another singular defining characteristic: Although terrorist acts involve many forms of traditional crime, they are political acts. The one possible exception to this is the recent scourge of what has been called "narco-terrorism" in which narcotic trafficantes in Latin America have targeted government officials for acts of violence and assasination. In these acts (while terroristic strategies are employed which have political consequences), the objective is more economic—applying pressure on anti-narcotic forces so as to disrupt any efforts to impede the enterprise of illegal narcotics trafficking. The political connection is mostly symptomatic of the drug enterprise—attacks on political officials who oppose the cocaine cartels.

This political characteristic of terrorism is important beyond the obvious. It imbues terroristic acts with an element of motivation—indeed a zeal that is not found in traditional criminal events. Some terrorists (and terrorist groups) are so extreme in pursuit of their causes that they are extraordinarily difficult to deter. Traditional methods of deterrence such as arrest, conviction, incarceration, and, in extreme cases, the threat of the imposition of the death penalty may not be effective deterrents. In addition to creating almost insuperable difficulties for these traditional forms of deterrence, this characteristic requires extraordinary counter-measures not typically found in the experiences or operating characteristics of most law enforcement agencies. This is especially the situation among those police operating in a free society and, as in the case of the United States, one in which we may be even more vulnerable because our nation's police are so fragmented. The ever-present threat is that effective counter-measures may, for example, require law enforcement agencies to abandon constitutional and legal constraints and to disregard procedural issues of due process. The police may feel (or worse, use the threat of terroristic activity) as a pretext for the need to step outside the law to deal effectively with terrorism. The chilling fact is that this might occur should widespread terroristic activities begin to take place more frequently in the United States. The implications are indeed ominous and thought-provoking and we shall return to this issue later.

Changing Characteristics of Terrorism

Terrorism, it would seem, persists because terrorists, cut off from normal contacts, talking only to each other, come to believe their own propaganda: government authority is vulnerable; the revolution is about to begin; victory, while not inevitable, is possible. These organizations also persist because a semipermanent subculture of terrorism has developed. Governments find it extremely difficult to identify and destroy the resilient web of personal relationships, clandestine contacts, alliances with other groups, suppliers of materials and services that sustain the terrorist underground.[14] In the process of long-term survival, some terrorist groups are changing their character. It costs money to maintain a terrorist group; those who do not receive support from foreign sponsors must get money through bank robberies, ransom kidnappings, extortion, smuggling, or participation in the trafficking of narcotics. Gradually, the activities become ends in themselves and terrorist groups begin to resemble ordinary criminal organizations hidden behind a thin political veneer.[15]

Modern communications and the relative ease and rapidity of world travel have heightened the potential for successful terroristic attacks. So has the proliferation and availability of weapons supplied by illegal arms traffickers. Along with this is the willingness of some terrorist groups to resort to unrestrained violence. Terrorism has become a major concern for at least one segment of the American criminal justice system—the police. In recent years, the most significant change in terrorist activities is their increasing sophistication. This poses significant danger to the nation. New technologies have offered the terrorist easy possession of advanced weaponry, easily concealable plastic weapons, and plastic explosives (some proving largely undetectable by conventional airport and public building screening devices including even technologically sophisticated thermal neutron analysis detectors).[16] The risk is also heightened by the availability of chemical and biological agents. Some experts are also concerned about possible nuclear devices, although this ultimate form of destruction is, according to intelligence sources, beyond the capabilities of terrorist groups at this time. Still, the availability of such lethal devices may only be a matter of time.

This development and availability of ''high-tech'' terrorism poses special problems for counter-terrorism efforts in advanced societies such as the United States. Highly developed nations rely on the existence and operation of a complex system of networks to provide esential services: electric power, oil and natural gas, telephone networks, major arterial highways, railroads, telecommunications, electronic financial data transmission, air travel, the shipping industry, and water supply. Such intricate and interdependent networks make such nations particularly vulnerable to a terrorist group. A major attack could seriously disrupt our nation's network infrastructure.

Fortunately, active terrorists in the United States have not yet begun to implement high-technology terrorism. It is known among federal authorities, though, that they are available. Such items include: high-order explosives; remote-controlled explosive devices; electromagnetic pulse generators to be used for the purpose of erasing computer data bases of the banking industry, finacial records, national security, and other essential records; and time-delay bombs with digital timers that can be set to detonate months later are available in the arsenals of more sophisticated terrorist groups.[17]

Terrorism is also unlike most other criminal events in that it is characterized by the fact that it involves a significant organizational network in order to be successful; a network that sustains and supports such activities. Experts in the area of terrorism are quick to point out that the lone terrorist or anarchist is a rarity today. The most threatening organizations are organized into groups or cells. There are the operatives or inner circle who actually select the target and then carries out the operation. This core is aided by other groups, or even nations, who supply them with weapons and training. Another level of organization is represented by a group of supporters who are responsible for ''logistics'': the rental of safehouses, the acquisition of automobiles or weapons, and the provision of fictitious documents and intelligence information on targets and existing security. A third level consists of those in sympathetic support of the activities or, at least, the objectives of the terrorist group. They may engage in protests, organize marches and demonstrations, and write articles that support terrorist efforts. Although often not directly invovled with the terrorists, these groups and individuals sustain the activities of the terrorist group by their support.

There is another issue of terrorism which can be described as jurisprudential in nature. Political acts of terrorism are directed at governments or surrogates of what is seen as government policies such as multinational corporations. This stands in contrast to traditional criminal acts which tend to victimize individuals. Although individuals in fact may be the direct victims of terrorism (e.g., a military attache at one of our foreign embassies is assasinated or a bomb is planted in the federal courthouse in Chicago), the purpose of such criminal actions is to strike a blow at government. Individual victims become the surrogate representatives of what is an attack on a nation's governmental structure or its policies. This is far different than most criminal events. While criminal law infers that criminal violations of an individual such as a rape, robbery, or homicide are within the theory of the law, an offense against a collective society bringing prosecution in the name of the state; in political terrorism, there is no such legal pretext. Government becomes the direct or indirect target and the victim becomes the medium. In conventional criminal prosecutions, the opposite occurs. This accounts for why terroristic acts are so repugnant. Like crimes of treason or sedition they are perceived as striking at the core of organized government or the activities necessary to sustain the state.

Finally, it should be pointed out that the United States must deal with two types of terrorist activity—international and domestic.[18] Usually, these are distinguished by where they are committed. *International terrorism* comprises those acts of terrorism committed against American citizens, property, and interests abroad. *Domestic terrorism* are those acts committed on American soil. This is generally the way the authorities treat the two. It is also the way they will be addressed here. Of course, this convenient classification doesn't take into account the fact that an element of internationalism may be involved in so-called ''domestic'' acts of terrorism; for instance, when the acts are committed on American soil by foreign nationals or by American citizens whose terrorist organization is supported or aided by foreign interests.

Along this line, there has developed in recent years an additional concern raised by a new form of terrorism: so-called *transnational terrorism*. This has been defined as a developing form of terrorism in which a terrorist group identified with a specific purpose will assume, at least temporarily, the goals of another group.[19] This seems to be a growing possibility in large part because of the greater cooperation which seems to be growing among certain terrorist groups; a situation that extends the web of terrorism throughout the world. A domestic terrorist group might, for example, take up the cause of a South African terrorist organization on U.S. soil. This, too, will require close attention in the years ahead.

Domestic Terrorist Groups and Characteristics

The United Freedom Front, the Covenant, Lord, the United Jewish Underground, Fuqra, the Revolutionary Armed Task Force, the Aryan Nations, the Armed Forces of the National Liberation (FALN), the Ku Klux Klan are just some of the many domestic terrorist groups which have operated in the United States during the 1970s and 1980s. Although most attention is focused on international terrorist organizations, the United States also has had to contend with domestic terrorist groups. Among the actions attributed to these groups have been bombings, armed robberies, drug trafficking, murders and arson.[20]

These groups are referred to as domestic terrorist organizations because they are not funded, directed, controlled, or supported by foreign sources.[21] Bruce Hoffman and the Rand Corporation in a major research paper prepared for the federal government identifies three categories of domestic terrorist groups:

1. The ethnic separatist/emigre groups;
2. Left-wing radicals; and
3. Right-wing racist, anti-authority, survivalist groups.[22]

The major domestic terrorist groups in each of these three classes are shown in Figures 4-5, 4-6 and 4-7.

Although such groups as the Ku Klux Klan have operated in the United States since the period of Reconstruction following the Civil War, most of the domestic terrorist groups are of much more recent origin. In recent years, over two-thirds of all terroristic acts in the United States have been the work of ethnic-separatist or emigre groups.[23] Except for Puerto Rican groups, their causes and grievances usually are not related closely to American foreign or domestic policies. The United States is simply the battleground where their nationalistic quarrels are fought.[24] Of the three types of terrorist organizations operating in the United States, the ethnic/emigre groups have shown themselves to be the most enduring and likely to resort to violence. They also have been the most active in the past several years.[25] Unlike ideological groups these terrorist organizations do not seem to have the same political following or attractiveness on an ideological basis. Their ethnic-centered support is found in scattered, tightly knit communities around the country. Almost all of the terrorist activity of the ethnic/emigre movements is carried out by these five movements: Puerto Rican separatists, Jewish extremists, Anti-Castro Cuban militants, Armenian radicals, and Islamic fanatics.[26] A smattering of politically

FIGURE 4.5. MAJOR ETHNIC/EMIGRE TERRORIST GROUPS AND SUBGROUPS

Purerto Rican	*Jewish*	*Cuban*
FALN	Jewish Defense League	Alpha-66
CRIA	Jewish Armed Resistance	Brigade 2506
FARP	Jewish Action Movement	Cuban Nationalist Movement
EBP (*Macheteros*)	Jewish Direct Action	FLNC
CRP	United Jewish Underground	Omega-7
COPAAN	*Hatikvah Le'umi*	
MAP	Jewish Defense Organization	
OVRP		
PACRF (Pedro Albizu Campos Revolutionary Forces)		
Armenian	***Islamic***	
ASALA	Libyans	
JCAG	Iranians	
ARA	Palestinians	
	Black Muslims	
	New World of Islam	
	Fuqra	
	A.M.I.	

Source: Bruce Hoffman, *Terrorism in the United States and the Potential Threat to Nuclear Facilities* (Santa Monica, Calif.: Rand Corp. 1986), p. 7. Updated with recent active terrorist groups as identified by the FBI. Adopted with permission.

motivated violence has also been attributed to Croatian and Taiwanese separatists and by Filipino and Haitian opponents of the former Marcos and Duvalier regimes.[27]

Puerto Rican separatists were the most active of the ethnic/emigre groups in the 1980s. Since 1898, when the United States acquired influence over Puerto Rico as a result of the Spanish-American War, violent criminal acts by a minority in support of independence have been directed against the U.S. government and private American corporations on the island and against private corporations, banks, and other targets on the U.S. mainland. Since the early 1970s, at least nine clandestine Puerto Rico-based terrorist groups have been waging an armed struggle to gain independence from the United States. The

Figure 4.6. Major left-wing radical groups.

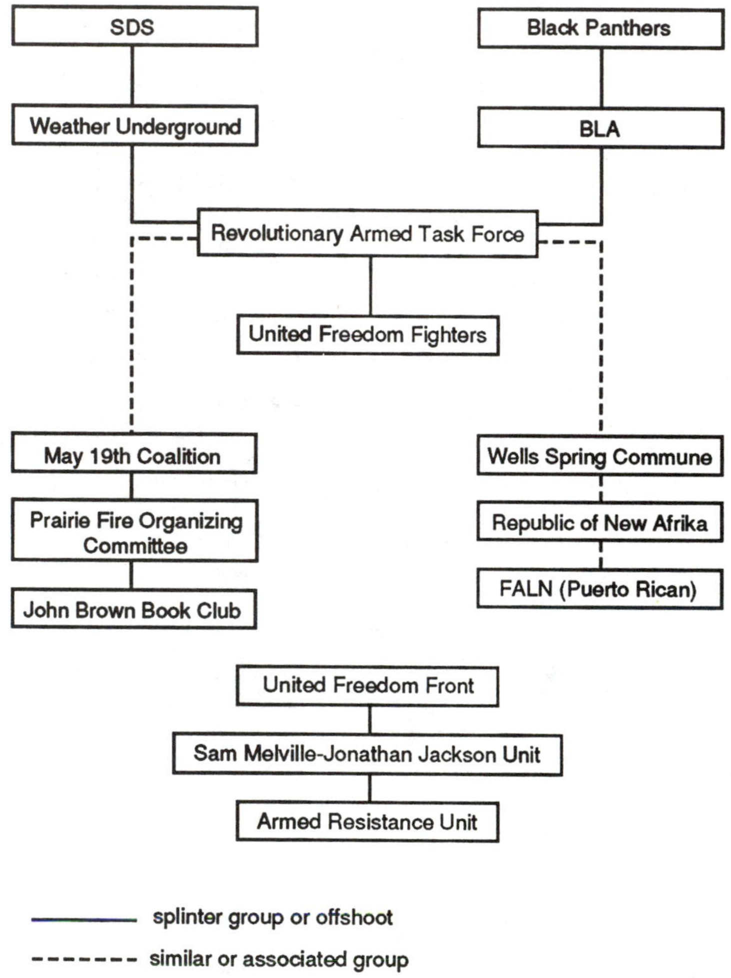

Source: Bruce Hoffman, *Terrorism in the United States and the Potential Threat to Nuclear Facilities* (Santa Monica, Calif.: Rand Corp., 1986), p. 27. Adopted with permission.

EPB-Macheteros, founded in 1978, has been until the last couple of years, the most active group. They have committed violent acts both alone and with other terrorist groups such as the Organization of Volunteers for the Puerto Rican Revolution (OVRP), Armed Forces of Popular Resistance (FARP), People's Revolutionary Commandos (CRP), and the Armed Commandos for National Liberation (CALN). The Puerto Rican Armed Forces of National Liberation (FALN) has also been very active on the U.S. mainland and in Puerto Rico.[28] The FBI claims that between the years of 1974 and 1987, more than 100 terrorist incidents or other crimes committed in the United States could be directly linked to the FALN. Included in these are bombings, assassinations, armed robberies, and rocket attacks. Targets have been military facilities and personnel (especially in Puerto Rico), U.S. Government facilities, and corporate interests.

Jewish terrorism has also been a problem. Fortunately, terroristic activities by Jewish extremists subsided in the late 1980s. The targets of Jewish extremism have been attacks on individuals and organizations considered to be anti-Semitic or opposed to Israeli interests. The issue of Jewish terrorism, for the most part, is centered around the activities of the Jewish Defense League (JDL). While the JDL has been most active in attacking Soviet targets including diplomatic installations, personnel and their property,

Figure 4.7. Major right-wing terrorist groups.

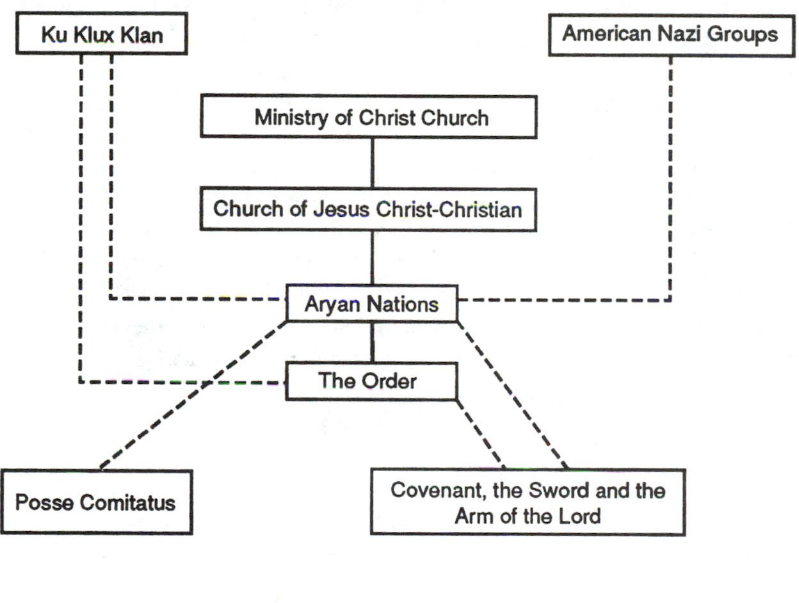

Source: Bruce Hoffman, *Terrorism in the United States and the Potential Threat to Nuclear Facilities* (Santa Monica, Calif.: Rand Corp., 1986), p. 38. Adopted with permission.

Soviet businesses, cultural events and exchange programs, with the loosening of immigration policies for Soviet Jews to leave the former USSR it has turned increasing attention to other ''unfriendly'' countries and their activities in the United States. The list includes Arab, Iranian, Iraqi, Egyptian, Palestinian, Lebanese, French, and German targets. In recent years, the JDL has focused much of its activity on sites in the Northeast states. Bombings are their favorite means of attack followed by shootings, arson, vandalism, and kidnapping. World events including the war with Iraq, growing unrest of the Arab countries, the festering Palestinian issue, the growth of acts of anti-Semitism in the world, and the publicity given right-wing anti-Jewish racial groups in the United States may be pushing the JDL into a new period of activity. Terrorism experts believe that these situations have made Jews more supportive of militant Jewish activity and heightened the possibility for a resurgence of terrorist attacks by this organization.[29]

Left-Wing Terrorism

Many of today's left-wing domestic terroristic groups seem to have been spawned out of the domestic left-wing terrorist activities which came into prominence during the 1960s. Although many of today's terrorist groups have no identity or sympathy with these earlier left-wing causes, the 1960s seemed to be a crucial turning point for the nation. This period led to the eventual formation of left-wing groups willing to use terroristic techniques to achieve their purpose. During that decade, the urban violence and its causes—our government's policies in Vietnam, the underlying racism which wracked many of the nation's major cities, existing social and economic inequalities, the spread of civil disobedience and demonstrations—gave impetus to the spawning and growth of such groups as the Students for a Democratic Society (SDS), and its even more militant offshoot, the Weather Underground. The 1960s also saw the growth of the militant anti-white Black Panter movement. During the post-Vietnam War era of the early 1970s, attacks focused on symbols of American imperialism and what these groups saw as capitalistic exploitation of Third-World nations by the United States. Their targets—banks, corporate offices, and military facilities—were chosen to publicize the terrorsts' cause and existence, as well as to symbolize their anti-imperalist/anti-capitalist ideology. Operations were staged to generate what these left-wing terrorists refer to as ''armed propaganda.''

The Revolutionary Armed Task Force

The abortive holdup of a Brinks armored truck in Nyack, New York in 1981 furnished the first evidence of a new and threatening development in left-wing terrorist activities. Evidence indicated that this robbery attempt was a cooperative effort between white radicals and black extremists. Until this time, law enforcement authorities thought that the small groups of radical leftists that had periodically engaged in terrorist activities in the Vietnam and post-Vietnam period were wholly separate and distinct with no connections to other domestic terrorist groups. The Brinks robbery indicated that two of America's most notorious revolutionary groups, the largely white Weather Underground and the exclusively black BLA, had formed an alliance known as the Revolutionary Armed Task Force (RATF).[30]

This Brinks robbery was the work of the RATF. Subsequent investigations and police raids on safehouses used by the robbers found documents that revealed the merger of the Weather Underground and the BLA. Although leftist radicals and black militants shared similar ideological orientations and views of American society and its government, they were never able to develop any bonds. The black militants looked contemptuously upon their white counterparts as white middle-class revolutionaries who lacked the real will and commitment to seek political change through necessary violence.[31]

It was actually the May 19th Coalition—a splinter group of the Weather Underground—which was primarily responsible for the creation of the RATF and the Brinks robbery. In the late 1970s, dissident elements within the Weather Underground formed this new offshoot. These elements were frustrated with the leadership of the Weather Underground and its inability to forge links with militant black and Hispanic groups who shared a similar ideology and demonstrated a greater willingness to use violence. The May 19th Coalition saw its mission as the development and strengthening of links between politically militant blacks and Hispanics and their white ideological counterparts. There is evidence to believe that the leader of the May 19th Coalition represented this group at a PLO-sponsored conference in Beirut, Lebanon a month before the robbery.[32] It had succeeded in forging a global link with other major international terrorist groups.

The RATF actively pursues its aims in American prisons where it seeks recruits from black inmates and parolees. The Coalition typically established contact by offering black, and to a lesser extent, Hispanic inmates free legal services and advice. Through this means, prisoners who accept this service are gradually drawn into "consciousness raising" meetings and sessions run by other indoctrinated prisoners where they receive rudimentary political indoctrination into the terrorists' ideological beliefs. Especially targeted for these efforts are black and Hispanic prisoners who see themselves as "victims" of a racist and unjust American society. These inmates are then identified for recruitment efforts by the RATF or BLA upon release.[33]

The May 19th cadres also function as couriers for the RATF and BLA, running a tight clandestine communication network among their members who are imprisoned and their organization on the outside. This has enabled the BLA to maintain cohesion. The network appears to be national in scope. Ties have been established with the Mississippi chapter of the Republic of New Afrika (a militant black organization that advocates armed struggle to establish an independent black nation in the American south), the New Afrikan Freedom Fighters (NAFF), and with the Wells Spring Commune (a group of paroled black prisoners operating in the San Francisco area).[34]

The RATF has been most active in the Northeast. The New York cell is thought to have accumulated significant financial resources through a series of bank robberies. The money is used for safehouses, food, and other living expenses as well as weapons and drugs. When police raided a network of safehouses in New York, they discovered detailed documents on several private companies and multi-national corporations identified as doing business with South Africa. These firms were clearly marked for terrorist attack.

Detailed plans have also been found to bomb at least a dozen federal offices in Washington—including the Old Executive Office Building in which President Bush had his office when he was vice-president and a building at the Naval Academy in Annapolis. Successful bombings attributed to the RATF include the bombing of an office of the South African Airways at Kennedy Airport, a bombing of an IBM facility in New York, and a bombing at FBI headquarters in New York City.

While it is believed that there are fewer than 50 active RATF members, this has not been confirmed. The group is so highly disciplined, and membership so carefully restricted, that it is almost impossible to infiltrate. Evidence uncovered in connection with the Brinks holdup reflected the security precautions, organizational skill, logistical support, and operational expertise of the group.[35]

United Freedom Front and the Armed Resistance Unit

These are two other left-wing groups which have been active during the 1980s. The United Freedom Front (UFF) is a group which has been formed to protest U.S. involvement in Central America and American corporations doing business with South Africa. In the early 1980s, this group was responsible for the bombings of several military reserve and recruiting centers in New York State. Also attributed to this group was a bomb which exploded in front of the Honeywell offices in Queens, three bomb attacks on IBM facilities in New York State, and the Union Carbide plant in Tarrytown, New York which was bombed for its business dealings in South Africa. The United Freedom Front also took credit for a bomb that wrecked part of the South African consulate in New York City.

The Armed Resistance Unit (ARU) came into prominence when it claimed credit for the planting of the bomb which exploded in the Senate wing of the U.S. Capitol in 1983. Shortly after the blast, an anonymous caller, purporting to represent the Armed Resistance Unit, called authorities claiming that the bomb had been set to protest the U.S. invasion of Granada a few days earlier and for the American presence in Lebanon. The bombings of several naval facilities in the the Washington, D.C. area also seemed to be the work of this group. Authorities are not convinced, however, that these bombings aren't really the work of the United Freedom Front masquerading under the name of the Armed Resistance Unit. The language of the communiques issued by the ARU and the UFF are very similar as are the targets chosen and the nature of the bombs and explosives used.[36]

The arrests of leaders and key members of groups such as the United Freedom Front during the early 1980s minimized their potential to engage in terrorist activities. Nearly a dozen left-wing terrorists were tried and convicted of various crimes during this period. Still, the authorities believe a number of supporters and associates of those who have been arrested, prosecuted, and imprisoned could become the next generation of terrorists. Domestic left-wing terrorism in the United States has historically been cyclical. There have been periods of terrorist violence, followed by arrests and prosecutions, followed by a regrouping stage. The cycle then starts anew. According to federal intelligence sources, left-wing terrorism in the United States currently appears to be in the regrouping stage.[37]

Right-Wing Terrorists

During the late 1970s and early 1980s, evidence came to light of a well-organized network of extremist right-wing groups in the United States all connected in some way to the so-called Christian Identity Movement which espouses a variety of anti-Semitic, racist, Christian fundamentalist, and anti-federalist beliefs. Certain features of these new right-wing groups are even more ominous than the more familiar threats from the Ku Klux Klan or the American Nazi Party. They espouse outright sedition and often engage in group paramilitary ''survivalist'' training where they practice developing their guerilla skills with a formidable arsenal of automatic weapons. According to the Center for Democratic Renewal (a private research organization that monitors domestic right-wing activity), it is estimated that these groups are made up of between 2,000 and 5,000 ''hard-core activists'' and between 14,000 and 50,000 sympathizers.[38]

Unlike most of their leftist counterparts, the members of these groups are, for the most part, not full-time terrorists. Rather, they see themselves as ''minutemen,'' the inheritors of the tradition of the American Revolution's Minutemen, who are available at a moment's notice to fight for their inalienable rights. They are bound together by their shared hostility to any form of government above the county level; their villification of Jews and non-whites as children of Satan; obsession with achieving the religious and racial purification of the United States; belief in a conspiracy theory of powerful Jewish interests controlling the government, banks, and media; and their advocacy of the overthrow of the government of the United States or as they refer to it, the ''Zionist Occupation Government.''[39]

The Aryan Nations

The International Association of Chiefs of Police describes the Aryan Nations as an ''extremist, anti-Semitic, Neo-Nazi group . . . [embracing] white supremacists, survivalists, militant tax resisters and Neo-Nazis.''[40] It operates from its secluded headquarters at Hayden Lake near the Couer d'Alene National Forest in Idaho. The group was founded by Richard Butler, a former aeronautical engineer from California who moved to Idaho in 1973. Butler is also the head of the Church of Jesus Christ-Christian which is also located on the Aryan Nations Idaho site. The church is based on the white supremacist dogma espoused by the church's founder, Dr. Wesley Swift. When Swift died in 1970, Butler assumed leadership. The church embraces the aggressive anti-Semitic beliefs found in the Christian Identity Movement. The religious spearhead of the movement is led by a retired U.S. Army officer and expert in guerrila warfare. The idea for the church's name came from the belief that Christ was not a Jew, but an Aryan. The sect also believes that white Anglo-Saxons and not the Jews are the ''chosen people'' and that the United States is the ''promised land.'' Jews are viewed as imposters and as ''children of Satan'' who must be exterminated.[41]

The Aryan Nations claim a membership of active supporters of over 6,000 members scatterd throughout the United States and Canada. Authorities see the number as much lower although it has been recognized that there is a scattering of sympathetic support for the movement throughout the United States.[42] It is difficult to determine accurately the group's membership partly because it is an umbrella-type entity that serves as a centralized, coordinating body for a variety of different, but similarly oriented, organizations.[43] Federal law enforcement officials believe that the Aryan Nations is "united more by ideology and theology than by organization and hierarchy."[44] Ties have been forged with Canadian white supremacist groups, West German neo-Nazi terrorists, Ku Klux Klan groups, the American Nazi Party, and other right-wing groups.[45] Its communication link to these various groups is through a code accessed computer network "bulletin board" known as the Aryan Liberty Net. It sees The Jewish Anti-Defamation League and the American Communist Party as its avowed enemy. Among its "race traitors" are liberal politicians, federal judges, federal prosecutors, and Internal Revenue Service agents.[46]

Its ideology is a combination of racism and sedition. In a published newsletter the group proclaimed its desire to "make it clear to ourselves and our ememies what we intend to do: We will have a national racial state at whatever price is necessary. We have to kill the bastards . . . the leadership of malicious bastardizing politicians . . . [in] modern, decadent America [where] millions of whites watch in abject dismay and hopelessness as their great culture, heritage and civilization evaporates in the steaming, stinking, seething milieu of so many alien races, cultures and gods."[47] The Aryan Nation professes the need to conduct Irish Republican Army (IRA) guerrilla tactics throughout the United States aimed at government officials and the corrupt Jewish (and black) influence. Special efforts are targeted among prison groups in the West and Southwest such as the prison-based Aryan Brotherhood to enlist their support for the cause.

The Order

The Order was founded in 1983 as a splinter group which broke off from the Aryan Nations when they felt more extreme tactics were required. Led by Robert Matthews, its purpose is to "pursue a more violent approach towards making the Unites States a pure white Christian country."[48] To Matthews and his followers, this could only be accomplished by the violent overthrow of the U.S. Government which has been taken over by Jews and other inferior races. The organization chose its name from the book, *The Turner Diaries,* in which a paramilitary group known as "The Order" carries out terroristic attacks against government buildings and the FBI. In its blueprint for revolution, government officials are assassinated, public utilities are bombed, and the U.S. nuclear arsenal is captured resulting in a mass nuclear attack then being launched on Israel. The Order regards all non-whites as "mud people," and its members swear an oath to eliminate "their enemies" (i.e., anyone of the Jewish race and white "traitors" who side with the Jews). Each member of the group can become an "Aryan Warrior" by accruing points based on the murder of Jews, blacks, federal judges, and FBI agents.[49]

In 1983, 17 members of The Order ambushed a Brinks armored car near Ukiah, California making off with $3.6 million. Later that year, they robbed another armored car in Seattle of $500,000. Several bank robberies were also attributed to this group. In each case, armed with automatic weapons, they struck with discipline and precision. Their most famous crime was the 1984 murder of a Alan Berg, a Jewish radio talk-show host, who was an outspoken and acerbic critic of the right-wing. Later that year, Matthews was himself killed after federal agents and police trapped him in a barricaded cottage on an island in Puget Sound, Washington. A search of the cottage found a veritable arsenal of weapons and explosives, a large amount of cash and a ''declaration of war'' against the United States signed by group members.

Special efforts were mounted by the U.S. Department of Justice to investigate, locate, prosecute, and convict the ''inner-circle'' and the leadership of The Order. Authorities located records which indicated that large amounts of money gained through their robbery efforts had been given to the Ku Klux Klan, the head of the White People's Political Association, and to Richard Butler, the leader of the Aryan Nations. Plans were also uncovered showing that The Order intended to support its activities through a series of robberies and by counterfeiting. It was also discovered that the organization had an extensive network of safehouses and support cells especially throughout the southwestern and southeastern states.

The Covenant, the Sword, and the Arm of the Lord

This group was founded in the 1970s and gained wide media attention in the early 1980s for the gunning down of an Arkansas State Trooper and the wounding of another. Subsequent investigation disclosed a CSA compound in Arkansas' Ozark Mountains. A police raid on its headquarters resulted in the death of the local sheriff leading the police raid. In the compound, the police found a cache of various weapons, materials used for the making of hand grenades, an anti-tank rocket, plastic and other explosives. A chilling paramilitary training area called ''Silouette City,'' complete with cutout figures of police officers with Stars of David on their chests, served as targets.

The search of the CSA compound disclosed evidence of their ties to other right-wing white supremacist survivalists groups including the Order. The CSA considers itself the paramilitary arm of the Church of Zarepeth-Horeb (the name of a Biblical ''purging place''). Its members are engaged in extensive paramilitary training for the coming ''Armageddon'' or race war they see as inevitable in the United States.

Posse Comitatus

The group Posse Comitatus takes its name from the Latin phrase meaning ''power of the county.'' It was founded in 1969 by a former member of the American Nazi Party. During the 1970s, chapters were found in almost every state. Initially, the organization practiced passive tax protest activities against the taxing policies of the federal government. In recent years, it has found a resurgence among some financially hard-pressed farmers in the Midwest and the Northwest based on the idea that a secret cabal exists consisting of Jews, bankers, and the federal government. The group is strongly anti-federal government and sees only county forms of government as legitimate. To members of Posse Comitatus, the state and federal governments are seen as usurpers of the rights of the people. It is estimated that its members number between 1,000 and 3,000 persons.[50] Leaders of the movement contend that there are chapters in every state but Hawaii and 2,000 members in the state of Wisconsin alone.[51]

The group is reported to hold "counterinsurgency seminars" throughout the United States, particularly in the Midwest. At these seminars, members practice as "killer teams" training in hand-to-hand combat techniques, the administration of poison, night combat patrol, murder by ambush, and the making of bombs and explosives. There is some evidence that they have obtained rocket-propelled grenades, mortars, explosive and protective equipment, and heavy-duty armor.[52]

There are two more recent developments in right-wing activities worth mentioning. Authorities consider anti-abortionist forces, the animal-rights oriented Animal Liberation Front (ALF), and the radical, environmentalist Evan Mecham Eco-Terrorist International Conspiracy (EMETIC) to be the most recent groups employing terrorist tactics. A number of bombings and acts of vandalism directed at abortion clinics or pro-abortion centers have occurred throughout the United States. A gunshot attributed to anti-abortion advocates was also fired through the window at the home of Supreme Court Justice Harry Blackmun who authored the Court's 1973 pro-abortion majority decision in *Roe v. Wade*. The ALF has used arson, vandalism, and theft against animal reserach laboratories and the EMETIC has taken credit for several terrorist incidents involving attacks on electric transmission sources and a uranium mine. There is a fear that the EMETIC may also target a nuclear generating facility.[53] There are also indications that emerging links between white supremacists and Black Muslims are occurring. Both find common ground on their antipathy toward the Jewish race and their feeling that powerful Jewish interests have taken control of the country; a situation which is at the root of America's problems. There is also common agreement by both groups that blacks and whites are different and each should live in separate countries under their own form of government.[54]

Terrorism and the Criminal Justice System

The leadership role for combatting terrorism has been given to the federal government largely because local and state law enforcement agencies are simply without the resources, specialized skills, or the jurisdictional sweep of authority to cope effectively with the problem. Still, some larger city police departments, such as Los Angeles, New York, and Chicago, have created special counterterrorist intelligence and investigative units. Some state police agencies have also specially trained investigative personnel to work with federal and municipal authorities in this area. For domestic terrorist activities occurring in the United States, the U.S. Attorney General has the responsibility for coordinating all federal law enforcement activities, with the FBI designated the lead agency for dealing with such occurrences. To a lesser extent, other federal agencies such as the Bureau of Alcohol, Tobacco, and Firearms of the Treasury Department, the United States Marshals Service, and the Immigration and Naturalization authorities play a part. In fact, some 26 federal investigative agencies have various degrees of jurisdiction over domestic acts of terrorism.[55] In some ways, this poses a problem. In trying to develop a national response to such threats, efforts have become somewhat divided, and those who are familiar with the "in-fighting" among federal agencies are concerned that such divided responsibility may dilute overall effectiveness.

The FBI is the lead agency in the investigation of domestic terrorist activities and counter-terrorism efforts. These include those occurring in Puerto Rico and the territories and possessions of the United States. By existing law and agency directives, they are authorized to commence an investigation if facts or circumstances reasonably indicate that two or more persons are involved in a continuing undertaking for the purpose of:

1. intimidating or coercing the civil population or any segement thereof;
2. influencing or retaliating against the actions of the government of the United States or any state or political subdivision thereof or of any foreign state, by intimidation or coercion; or
3. influencing or retaliating against the trade or economic policies of a corporation or other entity engaged in foreign commerce, by intimidation or coercion.[56]

The division of responsibilities is even more pronounced in our international anti-terrorist efforts. Existing federal laws and Presidential Executive Orders give the State Department (under its foreign relations authority) primary responsibility for handling terrorist activities directed at American citizens outside the United States. This has posed problems. The State Department is not an enforcement agency nor a specialist in anti-terrorist strategies, although it operates an Office for Combatting Terrorism and has created a special Diplomatic Security Service and a Anti-Terrorism Assistance Program for foreign governments.[57] In fact, its operating policies of diplomacy and statecraft may be at odds with effective programs of intelligence-gathering and enforcement efforts. There is some evidence that more enforcement-oriented agencies, such as those of the Department of Justice, are at odds with the State Department's role and handling of terrorist threats and actions. In addition, the CIA, the Department of Defense, the Department of Energy (for reasons of nuclear technology), the Department of Transportation, and the General Services Administration have all been designated roles in responding to international and, in some cases, domestic terrorist incidents.

Recently, a new weapon in global counter-terrorism has been introduced. The International Criminal Police Organization or, as it is now called, ICPO-Interpol has been developing greater response capabilities.[58] This organization began as the International Criminal Police Commission in Vienna in the 1920s. During WW II, the organization ceased functioning. In 1946, it was recreated in France and now operates out of its new headquarters the General Secretariat in Lyon, France. As a recognized international organization, Interpol is accorded privileges and protocols, is governed by its own rules, and remains wholly independent of French governmental control and regulation. Today, there are approximately 145 member states consisting of some 256 personnel, of whom 90 are police officers from 26 different countries.[59] ICPO-Interpol is not what many people conceive it to be. It is not an international police agency. Its primary mission is to gather, analyze, and disseminate law enforcement information and law enforcement-related intelligence to member nations. A member nation has a National Central Bureau

(NCB) (the United States' NCB is in Washington, D.C.) which is the only source authorized by the Interpol charter to request or receive Interpol-generated information or to transmit information to Interpol. At the General Secretariat, computers store vast amounts of information supplied by its member nations on such subjects as international criminals, major items of stolen property, and fugitives.

Until 1984, Interpol played a minor role in the area of international terrorism or terrorists. This was because Article 3 of its charter expressly prohibited the organization to "undertake any intervention or activities of a political, military, religious, or racial charcter."[60] For many years, this provision excluded counter-terrorism efforts or intelligence gathering by the agency because of the "political" nature of terrorism. Largely because progress had been made by other international conventions such as the European Covention on the Suppression of Terrorism, the Organization of American States Convention to Prevent and Punish Acts of Terrorism, and the League of Arab States Extradition Conventions—all of which had taken steps to exclude the long-standing exceptions for "political acts"—Interpol re-examined its position. Now, a specialized group, the Provisional Terrorism Unit, has been established within the ICPO-Interpol General Secretariat. All Interpol resources in terms of communication, intelligence, and support services regarding international terrorism (and terrorists) are now available to the National Central Bureaus of member nations.

Statutory Definitions of Terrorism

State Efforts

As interest in combatting terrorism has grown, so have efforts to counter the threat of terrorism. One result has been that some state governments have adopted laws aimed specifically at terrorist activity. Still, there is little uniformity from state to state. Although it is hard to imagine terroristic acts not incorporating conventional crimes which can be prosecuted under existing criminal statutes (e.g., robbery, assault, murder, burglary, extortion, possession of illegal weapons and explosives, and the like), a few states have passed specific legislation which creates the crime of "terrorism" or have construed their existing terrorist threat statute to include the "political" or "social" motivation for terroristic acts.[61] California's legislation is an example. In its terroristic threat statute, "terrorize" means:

> To create a climate of fear and intimidation by means of threats or violent action causing sustained fear for personal safety *in order to achieve social or political goals.*[62]

While such a statute tried to incorporate the "political" nature of terroristic acts, successful prosecution efforts under such specific political terroristic threat statutes has been a mixed-bag. The imprecision of the term, " . . . [to] achieve social or political goals" has not been looked upon favorably by some state courts. It also adds an additional burden to the government in prosecuting such cases. The state must show that the actions taken were in furtherance of a social or political goal. In this way, *individual motivation* and *political purpose* become elements of the particular offense. This adds a degree of difficulty to the problem of prosecuting such crimes as well as increasing statutory vagueness.

For example, most crimes do not require that the state demonstrate the motive for the crime. It is generally sufficient for conviction to merely show that the crime was committed and the accused intended to commit the crime with the latter being deduced from his or her behavior and the circumstances of the criminal event. In a more explicit anti-political terrorist statute, motivation and political purpose must not only be shown as an element of the offense, they also become interlocked. That is, motivation must be *independently shown as well as being linked to a political purpose which must also be proven by the state*. This definition arose in a California case, *People v. Mirmirani*.[63] The California Supreme Court, in reviewing the the term ''terrorize'' in the state's terrorist threat statute, said it was too vague in its phrase, ''in order to achieve social or political goals.'' The court struck down the entire statute because of the vagueness of this phrase.[64] It is perhaps instructive and appropriate—although disconcerting to law enforcement—that some courts don't uphold such vagueness. Otherwise government would be in a position to prosecute political dissidents as ''terrorists'' for acts which furthered ''social or political goals.''

Because of such problems, most states have eschewed creating a specific terrorism statute, especially one with the elements ''political'' or ''social'' purpose included. Instead, the majority of states attempt to define the offense under the broader classification of ''terroristic threat'' statutes. Since terroristic threat statutes are not directly aimed at the activities of terrorists who are politically or socially motivated, but are used to prosecute general non-political threats on the life or property of others, they seem to be more workable.[65] Many states have patterned their terroristic threat laws after the Model Penal Code which specifies that a person is guilty of terroristic threat if:

> He threatens to commit any crime of violence with the purpose to terrorize another or to cause evacuation of a building, place of assembly, or facility or public transportation . . . or in reckless disregard of the risk of causing such terror or inconvenience.[66]

The use of such general terroristic threat statutes for prosecution has not been without criticism. For one thing, the maximum penalties provided under such laws is often that of a lower-level felony. It could be argued that this is entirely inappropriate. But this criticism is questionable. Typically, states could prosecute domestic political terrorists for the predicate crimes they committed such as homicide, assault, or robbery as well as including the charge ''terroristic threat'' if the elements of this offense are also present which is highly likely. It would seem that in combination, adequate criminal laws then exist to prosecute for terroristic crimes. The one possible exception to this is in the case of the death penalty for homicides which occur as a result of an act of terrorism. Many death penalty states do not include ''in furtherance of a terrorist activity'' as an aggravating or specific circumstance calling for the death penalty. The reason for this is that such wording would impose another burden on the state and require the prosecution to show that the crime was specifically related to a terrorist activity. This raises certain issues and legal questions beyond the scope of required discussion here.

Federal Efforts

The prosecution of domestic terrorists by the federal government has followed a different path than that travelled by some state prosecutions for these crimes. Perhaps sensitive to possible civil rights issues, Congress has not enacted a specific all-encompassing domestic anti-terrorism law. It also may lie in the recognition by federal authorities (and Congress) that prosecution under conventional criminal statutes is less problematic and does not run the risk of dealing with the problems of "political" or "social" motivation as an element if these were incorporated into some federal anti-terrorism law. It can also be argued that there are enough conventional federal criminal laws in existence to cover domestic terrorist activities.

In his analysis of federal prosecutions of terrorist activities, Brent Smith found that the authorities were more likely, in the case of domestic terrorist groups or individuals, to use conventional federal statutes as the basis for prosecution. For example, prosecution was based on such crimes as firearms and weapons violations, bank robbery, transportation of explosives, escape, and Racketeer and Influenced Corrupt Organizations (RICO) charges.[67]

The federal government does indeed have an arsenal of crimes it can employ for prosecution. The Department of Justice in its official bulletin to federal prosecutors generally subscribes to the use of a number of federal statutes in their prosecution efforts against domestic terrorism and terrorists beyond those outlined by Smith. Together, they present a formidable array of federal criminal laws. Figure 4.8 is a list of what the federal authorities consider the most important and what has proven to be the most frequently used laws against terrorists.

In the area of international acts of terrorism, unlike domestic terrorism, specific anti-terrorist legislation has had to be adopted by the federal government. Since the mid-1970s, Congress has passed any number of specific statutes aimed directly at international terrorism. The 1980s were particularly busy years for the adoption of new federal laws in this area. Figure 4.9 lists the major federal laws in the area and their provisions.

Extradition of International Terrorists: Extending the Long Arm of the Law

The examination of anti-terrorism law and international terrorism would be incomplete without some discussion of the problems associated with returning international terrorists to the United States for the commission of terroristic acts on American citizens or property. One reason international terrorists have been successful in carrying out their campaigns of violence is their ability to exploit the international legal system by using

FIGURE 4.8. MAJOR FEDERAL DOMESTIC ANTI-TERRORISM STATUTES

Offense	*Violation*
Assault	Protection of foreign officials, official guests, and internationally protected persons.
Civil Rights	Conspiracy against rights of citizens; deprivation of rights under color of law; federally protected activities (e.g., voting rights).
Conspiracy	Conspiracy to commit offense or defraud United States; solicitation to commit a crime of violence.
Counterfeiting and Forgery	Dealing in or uttering counterfeit obligations or securities.
Importation, Manufacture, Distribution, and Storage of Explosive Materials	
Extortion and Threat	The use of interstate communications; mailing threatening communications.
Fraud and False Statements	Fraud and related activity in connection with identification documents.
Fugitives from Justice	Concealing person from arrest; flight to avoid prosecution, giving testimony, or damaging or destroying any building or other real or personal property.
Homicide	Protection of officers and employees of the United States.
Kidnapping and Hostage Taking	
Machine Guns, Destructive Devices, and Certain Other Firearms	
Racketeering	Interference with commerce by threats of violence; interstate and foreign travel or transportation in aid of racketeering activity; violent crime in aid of racketeering activity.
Racketeer Influenced and Corrupt Organizations (RICO)	
Robbery and Burglary	
Stolen Property	
Treason, Sedition and Subversive Activities	Includes seditious conspiracy; advocating overthrow of government.
Unlawful Possession or Receipt of Firearms	

Source: U.S. Department of Justice, *Terrorism in the United States* (Washington, D.C.: FBI—Terrorist Research and Analytical Center) December 31, 1989. pp. 31–32.

Anti-terrorism Act of 1987. Makes it unlawful to further the interests or assist the Palestine Liberation Organization (PLO).

Omnibus Diplomatic Security and Anti-terrorist Act (1986). Establishes extra-territorial jurisdiction over certain terrorist acts including homicide and the use of physical violence with intent to cause serious bodily injury against U.S. citizens abroad. Creates the Diplomatic Security Service and provides for increased security at U.S. Embassies and Consulates.

Victims of Terrorism Compensation Act (1986). Provides compensation for certain classes of American terrorist victims and their families.

Terrorist Prosecution Act (1986). Provides for the prosecution and punishment of persons who, in furtherance of terrorist activities or because of the nationality of the victims, commit violent attacks upon Americans outside the United States or conspire outside of the United States to murder Americans within the United States.

Comprehensive Crime Control Act (1984). Created a new crime of "hostage taking" and provides for the punishment of anyone who seizes a person in order to coerce a U.S. government agency to comply with some condition.

Anti-Hijacking Act of 1974. Imposes criminal sanctions for persons convicted of hijacking or attempted hijacking.

1984 Act to Combat International Terrorism. Authorizes rewards for information concerning terrorist acts.

Note: The United States has also ratified new anti-terrorist extradition agreements with several nations and ratified United Nations anti-terrorist Conventions and resolutions.

Figure 4.9. **Major specific federal international anti-terrorism laws.**

national boundaries as legal veils. International law does not require a nation to extradite an individual to the offended country. There must be an international agreement setting forth the terms and conditions necessary for extradition. Extradition treaties, however, normally contain an exception for "political offenses."[68] Generally, under international law in order to constitute an offense of a political nature, there must be some political disturbance or upheaval, or some struggle between two opposing political parties for the mastery of the government of the country.[69] Additionally, the crime in question must have been committed in furtherance of that disturbance or struggle with some connection between the conduct of the defendant and the political object.[70] From such a broad definition it can be argued that all terrorist acts constitute political offenses. Consequently, many perpetrators of terrorist acts may escape through this exception loophole.

In 1987, a suspected Shiite terrorist, Fawaz Yunis, was forcibly taken from a boat in the Mediterranean off Cyprus by FBI agents and brought to the United States to stand trial for the 1985 hijacking of a Jordanian airliner with four Americans aboard. He was lured by a contrived drug sale to a FBI-chartered yacht by a former associate-turned informer. This was the first time an international terrorist was successfully brought to trial in the United States. Several years before the Yunis arrest, the United States had tried to capture the hijackers of the Achille Lauro, but were frustrated when the Italian government let the alleged ringleader escape and would not extradite the other involved hijackers, choosing, instead, to try them in an Italian court.

However, once Yunis was returned to the United States, the federal authorities ran into some prosecution problems. After his arrest, he was transferred to a U.S. Navy ship. He spent four days aboard the ship during which time he confessed to the hijacking. The federal judge hearing the government's case ruled that the confession was taken in violation of Yunis' rights and, therefore, was inadmissable at trial. The ruling was based on the facts that Yunis, while violently seasick, had been questioned for more than nine hours during which time he confessed, that he had not received treatment for two broken wrists he had sustained during the arrest, nor had he been advised of his rights or provided an attorney during the questioning.[71]

In bringing Yunis to trial, the Federal government relied upon some recently adopted federal legislation which extended the jurisdiction of the United States for certain crimes committed outside its borders against United States citizens.[72] Although questions were raised by members of the world community about the legality of the United States to extend its criminal law and enforcement jurisdiction so broadly, the then U.S. Attorney General made it clear that America intended to use these new laws to combat international terrorism against American citizens.[73] The Yunis case was a departure from long-standing international law; a direction in which the U.S. government had been moving in recent years as it continued to increased the scope of its international jurisdiction.[74]

Congress, in providing the federal government with this new authority, sought to provide for the prosecution and punishment of persons who, in furtherance of terrorist activities or because of the nationality of the victims, commit violent acts upon Americans outside the United States or conspire outside the United States to murder Americans within the United States. Congress also intended to protect property against attack by terrorist groups with the new legislation. Also it seems to allow for the abduction of suspected terrorist within another country for the purpose of being brought to the United States for trial. Interestingly, this was the first federal law which specifically provided for prosecution of terrorists whose purpose it is to harm ordinary American citizens (previous existing federal law applied only to extraterritorial murder or assault on high-ranking U.S. officials) and it does this as in the case of the Jordanian hijacking regardless of whether the terrorist action was directly aimed at Americans, American interests or the American government.

Problems of International Extradition

A lot of Americans get upset when they feel that our so-called allies will not extradite a terrorist to the United States for trial. This has periodically occurred among our West European allies and with nations of Latin America. The idea underlying their refusal to extradite is that "political offenses" are not extraditable. Without getting too deeply emeshed in the international law which governs this provision, it is enough to understand that there are several important reasons why nations have refused to extradite "political offenders." The first is the idea of fairness and justice: Political offenders are thought to be vulnerable to retaliatory justice if returned to the requesting state. Along this line there is the argument that nations should avoid assisting countries acting in revenge upon unsuccessful dissidents. There is also the issue of the preservation of state neutrality toward foreign conflicts. An in-depth inquiry by the asylum state into the offender's alleged crime is seen as requiring a judgment on the legitimacy of the particular political conflict and is deemed inappropriate for a nation. Of course, it is another issue if the offense isn't a "political crime" (which is contended in our efforts to extradite certain narotics traffickers). Still, the United States has also refused such extradition requests and more often than most Americans realize.

In 1981, Britain sought to extradite a member of the Provisional Irish Republican Army (IRA) who had been arrested in Belfast, Northern Ireland for the murder of a British soldier and for illegal possession of firearms and ammunition. He escaped from the British authorities and fled to the United States. The Immigration and Naturalization Service arrested him and Britain requested extradition. The federal government refused finding that the alleged crimes were incidental to and part of the IRA's political opposition in Northern Ireland.

In 1984, the British government again fared no better. A group of IRA supporters ambushed a group of British soldiers in Belfast killing one of the soldiers and wounding several others. Doherty, a member of the ambush was later arrested by British authorities. He was tried and convicted, but before he was sentenced, the IRA managed his violent escape from prison. He then found his way to the United States where he was arrested by American authorities. The United Kingdom asked for his extradition based on his convictions and the additional offenses commited in the course of his escape. The federal court which examined the request held that both the offenses committed during the ambush and during the escape were within the scope of the political offense exception and refused to extradite.*

**Author's note:* In 1986, the United States and the United Kingdom signed a Supplementary Treaty on Extradition which restricts the "political offender" defense by eliminating its availability in crimes of violence and removes the decision to extradite from the federal courts to the U.S. Secretary of State. These two departures from established precedent have been very controversial issues and caused some criticism among international law scholars.

To some legal sources, the appropriateness of this and similar future actions by the United States has led to the proposal for the creation for an international criminal court to prosecute terrorists.[75] As in other areas of transnational and international crime, however, this is an unlikely occurrence. The individual interests of nations and the geopolitical situation in the world community today argues against the possibility of such a court becoming a reality.[76] As discussed in the issue of transnational environmental crime in chapter 10, neither the will nor the legal structure for any such acceptable and workable solution exists.

Issues of Enforcement

Among criminal justice agencies, the major responsibility for combatting terrorism must rest with law enforcement. And among law enforcement agencies, the primary and most fundamental counter-terrorist strategy relies upon effective intelligence gathering efforts by the police. The gathering of intelligence is just one problem, however. Associated with this must be a workable and secure means to share this kind of information and to enlist cooperation among law enforcement agencies. This can be seen in The FBI's creation of a special Terrorist Research and Analytical Center and the newly created efforts of Interpol as previously discussed.

Still, as mentioned previously, there are hidden dangers present, especially as the need for intelligence focuses on domestic forms of counter-terrorism efforts by the police. Intelligence-gathering efforts are, by their very nature, potentially threatening to civil liberties. For example, the FBI has come under a great deal of criticism for its own intelligence-gathering "lawlessness" during the history of this agency. The notorious Palmer Raids in 1920 in which thousands of so-called "anarchists" and "Communists" were rounded up by the federal authorities and jailed with little regard for their constitutional rights. After WW II, during the McCarthy era of anti-communist hysteria, further excesses were committed by the FBI against suspected Communists and Communist sympathizers.

More recently, revelations have come to light that the FBI engaged in both illegal and certainly unconstitutional actions in such areas and against such groups as anti-Vietnam protesters and in furtherance of "the law and order" crisis of the 1960s to early 1970s (a period characterized by the "black bag" jobs of illegal break-ins by FBI agents seeking intelligence information). These revelations led to important concerns about constitutional excesses and violations of First and Fourth Amendment rights by overzealous domestic intelligence activities.[77] In response to such excesses, more controlling domestic security guidelines were imposed on the operations of the FBI in the 1970s. Under the Reagan administration, however, there is some evidence that amended guidelines which went into effect in 1982 have given the FBI additional authority to conduct domestic security and terrorism investigations.[78] The spreading involvement of state and local police in counterterrorism activities could significantly heighten the risks.

More recently, these concerns arose again. During the Gulf War, heightened fears arose over the widespread domestic adoption by the FBI of increased use of electronic surveillance and eavesdropping directed at Americans with a Middle East heritage and resident aliens from that region. Even members of Congress were concerned that the FBI during this crisis had reverted to policies and practices reminiscent of its operations under J. Edgar Hoover. Representative Don Edwards who is chairman of the House Judiciary subommittee on Civil Rights expressed this fear when he said at the time, "we want the FBI to be vigilant, and we support the FBI's anti-terrorism effort . . . [but] we must avoid infringements of our civil liberties."[79]

The need for effective intelligence and the requirement that the police work within acceptable Constitutional and legal guidelines poses something of a dilemma for law enforcement. Elements of organization, secrecy and the willingness to resort to violence among terrorist group members increase the difficulty of obtaining effective intelligence. The ability to penetrate some terrorist groups is made increasingly difficult under these circumstances. This has made it necessary to rely on informants for information, especially when dealing with foreign terrorist groups whose members consist only of nationals of a particular nation or area. Although it is true that "organized" criminal activity has certain weaknesses as compared to the lone or solitary criminal action (e.g., greater dispersion of incriminating knowledge among members, the possibility of a member of the group becoming an informant, ability to penetrate the group through its weakest link), it still remains a two-way street. With some of the terrorist groups now in operation we cannot expect such techniques used to combat traditional forms of organized crime to work.

We cannot, for example, rely upon our so-called "Mafia experience." We were able to first penetrate this organization in the early 1960s when a member of the Mafia who had turned informer broke "Omerta" (the code of silence) which permitted infiltration by law enforcement authorities. Counterbalancing such techniques are factors operating that also impede successful penetration among the most dangerous terroristic organizations. Many of the most dangerous terrorists hold deep-seated convictions and resort to such unrestrained violence that inroads are difficult to make. This not only makes them more difficult to deal with initially but less likely to cooperate when arrested.[80]

This largely explains why authorities have been more successful in dealing with certain domestic terrorist groups than with international terrorists who commit domestic terrorist acts, acts against American citizens, or interests abroad. Witness our government's inability to initially identify the terrorists responsible for blowing up Pan American's Flight 103 over Scotland. While it has generally been determined that this atrocious act was committed by the Popular Front for the Liberation of Palestine—General Command, and federal indictments of at least two who are allegedly involved have been handed down, no arrests have as yet been made of those responsible. Fortunately, many indigenous (domestic) terrorist groups are not bound together by the same dedicated fervor that exists among say, anti-Zionist or anti-American Middle Eastern terrorists or the Irish Republican Army (IRA). Although professing strong loyalty to the ideals of the organization, many members of indigenous terrorist groups are quick to break under the pressure of prosecution.

Terrorism may affect other aspects of the criminal justice system as well. Agencies of criminal justice as well as those employed within the system may become primary targets for terrorist attack. Law enforcement and judicial officials always run the risk of being singled-out as do courtrooms where such cases are tried and jails and prisons which hold convicted terrorists. Another frequently expressed concern is that terrorist cells or terrorist sympathizers among correctional populations may serve as a catalyst for increased problems and violence within institutions. In this way, the spread of terrorism will expand beyond its mere relegation as a problem for law enforcement authorities.

In dealing with terrorism as with many newly emerging crime issues, the criminal justice system has an important role to fulfill. But it is only a one aspect of an overall strategy. Counter-terrorism efforts must incorporate the efforts of other agencies of government, non-criminal justice efforts, and legislative authority in both the enforcement and non-enforcement areas. For example, while it is important that criminal justice community be given appropriate statutory authority to counter terrorism—including investigative, prosecutorial, and sentencing authority—it cannot end here. Counterterrorism experts point out the need, for example, to strictly control the sale of weapons or the transfer of technology to sources that might divert such materiel to terrorist groups. Although such laws generally exist, their enforcement efforts are scattered among various government agencies and ensuing regulatory efforts are not wholly satisfactory. Likewise, a re-examination of policies for obtaining information under the Freedom of Information Act which has been used by some terrorist groups must be cautiously examined. Without curtailing the rights of the media and citizen access, experts point out the need to focus efforts to work out an acceptable accomodation between a free press and the problems of publicity which attend a major terrorist act and seem to play a contributing role in terrorist actions. It is also recommended that international law must be examined to develop accords and agreements among nations as to the status of terrorists and the rights of victim nations to employ law enforcement or even military force as a counterterrorist response.

The Danger of Counter-Terrorism Efforts

No discussion of terrorism or counter-terrorism efforts would be complete without recognizing that strategies and policies to combat terrorism contain within themselves hidden dangers which are not always obvious. Government officials and their supporting power structure may be tempted to define situations as potential terrorist targets and to employ the term "terrorist" to actions and individuals in order to maintain their position of authority and to impose control. This has happened frequently in history. It is a well-recognized fact that the chief executive and the executive organs of government have a tendency to take power unto themselves, especially in times of danger or perceived danger.[81]

This has already occurred in the United States in response to the threat of terrorism and hijacking aboard aircraft. Luggage checks at airports have been imposed in response to this danger. Although an acceptable procedure in response to a real threat, such efforts can "ripple out" into other less warranted invasions of privacy and civil rights. Such actions have the direct effect of arrogating power. Organizations and individuals who express dissent can be stifled by defining them as "terrorists" and their actions as "terrorism." Although subsequent prosecution action is framed in the context that the so-called terrorist committed a conventional criminal act such as a robbery, burglary or the destruction of property, the criminal justice system—especially the courts—are encouraged by the government to deal more harshly with these defendants. The criminal justice system then becomes a mechanism for this form of threat.

Some scholars warn about our nation's penchant to overreact to the threat of terrorism and what they see as the manipulation of people's fears about the dangers of terrorism which can then be used to accomplish foreign policy or domestic ends. Many, if not most, nations exploit these fears to justify their own acts of criminal terrorism, in which they then become terrorists to fight terrorism.[82]

The United States is not immune to such criticism. For example, former President Reagan and his advisors are criticized in some quarters for his ordering of the raid on Libya as a retaliation to what the Reagan Administration saw as the formenting of terrorism and the providing of terrorist support and sanctuary by the Libyan leader, Qaddifi. In the raid, over 100 innocent people including Qaddafi's adopted infant daughter were killed. The sordid Iran-Contra Affair also gave little assurance that our nation wasn't above reproach. Not only were arms sold by Oliver North and others to Iran (a nation which considered the United States its arch-enemy and a country which openly gave support and sanctuary to Middle East terrorists), but the money received for the arms were funneled to the Contras who had a record of committing terroristic atrocities against the Nicaraguan people. In the Libyan raid, the United States could be considered employing a form of "terrorist" response and in the Contra case, an argument can be made that we were a nation that at least abetted terrorism.

It must be recognized that a real danger exists in any counter-terrorist strategy. Too often, government reaction to terrorism has been to develop an executive-controlled security state through the evisceration of civil liberties in the name of combatting terrorism. A major danger posed by terrorism beyond the obvious to America's democratic institutions and to our constitutional republic may be our executive branch's overreaction to terrorism and its use of terrorism to erode constitutionally mandated checks and balances and sharing of powers in foreign affairs, war powers and combatting international crime. The precedent set by the 1986 Supplemental Treaty with Britain that removed the authority from the federal courts and transferred this to the Secretary of State (an Executive Branch agency) to determine the extraditability of so-called terrorists sent a chill through the international law and international civil rights communities. If terrorism should prove to become a serious problem for America in the years ahead, this threat to civil rights must be watched carefully.

The Threat of Counter-Terrorist Activity

Some observers of America's counter-terrorism activities are concerned about the federal government's growing domestic anti-terrorist activities.[†] These efforts became most pronounced during the 1980s under the Reagan Administration. Although ostensibly created to prevent anti-government political violence, these efforts have created a counter-terrorism organizational network with significant capacity for information gathering, surveillance activities, and pre-emptive control of legitimate forms of political dissent. The threat of terrorism has spawned an almost anti-insurgency-like response from the federal government. It has been suggested that this has included among other things: an extension of intelligence prerogatives, an erosion of constitutional rights, and a subtle (but existing) heightening of political repression—all for the purposes of monitoring, discouraging and disrupting "radical activity." In the past fifteen years, for example, the federal government has, among other things, taken the following counter-terrorism steps:

- The development of A Reorganization Plan for the Federal Emergency Management System (FEMA) which makes this system responsible for coordinating efforts in case of a terrorist incident including responsibility for improving construction and security of "strategic" installations—financial institutions, government buildings, and high-technology utilities.
- The creation of a special coordinating committee and a policy review committee of the National Security Council to facilitate the development and coordination of anti-terrorist programs among federal agencies.
- Authorization for FBI-operated anti-terrorist training programs for local law enforcement agencies.
- Ongoing grand jury investigations of domestic groups labeled "terrorist groups" and the use of civil contempt charges to jail uncooperative grand jury witnesses.
- Adoption of an amendment to the Bail Reform Act of 1966 which qualifies "terrorists" for pre-trial or preventive detention.
- Creation within the FBI of the Terrorist Research and Analytic Center.
- Creation within the FBI of the Special Operations and Research Unit (SOAR), which trains agents and state and local police in the principles of criminology and psychology as relevant to terrorism such as profiling terrorists, negotiations, and prevention.
- The establishment of the Joint Terrorist Task Force (JTTF) which targets domestic terrorists. This is a cooperative venture between federal agents, intelligence analysts, and state and local police. Besides being trained in tactics and weapons at the FBI Academy in Quantico, Virginia, trainees in the program are indoctrinated in social science subjects relevant to counterterrorism activities. This program has expanded to a number of major cities in the United States.

- The creation of Special Weapons and Tactics (SWAT) teams assigned to many FBI field offices.
- Provisions with the Federal Bureau of Prisons (FBOP) for ''special handling'' of high security risk prisoners. Among other things this includes: numerous restrictions, lengthy periods of solitary confinement, limited access to visitors, phones, and recreation, the use of handcuffs and leg irons when outside cells, searches of all visitors, constant surveillance, and limited access to legal materials and media. The FBOP uses a Central Inmate Monitoring System (CIM) to monitor these ''high risk'' prisoners which includes all prisoners associated with political ''terrorist'' organizations.
- Special Control Units within specific FBOP institutions. For example, in 1986, the agency announced the completion of a new, 16-bed high-security unit for women in the basement of the federal penitentiary at Lexington, Kentucky. Some civil rights groups contend that several of the women in this tomb-like unit are there for their ''political'' affiliations.

[†]For example, see Gilda Zwerman, ''Domestic Counterterrorism: U.S. Government Responses to Political Violence on the Left in the Reagan Era,'' *Social Justice*, Vol. 16, No. 2, pp. 31–60. (1988).

Conclusion: The Future of Terrorism

Our vulnerability to terrorism and the continued instability of the world in spite of the apparent end of the cold war assures that the United States will still be susceptible to terrorist activities in the years ahead. Although the dismanteling of the Soviet Union and its Eastern European bloc and the thawing of relations with the Commonwealth of Independent States may curtail this source for supply of weapons, training and asylum for terrorists, sporadic acts of terrorism still remain an important crime issue facing our nation. Acts of terrorism will never be eradicated. America's incursion into the Middle East as a result of the Iraq conflict always threatenes to assure some form of terroristic retribution from the Arab world.

Terrorism must also be considered as a major crime issue of the present and for the future because of the fear it generates and its possible consequences. Unlike most conventional crimes, a major and successful terrorist attack or series of attacks, could be devastating in its consequence. Not to recognize it as a continuing challenge to be faced by our nation and its criminal justice system would be an oversight of unacceptable proportions.

There is another somber postscript on terrorism. Increasingly, the United States appears to be a nation of polarizing interests. Its absorptive character, mentioned earlier, seems to have dangerously eroded. Growing cleavages in our social, economic, and political fabric have increased tensions among the American people. It is seen in many aspects of daily life: Deep and threatening fissures along racial lines, a widening gulf between the wealthy and the poor, a growing sense of strain on the moderating and stabilizing influence of the middle class, special interest groups pitted against each other including environmentalists against commercial interests, pro-abortion activists against pro-life and fundamentalist groups, and avowed white and black racist groups who espouse violence. The growth in the incidence of hate crime to be discussed in the next chapter is but one manifestation of the growing cracks in America's social structure. To the extent that this continues and to the extent that the nation is unable to deal effectively and satisfactorily with the complex issues underlying this growing social polarity, serious consequences loom. Growing dissatisfaction and alienation can openly lead to increased tension, hostility and ultimately violence. The risk of terroristic acts directed at opposing groups and classes—and at government—grow in such an environment. Significant challenges lie before the American people and its government. The social, economic, and political strains unless addressed, could erupt with dire consequences in the years ahead.

The fact remains, however, that fundamentally neither the world community of nations, the United States and its government, nor the American criminal justice system has been able to forge an effective strategy to deal with the threat of terrorism anymore than its causes. It has neither developed the capacity to act proactively to solve the grievances that contribute to terroristic violence or reactively to deal with terrorism (and terrorists) when it occurs. Many important issues exist and still remain unanswered. The direct threat of terrorism and resulting loss of lives and the destruction of property through terrorist activity and the anxiety this crime issue provokes are the direct and obvious manifestations of terrorism. The less obvious manifestations are, however, equally as thought-provoking: How to deal with acts of terrorism both before and after the fact while maintaining the rights of acceptable dissent.

What challenges these concerns face and the significance of terrorism as a continuing crime problem will depend a great deal on the face of future acts of terrorism. Both its frequency and its nature will govern our nation's future response to the problem. If we are fortunate it may be a crime issue that will continue only with sporadic frequency. On the other hand, significant outbreaks of international terrorism may propel us into costly conflicts. Domestic terrorism by disaffected political/ideological factions in our country may pose even graver threats to our personal safety and our liberties. In this way, the 1990s may be a very critical decade for our efforts against this form of crime.

NOTES

[1]This "third-level" refers to the general feeling in the counter-terrorism community that the United States ranks behind the Middle East and Europe as a possible target as an aftermath of the outbreak of hostilities in the Gulf War. This was the position of Brian Jenkins, a noted authority on international terrorism, as expressed on the ABC Nightly News, January 18, 1991.

[2]For example, see Jenkins, Brian M. "The Future Course of International Terrorism," *The Futurist,* Vol. 21 (July–August 1987), pp. 8–13.

[3]Cetron, Marvin J. "The Growing Threat of Terrorism," *The Futurist,* Vol. 23 (July–August 1989), pp. 20–24.

[4]For example, see Radenour, James M. "The Potential Threat of Terrorism," *Newsweek,* (October 18, 1989), p. 34.

[5]Ross, Jeffrey Ian, and Gurr, Ted R. "Why Terrorism Subsides: A Comparative Study of Canada and the United States," *The Journal of Comparative Politics*, Vol. 21 (July 1989), p. 405.

[6]For an example of this kind of thinking, see Revell, Oliver B. "International Terrorism in the United States," *The Police Chief*, (March 1989), pp. 16–22; and Schwartz, Donald R. "The Potential for Violence in the United States," *The Police Chief*, (June 1991), pp. 38–39.

[7]Trick, Marcia M. "Chronology of Incidents of Terroristic, Quasi-Terroristic, and Political Violence in the United States, January 1965 to March 1976," in National Advisory Committee on Criminal Justice Standards and Goals, Disorders and Terrorism: Report of Task Force on Disorders and Terrorism (Washington, D.C.: U.S. Department of Justice, 1976), pp. 509–10.

[8]Ross and Gurr, *op. cit.*, p. 417.

[9]Hoffman, Bruce. *Terrorism in the United States and the Potential Threat to Nuclear Facilities* (Santa Monica, CA: Rand Corporation, 1986), pp. 3–4.

[10]Bender, David L. and Leone, Bruno (eds.) *Opposing Viewpoints: Terrorism* (St. Paul, MN. Greenhaven Press, 1986) p. 14.

[11]Flynn, Edith. "Political Prisoners and Terrorists in American Correctional Institutions," in Crelinsten, R.A. Laberge-Altmejd, D. and Szabo, D. *Terrorism in Criminal Justice* (Lexington, Mass., Lexington Books, 1978), p. 87.

[12]For an excellent discussion of this issue and the concept of terrorism itself, see Poland, James M. *Understanding Terrorism: Groups, Strategies, and Responses* (Englewood Cliffs, NJ: Prentice-Hall, 1988), esp. Chapter 1.

[13]Schmid, Alex P. *Political Terrorism: A Research Guide to Concepts, Theories, Data Bases, and Literature* (New Brunswick, N.J.: Transaction Books, 1983), pp. 110–11.

[14]Ibid., p. 193.

[15]Ibid.

[16]Popkin, James and Brownlee, Shannon. "Holes in the Security Web," *U.S. News and World Report*, (February 18, 1991), pp. 39–42.

[17]U.S. Department of Justice, *Terrorism in the United States* (Washington, D.C.: FBI—Terrorist Research and Analytical Center, December 31, 1989), pp. 21–22.

[18]Some students of terrorism break this down even further by including the category of transnational terrorism. For example, see Farrell, William R. *The U.S. Government Response to Terrorism: In Search of an Effective Strategy* (Boulder, CO: Westview Press, 1982), pp. 12–13. Since this seems to only confuse the issue, it is not being used here.

[19]Crelinsten, Ronald D. Laberge-Altmejd, D. and Szabo, Dennis. *Terrorism and Criminal Justice* (Lexington, MA.: Lexington Books, 1978), p. 10.

[20]Revell, Oliver B. "Terrorism Today," *FBI Law Enforcement Bulletin*, Vol. 56 (October 1987), pp. 3–4.

[21]Ibid.

[22]Hoffman, *op cit.*, p. 4.

[23]Cordes, Bonnie. *Trends in International Terrorism, 1982 and 1983* (Santa Monica, Ca: Rand Corporation, 1984), pp. 2–3.

[24]Hoffman, *op cit.*, pp. 5–6.

[25]Terrorist Reserach and Analytical Center, *Terrorism in the United States—1990* (Washington: U.S. Department of Justice, 1991), p. 22.

[26]Cordes, *op cit.*, p. 4.

[27]Hoffman, p. 5.

[28]U.S.Department of Justice, *Terrorism in America* (Washington, D.C.: Federal Bureau of Investigation, Terrorist Research and Analytical Center, December 31, 1989), pp. 16–17.

[29]See Hoffman, *op cit.*, p. 16. For a good discussion of the JDL (and other extremist groups) see his pages 7–51.

[30]*The Wall Street Journal,* July 26, 1984.

[31]Arostegui, Martin C. "Terrorism in the United States," *Clandestine Tactics and Technology: Group and Area Studies,* No. IX, pp. 1–2.

[32]Ibid., p. 4.

[33]Ibid., p. 2.

[34]Hoffman, op. cit., pp. 29–30.

[35]Ibid., p. 30.

[36]Arostegui, *op cit.*, Vol. X, p. 3. *Author's note:* In 1990, Jean Buck, Laura Jane Whitehorn and Linda Sue Evans pled guilty to charges relating to the 1983 bombing of the U.S. Capitol and other bombings in the Washington, D.C. area. They are members of the May 19th Communist Organization (M19CO).

[37]U.S. Department of Justice, *Terrorism in the United States—1987* (Washington, D.C.: Federal Bureau of Investigation, Terrorist Research and Analytical Center), December 31, 1987, p. 31.

[38]*The New York Times,* September 20, 1985.

[39]Hoffman, *op cit.*, p. 38.

[40]International Association of Chiefs of Police, *Terrorist Trends: The Quarterly Intelligence Reporter* (Gaithersburg, MD: IACP, 1985), p. 13.

[41]Ibid., p. 39.

[42]*The New York Times,* Dcember 27, 1984.

[43]Hoffman, p. 40.

[44]*The New York Times,* December 27, 1984.

[45]Ibid.

[46]*IACP Terrorist Trends*, p. 14.

[47]*Aryan Nations Newsletter*, No. 42, 1982, quoted in Anti-Defamation League of B'nai B'rith, Hate Groups in America: A Record of Bigotry and Violence, 1982, p. 58.

[48]*The Washington Post*, December 26, 1984.

[49]*The New York Times*, April 12, 1985.

[50]Audsley, David. ''Posse Comitatus: An Extremist Tax Protest Group,'' *TVI Journal* (Spring 1984), p. 9.

[51]*The New York Times*, June 4, 1983.

[52]*The New York Times*, June 11, 1983.

[53]U.S. Department of Justice, *Terrorism in the United States—1989* (Washington, D.C.: Federal Bureau of Investigation, Terrorist Research and Analytical Center, December 31, 1989), pp. 19–20.

[54]Hoffman, *op cit.*, pp. 49–50.

[55]Motley, James B. *U.S. Strategy to Counter Domestic Political Terrorism* (Washington, D.C.: The National Defense University Press, 1983), p. 42.

[56]The FBI considers terrorist activity to mean activity involving a violent act that is dangerous to human life or risks serious bodily harm or one involving aggravated property destruction, for the purpose of coercion or intimidation. That such purpose is to be accomplished wholly or in part in violation of a criminal law of the United States or a political subdivision thereof.

[57]For a description of the State Department's efforts in this area, see Putney, Rufus D. ''Enhancing Anti-Terrorism Skills,'' *Police Chief*, (June 1991), pp. 40–42.

[58]*Author's note:* The name was changed in 1956 from The International Police Organization (Interpol) to The International Criminal Police Organization—Interpol but still retains its earlier designation as simply Interpol.

[59]Overton, James. ''Interpol's Perspective on International Terrorism and Drug Trafficking,'' in Ward, R. and Smith, H. (eds.) ''International Terrorism,'' *University of Illinois—Chicago Circle*, 1988. p. 168.

[60]Ibid.

[61]For an excellent discussion of this issue, see Smith, Brent. ''State Anti-terrorism Legislation in the United States: A Review of Statutory Utilization,'' *Ibid.*, pp. 23–46.

[62]California Penal Code 11.5.422.5

[63]*People v. Mirmirani*, 636 Pac. Rpt. (1982)

[64]Smith, Brent. *op cit.*, p. 28.

[65]Ibid.

[66]Model Penal Code Sec. 211.3

[67]Smith, p. 34.

[68]Gardes, Jeannemarie. ''Jurisdiction Over Terrorists,'' *Criminal Justice Journal,* Vol. 10 (1988), p. 335.

[69]*State v. Schumann,* 39 Int'l L. Rpt. 433 [Ghana Court of Appeal of Accra, 1966, 1970].

[70]Ibid.

[71]*Author's note:* The extending of the power of the U.S. Government also means extending Constitutional guarantees. A terrorist arrested in a foreign country by U.S. agents has the same Constitutional guarantees as a citizen of the U.S. or an alien living in the United States. In 1990, however, a Supreme Court decision *U.S. v. Verdugo-Urguidez,* (110 S. Ct., 1056) held that the Fourth Amendment does not apply to searches by U.S. officials of nonresident aliens in foreign countries.

[72]18 U.S.C. Sec. 7 (1982 as amend. 1985); and 18 U.S.C. Sec. 2331 (1986).

[73]Some international legal scholars argue that United States action in abducting suspected terrorists violates the United Nations Charter. See Paust, Jordan J. ''Responding Lawfully to International Terrorism: The Use of Force Abroad,'' 8 *Whittier Law Review,* (1986), pp. 711–33.

[74]For a brief discussion of the extension of U.S. jurisdiction in this area and some of the justifications for such changes, see Gardes, *op. cit.*, esp. pp. 317–23.

[75]''A Court to Try Terrorism?'' An editorial, *New Jersey Law Journal* 119 (January 8, 1987), p. 4.

[76]For a discussion of this issue, see ''Problems of Judicial Processing and Selection,'' in Crelinsten, Laberge-Altmejd, and Szabo, *op cit.*, pp. 29–38.

[77]For example, see Belknap, Michael. *Cold War Political Justice* (Westport, CN: Greenwood Press, 1977); and Crewdson, John. ''Burglaries Laid to Agents of FBI in 30-Year Period,'' *The New York Times* (August 24, 1973).

[78]Poveda, Tony G. *The FBI in Transition* (Belmont, CA.: Brooks/Cole Publishing, 1990), p. 133.

[79]Johnston, David. ''FBI Increases Its Attempts to Block Terrorist Acts,'' *The New York Times* (January 20, 1991), p. 18-A.

[80]Pursley, Robert D. *Introduction to Criminal Justice, 5th ed.* (New York: Macmillan Publishing, 1991), p. 681.

[81]Petrowski, Frank. ''Dangers in Anti-Terrorism Efforts,'' *The Commentary* (July 1987), p. 17.

[82]Blakesley, Christopher. ''Terrorism, Law and Constitutional Order,'' 60 *Colorado Law Review* (1989), pp. 471–532.

CHAPTER 5

Public Integrity Offenses and Bias (Hate) Crime

CONTENTS

- The Face of Political Corruption
- Classifying Government Corruption
  - Judicial Corruption
  - Corruption in Government Contracts
  - Regulatory Agency Corruption
  - Narcotics-Related Corruption
  - Legislative Corruption
  - Police Corruption
  - Election Crimes
  - Conflict of Interest Crimes
- The Feds: The "Shakers and Movers" in Public Corruption Cases
  - Prosecutorial Craftsmanship
  - An Overview of Major Federal Anti-Corruption Laws
  - Criticism of Federal Efforts
  - The Nature of Federal Corruption Investigations
- The Ugly Shadow of Hate Crime
  - Growing Legal Efforts to Stem Hate Crime
  - Federal Laws
  - State Laws

The Face of Political Corruption

During recent years, there have been shocking disclosures such as those represented in the home loan industry involving elected members of Congress, the ABSCAM investigations, the HUD scandals, recurring revelations involving government abetted defense-related corruption, and $600 toilet seats. But these are only the tip of the iceberg. Government corruption has not been merely relegated to what some social commentators call "the runaway 1980s"; a decade which saw serious examples of the open maw of this problem. Any student of American history knows that our nation has been anything but a stranger to government perfidy. It has existed for longer than we care to remember. Public corruption has touched all periods and is rooted in all levels of government. It has fallen on Presidents, members of Congress, governors, mayors, cops, local building inspectors, and low-level clerks who issue governmental permits.

Just as it has touched all periods and levels of government, so too has it cast a long shadow across America. No area of our country has been immune to the problem. It is represented in Boston where public buildings may have to be closed because of shoddy construction brought about by a corrupt system of selecting architectural and construction firms. Government corruption is found in Florida where public officials, in collusion with construction firms, approved the dangerous use of substandard electrical wiring and low-grade building materials in publicly assisted homes for the elderly. It has undermined the administration of justice in Chicago and Philadelphia, where judges have been investigated and imprisoned for fixing criminal cases. Corruption has been found in Alabama and Louisiana where voter fraud and ballot box stuffing deprive citizens of their right to vote and ensured the election of corrupt state and local public officials. It stalks the corridors of Capitol Hill and in State Houses across the nation as lobbyists and special interest groups have corrupted legislators with a wide array of "payoffs." It has surfaced in a disturbing number of American communities where police officers have been put on the payroll of narcotic traffickers so that drugs can flow into our nation and unto our streets.

Although such governmental crimes are sometimes considered as "victimless" offenses or "consensual" crimes, such a label is inappropriate. It masks the seriousness of these actions and the direct and indirect victimization which lies in its wake. If left unchecked, it poses a threat to democratic society. It erodes citizen confidence in the institutions of government and government itself. It distorts the the democratic process—a system that is supposed to fairly resolve competing meritorious claims to limited public resources on a rational basis. What it does is substitute meretricious government decision making. Too often, such corruption also operates to the detriment of the most disadvantaged members of society; it always works to deprive taxpaying Americans of honest and effective representation. This undermines the legitimacy of government and short-circuits the hopes of those who have not prevailed or benefitted that there is someone in government who will faithfully serve, rather than sell out, their interest.

Governmental corruption also operates like a political Gresham's Law—driving out the good and substituting the bad. A perception that the system is rigged, unfair, or corrupt eventually forces the good players out of the game. It does this in two ways:

1. By initially deterring honest and able citizens from seeking public office or from seeking careers in the public service.
2. It operates as in Massachusetts where a blue-ribbon commission found that corruption was one of the principal reasons why so many public buildings, including government offices, parking garages, courthouses, hospitals, libraries, and prisons were in substandard shape and why many had to be closed. Over time, many reputable contractors in this state knowing how "the system" worked refused to bid on government contracts.[1]

This part of the chapter will primarily focus on the federal government's efforts to deal with criminal acts of political corruption. Aspects of state and local anti-corruption efforts will not be examined. Although state and local jurisdictions make periodic efforts in this area, such undertakings are very sporadic and highly variable. It has been the federal government in recent years which has made the most significant effort to deal with public corruption and prosecute government officials. Singled out for particular examination will be such issues as what forms of behavior are typically considered public integrity crimes, how the federal government deals with such offenses (including statutory authority, organization, investigative and prosecution strategies), and issues that surround these criminal events.

Classifying Government Corruption

Corruption by government officials comes in many guises. In an effort to deal with this subject, it is necessary to classify these forms into major categories. An examination of the criminal justice system's involvement in such cases in recent years provides evidence that efforts against public corruption fall into eight broad categories:

1. judicial corruption;
2. corruption in government contracts (e.g., bribery, kickbacks, bid-rigging, and the like);
3. regulatory agency corruption;
4. narcotics-related corruption;
5. legislative corruption;
6. investigation and prosecution of police corruption cases;
7. election crimes; and
8. conflicts of interest crimes.

Judicial Corruption

During the 1980s, public attention focused on the City of Chicago. The Department of Justice cracked open widespread corruption involving a number of judges in that city. This was the famous *Greylord* case. The corruption in these courts was open and notorious. Although widespread corruption in Chicago's courts was frequently alluded to by members of the legal community in that city, local and state efforts to investigate were non-existent. No single investigation in American history has exposed so much judicial corruption. This seven-year federal probe, which centered on the Circuit Court of Cook, County Illinois, resulted in the convictions of 65 defendants including 10 judges. Remnants of the investigation are still on-going. A local newspaper columnist for the *Chicago Sun-Times* related an interesting anecdotal story of judicial corruption in that city.

> They tell a story about a judge who called the parties into his chamber and announced: 'I have received $1,500 from the plaintiff to decide the case in his favor and $1,000 from the defendant to decide the case for the defense. In fairness to the parties, I will return $500 to the the plaintiff and decide the case on the merits.'[2]

What set Operation Greylord apart from other problems and investigations of judicial corruption was the scope of involvement and the numbers of court officials eventually indicted and convicted. The federal authorities found several common forms of judicial corruption occurring. The most common form of judicial corruption involves the "fix." This is a promise by the judge, or someone acting on his behalf, that the judge will give a specific disposition or consideration to a case in exchange for money or other things of value.

In *Greylord,* it was revealed that substantial corruption existed especially within the traffic courts in Chicago. In these courts, a corrupt chief judge assigned other judges to the "big rooms" (courts where driving under the influence cases were heard). The assignment to these cases was based on the willingness of such judges and court officials to accommodate the equally corrupt defense lawyers who practiced there. These attorneys were known as "miracle workers" because they never lost a case. These defense lawyers, often operating through middlemen, got favorable results for their clients by paying off the judges to reduce or dismiss cases. Police officers were also part of the scheme. Arresting officers were paid to testify in a way that created a "reasonable doubt" which then gave the judge a justified basis for dismissing the charge. An interesting insight into the pervasiveness of the corruption in these courts was cited by the Federal Court of Appeals which was asked to rule on an appeal filed by one of the convicted judges. In one example cited by the Court, the judge openly complained that the defense lawyer had just let his client confess, giving the judge no basis to rule in his favor. This didn't stop the judge, however. Since "the fix" was on, the judge dismissed the case anyway.[3]

Many examples of the judicial "fix" are a little less obvious then what generally occurred in these Chicago courts. In one of the *Greylord* cases, for instance, a convicted chancery judge was found guilty for arranging for "loans" from attorneys who regularly practiced before him.[4] Judges may be a little more subtle in obtaining what is, in essence, a form of extortion for deciding cases. Although not directly threatening lawyers who practice before them with adverse rulings should they not comply, there may be an implied threat that this could occur if some form of payment is not made—regularly practicing attorneys "get the message" when they see how (and they can soon figure out why) the judge rules in a particular way.

Another corrupt practice that goes on in some of our nation's courtrooms is the practice of "hustling." Lawyers pay off judges who let them "hustle" clients in the courtroom. Although this is, strictly speaking, a violation of the legal profession's code of ethics, it occurs. Often it also involves other members of the court such as baliffs and clerks who receive a "finders fee" for each case referred. In the Chicago investigations, the lawyers actually formed a hustlers' bribery club where the attorneys paid the chief judge of the district $500 a month to work the courtroom and for leads. It can also involve probate court judges who have the authority to assign estate cases to lawyers when someone dies without a will naming an executor. "Favored" lawyers are asigned by the court to handle the estate.

Another common form of judicial corruption is what is called "brokering." Some corrupt judges in an enterprising entrepreneurial spirit, not only fix cases in their own court rooms, but in the courtrooms of other judges as well. This can arise in a number of situations. It can involve judicial colleagues asking for "favors" from each other for financial or political considerations, it can be a chief judge pressuring another judge for special consideration in a particular case, it can be so seemingly innocuous an occurrence as one judge introducing an attorney to another judge so that they can "work out their own deal."

Corruption in Government Contracts

Corruption in government contracts seems to be a rather frequent occurrence in spite of federal and state laws prohibiting this form of crime. Equally unworkable are efforts to control it through such practices as government purchasing policies and regulations (at least, as judged by how often questionable and outright criminal acts in this area occur). Two of the most notable and widespread cases in this area occurred during the 1980s in the States of Oklahoma and Mississippi. Both of these cases developed in large part from people—sometimes vendors—approaching the authorities contending that government contracts were being awarded for less than legitimate reasons. In both the Oklahoma and Mississippi cases, allegations came to the authorities that county judges (an administrative position in Oklahoma) and county supervisors in Mississippi were corrupt in awarding contracts. In Oklahoma during the early 1980s, more than 100 county officials were ultimately convicted for receiving bribes and kickbacks.

Most of these crimes involve acts of bribery, extortion, "kickbacks," the use of "phantom invoices," and bid-rigging. Bribery is the most common offense charged. Here an unscrupulous vendor bribes a public official to receive a contract. Sometimes this bribe, rather than being a payment up-front, is in the form of a kickback in which a certain percentage (say, five percent of the value of the awarded contract), is kicked-back to the official. The extortion angle comes in when a public official obtains the property of another with consent by force, violence, fear, or *under color of official right*. This latter requirement simply means that a public official obtained property that was not due him or his office.[5]

In some cases, the "kickbacks" become even higher as greedy public officials demanded more. This can lead to the situation where the supplier must raise the price of his product but, in so doing, they run the risk of inquiry from competing firms and subsequent focusing of attention on the submitted bids and contracts issued. At this point, the game plan can switch to the use of "phantom invoices." Here the purchaser and supplier merely agree to charge on phony invoices for property not received. A local government official may order 100 55-gallon drums of chlorine for municipal swimming pools but only 80 are delivered. The supplier is paid for 100 drums and they split the cost of the additional 20 drums equally.

Bid-rigging ventures are much like anti-trust violations. They often operate in conjunction with bribery. Here suppliers get together in collusive deals to divide government business in the geographical area for defined periods of time to avoid competition and to inflate prices.[6] In the Mississippi cases, suppliers of gravel or asphalt met privately and agreed on how much each would price their bids to particular local governments to furnish materials for road building. Each agreed never to underbid another and each in return was guaranteed that it would non-competitively "win" one or more bids at these exorbitant prices. Entire states have fallen victim to rigged-bid schemes, especially where markets are dominated by a few large companies as in the highway construction and heavy equipment industries.[7] Because of the large sums involved, local politicians can easily be bought and a closed non-competitive system wreaks havoc on the costs of taxpayer-borne services.

Regulatory Agency Corruption

The myriad regulatory apparatus and activities carried out by government agencies and employees along with their licensing and inspection responsibilities have opened up vast opportunities for public corruption. The multi-layered bureaucracies which often conduct such regulatory oversight functions find this problem difficult to control. An agency may be responsible for seeing that construction projects in Phoenix are periodically inspected and are meeting code requirements. To do this, they have a number of inspectors on their payroll. The only way to really check to see if an inspector is properly doing his or her job is to have another inspector or a member of supervision inspect the site after a report has been turned in. The problem is that such "quality-control" checks are very infrequent especially in today's period of austere operating budgets among state and local governments.

In contrast to other types of public corruption cases, regulatory corruption cases often involve lower-level officials who accept illegal payments without the knowledge of their superiors. It is also insidious in that it could conceal serious problems with drastic consequences as when our Phoenix code inspector overlooks serious structural or safety violations in a building. And, for purposes of prosecution, there is always the problem of proving that the inspector in this case purposely ignored the problem for some kind of financial inducement rather than it being merely a case of the inspector being incompetent or careless.

The fact that such inspectors are often given a great deal of discretion also complicates the issue. Since the person or firm being regulated has a real interest in continuing the non-compliance and willingly pays for such oversight (in addition to running the risk of being charged with a criminal offense himself for offering a bribe), there certainly is no incentive to report the crime or cooperate with the authorities in the investigation or prosecution. In spite of this problem, prosecutors point out that in these cases, the assistance of credible cooperating witnesses who either paid a bribe, accepted a bribe, or saw an act of bribery occur are indispensible.[8]

Narcotics-Related Corruption

The drug problem in the United States and the massive profits generated by narcotics trafficking have had a tremendous corrupting influence over almost all aspects of the law enforcement and the criminal justice process. The drug traffickers know that "official protection" along the entire line—from importation to receipt of the drugs to sale—significantly increases their chances for success and the continution of the drug enterprise. Although law enforcement and other criminal justice personnel may not be compromised in their actual sale or distribution of the illegal drugs, they offer the services of protection and information to drug dealers.

There are many ways this can occur beyond the obvious. In several areas throughout the country, there have developed what are called instances involving "snitch busters." Evidence has been uncovered of police officers providing investigative information to drug dealers. This practice has also involved ex-law enforcement officers who have maintained corrupt contacts in local and even federal police agencies. Often these ex-cops are involved in the private detective or private security business. They "contract" with drug dealers to protect their operations by using their contacts within law enforcement agencies to determine the identity of informants and undercover agents and operations.[9] This is a valuable service to drug dealers. They are only too willing to pay corrupt police and ex-cops and their "inside contacts" who supply them with the information.

Police personnel have also been convicted for stealing, destroying, or tampering with evidence. This latter act is done to contaminate and compromise its value to the case. The police may also be employed to transport narcotics. Situations have occurred where cops while on duty and in uniform and while using a police vehicle have been caught doing this. And, as we shall see from our discussion on corruption in the chapter on narcotics, the police are increasingly falling victim to such corruptive practices as seizing large quantities of drug money which is not confiscated, but goes into their pockets. Police oficers have also been found keeping drugs for their own personal use or to sell.

Cross-over corruption has also been a problem. This involves corruption of both law enforcement and the judicial system. Corrupt law enforcement officers or "snitch busters" have established corrupt links to the judicial system. They may, for example, develop contacts in the court clerk's office or with judges to gain access to sealed pleadings, such as wiretap authorizations and the evidentiary information these applications contain or cooperation agreements involving informants (e.g., members of the drug dealing network who have agreed to cooperate with the authorities in gaining evidence). Drug dealers also are interested in protecting members of their organization from prosecution or the possibility that facing conviction and a lengthy sentence, these organizational members might cooperate with the authorities. Often corrupt police officers are associated with corrupt defense attorneys and judges. Police officers or their corrupt agents may refer an arrestee to the ''right'' defense attorney who can pay off a judge to reduce the bond, dismiss charges, supress evidence, or impose a light sentence. The corruption may involve a prosecutor willing to ''throw'' a case or falsely acknowledge ''substantial assistance'' given to the government that could result in a significant reduction of a sentence.[10]

Legislative Corruption

Most readers are familiar with the so-called ABSCAM corruption scandals involving members of Congress. The investigation, prosecution, and Congressional inquiries which followed in their wake were widely publicized by the media. Problems of legislative corruption are not confined only to Congress. Legislative bodies exist at all levels of government and criminal corruption cases can involve state as well as county and city legislative bodies. Periodic scandals in New York State and Illinois and recent corruption prosecutions of state legislators in South Carolina show that states are no strangers to cases of corruption and attempts to prosecute state legislators.

The federal government and all states have laws which provide for criminal penalties for specific corrupt actions by legislative officials or they can be prosecuted under existing conventional statutes such as bribery. There have also been efforts in recent years to strengthen such anti-corruption measures as ethics acts and public financial disclosure laws. Still, no one would suggest that these efforts have solved the problem. There are many difficulties associated with the prosecution of legislators for criminal acts involving a violation of the public trust. In addition to the political sensitivity of these cases (and how ''politics'' might thwart such efforts), there are also some unique legal hurdles of a Constitutional, statutory, and procedural nature that are not involved in investigating and prosecuting other public officials.

The prosecution of a member of Congress is a case in point. This will be used to show the inherent complexity of prosecuting a case. Often, similar protections are found in the laws of states. One such obstacle is the Speech or Debate Clause of the Constitution.[11] This clause, which has its roots in the 1689 English Bill of Rights, has been interpreted by the U.S. Supreme Court as:

> . . . [The purpose of the protection afforded legislators by this clause] is not to forstall judicial review of legislative action but to ensure that legislators are not distracted from or hindered in the performance of their legislative tasks by being called into court to defend their actions.[12]

The Supreme Court has interpreted this clause broadly. Among the actions deemed protected under the clause are voting by members of Congress, the preparation of committee reports, and conduct at legislative committee hearings.[13] In addition, the Court has held that the clause protects legislative aides as well as legislators.[14]

In 1969, the Supreme Court first interpreted the clause in the context of a criminal charge brought against a member of Congress.[15] A Congressman was charged with assisting savings and loan officials in return for a bribe. Part of his help came from a speech made by the Congressman on the floor of the House of Representatives. This speech became the subject of extensive government cross-examination of the Congressman at his trial. The government contended, among other things, that the speech was meant to persuade Congress to act favorably on pending legislation supporting the savings and loan industry and this was motivated by the bribe he received. The Court held that even if the Congressman's speech was motivated by the bribe, the cross-examination violated the clause.

Without venturing too deeply into the complex Constitutional case law which has surrounded this issue, it has been pointed out by prosecutors faced with overcoming this formidable clause, " . . . [it should be anticipated] . . . that Congress, as an institution, will take every opportunity to expand the reach of the Speech or Debate Clause. Both Houses have legal staffs who view, as an integral part of their work, the development of the clause."[16] For example, although the government successfully prosecuted former Congressman George Hansen for filing false financial disclosure forms to Congress, prosecutors sought from the Clerk of the House evidence of how such financial disclosure forms were processed, the Counsel for the House resisted, claiming that the use of the forms by Congress was an "internal matter" and thus protected by the clause. The trial court agreed. It is also the case through a long-standing informal agreement with the Department of Justice—much to the consternation of the FBI—that lawyers for the House of Representatives may automatically attend FBI interviews of members of Congress or staff that pertain to official business.

Other obstacles are the Publication Clause of the Constitution[17] and the immunity from arrest clause which surrounds Congressmen and similar state laws which protect state legislators when in session.[18] The Publication Clause has been cited as constitutional support for Congressional claims of a privilege to resist requests for certain types of documentary evidence such as transcripts of testimony given to executive sessions of Congressional investigating committees.

The courts have examined the relationship of this clause to refusals to give up such transcripts in two important cases. The first case was one of the Watergate trials. The defendant, G. Gordon Liddy, was being prosecuted for the warrantless search of a psychiatrist's office which had been instigated by White House officials. Liddy issued subpoenas for transcripts of testimony by government witnesses who had appeared before a House subcommittee. The House refused to supply the transcripts. Consequently, the trial court ruled that the transcripts were privileged and Liddy had no right to require their production.[19]

The second case was the famous court-martial trial of Lt. William Calley, Jr. for the

1968 mass murder of Vietnamese civilians in the village of My Lai. The military judge requested that the House release evidence and testimony given in an executive session of the Armed Services Subcommittee. The House refused and the military court held that the House's failure to release the papers was within the scope of the privilege. Although a subsequent federal civil court agreed with the interpretation by the military court, it disagreed that the House had the right to invoke the privilege of confidentiality at the expense of the accused's right to evidence at his criminal trial.[20]

Much of what passes for legislative corruption revolves around the issues of bribes, gratuities, and campaign contributions. Each of these present specific problems for prosecution. Although laws exist to prohibit legislators from accepting anything of value to influence his/her official actions, problems abound. There is the question, of course, of showing the connection between accepting a bribe and resulting bribe-influenced behavior although accepting (or soliciting) a bribe is, itself, an illegal act. The issue is even more murky in the area of gratuities. A gratuity may be an "after the fact" payoff for performing a certain act whereas a bribe is "forward looking" (i.e., a payment for a future act). Campaign contributions are a particularly slippery slope for prosecutors especially if the contribution, while they may be veiled attempts to "bribe" a legislator, falls within the permissable guidelines of existing campaign contribution laws.

Police Corruption

Although we have mentioned police corruption in terms of narcotics-related corruption, there are many other forms of police corruption—all of which fall within the classification of "public integrity offenses." Some of the more common are:

- "shakedowns" (extortion) efforts for protecting certain illegal activities such as prostitution or gambling;
- extortion payments from bars and acts of harassment such as harassing operators of gay bars;
- evidence tampering;
- case fixing and civil rights abuses; and
- organized theft rings involving police officers which occasionally surface in scandle.

One of the most difficult problems to overcome in these type investigations is the so-called "conspiracy of silence" among police officers and the problems this poses for a successful investigation and prosecution.

Election Crimes

Election crimes generally fall under the broad umbrella of what are called "ballot fraud crimes." For example:

- it is illegal to bribe voters;
- to cause ballots to be cast in the names of individuals who did not personally subscribe the ballot;
- to falsely report or fraudulently alter voting tallies;
- to steal ballots;
- to stuff ballot boxes with fraudulent or illegal votes;
- to tamper with voting equipment or vote tabulating machines;
- to fraudulently change a voter's ballot;
- to intentionally prevent a qualified voter from casting a ballot;
- to intimidate voters; and
- to physically assault voters for having exercised their franchise.[21]

Often, these crimes are sanctioned by local officials and, in turn, aided by the local police. The existing political power structure in the community or the state use these tactics to ensure that they remain in office. History is replete with examples of this occurring in days past in the South to disenfranchise blacks. But it has not only been in the South where this has taken place. Significant instances of corruption have occurred in maintaining the power of the political machines in such cities as Chicago, New York City, New Orleans, and Kansas City. It occurred in Texas during the election of a Sènator who went on to become President.[22] Fortunately, the federal government has exercised more oversight of election laws in recent years and such notorious instances of ballot fraud have diminished.

Conflict of Interest Crimes

This is another form of public corruption which has grown in recent years. Generally speaking, ''conflict of interest'' laws are designed to foster confidence in the integrity and objectivity of public officials and the fairness of the decision-making process of government. Conflicts of interest are not only governed by federal and state laws in this area, but by such agencies as the federal government's Office of Government Ethics.[23] A few states also have agencies who oversee and investigate violations of similar state ethics laws.

During the Reagan Presidency, a great deal of criticism focused on Reagan appointees who left the ''revolving door'' of high-level government appointment and tried to cash-in on their ''insider'' contacts and knowledge for personal gain. Perhaps most notable of the prosecutions was that of Michael Deaver, who served as White House Chief of Staff during the Reagan Presidency. Deaver was ultimately convicted by an independent counsel for such conflicts allegations. Deaver had been accused of using his influence and garnering substantial consulting fees after he had left his position to represent certain private interests who sought to influence the administration.

Broadly, laws prohibiting conflict of interest make it illegal for officers and employees (and certain categories of ''special government employees'') to represent individuals in matters before government. It also prohibits government officials and employees from receiving private compensation other than their government salaries for services rendered before government agencies.[24] Public officials are also prohibited from representing others in claims against and other matters affecting government.[25] An official cannot, for example, act as an agent or attorney for prosecuting a claim against the government and he or she cannot receive a gratuity for this assistance or from receiving any share of or interest in the claim because of their representation. Federal law also places restrictions on post-federal employment activities (such as in the *Deaver* case) as well as their official participation in a matter in which they have a financial interest. An interesting case in this latter area involved the former director of the United States Bureau of Engraving and Printing. This official advised and aided a firm in obtaining a contract with the Bureau. It was shown that at the time he assisted the firm, he had an arrangement for a job with them when he left government service. In the eyes of the court, this job arrangement constituted a financial interest.[26]

The Feds: The "Shakers and Movers" in Public Corruption Cases

While political corruption in state and local governments is a time-worn phenomenon, one aspect of weeding it out is relatively new. Federal efforts of prosecuting corruption in this area has come of age. It was not always this way. With few exceptions, the repeated campaigns against state and local political corruption had been led by citizen committees, good government associations, local prosecutors, county grand juries, and reform governors and mayors. These anti-corruption campaigns were conducted under state laws and in state courts. When corrupt public officials were convicted, they were sent to state prisons. Reform efforts were instituted by state and local bodies. The federal government was merely a sideline observer. Except for a few noted instances, such as the politically inspired efforts of the federal government in the early 1930s to investigate the corrupt political machine of Senator Huey Long of Louisiana and sporadic attempts to investigate and occasionally prosecute state and local officials for the violation of the Hatch Act or federal contract and grant requirements, little activity emanated from Washington.[27] This began to change in the 1970s when the federal government became a major player.

There were probably several reasons why the federal authorities took such a hands-off policy toward state and local political corruption. For one thing, it was not considered a special province of the federal government. Such corruption problems were traditionally seen as the responsibility of states and localities. This also has to be coupled with the fact that there was little in the way of a "federal interest" involved—a situation which would develop later under a rapidly changing concept of fiscal federalism as federal grants and contracts became an ever-larger share of state and local operating funds and program support monies. Also, it was a fact that the federal government had no specific legislative authority to investigate and prosecute such crimes. Specific federal statutes did not exist conferring federal criminal jurisdiction for such violations. In 1970,

John A. Gardiner, in a study of political corruption in American cities, was to note that the federal government has ''seldom been able to act against official corruption since bribery and extortion involving local officials (unless they affect interstate commerce) are not federal offenses.''[28]

There were also some other significant happenings which would change this situation. One was the public moral outrage resulting from the Watergate scandal. Associated with this was the attention given to several widespread local and state corruption scandals which occurred about the same time. The mood was one of change: It was time to clean up government. Both President Gerald A. Ford and his newly appointed assistant attorney general in charge of the Criminal Division for the Department of Justice signaled that ''conscious efforts presently are being exerted by the Department of Justice to bring federal investigative and prosecutorial resources to bear in increasing quantity and quality in the area of governmental and institutional integrity.''[29] An important part of this reform effort was the 1976 creation within the Criminal Division of the Department of Justice a Public Integrity Section with responsibility for overseeing the federal effort to combat corruption through the prosecution of elected and appointed public officials at all levels of government.[30] The almost simultaneous confluence of these factors chartered a new course for federal involvement in this area.

Prosecutorial "Craftsmanship"

The signal was given and aggressive anti-corruption attorneys in the Public Integrity Section, assisted in their efforts by some equally aggressive local U.S. attorneys in the field, began concentrating on crimes involving state and local government officials. Still, they were hindered initially in their efforts by the lack of specific federal statutory authority under which prosecutions could be brought. In a creative and enterprising spirit, these legal minds began searching existing federal laws which could be applied in public corruption cases.[31] They found them. Table 5.1 shows indictment and prosecution activity since 1980. To appreciate the growing federal involvement in this area, consider the fact that in the entire preceeding decade (1970 to 1979), there were only 359 indictments and 251 convictions of state officials and 1,265 indictments and 906 convictions of local government officials.[32] Compare these figures with what has occurred in the past 10 years.

The prosecutors chose for their arsenal four specific federal laws: mail fraud, the Hobbs Act, the Travel Act, and the Racketeer Influenced and Corrupt Organizations Act (RICO).[33] However, neither the statutory language nor the legislative histories of these laws indicated that they were to be used to prosecute public corruption. Nonetheless, in a spirit of legal craftsmanship, these laws were used as the basis for conducting federal investigations and obtaining indictments and convictions of state and local public officials. It would seem that the Department of Justice took special pride in the innovative efforts of its attorneys to craft new prosecution strategies under these laws. The former chief of the Justice Department's Criminal Division celebrated the legal craftsmanship of the successful prosecutors. ''It is the creativity of the prosecutor/craftsman that is responsible for a number of relatively recent legal developments which can only be

TABLE 5.1 PROSECUTION OF CORRUPT STATE AND LOCAL PUBLIC OFFICIALS 1980–1989

	1980	*1981*	*1982*	*1983*	*1984*	*1985*	*1986*	*1987*	*1988*	*1989*	*Total*
State Officials											
Indicted	72	87	49	81	58	79	88	102	66	71	(753)
Convicted	51	66	43	65	52	66	71	76	69	54	(613)
Awaiting Trial on December 31st	28	36	18	26	21	20	24	26	14	18	(231)
Local Officials											
Indicted	247	244	257	270	203	248	232	246	276	269	(2492)
Convicted	168	211	232	226	196	221	207	204	229	201	(2095)
Awaiting Trial on December 31st	82	102	58	61	74	49	55	89	79	122	(771)

Source: Report to Congress on the Activities and Operations of the Public Integrity Section, 1989 (Washington, U.S. Department of Justice, November 1990), p. 26.

characterized as breakthroughs in the federal effort to insure the integrity of state and local governments.''[34]

An Overview of Major Federal Anti-Corruption Laws

Although federal prosecutors now rely upon more than the four major laws indicated previously, these four laws have played a prominent role in the prosecution of state and local officials. The most frequently used law has been the Hobbs Act with the prohibition against extortion contained in this law. The Hobbs Act was an amendment to the Anti-Racketeering Act of 1934. In 1945, the Supreme Court excluded certain types of labor racketeering under the 1934 Act and Congress responded to restore this authority by the adoption of the Hobbs Act the following year. Because of the ease of proof and severity of punishment, its use is recommended by the Department of Justice to its U. S. attorneys in the field.[35]

The Hobbs Act prohibits any obstruction, delay, or effect on interstate commerce by robbery or extortion in which property is obtained from another with consent by force, violence, or under color of official right. Of course, ''the interstate commerce, the extortion element, and under color of official right'' clauses play the crucial role in prosecuting public officials under the Act. This law can work successfully in a number of ways. If for example, a contractor refuses to pay a bribe to a public official and ends up not getting the contract, the effect may be that building materials are not brought in from out of state so there is an actual effect on interstate commerce. If he does pay the bribe, there is still an effect upon interstate commerce because the building materials would not have come in from out of state otherwise. ''Under color of official right'' has been held to mean that a public official obtained property not due him by virtue of his office. It should be noted, however, that in recent years the courts have been a little reluctant to let federal prosecutors push the Hobbs Act too far in prosecuting public corruption cases and federal authorities have grown a little more cautious in its use.[36]

The mail fraud and companion wire fraud statute have also been major anti-public corruption tools. Until an important Supreme Court decision in 1987, these laws could reach any scheme by a public official to deprive citizens of their intangible right to the public officials' honest and faithful services.[37] The 1987 decision limited its use to the protection of certain "property rights" which affects the government's interests as a property holder.[38]

Readers may wonder how a travel act may get into this. Generally speaking, it requires an act of interstate travel or use of an interstate facility in order for a scheme to bribe a public official to influence the performance of an official act to work.[39] In addition to traveling interstate to convey (or accept) a bribe, a letter mailed between states, an interstate telephone call, an interstate express delivery, and even the use of interstate banking facilities are uses of commerce facilities sufficient for the Travel Act.[40]

The Racketeer Influenced and Corrupt Organizations Act (RICO) has been used to prosecute public officials at all levels of government. This law which was adopted by Congress to add to the arsenal of federal powers to combat organized crime has been employed to prosecute and convict the mayors of Syaracuse, New York, Chester, Pennsylvania and the Village of Fox Lake, Illinois. Also falling to RICO have been members of the Philadelphia City Council and a Pennsylvania State representative. Police officers in Chicago, Philadelphia, and Miami have been convicted of conducting the affairs of their respective police departments through a pattern of racketeering activity.

There are several advantages to be gained by charging a RICO count in a public corruption case. RICO allows for federal prosecution of local officials based on state charges even if there are no other applicable or easily provable federal charges. In Chicago, a series of RICO prosecutions involving the police in that city ended in convictions when a pattern of racketeering activity for extorting money from citizens involved in hit-and-run accidents was shown. The federal authorities could not charge the offending police officers with extortion violations under the Hobbs Act because these extortions had no appreciable effect on interstate commerce. However, there was an Illinois law which made bribery illegal—and since the employing agency (the Chicago Police Department) was involved and since the department did have an effect on interstate commerce—RICO was used to obtain the convictions.[41]

Another advantage of RICO is that it permits the government to escape the statute of limitations which exist on most federal offenses. As long as one act falls within the five-year limitation period, other related offenses can be included as long as the last act was committed within 10 years of a prior act (excluding any period of imprisonment). A third advantage of RICO is that, in public corruption cases, a RICO charge can be used to present the whole corrupt scheme as a criminal enterprise and provide a unifying effect to an indictment.[42] In this way, the entire corrupt enterprise can be brought into focus for prosecution as was the case with the *Greylord* judicial corruption investigation in Chicago. RICO is also noteworthy in that it lets the prosecution join several corrupt schemes under a single prosecution and the statute provides for serious penalties upon conviction and forfeiture possibilities which includes not only the proceeds of the racketeering activity (e.g., bribes earned) but, in some cases, it can be used to forfeit pension, retirement benefits, salaries, and even the defendant's political office.[43]

In addition to these formidable tools, there are federal bribery statutes which can be used against corrupt federal officials and persons who have the power to allocate and spend federal grant funds.[44] There are also federal conspiracy laws including conspiracy to defraud the United States. These have resulted in a sizable number of indictments and convictions. Finally, there is the availability of conflicts of interest statutes, perjury, false statements, election crime statutes, and tax charges.

Criticism of Federal Efforts

Still, federal efforts in this area have not been without criticism. Arthur Maass, writing in the journal, *Publius,* argues that this is an inappropriate usurpation of the powers of the federal government. Without really addressing the moral issue of state and local public corruption—he was more concerned about the seeming violation of expressed federal powers—he argues that this has occurred without meaningful benefit of Congressional approval or oversight. In these cases, a federal agency (i.e., the Department of Justice and local U.S. attorneys) have taken it upon themselves to carve-out a new area of federal involvement and prosecution. Maass is also critical of the lack of effective oversight on these activities. He says,

> [T]he combination of these three factors—lack of authorization, independence of U.S. attorneys, claims for autonomy based on prosecutorial discretion—appear to have weakened departmental control as well as Congressional control over the program to combat state and local corruption.[45]

He goes on to say,

> The Department of Justice has not promulgated guidelines for screening local corruption prosecutions as it has in other areas, such as labor racketeering and prosecution of election offenses.*[46]

In a sharp rejoinder to Maass's position in a later article in *The Public Interest,* Philip B. Heymann argues,

> In the area of federal law enforcement, there are many more acts chargeable under federal statutes than investigators and prosecutors can pursue . . . The attorney general has announced the broad areas of emphasis such as narcotics, organized crime, fraud and public corruption. Federal priorities are chosen as important matters that the localities either cannot or will not make the focus of extensive, effective enforcement effort. [Under such circumstances] the individual U.S. attorneys throughout the country are left with substantial independence to the weight to be given to each of the priority categories, the emphasis to be given within each broad category and the wisdom and fairness of pursuing any particular case. Realistically,

**Author's note:* This situation has significantly changed since he relied upon his source of information.

> a great deal also turns on what the next levels—the line attorneys and the investigative agents—think about a particular charge in terms of both the moral outrage it arouses and the strength of evidence that supports it. If there is relatively little control from above, it is because higher bureaucratic levels are not better able to assess what are generally the crucial variables: moral outrage and strength of evidence of illegality.[47]

Federal prosecutors have countered with the argument that they have had to step-in because states and local governments have too often ignored their responsibilities to ferret-out public corruption in their jurisdictions. It is contended that because of existing "politics," state and local authorities are often reluctant to move on such cases. It is particularly sensitive when local public officials are themselves part of the enforcement mechanism such as corrupt law enforcement and judicial authorities. Federal prosecutors also argued that the idea that they are active in the pursuit of such cases may be a deterrent that otherwise would not operate.[48]

The Nature of Federal Corruption Investigations

The primary responsibility for overseeing the investigation and conducting prosecution of corruption cases involving state and local public officials rests with local U.S. attorneys. These federal prosecutors are assisted by the Public Integrity Section which provides prosecution specialists from the Department of Justice. These specialists assist local federal prosecutors as co-counsels in special cases and under circumstances where the local federal prosecutors do not have sufficient resources to carry out their efforts. They also assist in cases which are politically sensitive or of particular importance as well as cases that are multi-jurisdictional in nature (i.e., involve the offices of two or more local U.S. attorneys). Whenever an integrity investigation involves a federal judge or any judicial officer in the U.S. attorney's district, the case is always handled by the Section.[49] Field investigations are conducted by the FBI and supported by other federal investigative units such as the IRS if a tax violation is involved.

In recent years, we have seen increasing use of what are called "independent counsels" in federal integrity cases such as the Iran-Contra affair. When a very sensitive integrity issue such as the involvement of specific high-level government officials is involved, the Section is authorized to recommend to the Attorney General that a special independent counsel be appointed. The responsibilities of this office are contained in the provision dealing with independent counsel in the Ethics in Government Act.[50]

A wide range of conventional and some less typical investigative strategies are used in the conduct of public corruption investigations. These include, but are not limited to, such techniques as undercover operations, the use of informants, telephone toll records, pen registers, mail covers, mobile tracking devices, the use of investigative grand juries, closed-circuit television monitoring, consensual audio recordings, body "wires," wiretaps, grants of immunity for testifying, and financial records investigations. All of these investigative techniques have been used successfully in public corruption cases.

Many of these techniques are regulated by existing laws, court holdings, and policies of the Department of Justice. The rule is, generally, the more covert and intrusive the activity (e.g., the use of wiretaps), the more regulations are imposed on their use. Federal investigative agents, for example, cannot merely take it upon themselves to tap a suspect's telephone. If it is thought necessary to use this method against a suspected public official, approval must be sought from both the Office of Enforcement Operations in the Department of Justice as well as the Washington headquarters of the FBI. Here both agencies simultaneously considered the request and the need. If both concur in its need, the request is sent to an Assistant Attorney General for approval. If approved the local federal prosecutor then goes before a federal judge for final approval and authorization to establish a phone tap. The judge may well require additional testimony or documentary evidence before issuing the wiretap.

In fact, federal law requires that in all federal wiretap applications, the judge must satisfy himself/herself that normal investigative proedures have been tried and failed or reasonably appear unlikely to succeed if tried or are too dangerous before an authorization can be given.[51] The investigators will also find that they can only run the wiretap for a prescribed period and they must report periodically to the authorizing judge. When the prescribed time is up, they must go through the application process again. Also, all taped evidence must be presented to the judge to be sealed upon conclusion of the wiretap.[52]

Most representatives from the Department of Justice with whom we spoke while compiling the research for this section of the chapter, were unanimous in their acknowledgment that public integrity cases are particularly sensitive and had to be handled as such. While they were concerned with preventing corruption and weeding-out corrupt public officials, they were also sensitive to the need not to compromise the reputation of public officials and the public service needlessly. The fact, for example, that a local, state, or federal elected official was under federal investigation could have a chilling effect on their political careers which might be jeopardized even if the official was not found guilty of the allegations which prompted the federal inquiry. It is these kinds of consequences which must be carefully considered in any such investigation.

It should also be recognized that the realities of criminal investigation and prosecution give the federal establishment a virtual insurmountable advantage in public corruption cases. Information about criminal activity is fed into the law enforcement system from an endless variety of sources: Internal Revenue agents conducting civil or criminal tax investigations, bank auditors, investigators from the regulatory agencies, and forms filed with government pursuant to any of hundreds of registration and disclosure requirements. There is also information available from federal enforcement agencies themselves such as the FBI, the DEA, the Customs Service, and the Criminal Investigation Division of the IRS. The information is then funneled to a prosecutor whose caseload is only a small percentage of that of the typical district attorney.

The federal government also has assistant prosecutors in many of its districts specially trained in these types of investigations and prosecutions as well as the expertise and resources of the Public Integrity Section in Washington. Most importantly, the federal prosecutor has at his command the power of the grand jury—the most effective vehicle for the investigation of complex criminal operations which is not available to many local district attorneys even in major metropolitan areas.[53] He or she may have another important leg up on their local district attorney counterpart: The motivation to act against individual whom his state or local counterpart may be reluctant to challenge.

It is likely that the prosecution of corrupt public officials will continue to remain a priority of the federal government. Increased efforts to root out governmental corruption will, in all likelihood, be looked upon favorably by the American people who are growing increasingly restive about the failures of the public sector and the corruption among public officials. The fact that Congress has still not seen fit to authorize more comprehensive anti-corruption legislation that can be used to prosecute state and local government officials will continue to be something of a handicap. Federal prosecutors will continue to have to rely on existing federal laws which have been innovatively applied. The concern is that the federal courts may limit some of these tools under the doctrine of "expressed intent;" a situation which arises when they rule the law's application is beyond the scope of legislative intentions. There is a danger that this could occur should federal prosecutors become too zealous and push these laws too far as a basis for prosecution.

Still, important develops and inroads have been made into the investigation and prosecution of these crimes in the past 20 years. At least in a defacto sense, the federal government, in spite of the absence of a specific legislative mandate, has created a special federal "sphere of interest." This has taken place through the combining process of successful prosecution efforts, the apparent inability for state and local governments to police government corruption, and the public's growing sense of outrage. There is every indication that these offenses will continue to be aggressively pursued. The Department of Justice has announced plans to increase its efforts to devote special attention to these types of crimes in the years ahead. Public integrity offenses and their investigation and prosecution promise to be another important crime issue of the future.

The Ugly Shadow of Hate Crime

A new kind of crime is attracting attention from Congress and from state legislatures, social agencies, and police departments throughout the country. The "hate crime"—any assault, intimidation, or harassment that is due to the victim's race, religion, ethnic backgound, and, in some legislation, the victim's sexual preference—is emerging as an area of rapidly growing interest. Such crimes are seen by those advocating a crackdown on this new classification of crimes as particularly harmful in their effect on the victims and the tendencies for such actions to worsen the racial tensions that already grip some communities.[54] In this section, we will examine what little is known about these crimes and the initial steps being taken by legislation and the administration of justice to come to grips with this developing issue.

In spite of years of efforts to deal with racial, religious, and ethnic prejudice in the United States, many commentators are worried that the problem in recent years is becoming worse. The spectre of growing racial animosities is everywhere: in the workplace; in integrated neighborhoods where residents hurl racial epithets at minority members of the community, where houses are torchbombed and property is vandalized; and in clashes between young members of different racial groups on city streets and in public parks. It is represented by arson attacks and the appearance of swastikas on Jewish synagogues. Recently, a wave of anti-Catholicism has occurred with attacks on Catholic churces by abortion advocates and homosexuals who are angry at the church's position on abortion and its doctrinal intolerance for homosexual behavior. It is even becoming a problem on college and university campuses which have witnessed a smattering of racial confrontations including assaults and the less overt, but still insidious examples of racial and ethnic slurs which appear in underground campus newspapers and on dormitory walls.

Although there are no accurate data on the number of hate crimes committed each year, every national indicator shows that threats, intimidation, and violence directed against individuals based on their race, ethnicity, and sexual orientation is increasing.[55] Such organizations as the Puerto Rican Legal Defense and Education Fund, the National Gay and Lesbian Task Force, the Anti-Defamation League of B'nai B'rith, the Klanwatch Project of the Southern Poverty Law Center, and local and state commissions on civil rights all report sharp increases. The homosexual community claims that one in five gay men and nearly one in 10 lesbians have been physically assaulted because of their sexual orientation.[56] There are also reports of increased attacks on blacks, Asians, Hispanics, and Jews.[57] This is only the tip of the iceberg. It is well recognized that many crimes which could be considered hate crimes are not reported to the authorities. And many of those which are reported, which could be considered as a form of this offense, are not classified as such by the police. In both cases, they never end up in the official crime statistics.

The reasons behind this growing problem are unclear. Some observers generally attribute its rise to several things occurring in American society. Many white Americans, especially young white males, are increasingly frustrated with what they see as the inequality and unfairness of government attempts to promote equality through such programs as affirmative action. With the worsening of the economic situation and the growing scarcity of well-paying jobs, an increasing number of young white Americans feel threatened. Such programs are seen as providing preferential and unfair adavantages or treatment to minorities. This feeling may be most pronounced among working class

FIGURE 5.1. **ANTISEMITIC INCIDENTS (Number of Reports in 1989 and Change ( ) from Previous Year)**

Rank	*State*	*Vandalism*		*Harassment*	
1	New York	213	(+5)	115	(0)
2	New Jersey	112	(+45)	42	(+2)
3	Massachusetts	95	(+60)	45	(+17)
4	California	75	(−46)	82	(+33)
5	Florida	66	(−23)	40	(0)
6	Michigan	39	(+23)	18	(+8)
7	Pennsylvania	30	(−3)	22	(−3)
8	Maryland	25	(−11)	22	(+9)
17	Virginia	9	(+2)	3	(−4)
42	District of Columbia	0	(−3)	1	(0)

Source: Anti-Defamation League of B'nai B'rith. Adopted with permission.

youth who feel especially vulnerable to economic inroads made by minority groups. These fears may sometimes be nurtured by stories and experiences related by their parents and friends who have felt themselves discriminated against. It is also said that certain statements and the efforts of the Reagan Administration to weaken the protective effect of civil rights legislation and affirmative action programs have encouraged less tolerance for minority groups.[58]

Part of the problem may also be attributable to the growing visibility of interest groups, the increased militancy of minority activists, and their willingness to be more confrontational. It is more than mere coincidence that the confrontational tactics of Gay Rights groups, who have "come out of the closet" in recent years, and marches and demonstrations by militant blacks have been accompanied by a corresponding increase in at-

Figure 5.2. Hate crimes 1980–1989

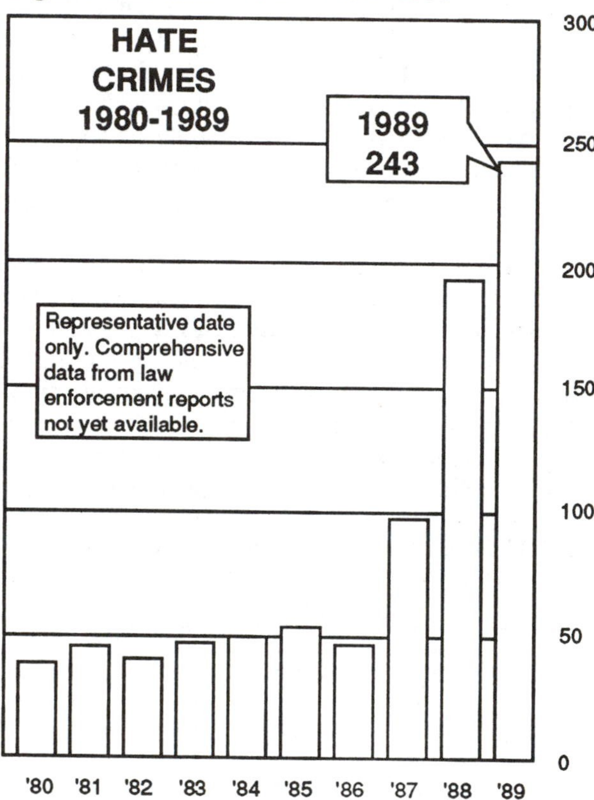

Violent crimes, threats, and the like, with evidence of bias motivation, as gathered by the Klanwatch Project of the Southern Poverty Law Center from its own sources plus the Anti-Defamation League of B'Nai B'rith and the National Gay and Lesbian Task Force. Note: This is representative data only because of the unavailability of law enforcement data. Printed with permission from *The Christian Science Monitor,* (October 5, 1990), p. 6.

tacks on members of these groups. These hate crime incidents may represent a backlash among whites who feel threatened by these new tactics. There is also the AIDS issue as it relates to the threat seen among homosexuals—a situation which galvanizes prejudice and fosters violence. In California, increasing incidents of hostility and attacks have occurred against Asians. This has led some observers to offer the opinion that some Americans feel increasingly threatened by the success of Asian groups in our society who, through hard work and thrift, excel in financial ventures and in the classroom—all of which antagonizes some Californians who are jealous of such success.[59]

There is also a growing racism among many minority groups—especially in certain segments of the black and Hispanic communities toward white society. Racial antagonisms and prejudice are not the sole province of only white America. And given the greater propensity toward violence in some of our urban neighborhoods, a dangerous fusion exists.

This can be seen in the rage directed by black youths against members of the Hasidic Jewish sect in the Crown Point section of New York City in the Summer of 1991. Many members of the black community expressed support for the violence and demonstrations directed at the police and the Jews in the neighborhood. The outcome was predictable: One Jew was stabbed to death by a group of black youths, others taunted the community with Nazi slogans and rampaged through the area destroying property and attacking the police. Indiscriminately, a group of youths roved the streets searching for targets turning over a police car, attacking a news crew, burning a van, and hurling rocks, bottles, and racial insults at the police. Many blacks felt they were justified because the Jews had lives and economic opportunities they resented.[60]

Whatever its cause, such attitudes lead to increasing polarization in our society. It is an issue which is both timely and in need of attention. As we have seen from our discussion of domestic terrorism in Chapter 4, the fostering of hate ultimately leads to the development of hate groups. This has important consequences for our society and for the administration of criminal justice.

Growing Legal Efforts to Stem Hate Crime

The recognition that racially motivated violence is on the rise has led Congress to pass legislation which requires the federal government to collect and publish statistics on "hate crimes" involving race, religion, ethnic origin, and sexual orientation. In 1990, the federal Hate Crimes Statistical Act was adopted. Although this is the first attempt by the federal government to gather such data, some states had already passed similar data-gathering laws. At the time of the law's adoption, nine states were already in the business of gathering similar statistical reports from the police.[61]

The proposal for such a clearinghouse on crimes of prejudice was not, however, without its opposition. An earlier proposal was criticized by former President Reagan who expressed opposition to any such new legislation. His successor, George Bush, supported the proposal and encouraged Congress to pass legislation which would establish a federal center for the gathering and analysis of such crime data. There was also opposition to the proposal from some members of Congress. They argued that the adoption of

Hate Crimes Move Out of the Shadows

The past several years has seen increased public discussion on the subject of hate crimes. Such cities as Philadelphia, San Antonio, Houston, Boston, and New York have held hearings and open public forums on the problem of hate crimes in their communities and how to stem the growth of associated violence. New York is a good example of the problems and concerns that this new form of crime poses.

New York City is no stranger to hate-induced violence. In 1986, the city experienced the widely publicized Howard Beach incident in which a group of white youth attacked a group of blacks. This was followed by the Bensonhurst outbreak in which 30 white youths attacked and killed a black teenager. In both cases, white youths were ultimately convicted of manslaughter and assault. Although these are the most sensational cases, these attacks and their resulting trials were only symptomatic of the underlying problem. A series of race-related incidents gripped the city: random beatings, firebombed houses, a synagogue painted with swastikas, a wide assortment of crimes against black, gay, Hispanic, and Jewish people all had come to the attention of the authorities. Together, they were recounted at a City Hall hearing on ''hate crimes'' in Manhattan.

Testimony indicated the vicious and random nature of these acts. ''They stabbed him, they slit his throat, they threw him in the water,'' Peggy Marlow told the hearing as she choked back sobs. ''They slaughtered him, all because he was gay.''* Mrs. Marlow was speaking about the slaying of her brother, James Zappalorti, a 44-year old Vietnam veteran with emotional problems. He was found dead on a recent cold January morning on the Arthur Kill beach section of Staten Island where he lived in a small shack he had built from scrap lumber.

Mrs. Marlow said her brother lived in constant fear since he had been attacked and beaten before the fatal attack because of his homosexuality. His emotional problems seemed to make him particularly vulnerable to homophobic violence. Two men, Michael Taylor and Phillip Carlo have been accused of his slaying and are now awaiting trial. The police say that the two began insulting Mr. Zappalorti as he left a delicatessan, calling him a ''queer'' and a ''faggot,'' and then, after following him, slashed his throat and stabbed him in the chest.

City Council President Andrew J. Stein, who called the hearing, described bias-related crimes as ''among the most frightening kinds of violence because they are motivated by prejudice and bigotry.''**

Mr. Stein and those who appeared at the session urged the state to enact legislation supported by Governor Mario M. Cuomo and State Attorney General Robert Abrams, to provide tough penalties for those found guilty of bias-related violence or intimidation. These penalties would be in addition to any others resulting from the same criminal act.

Matt Foreman, the executive director of the New York City Gay and Lesbian Anti-Violence Project, told the hearing that, unlike other crimes, ''hate crimes'' were not committed for economic gain, for a drug fix, or out of passion or sometimes because of provocation. ''Hate crime,'' he added, ''is what it says it is: crime committed for no reason but hate—inexcusable hatred for the color of one's skin, one's religion or disability, one's sex, or one's sexual orientation.''***

He related the fact that in 1989, 688 victims had come to the Anti-Violence Project, a 300 percent increase from five years earlier. Foreman argued that the situation is far more serious than the data shows. Seventy-five to 80 percent of crimes against gay men and lesbians are not reported because of their fear of the authorities and their feeling that the police and the courts are, themselves, openly hostile to gays.

Another speaker was Wilfred Phillip, whose newly purchased house in the Carnarsie section of Brooklyn was firebombed in February shortly before Mr. Phillip and his family were to move into it. The family is black and the neighborhood is largely white.

Another person testifying was Roger Wareham of the Center for Law and Social Justice afiliated with Medgar Evers College in Brooklyn. He spoke of the slaying of Yusuf K. Hawkins in Bensonhurst and other killings of African-Americans by whites. He described white and Hispanic neighborhoods that black people were afraid to enter because of the risk of harm if they went into these areas.

Howard Jordan, chairman of the Latino Rights Project, described incidents of bias-motivated violence against people of Hispanic background, many of which he said, do not attract public attention. ''Two Latinos,'' he said, ''were attacked and beaten only blocks from where Yusuf Hawkins was killed.''**** Mr. Jordan and Mr. Wareham were also critical of what they described as abuses and brutality by police officers toward minority groups.

Rabbi Alvin Kass, of the East Middlewood Jewish Center in Brooklyn, related that in recent years there had been 12 to 15 incidents of an anti-semitic nature directed at the synagogue, including the painting of swastikas and hate messages on the front of the building.

Gary Zaslav, of the New York Regional Board of the Anti-Defamation league of B'nai B'rith pointed out the need for increased legislative and criminal justice attention to the problem; that although prejudice and hatred cannot be legislated or prosecuted out of existence, there was a need for the state legislature to ''send a clear signal to society as a whole that acts of bigotry would not be tolerated.''

*Buder, Leonard. ''Stein Holds Hearing on Hate Crime,'' *The New York Times* (May 13, 1990), p. 9-A.

**Ibid.

***Ibid.

****Ibid.

such legislation would be a capitulation to homosexual and gay rights interests and would give sexual orientation protected status for the first time under federal law. A small group of ultra-conservative members of Congress and their supporters contended that the law amounted to the "flagship of the homosexual-lesbian legislative agenda which was an attempt to broaden civil rights protections to include gays."[62] In spite of such attempts to defeat the bill,it was ultimately passed. The legislation requires the Attorney General to gather and release data during each of the next five years on cases of murder, rape, assault, arson, vandalism and other crimes where "there is manifest evidence of prejudice based on race, religion, sexual orientation, or ethnicity."[63]

The growing concern about incidents of hate crimes and the adoption by some states and the federal government of statistical record keeping together with the passage by some states of specific anti-hate crime legislation, promises greater criminal justice system involvement in this area in the future. In spite of these efforts, it is widely recognized that there exist important limitations on the effect of such efforts. The anti-hate laws themselves are often ambiguous and are proving difficult to successfully enforce and prosecute. Observers are also pointing out that simple awareness of such crimes by the federal government as provided under the Statistical Act is not going to put more people behind federal bars. While keeping tabs on the growing number of crimes of prejudice will in all likelihood increase pressure on the Department of Justice to instigate more prosecutions against hate mongers, the bill does nothing to make that difficult job any easier.[64]

Federal Laws

In order to successfully win these cases, federal prosecution specialists in this area point out that it is not enough simply to prove that prejudice was the main motivation behind the crime. There is no special penalty currently on the federal books for most bias crimes. This hampers the efforts of local federal prosecutors and the Criminal Section of the Civil Rights Division of the Department of Justice to take action. Today, the most frequently relied upon laws used by federal prosecutors are provisions in existing civil rights laws especially pieces of the landmark 1964 civil rights legislation that attaches penalties for interfering or conspiring to interfere with such federally protected activities as voting, jury duty, conducting civil rights protests, and enrolling in public schools and colleges.[65] Under this latter civil rights law, for the federal government to conduct a successful prosecution, their lawyers need to show that the victim was deprived or there was a conspiracy to deprive someone of specific, federally protected rights. The simple freedom from such acts as hateful harassment is not among them. Although Congress added an important arrow to the prosecutor's quiver in 1988, passing a law that specifically outlawed acts of violence motivated by religious bias, by late 1990, there was not as yet a single prosecution under that law.

Existing federal law in this area is also criticized for being mainly effective in confronting conspiracies of extremist group violence, epitomized by the tactics of the "skinheads," the Ku Klux Klan, or neo-Nazi groups, not the scattered racial violence that suddenly erupts in urban settings.[66] But increasingly, hate crimes are being committed by people with no affiliations with these groups. It is "average Americans," not organized racist extremists, that are now often committing these crimes.[67] If this is the case, however, this situation may be an important argument for the role of the criminal justice system in dealing with these offenses. By prosecuting and convicting hate crime offenders and widely publicizing such prosecutions, some are suggesting that such efforts may serve as a deterrent.[68] Publicized prosecution efforts and the threat of increased prosecutions in the future, may make some of these ''average Americans'' think twice before they're involved in such acts; it might turn them around before their hatred channels them into paramilitary racist organizations or to radical racist or homophobic political groups.

State Laws

As of 1990, 46 states had passed criminal laws specifically aimed at crimes that are racially and/or religiously motivated which result in violence.[69] For non-violent crimes such as threats and intimidation, harassment and property damage offenses, some states have passed specific hate crimes offenses to cover these acts. Other states rely on conventional criminal statutes for the prosecution of these non-violent crimes regardless of the motive for the act. Still other states have enhanced penalties for these crimes if they are motivated by bigotry or bias. Some states have passed specific legislation aimed at protecting certain types of property or laws obviously aimed at certain hate groups. For example, 21 states and the District of Columbia specifically prohibit property damage to places of worship and cemeteries; six states have laws prohibiting cross burnings; 11 states have anti-mask or hood laws; and 21 states ban the formation of private paramilitary organizations.[70] At least three states have criminal laws which broadly proscribe interference with a person's civil rights.

It has been suggested by some legal commentators that states permit cross-filings in both civil and criminal courts for acts constituting bias-motivated crimes. As an example, the State of Massachusetts now permits, in addition to criminal prosecutions, the victim's right to sue for civil damages. The Commonwealth of Massachusetts goes one step further. The Commonwealth's Attorney General can also sue in civil court on behalf of the victim to restrain the future behavior of the offender.[71] Although several states have introduced such legislation, only a handful of states have laws allowing the victim to seek civil damages from an offender.[72]

This uneven approach, while not unusual, has encouraged criticism from those who want to see the state authorities deal more harshly with bias-related crime. In the first place, they would like to see all states develop specific criminal laws which would contain the element of racial/religious/ethnic bias as a motivating factor. Rather than prosecuting an attack on a church or synagogue as a conventional arson or malicious destruction of property crime, it should be prosecuted as a particular bias-related act. If the authorities are unwilling to write specific laws around this particular element of motivation, than it is argued, the sentence that can be imposed under existing criminal law violations should be increased if it resulted from a hate-induced motivation.[73]

Several states have done this. The most researched state law is probably Oregon's which was passed in 1981. Oregon's law created special enhancements for the crimes of criminal mischief, harrassment, assault, and menacing when they are committed by reason of race, color, religion, or national origin of the victim.[74] One that is receiving a lot of attention is the Florida Hate Crimes Act which was adopted in 1989 and is considered the toughest in the nation. Under this law, conviction for a crime which evidences prejudice during its conviction calls for an automatic enhanced penalty for both misdemeanor and felony offenses.[75] If the crime committed is a third degree misdemeanor, it is sentenced as a second dgree misdemeanor; a second degree felony would be sentenced as a first degree felony. The Florida law also has another feature which appeals to the ''get-tough'' on hate crimes group: civil provisions which award triple damages to victims. In this way, it allows for civil damages to be awarded in addition to any criminal penalties imposed. In 1990, the first year for which figures are available, 306 hate crimes were reported in Florida, 72 percent of which were classified as racially motivated. There is no available breakdown of how many of these cases were prosecuted under the law.[76]

A new element has been introduced which may have an effect on bias-crime legislation. The U.S. Supreme Court, in its 1991 to 1992 term, has agreed to consider the First Amendment constitutionality of a case in Minnesota. A local community in that state, like some other communities across the nation, has enacted a content-based hate crime ordinance that prohibits the display of symbols including the Nazi swastika or a burning cross on public or private property which one knows or has reason to know arouses alarm, anger, or resentment based on race, color, creed, religion, or gender. This is being challenged. How the Supreme Court decides this case—and if the Court broadly disapproves of such efforts under the Freedom of Expression Doctrine—might well restrict the ability of governments to regulate bias or hate-related acts under such specific legislation.

As we saw in the discussion of the legislation creating the federal government's Hate Crimes Statistics Act, politics and political considerations also are playing a role in dealing with state hate crime laws. Only the state of California specifically protects a special group—in this case, homosexuals and lesbians—from bias acts. No other state has sought similar extension of its laws to cover a specific group. Even the liberal State of New York has found state legislative action to protect homosexuals impossible to pass in spite of gubernatorial support for such a law and concerted efforts by Gay Rights' groups in that state. Feminist groups have also gotten into the act. Some such groups have been demanding that rape be considered a form of ''hate crime'' and come in for special statistical reporting, analysis, and prosecution efforts by the authorities.[77]

Problems for the Criminal Justice System

Following outbreaks of major hate crime violence, several cities in the United States such as Boston and New York have created special hate crime investigative units in their police departments. The New York Police Department now has 22 detectives assigned to the Bias Investigation Unit which was first formed in 1980. Investigations in Boston are conducted by the Boston Police Department's Community Disorders Unit. Some smaller cities faced with the same problems have tried to train a specialist investigator to handle these crimes. These crimes are proving to be very hard to investigate and prosecute. Investigators are plagued with the problem of determining whether a crime was mainly the result of prejudice. This is important as it relates to the intent of the offender and the success of the prosecution under a hate crimes statute.

Proving this is often difficult unless the arrested offender admits to this motive by way of a confession or admission that is itself admissable in court. Perhaps the detectives will be fortunate enough to find a symbol of bigotry—a swastika or KKK symbol—at the scene of the crime from which motive can be inferred. The investigator will also examine other factors such as did the crime involve two ethnic groups? Trying to rule-out other possible motives such as money or jealousy is also important. Seasoned police investigators also follow such procedures as checking the incidence of similar attacks on others in the neighborhood who have the same background in order to develop a pattern to support the motive that it is hate-related. Such questions as did the attacker select the victim from others of different background is also an important investigative element. While the police will tell you that they suspect it was bias which led to the crime, they will also admit that proving it is very tough but absolutely indispensible to the case.[78]

The same problems are carried over into the prosecution of these offenses. Prosecution authorities are finding that their chances are hinged on the same evidentiary and motive considerations that hinder the police. They, too, even to a greater degree than the police, must "prove"—and as in all criminal cases, beyond a reasonable doubt—that the intent to commit the crime was the result of a bias-directed motive on the part of the offender. Prosecutors faced with such difficulties might resign themselves under such circumstances to merely prosecute an offender for an assault, malicious destruction of property, or arson offense under conventional statutes in lieu of trying to prosecute for a bias-related offense which requires the showing of such a specific motive. When we move into the "gray area" of trying to prosecute for specific bias-induced crimes such as acts of harrassment, threat, or intimidation, it is here that even more difficult problems loom. Just as such conventional (non-bias related) crimes of this nature are difficult enough in and of themselves to successfully prosecute, adding the qualifier that it was inspired by racial, ethnic, or homophobic motives, ratchets the proof in such a case up to a new level of difficulty.

Experienced prosecutors follow certain guidelines for identifying whether a crime is bias-related. The first is merely common sense, for example, when a cross is burned on the lawn of a minority family that has just moved into an all-white neighborhood. Likewise, the language used by the suspects may be important. Although language by itself may not always prove bias—racist slurs may be uttered in the heat of an argument or fight that was initiated for another reasons, and language that is not threatening may not be a crime—still, what was said and under what circumstances may carry the required probative weight. The severity of the attack is important as is any evidence of lack of provocation. The previous history of similar incidents in the same area and the absence of any other apparent motive such as a battery occurring without an attendant robbery may also be crucial to the case.[79]

Prosecutors also are finding they are having some problems obtaining convictions in hate crime cases because they can't escape the typical problems found in the prosecution of conventional assault crimes coupled with the particular difficulties (other than the motive angle discussed previously) which are associated with hate crimes. Uncooperative, complaining witnesses who want to drop the case is a major prosecution hurdle. Whether this is brought about by future fears of another incident or merely wanting to forget an unpleasant occurrence, the result is the same. A few prosecutor's are attempting to deal with this problem by working closely with minority groups, victims assistance programs, by fostering a close working relationship between the prosecutor's office and the victim, and employing, in some jurisdictions, vertical prosecution efforts directed at hate crime offenders.

There has also arisen special defense issues in several areas of the country involving attacks on gays. The "homosexual panic" or "gay advance" defense—claiming self-defense or temporary insanity in response to a sexual advance—has resulted in lenient sentences or acquittals for defendants charged with assaulting or murdering gay men in several communities in California.[80] In Kalamazoo, Michigan at the end of a jury trial in which this tactic resulted in an acquittal on all charges, the judge, exasperated with the jury's finding, told the press that had it been a benchtrial, he would have have found the defendant guilty of first degree murder.[81]

Peter Finn, a prosecuting attorney in New York City, who has been relatively successful in the prosecution of hate crimes involving gay victims, has developed some guidelines to assist other prosecuting attorneys in their efforts to deal with the problem. He points out that in New York City, the Manhattan District Attorney's Office developed several approaches to countering the homosexual panic defense. A key factor is the selection of the jury. During the jury selection process, efforts are made to select jurors who are politically and socially liberal. He warns prosecutors not to play or sidestep the issue that the victim is gay. Jurors must be prepared for the defense tactic of bringing out, in the courtroom, the fact that the crime victim is homosexual. Jury candidates are asked, "If I told you this case would involve a homosexual victim, could you be objective? I know some people have moral problems when it comes to homosexuality, so please be honest and step forward to let us know if you can't be fair." During the trial, the prosecutors take a common sense approach toward the defendant. For example, asking what prevented him from simply leaving the scene rather than assaulting the victim. Finally, prosecutors use the summation to remind jurors that they took an oath to be fair and to emphasize again that every victim has a right to justice."[82]

A final problem that prosecutors report is one involving judicial leniency. Judges are often reluctant to impose maximum sentences, especially since many times hate crimes are committed by juveniles. In New York City from 1987 to 1990, the NYPD's Bias Investigation Unit has invested 1,554 cases and made arrests and found suspects in about one-third of these. Two-thirds of those arrested were under the age of 19 and 40 percent younger than 16.[83] Judges in many jurisdictions are reluctant to impose a criminal record on a young defendant. Many times, they do nothing but lecture the offender and possibly place him or her on probation. One way to deal with this judicial leniency is for prosecutors to argue for the imposition of more intermediate sanctions in such cases. These can include fines, restitution, and community service activities in the setting where the offense occurred.

Conclusion: Charting a Future Course

The investigation and prosecution of sporadic hate-induced acts may well grow in the future as further strains in the economic and social structure of our nation continue. There is little indication or optimism that these pressures will subside. One consequence of this is that class, race, ethnic, and ''lifestyle'' cleavages and expressed hostility will continue to escalate in threatening ways. The problem of bias-induced hatred and the acting-out of this hatred seems to be growing. As with many other criminal events, we also need to learn more about these crimes including their motivation and ways to more effectively deal with them.

It is questionable, however, how effective the criminal justice system can be in stemming these kinds of acts. The conditions that give rise to such acts are deeply imbedded in the social structure of our nation. Efforts by the criminal justice system, in fact, may cause the problem to worsen. For example, the smouldering hatred some blacks—especially a disturbing number of young black males—seem to be expressing toward white society and the police run a risk of erupting if arrests were made of young blacks for hate crimes. Although society cannot permit itself to be intimidated by such threats no more than it can condone or disregard such actions whether committed by white racists, homophobes, black racists or other minorities, there are some important and thought-provoking issues involved in this area that need to be carefully thought out by policymakers and legislators.

It would seem that there are two roles for the criminal justice system in the future. The federal government must play the major role in dealing with organized traditional hate groups such as the Klan, the White Aryan Resistance, and the burgeoning skinhead movement where this latter phenomenon is affiliated with a national racist organization. These are best attacked through the resources and the jurisdictional breadth of federal authorities. To do this, however, Congress must review the weakness of existing federal civil rights law to effectively address the problem. Perhaps more specific federal anti-hate crime legislation is needed.

But there are dangers in trying to over-extend federal authority specifically for hate-induced crimes, thereby making such acts federal offenses. In addition to questions of propriety and available resources, the fundamental fact remains: The primary responsibility to deal effectively with the growing menace of these crimes is by state and local investigations and prosecution efforts. A gang of attacking white (or black) youth such as the Bensonhurst incident in New York or the Confederate Skinheads in Dallas must be shown that their actions are intolerable by the standards of the local community. And because the problem often emenates from the local community, it needs to be addressed at this level.

There is also a need for the states to carefully experiment with different legislative approaches to the problem in an effort to determine what laws seem to work best and show the greatest promise of deterring these acts and dealing appropriately with offenders who commit these crimes. Perhaps greater insight into such successful legislative strategies will be forthcoming as states grow more experienced in their use and as we learn more about these offenses through our efforts to gather a national depository of data on their occurrence for study. This should also provide better insight into the appropriate role of the administration of justice in dealing with this growing problem.

NOTES

[1]Weld, William F. "Introduction: Why Public Corruption is Not a Victimless Crime," in U.S. Department of Justice, *Prosecution of Public Corruption Cases* (Washington: U.S. Government Printing Office, February 1988), p. iii.

[2]Chicago Courthouse folklore as related by Irv Kupcinet, columnist for *The Chicago Sun-Times* as related by Anton R. Valukas and Ira Raphaelson, "Judicial Corruption" Ibid., p. 3.

[3]See *United States v. Murphy,* 768 F.2d 1518 (7th Cir. 1985).

[4]Valukas and Raphaelson, p. 4.

[5]This area is a little unsettled in the law. Some courts have held, for example, that although a public official receives property under color of official right, there must be an inducement or a demand made by the defendant to constitute a form of extortion. See *United States v. O'Grady,* 742 F.2d 682 (2d Cir. 1984) and *United States v. Aguon,* 813 F.2d 1413 (9th Cir. 1987).

[6]Hailman, John R. "Corruption in Government Contracts: Bribery, Kickbacks, Bid-Rigging and the Rest," *Prosecution of Public Corruption Cases, op cit.*, p. 23.

[7]Ibid.

[8]Giuliani, Rudolph W., and Kemble Brecher, Rhea. "Regulatory Agency Corruption," in *Prosecution of Public Corruption Cases, supra* p. 32.

[9]Kellner, Leon B. "Narcotics-related Corruption" in Ibid., p. 42.

[10]Ibid.

[11]See Article 1, Section 6.

[12]*Powell v. McCormack,* 395 U.S. 486, 505 (1969). See also *Dombrowski v. Eastland,* 387 U.S. 82, 85 (1967).

[13]*Gravel v. United States,* 408 U.S. 606 (1972).

[14]Ibid., at 616.

[15]*United States v. Johnson,* 383 U.S. 169 (1966).

[16]Weingarten, Reid H. "Legislative Corruption" in *Prosecution of Public Corruption Cases, op cit.*, p. 59.

[17]Article I, Section 5.

[18]Article 1, Section 6 of the U.S. Constitution provides that members of Congress shall, in all cases except treason, felony, breach of the peace, be privileged from arrest during their attendance at the Session of their respective Houses, and in going from and returning to the same.

[19]See *United States v. Liddy,* 452 F.2d 76 (D.C. Cir. 1976).

[20]For case law related to the *Calley* case and this issue, see *United States v. Calley,* 8 Crim L. Rep. (BNA) 2054-55; *Army GCM,* 5th Jud. Cir. 1970); *Calley v. Callaway,* 382 F. Supp. 650 (M.D. Ga 1974), *rev'd* 519 F.2d 184 (5th Cir. 1975, *cert. denied,* 425 U.S. 911 (1976).

[21]Donsanto, Craig C. "Election Crimes" in *Prosecution of Public Corruption Cases, supra.* pp. 79–80.

[22]This latter instance refers to the election of Lyndon B. Johnson. See Caro, Robert A. *The Years of Lyndon Johnson—Means of Ascent* (New York: Alfred A. Knopf, 1990).

[23]This agency housed in the Office of Personnel Management was created by Title IV of the Ethics in Government Act of 1978. (Pub. L. 95-521, October 26, 1978).

[24]For example, see 18 U.S.C. Sec. 203.

[25]For example, see 18 U.S.C. Sec. 205.

[26]*United States v. Conlon,* 628 F.2d 150 (D.C. Cir. 1980).

[27]The Hatch Act which was extended to state and local governments in 1940 prohibited certain political acts by non-elected state and local public employees.

[28]Gardiner, John A. *The Politics of Corruption* (New York: Russell Sage Fund, 1970), p. 101.

[29]As cited in Maass, Arthur. "U.S. Prosecution of State and Local Officials for Political corruption: Is the Bureaucracy Out of Control in a High-Stakes Operation Involving the Constitutional System?" *Publius,* Vol. 17 (Summer 1987), p. 201.

[30]Thornburgh, Richard L. "Preface to the United States Court of Appeals: 1974–75 Term: Criminal Law and Procedure," GEORGETOWN LAW REVIEW, Vol. 64 (1975), p. 173.

[31]See, for example, Ruff, Charles F. C. "Federal Prosecution of Local Corruption: A Case Study in the Making of Law Enforcement Policy," GEORGETOWN LAW JOURNAL 65 (June 1977), pp. 171–228.

[32]Report to Congress on the Activities and Operations of the Public Integrity Section for 1989 (Washington: Public Integrity Section, U.S. Department of Justice, November 1990), p. 25.

[33]These respective statutes are 18 U.S.C. Sec. 1341; 18 U.S.C. Sec.1951; 18 U.S.C. Sec. 1952; and 18 U.S.C. 1962 *et sec.*

[34]Henderson, Thomas H. Jr. Chief of the Public Integrity Section, "The Expanding Role of Federal Prosecutors in Combatting State and Local Political Corruption," CUMBERLAND LAW REVIEW, Vol. 8 (1977), p. 385.

[35]Radel. Lee J. "Hobbs Act," in *Prosecution of Public Corruption Cases, op cit.,* p. 415.

[36]Ibid., p. 419.

[37]Cole, James M. "Mail and Wire Fraud," Ibid., p. 447.

[38]See *McNally v. United States,* 107 S.Ct. (1987).

[39]*Author's note:* This is a very broad overview of the provisions of the Travel Act and caution is warranted. The courts have different interpretations and restrictions. See, for example: *United States v. Karigiannis,* 430 F.2d 148 (7th Cir.) 1970; *United States v. Isaacs,* 493 F.2d 1124 (7th Cir. 1974); and *United States v. Herrerra,* 584 F.2d 1137, 1146 (2nd Cir. 1978).

[40]Coffey, Paul E. "RICO and the Travel Act," in *Prosecution of Public Corruption Cases, supra.,* p. 441.

[41]Ibid., p. 433.

[42]Ibid.

[43]Ibid., p. 435.

[44]This has been interpreted by the Supreme Court to apply to such officials in *Dixson v. United States,* 465 U.S. 482 (1984).

[45]Maass, *op cit.*, pp. 220–21.

[46]Ibid., p. 221. Maass is not alone in this criticism of lack of DOJ guidelines governing such cases. See U.S. General Accounting Office Report, ''Justice Needs to Better Manage Its Fight Against Public Corruption,'' *Report to the Chairman,* Subcommittee on Crime, Committtee on the Judiciary, House of Representatives (Washington: U.S. Government Printing Office, 1980).

[47]Heymann, Philip B. ''The Risks of Corruption,'' *The Public Interest,* Vol. 23 (1988), pp. 128–29.

[48]From the author's discussion with federal prosecutors about the claims of usurpation of authority, November 11, 1990.

[49]Public Integrity Section, U.S. Department of Justice, Report to Congress on the Activities and Operations of the Public Integrity Section for 1988 n.d.

[50]See 28 U.S.C. Secs. 591–598.

[51]See 18 U.S.C. Sec. 2518 (3) (c).

[52]This section is adopted from Keefer, William A. ''Additional Covert Techniques in Corruption Investigations,'' *Prosecution of Public Corruption Cases, op cit.*, pp. 140–41.

[53]Ruff, *op cit.*, p. 635.

[54]Malcolm, Andrew H. ''New Efforts Developing Against Hate Crime,'' *The New York Times,* May 12, 1989, A-12.

[55]''Bias Crime Shows Sharp Increases,'' *Criminal Justice Newsletter* (June 15, 1988), p. 3.

[56]*Dealing with Violence: A Guide for Gay and Lesbian People,* National Gay and Lesbian Task Force, 1986 p. 1.

[57]For example, see Barrett, Paul M. ''Hate Crimes Increase and Become More Violent: U.S. Prosecutors Focus on 'Skinhead' Movement,'' *The Wall Street Journal,* (July 14, 1989), p. A-12.

[58]Ibid.

[59]Roslyn, William A. ''California's Growing Anti-Asian Sentiment,'' *The Californian* (June 12, 1989), p. A-1.

[60]''Crowd Changes Mood and Makeup,'' *The New York Times* (August 25, 1991), p. 34.

[61]The first such state was Maryland in 1981. The other states are Pennsylvania, Illinois, Minnesota, Connecticut, Oklahoma, Virginia, Maine, and Missouri.

[62]Dewar, Helen. ''Senate Passes Bill Requiring Data on Hate Crimes,'' *The Washington Post,* August 4, 1990 p. A-6.

[63]Ibid.

[64]Watson, Tom. "New Reporting Requirements Only the Beginning," *Legal Times*, Vol. 13, (April 16, 1990), p. 2. *Note:* The federal government primarily uses federal criminal statutes directed at racially or religously motivated violence by private individuals. 18 U.S.C. Sec. 241, Conspiracy to Interfere with Civil Rights; 18 U.S.C. Sec. 242 and 245, Deprivation of Civil Rights Under Color of Law and Forcible Interference with Civil Rights; and 42 U.S.C. Sec. 3631 which pertains to Willful Interference with Civil Rights Under the Fair Housing Act. There are also four federal statutes which provide for civil causes of action for victims of racially and religously motivated violence by private individuals.

[65]Ibid., p. 23.

[66]Kateri Hernandez, Tanya. "Bias Crimes: Unconscious Racism in the Prosecution of Racially Motivated Violence," THE YALE LAW JOURNAL, Vol. 99 (January 1990), pp. 845–64.

[67]Ibid., p. 847.

[68]Hazelwig, Robert A. "Turning Attention to Hate Crimes," *Washington Lawyer,* Vol. 24 (June 14, 1990), pp. 7–9.

[69]Only the states of Arkansas, Nebraska, Utah, and Wyoming have no specific hate crime statutes at this writing. See Sherman, Rorie. "Hate Crimes Statutes Abound," NATIONAL LAW JOURNAL (May 21, 1990), p. 3 and p. 28.

[70]Pitts, M. Bruce. "Eliminating Hate," LAW AND PSYCHOLOGY REVIEW, Vol. 14 (Spring 1990), p. 144.

[71]Finn, Peter. "Bias Crime: A Special Target for Prosecutors," *The Prosecutor,* Vol. 21, No. 4 (Spring 1988), pp. 9–15.

[72]For an excellent review of federal and state laws dealing with hate-motivated violence, see National Institute Against Prejudice and Violence, *Striking Back at Bigotry: Remedies Under Federal and State Law for Violence Motivated by Racial, Religious, and Ethnic Prejudice* (Washington, D.C.: 1986).

[73]Fleischauer, Marc L. "Teeth for a Paper Tiger: A Proposal to Add Enforceability to Florida's Hate Crimes Act," FLORIDA STATE UNIVERSITY LAW REVIEW, Vol. 17 (Spring 1990), pp. 697–711.

[74]See Oregon Revised Statutes Secs. 164.345, 166.065, 163.160, and 163.190.

[75]This is defined as, "evidences prejudice based on the race, color, ancestry, ethnicity, religion, or national origin of the victim. See Ch. 89–133, Sec. 2, 1989 Fla. Laws.

[76]Rother, Larry. "Without Smiling, to Call Floridian a "Cracker" May be a Crime," *The New York Times,* (August 25, 1991), p. 26.

[77]Roberts, Charlie. "Senate Trying to Make Rape a 'Hate' Crime," *The Los Angeles Daily Journal,* (October 8, 1990), p. 1.

[78]McKinley, James C. Jr. "Tracking Crimes of Prejudice: A Hunt for Elusive Truth," *The New York Times* (June 29, 1990), p. A-1 and B-4.

[79]Finn, Peter. *op cit.*, pp. 13–14.

[80]Ibid., p. 14.

[81]"Jury Acquits in Bryban Case," *Kalamazoo News* (February 21, 1986), p. 3.

[82]Finn, p. 14.

[83]McKinley, James C. Jr. *op cit*.

CHAPTER 6

Developing Problems for the Administration of Justice? Aspects of AIDS and the Perinatal Drug Issue

CONTENTS

This chapter deals with two important social problems which are causing concerns for society. The first is the issue of willful and deliberate transmission (or the possibility of transmission) of the deadly virus AIDS to unsuspecting sex partners or third parties. Although there is a related concern about the transmission of the virus to the fetus of AIDS-infected mothers, this topic will not be discussed. What will be examined in the second part of the chapter, however, is related: The perinatal transmission of drugs to neonates by mothers. Both of these health concerns have significant implications for our nation. Neither of these issues—especially this aspect of the AIDS situation—has begun to be addressed by effective public policy initiatives. What role, if any, the criminal justice system will play in these areas is just now beginning to be examined. Even so, the discussion shows deep fissures of both public and professional opinion on these issues. The picture at this time is unclear. Still, it is entirely conceivable that the continued unabated spread of these problems will see increasing efforts by the criminal-legal system to be used as a mechanism to deal with these concerns.

Another aspect of the AIDS situation is its effect upon those operating in the criminal justice system. Police officers, jailors, and correctional personnel through their contact with HIV positive carriers are expressing increasing apprehension over the risk. This subject has generated widespread attention and controversy among these members of the criminal justice community. This chapter will not examine that consequence of AIDS. The reader interested in this aspect of the problem is encouraged to examine the developing literature on this subject.

We want to examine what little we know to date about the involvement of the administration of criminal justice in these two areas. Most of the present debate focuses on evolving legal issues amid the social turmoil that attends these problems. It is the law that is the arena of interest at this time. The focus will be on the arguments that surround these two areas and the developing and often unsystematic and emotionally charged concerns for criminal justice involvement. It will serve as an overview for what is unfolding in these still unchartered and turbulent waters.

The Controversy over AIDS

Public health officials who are willing to speak out see AIDS as the number-one health priority in the nation. These disease specialists also express the opinion that this disease will continue to be so for many years to come.[1] Since June of 1981, when the Centers for Disease Control (CDC) first announced the existence of a new virus that we now call AIDS, much has happened. Nine years after the CDC's initial report, nearly 400,000 cases of AIDS has been diagnosed and reported in the United States. More than 50,000 Americans have died of the disease, about the same number who died in the Vietnam War and about the same number of people killed on our highways each year. Although the CDC has recently downgraded its earlier projections, it is still estimated that from 800,000 to 1.3 million persons are infected with the Human Immunodeficiency Virus or HIV.[2] All evidence to date indicates that the majority of those people will eventually develop the full-blown AIDS syndrome. The current estimate is that over a half million Americans will have developed AIDS by the end of 1993.[3] In some of our nation's major urban centers, the problem threatens to overwhelm the health care system. In New York City, for instance, one in every 12 hospital beds is filled by an AIDS patient a cost of $1 million dollars a day—much of it paid for by taxpayers and the hospitals themselves.[4]

Experts clearly recognize that the primary transmission of the disease is among homosexuals and intravenous drug users who employ contaminated hypodermic needles. But fear is growing in other areas. There is the fear that AIDS will also become a significant transmission risk among heterosexuals. The Hudson Institute, a conservative think tank, has developed a worse-case scenario in which they project by the year 2002 the number of people infected could rise to nearly 15 million unless there is a medical breakthrough and if risk reducing behavior changes do not occur. In this gloomy forcast, 2.9 percent of whites, 9.2 percent of Hispanics, and a staggering 41.8 percent of blacks between the ages of 15 and 50 could carry the disease. By then, the Insitute predicts, at least half of all those infected will be non-drug using heterosexuals.[5] Others argue that such projections are nonsense and the threat to non-drug using heterosexuals is extremely small.[6]

While such arguments continue, one fact remains: This health tragedy has begun to affect the criminal justice system in several ways. It is already a major problem for one component of the system, namely, corrections. The Federal Bureau of Prisons alone spent $3 million in 1990. The money was used for randomly testing asymptomatic inmates entering federal prisons, and uniformly testing all persons being released from federal prisons. It also covers the costs of medical treatment for AIDS, including Azidophinadine (AZT) treatment.[7]

State prison systems and large city jails are also feeling the effects. It is estimated, for example, that approximately 10,000 to 15,000 inmates who passed through the New York City prison system in 1988 were HIV-positive.[8] Still unknown, and less understood, are other ways the AIDS epidemic may affect other parts and operations of the criminal justice system. This concern led to a 1989 National Conference on AIDS, co-sponsored by the State Justice Institute and the National Institute of Justice. This conference brought together experts from many areas to discuss the impact of this burgeoning problem on the legal system and the administration of criminal justice and what could be done to deal it.

A Policy Issue: Trying to Peer Through the Thicket

There is increasing concern that some individuals afflicted with AIDS will knowingly engage in sexual activities with others, thus significantly heightening the risk that these innocent sex partners will themselves be afflicted with the disease. Whether such transmission occurs by means of rape or consensual homosexual and heterosexual behavior is inconsequential. There is also the concern that infected individuals will purposely try to transmit the disease to criminal justice and medical personnel who come in contact with them. It is, however, the concern that knowing and willful sexual transmission of the disease may be the most serious and prevalent consequence; a situation of such gravity that it will require the intervention and protection of the criminal law.

The President's Commission empaneled to study the AIDS problem and make recommendations realized the possibility of such grave consequences. It has suggested that states move to enact HIV-specific statutes. While the Commission recognizied the difficulties in applying traditional criminal law in this area as a regulatory mechanism, it has recommended that the states adopt criminal statutes whose sanctions would be imposed on those HIV-infected individuals who know they are infected and engage in behaviors which they know according to scientific research are likely to result in the transmission of AIDS. These suggested laws would clearly set forth what specific behaviors are subject to criminal sanctions.[9]

About 20 states have passed such laws.[10] These laws criminalize certain behavior when engaged in by persons who have tested positive for HIV or who actually have AIDS or AIDS-Related Complex.[11] These generally fall into several types of laws:

- statutes which make it mandatory to disclose HIV status;
- laws which prohibit certain activities such as sharing needles or the donation of infected blood; and
- statutes enhacing penalties for activities already illegal such as prostitution when committed by an HIV carrier.[12]

How contentious the subject is can be seen in cases of rape. Victim rights groups are calling for the mandatory testing of arrested or indicted suspects in rape cases. Opposed to such testing on grounds of the accused's rights of privacy and the presumption of innocence which surrounds defendants are civil rights groups and many members of the defense bar. Today, only 10 states require such an automatic test of rape suspects or require testing upon the request of the victim. Twenty-eight states require the test for those convicted of rape.

In New York State, for instance, the alleged or convicted rapist cannot be tested without his permission. This has led to situations where suspects later convicted for rape have plea bargained the charge down by agreeing to submit to an AIDS test. This has heightened the controversy around mandatory testing laws and created further criticism of the criminal justice system and the practice of plea bargaining.

Proposals to impose criminal penalties on aids carriers raises an important policy issue. Is it appropriate to use the criminal law and the criminal justice system to respond to a medical problem? Can such a system be workable? Proponents argue that criminal penalties provide the strongest means available of protecting society from the dangers posed by AIDS carriers who deliberately or recklessly engage in conduct which threatens to transmit the deadly virus to innocent or unspecting victims. Such actions in addition to the harm done to innocent parties, ultimately poses a serious threat to public health. In the interests of public safety, the legal system must move immediately and clearly to impose sanctions.

Existing Criminal Sanctions

We have seen that about 20 states have specific criminal laws pertaining to aspects of AIDS. Still, there are other criminal laws that could be employed. While all states have adopted laws which require that AIDS cases be reported to the health authorities who in return are required to report these to the CDC, about half the states have laws that criminalize the exposure of others to sexually transmitted diseases. These generalized sexual transmission laws are for the most part, however, rarely enforced. In most states that have such laws, the offense is also treated as a misdemeanor.[13] Thus, existing sanctions which could be imposed are minimal. While most states punish the act of exposing another person to a sexually transmitted disease, they are possibly weakened by the fact that a defense would be that the defendant took reasonable precautions.[14] Some of these laws also impose broad bans which prohibit infected persons from marrying or engaging in sexual intercourse. This may prove to be unreasonable in AIDS cases, since given the nature of HIV infection, the ban could last a lifetime.

Several states impose a strict liability doctrine that theoretically permits the prosecution of the defendant even if he or she did not know they had the disease.[15] Such provisions, however, are likely to make successful prosecution that much more problematic. For example, given the fact that HIV tests are sometimes unreliable and the HIV carrier may not be aware that they are infected, these facts call into question the fairness of prosecutions based on such a standard.

The major weakness of such laws is that they have been adopted for more conventional forms of sexually transmitted diseases. When they were adopted they did not anticipate the terrible consequences of AIDS. The implications of AIDS in terms of its life-threatening medical implications is of much graver consequence than other forms of sexually transmitted disease. Existing general sexual transmission statutes could not have forseen the epidemiological nature of AIDS and such consequences were not taken into consideration.

Some Case Precedents Employing Conventional Criminal Statutes

Without adequate legal remedies for the prosecution of such cases, there have been a smattering of initial attempts to criminally prosecute by the use of more conventional criminal laws, AIDS-infected individuals who either negligently or purposely attempt to infect others. An airman at the Lackland Air Force Base in San Antonio was charged with aggravated assault. The deadly weapon was his own bodily fluids. In Lafayette, Indiana, the local prosecutor successfully prosecuted an AIDS-causing human immunodeficiency virus (HIV) carrier for attempted murder. ''We're trying to control the spread of murder,'' was the prosecutor's response to critics of his action. In Genesee County, Michigan, an HIV-positive drug user was charged with attempted murder for spitting at the police officer who tried to arrest him. The charges were later reduced to resisting arrest.[16]

In the Indiana case, a superior court judge sentenced Donald J. Haines to six years in the state penitentiary after he was convicted on three counts of attempting to murder the policeman and emergency medical technicians who came to his aid during an unsuccessful suicide attempt. According to testimony at the trial, both the police and the emergency medical personnel knew Haines was HIV-positive when they tried to help him. Haines, who had slashed his wrists, battled the policeman who was first at the scene. He threw a blood-drenched wig at the officer and spat at him. After almost an hour of trying to subdue Haines, the officer was, according to court records, covered in Haines' blood. The officer was also cut in the struggle and had Haines' blood in his mouth. The medical personnel, although they wore gloves, also suffered cuts in trying to subdue him. The struggle did not end at the scene of arrest. It continued in the hospital emergency room, where Haines reportedly told the emergency room physician that he wanted other people to know what it was like to die from AIDS.[17]

In a highly publicized case in which community outrage against the defendant was palpable, Terry Lee Phillips was indicted in Columbia, South Carolina for rape, attempted murder, assault and battery with intent to kill, and first-degree sexual conduct after sexually assaulting a woman. Phillips had been diagnosed earlier as having AIDS and was informed of this fact. He allegedly said that he intended to give someone else AIDS. The prosecutor contended that Phillips was intentionally trying to transmit the fatal disease to the woman he raped.[18]

Probably the most discussed case, from a legal standpoint, involved an AIDS-infected inmate in a federal correctional institution who, in a scuffle, purposely bit two correctional officers who were trying to subdue him. The inmate later informed a nurse that he was deliberately trying to infect the guards. This led to a controversial ruling by the court. The defendant was found guilty of assault with a deadly and dangerous weapon (in this case, his teeth and mouth). The court sidestepped the issue of the inmate's seropositive AIDS condition, merley relying on a finding that the inmate's teeth and mouth were dangerous weapons. The jury's conviction was upheld by the federal Court of Appeals.[19] This has generated considerable controversy in the legal community. Some law scholars feel that the proper ruling should have been to move to classify HIV itself as a deadly and dangerous weapon.[20] Others feel the court and the jury grossly erred in thinking that the AIDS virus can be transmitted from one human being to another by a bite and, if so, the mouth and teeth according to established legal precedent, cannot be considered a deadly and dangerous weapon.[21]

This precedent has not held in similar cases. In New York City, the local prosecutor refused to apply this doctrine. Choosing to ignore the Federal Court of Appeals ruling, the prosecutor reduced aggravated assault charges against a prositute alleged to have bitten a police officer because of the lack of medical evidence showing that the virus can be transmitted through biting.[22]

Arguments Against the Use of the Criminal Law

Opponents argue that criminal penalties will be ineffective. First, their use will neither inhibit the spread of the disease nor deter the conduct sought to be prohibited. History

Prostitute is Jailed After Disclosing AIDS

It all began innocently enough with an article in *Newsweek* magazine about AIDS. Linda Kean, 36, a prostitute in Oakland, California allowed herself to be photographed for the article while working the streets. She appears leaning against a building looking directly into the camera dressed in skimpy ''working clothes.'' To the *Newsweek* journalists working on the story, she acknowledged that she was a heroin user and had AIDS. This is how she was described in the article's caption. She also admitted in the article that she doesn't tell her ''customers'' about her condition because to do so would be ''professional suicide.'' There is no indication of whether she requires her clients to use a condom during sexual encounters or whether she takes any other kinds of precautions.

Her moment in the sun was soon to prove costly. The photograph and the story came to the attention of the police vice squad and the local district attorney's office. Ms. Kean had several prior convictions for prostitution and, at the time, was on probation from her most recent conviction. The police successfully sought an arrest warrant for probation violation. When they arrested her, she was getting into a client's car. The police admonished the visibly shaken man with the suggestion that he read the *Newsweek* article. Although Kean was arrested for violation of her probation, the police want her charged with attempted murder. The continued practice of prostitution in light of an admission of being infected with the AIDS virus forms the basis for the charge.

The judge remanded her to the custody of the Alameda County Jail while the prosecutor's office huddles over what can be done. Her court appointed public defender doesn't think the state has a case. In California, as in other states, attempted murder requires the state to prove that the accused had the intent to kill someone. Her attorney scoffs at the idea that she could be convicted under such circumstances and blames it all on the hysteria of the police who, like most of the population, are ignorant of the disease and how it is spread. Kean, perhaps now realizing she made a mistake, denies telling the journalist that she had AIDS; she also denies any knowledge that she has the disease. *Newsweek* had no comment to make other than to say, ''we stand by our story.''

The police and the district attorney's office have a lot of public support for their efforts; people who encourage prosecution on the attempted murder charge. Not all sources, however, are so supportive of such police action. Although California is one of several states which have passed laws in recent years which require that prostitutes as a condition of probation be tested for HIV and, if found seropositive and are later engaged in prostitution, can be charged with a felony, the county Health Department has not been cooperating. The Department, like similar departments in other big city areas across the country, says it doesn't have the resources to test prostitutes. The head of its communicable diseases division also says the problem of testing is one of giving a false impression: It tends to send a message that the government is making it safe out there. It conveys the idea that the hookers who are still on the streets have been certified as clean.

The head of the Health Department's communicable diseases section considers the police action to be "witchhunting." The reponsibility to remedy the situation must be taken by the client to use appropriate precautions such as condoms. It is a problem which has to be handled by education rather than by the criminal law he suggests. Judging by the public reaction to his statement when it appeared in the local paper, many would disagree.

shows that that attempts to use the mechanism of the law in the guise of sodomy statutes to deter private consensual sexual activity has not been effective. Instead, it is argued that the threat of criminal penalties may discourage people from seeking AIDS testing and treatment and, thereby, increase the risk that the disease will be spread. It is also suggested that the prosecution of AIDS carriers may lull the public into a false sense of security by misleading the American people into believing that effective measures are being taken by the government against the disease. Opponents of criminalization contend that the government's efforts should focus on mass public education and search for a cure to the dread disease rather than the futile attempt to use the criminal law as a deterrence.

There are also legal questions in any attempt to invoke criminal sanctions. Critics feel that proposed criminal measures against AIDS carriers are virtually impossible to successfully prosecute because of overwhelming evidentiary and constitutional issues. And as the situation exists in rape cases there is also the legal issue of privacy involved. The enactment of even a narrowly defined criminal law would create grave risks to sexual privacy throughout the population, homosexual as well as heterosexual. Enforcement of such a law would implicate not only the purposeful, knowing and reckless AIDS transmitter who are the law's ultimate target, but also a vast number of others who are or have been sexually involved with them.[23]

As Field and Sullivan ask:

> . . . If all it took to trigger such a law was a complaining witness' allegation against a named defendant—as in the case, for example, in date-rape charges—then it might seem that only the witness and the named party's sexual privacy would be breached, the witness' voluntarily and the suspect's justifiably. But suppose that the complaining witness had recently had sex with more than one partner. Would the criminal law stop with the initial complaint? Or would the complainant's other sexual partners now be subject to investigation or surveillance? And what about the defendant's other sexual partners, if any? Should the authorities seek them out if they have not come forward?[24]

Some critics of criminalization go even further. Some contend, for example, that this would lead to selective enforcement and harassment of homosexuals and intravenous drug abusers by the authorities—especially the police.[25] Being gay is not illegal and sodomy has been decriminalized in many jurisdictions. Even so, the adoption of criminal laws would likely result in greater surveillance of these groups and the use of anti-AIDS laws as a pretext to harass such groups in the absence of sodomy statues the authorities could (and did) use in the past. Even in those jurisdictions which still enforce sodomy statutes, these are rarely used to prosecute. However, a renewal of such prosecutions could commence using the criminal anti-AIDS laws as justification for a greater degree of arrest activity than exists under conventional anti-sodomy statutes.

It is also argued that much of the apprehension surrounding the potential for transmission of AIDS through criminal activity is unwarranted. As Blumberg points out, "While the AIDS epidemic has been with us for almost a decade, there have been no documented cases in which the virus has been transmitted through an assault—whether it be a bite, a spitting incident, or a case of rape."[26] His argument tends to support the proposition that unsubstantiated fear, rather than a clear and present danger, is propeling us toward criminalization.

Sanctions Other than the Criminal Law

Before exploring the possibility of the use of the criminal law as a means to deal with AIDS-infected individuals who pose a risk of infecting others, a brief discussion of other available sanctions is in order. Many states have public health laws which permit authorities to impose restrictions on persons with contagious diseases.[27] One such frequently mentioned remedy is a quarantine law. These laws, passed in an effort to impose quarantines during epidemics, have generally not been used in recent years because advances in medical science, innoculations, and antibiotics have replaced the "pesthouse" as the primary means to deal with contagion. There is also the issue that evidence indicates that AIDS cannot be casually transmitted. This being the case, important legal problems exist for invoking these laws and imposing quarantines on persons unable or unwilling to refrain from behavior which is risk inducing. The use of quarantine measures also would punish—as compared to even a criminal law approach to the problem—AIDS carriers for the mere status or condition of being infected.[28]

Still, these laws remain and are, at least theoretically, available to public health officials. To date, however, quarantine has been imposed in only a few rare instances where HIV carriers have been characterized as unable or unwilling to forego activities which impose a significant risk of viral transmission.[29] However, as the American Bar Association points out in its task force report, if the goal is to incapacitate HIV carriers who refuse to desist from behaviors which expose others to harm the use of quarantine measures has at least one theoretical advantage over relying on criminal sanctions. Because such quarantines would be permissable only so long as the subjects were unwilling to change their behavior, health officials could be required to provide individualized counseling and education, and to release individuals if and when such efforts were successful.[30]

There is also the possibility of using the civil law in which tort actions could be filed for imposing liability under negligence or battery theories, upon HIV carriers who fail to disclose their infection to sex partners, or to take appropriate precautions to safeguard partners against transmission of the virus.[31] The use of tort law has certain advantages over criminal sanctions. People who engage in high-risk behavior could be held responsible for their negligence and civil damage awards could provide financial relief to plaintiffs who face shortened life spans, reduced earnings and staggering medical bills.[32]

Still, the use of civil law is not without certain disadvantages which may make it less effective as a meaningful alternative. Civil damages may be meaningless because the potential defendant may be impoverished or dead. Many actions may also be barred by statutes of limitations because of the lengthy period that HIV may lie dormant before it produces detectable infection and because of the additional latency period between infection and the onset of symptoms. And like problems in the criminal law to be discussed, the latency aspects of HIV infection also complicate proof of causation and damages and there is posed privacy questions, especially in cases alleging sexual transmission in that the plaintiff will have to prove that he or she was not infected prior to contact with the defendant, and that he or she did not contract the virus in any subsequent encounter. Thus, such litigation may well involve the ever-present issue of the privacy of numerous third parties.[33]

The Use of Conventional Criminal Laws to Prosecute

Most attention today focuses on the viability of the use of conventional criminal laws—homicide (including this crime's variations), assault, reckless endangerment, sodomy, and even fornication and adultery—as prosecution tools against HIV-positive individuals who knowingly and recklessly endanger others. Legal attention is focusing upon the propriety and effect of using such laws and the legal problems this may pose if we turn to such laws as a means to prosecute.

Before examining the use of conventional criminal laws, a brief introduction into this area is warranted. Legal scholars point out that there are two basic yet general approaches which might be taken in criminalizing AIDS transmission. The first of these is the *classic culpability approach* and the *affirmative duty approach.*[34]

The Classical Culpability Approach

This is the traditional criminal law approach that would criminalize the act of transmitting AIDS by any means, sexual or non-sexual, as long as it is accompanied by the required specific state of mind. This is sometimes called the *proof of criminal intent* or the *requisite mens rea* standard. The advantage of such an approach is that it focuses on acts, not persons; it would thus focus on all rather then merely singling out persons with AIDS or those who carry the virus. The problem with this approach is the difficulty of showing that the individual intends or knows that his behavior will likely transmit AIDS. Since his intention becomes a crucial element, it must be proven before a conviction could result. This poses some problems.

Another way to approach this problem is through a standard of "recklessness" and "negligence." AIDS transmission could be "reckless" if a person was aware of the fact that he was afflicted with AIDS and he knew that there was, therefore, a substantial risk that by engaging in certain forms of conduct, he ran the risk of infecting others. AIDS transmission could be "negligent" if one took the risk even if he was not aware that he had the virus or that his conduct might transmit the disease—as long as the jury finds that one should have been aware of these risks.[35]

The problem with such "reckless" and "negligent" standards in the criminal law as these doctrines might be applied to defendants in AIDS-related cases, is it runs the risk of targeting certain groups who are already unpopular such as gays and intravenous drug abusers to the anxiety and irrationality that surrounds these groups. In much of the public's eye, these groups are seen as the creators of the "AIDS problem." Such hysteria leaves little assurance that juries can be rational when considering the fate of such defendants. Moreover, even the most rational jury may be confused by the ever-evolving scientific understanding about the nature of the disease and its transmission. Where science is uncertain, some juries may want to impose some very strict norms of conduct.[36]

Criminalizing AIDS under the reckless or negligent standards not only threatens to punish those who did not know they had it; it also threatens to punish those who did not know they were transmitting it. As Field and Sullivan say about this issue:

> The reckless AIDS transmitter—because he was aware that there was substantial risk—may seem sufficiently culpable for punishment to be appropriate, but negligence liability would be troubling. Negligence liability would punish any act a jury believes "unreasonably" risked transmission, regardless of the defendant's own knowledge or state of mind. It would thus risk branding an individual a criminal because of his ignorance or stupidity rather than because of any malice.[37]

While negligent liability may seem too strict, there is also the situation where it might prove too lenient. If an AIDS carrier used precaution, such as wearing a condom during sexual intercourse, that might negate "conscious disregard" of risk.[38] However, the use of a condom is not a total assurance that safe sex is possible since condoms are not themselves completely fullproof. Under such circumstances, some legal scholars while agreeing that it is appropriate for the law to encourage precautions, it would not be appropriate for a law to make the taking of precautions alone negate the offense.[39]

The Affirmative Duty Approach

It has been suggested that instead of the classical culpability approach, that the law might want to take an affirmative duty approach. This would impose the requirements of disclosure and precautions on persons with AIDS and AIDS carriers. The law might specify these specific duties and punish AIDS transmission when, for example, the accused actually knew from testing or diagnosis that he or she had AIDS or was an AIDS carrier and failed to disclose this fact to a sex partner or failed to use appropriate precautions. Rather than relying on a specific state of mind, evidence would concentrate on knowledge and failure to disclose. This would leave less discretion to juries to attempt to wrestle with the sticky issue of state of mind.[40]

In this way, it imposes a kind of strict liability by which offenders could be held accountable without getting into the vagaries of culpable mental state. All it would require is, as pointed out, a knowledge and an act of transmission without disclosure or precautions. Like other strict-liability crimes, the purpose is to mold behavior, to take care with a dangerous disease when they are in a position to do so.[41] This approach which would have legislative bodies rather than juries set the rules in this area and would exhibit far less of a concern for jury arbitrariness and imagination than what exists today. A real danger here is that legislative bodies, by defining ''certain acts'' are, themselves, entering the gray area of intruding too deeply into private sexual decision making.[42]

This approach would also avoid punishing someone for ignorance. Although it would single out a particular group, much like an enforced quarantine practice, this would be fairer than subjecting an unknowing person to criminal sanctions. And even those singled out would still be permitted to have sex as long as they disclose their condition and, under such circumstances, the sexual partner was aware of the condition and the risk.[43]

Using Conventional Criminal Laws

A number of states and legal experts in criminal law have looked at this issue of using conventional criminal law statutes.[44] The use of homicide and attempted homicide laws are highly problematic. Although it is pointed out that existing homicide laws could be used to prosecute AIDS carriers who intentionally or recklessly transmit the AIDS virus to another person thereby causing the victim's death, the evidentiary problems associated with proving intent and causation make the success of homicide prosecutions unlikely.[45] A prosecutor could avoid some of these evidentiary problems by reducing the charge to attempted homicide, but probably would still have difficulty proving that the defendant had the required mental state to be guilty of the crime charged.[46]

The evidentiary issues boil down to this: The first requirement that the prosecutor faces is proof beyond a reasonable doubt that the defendant had AIDS or the AID virus at the time of the alleged act. The prosecutor would be unable to prove this fact directly unless the defendant admits it or there is contemporaneous medical evidence supporting it. If evidence of the defendant's infection is unavailable from either of these sources, the prosecutor could seek a court order requiring the defendant to submit to an AIDS test. The problem with this is that the prosecutor is placed in the position of trying to prove by circumstantial evidence, if possible, that the defendant had the virus at the time of the alleged crime.

The proof of causation is also a problem. The prosecutor must prove beyond a reasonable doubt that the defendant caused the victim's death by transmitting the AIDS virus to the victim. This may well be the most difficult evidentiary problem because, practically speaking, the prosecutor must prove two ''negative'' facts: Proof must be shown that the victim was not infected with AIDS before the defendant's alleged conduct; and that the victim did not become infected afterward from some other source. Because of this difficulty of proving causation, prosecutors may choose to reduce homicide charges against the defendant to attempted murder or attempted manslaughter and, thereby, avoid having to prove that the accused caused death.[47]

Third, the prosecutor must prove that the defendant had the required criminal intent (*mens rea*) to be guilty of the crime charged. The type of criminal intent that must be proven varies, depending upon the severity of the offense charged. In intentional homicide cases such as first or second degree murder, the prosecutor must prove beyond a reasonable doubt that the defendant knew that he or she had the AIDS virus at the time the offense was committed and specifically intended to cause death by transmitting the virus to the victim. The intentional homicide charges would apply only to the most extreme fact situation. In unintentional homicide cases such as lesser degrees of murder or manslaughter, the prosecutor must only show that the defendant knew he or she had AIDS or the AIDS virus and either ''evinced a depraved mind'' or was ''culpably negligent'' in engaging in the conduct. Whether such extreme recklessness can be shown depends on the particular facts in each case. For example, a single act of heterosexual intercourse might not be enough to show that the defendant had the requisite *mens rea* to be guilty of the crime since studies purport to show that the odds for transmitting the AIDS virus through this means is only one in 1,000.[48] On the other hand, multiple acts of anal intercourse or the sharing of hypodermic needles carry higher risks of transmission which may make these acts more culpably reckless and prosecutable under lesser degrees of murder and/or manslaughter charges.

In some states, the common law year-and-a-day rule may also be an obstacle to a successful prosecution. In those jurisdictions, the victim's death must occur within a year and a day of the alleged assault in order for it to be considered caused by the accused's actions. Other states have felony-murder laws. These basically provide that a person can be charged with this serious form of homicide if the death resulted from the commission of a felony or a specific named felony. If the defendant caused the victim's death during the commission of a violent felony such as a rape, the prosecutor could charge the accused with felony-murder and not have to prove that the defendant intended to cause the victim's death—only that rape was intended. Here again, however, another problem is raised. The state would have to prove that the victim's death occurred in the course of the underlying felony. Because the disease may lie dormant and undiagnosable for several years, a number of years may further lapse before the victim dies, and the victim's death may be too attenuated to permit a successful prosecution under this type of murder charge.

What about assault statutes? Most states break down their assault statutes into various degrees. These are usually determined by the degree of injury incurred. The Model Penal Code also uses this general classification with aggravated assault reserved for more serious cases.[49] Criminal prosecutions against AIDS carriers under the assault statutes, while rare, have been the most common type of criminal prosecution brought against AIDS carriers to date.[50] Many legal experts believe this is the most practical vehicle for criminal prosecution.[51]

The prosecutor using an assault charge would have to again show that the defendant was a knowing carrier of the AIDS virus at the time of the alleged conduct. Such proof is required not only for purposes of causation, but also for proving the necessary *mens rea* of the assault crime—that the individual intended to cause harm to the victim or intended to create fear in the victim of immediate harm. In order to prove aggravated assault, the prosecutor must show that the victim suffered either ''great bodily harm'' or ''substantial bodily harm'' as a result of the defendant's conduct. To meet this burden of proof, the state must show that the victim was infected by the actor and probably must show that the victim has or is likely to develop AIDS as a result. In those rare cases where the victim of the alleged assault has already developed AIDS by the time the criminal charges have been filed, proof of great or substantial bodily harm is relatively easy to provide since all persons with AIDS either die as a result of the disease or suffer bodily harm caused by those diseases that their immune systems are unable to combat.[52]

The prosecutor might avoid the problem of proving victim harm by charging the defendant with assault with a deadly weapon as was done successfully in the case of the prosecution of the federal prisoner dicussed previously. The aggravated assault crime does not turn on the extent of bodily harm. Rather, it is based on the deadly nature of the weapon or other instrumentality used in committing the assault. To prove this crime, the prosecutor must convince the jury that either the AIDS virus itself or the means through which it was transmitted (e.g., sexual intercourse, biting, and the like), is a deadly weapon. Again, this may be difficult given the lack of medical evidence supporting the transmission of the AIDS virus through saliva or biting, and the relatively low likelihood of either transmitting the AIDS virus through a single sexual contact or developing AIDS as a result of infection with the virus.[53]

One last comment about an assault is in order. If the victim consented to contact by the defendant, as is likely in most sexual transmission cases, some courts would undoubtedly rule that this consent bars criminal prosecution of the defendant for assault. Other courts take a different view, however, and would rule that consent to physical contact is not equivalent to consent to bodily harm.[54]

Prosecution for the offense of reckless endangerment may not encounter the same limitation imposed on other crimes. Reckless endangerment occurs when a person ''recklessly engages in conduct which places or may place another person in danger of death or serious bodily injury.''[55] Thus, the prosecutor is not required to prove that the defendant's conduct actually harmed the victim, and consent is not a defense. Guilt turns upon the the fact finder's evaluation of how a person should act. For this reason, reckless endangerment may be thought susceptible to jury overreaction concerning risk-creating behavior, particularly if the victim has not actually suffered any harm.[56] This may be offset by the fact that such reckless endangerment statutes are usually only misdemeanors.

There are of course, other criminal statutes that could be employed. These include sodomy statutes which are still on the books in about half the states. In 1986, the Supreme Court ruled that state anti-sodomy statutes are constitutional under the federal Constitution.[57] A number of states also make it a crime to knowingly transmit or expose others to a communicable disease. These laws generally limit its application to exposure in public places which means they are aimed at those communicable diseases which can be spread by casual contact. Since AIDS cannot be spread by casual contact but only by exchange of bodily fluids, it has limited effect as a prosecution tool. It would also require that this exchange of bodily fluids occurred through unsafe sexual conduct in a public bathhouse or other public place, or the the sharing of hypodermic needles in a public location. Finally, there are prostitution laws which could be used as well as greater efforts to enforce illegal use of drugs and hypodermic needle laws.

As we can see, this issue is just beginning to be addressed. The issues and the developing criminal law in this area are still unfolding. Many concerns abound about the proper or appropriate use of the criminal law and the criminal justice system in this area. This will be the major arena of debate for the future. The remainder of this chapter will address another problem that like the prosecution of this aspect of AIDS raises similar concerns. Together they raise many of the same questions and pose strikingly similar problems for the administration of justice.

Perinatal Addiction: The Case of "Crack Mothers"

There are many insidious sides to the crack epidemic in America. Perhaps none is so hotly debated as what to do with mothers who, as addicts, give birth to crack babies. Medical researchers are only beginning to study the physical and developmental effects of cocaine exposure during pregnancy, but the preliminary results of the research are alarming. While it was once thought that the placenta served as a barrier to protect the fetus from toxic substances during pregnancy, it is now known that many drugs, including cocaine and heroin, invade the placenta and find their way into fetal circulation. In fact, research has shown that the fetus may be exposed longer to drugs than the mother herself because the drugs are not metabolized as rapidly by the immature fetal liver and kidneys.[58]

What we know is that crack babies seem to be everywhere—especially in the large public hospitals in those urban areas where the drug problem has been most ravaging. We have all seen video clips of shrieking bug-eyed infants kicking spasmodically in incubators and postnatal critical care wards. These underweight children run extremely high risks of having respiratory and neurological damage. While it has long been suspicioned that cocaine use during pregnancy is associated with serious physiological and behavioral problems because of the higher incidence of miscarriage by cocaine using mothers, studies conducted at the Boston City Hospital during the 1980s and by the federal government's Center for Disease Control seem to confirm a relationship. These studies concluded that a mother's use of cocaine (and marijuana) is often associated with low birth weight (and along with this a higher risk of respiratory disease syndrome, brain hemorrhages, chronic lung disease, and neurodevelopmental problems), smaller head circumference, and seriously malformed kidneys.[59]

It is estimated that as many as 70 percent of Pennsylvania's dramatically increasing number of child abuse cases, and as yet unknown foster care placements, are attributable to mothers cocaine addiction.[60] Nobody has any idea of the extent of the problem on a national basis. Statistics by the Federal government are incomplete as to the number of perinatal (transmission from mother to child) crack babies born each year. A 1988 report conducted by the National Association for Perinatal Addiction, Research, and Education (NAPARE) found that 10 percent of new mothers had used drugs, usually cocaine, during pregnancy.[61] At many hospitals, especially public hospitals in our nation's large cities, the percentage is much higher. Private agencies such as the American Hospital Association peg the number of drug-impaird children being born annually in the United States at between 50,000 to 100,000. A much-cited report, released in 1989, claimed that 375,000 children may have been affected by their mother's drug use during pregnancy.[62] This, too, is only a guess as many hospitals are not in the business of routinely keeping records of the number of such births. Also lacking is a central clearinghouse for such data even if it was routinely gathered by the nation's hospitals and health care providers.

One fact is apparent: Crack babies and their mothers have become a social dilemma. Most of the babies are illegitimate, the majority are black, and they are all, by definition, addicted to drugs. Many are simply abandoned by their mothers. Preliminary evidence seems to suggest that these children may suffer a variety of medical, developmental, and behavioral problems depending on the nature of their mother's substance abuse. Short-term effects include premature birth, low birth weight, stroke, and withdrawal symptoms.[63] According to NAPARE, babies exposed to cocaine have a tenfold greater risk of suffering sudden infant death syndrome. The harm may be long-term as well—mental retardation, congenital disorders and deformities, hyperactivity, and speech and language impairment. These long-term effects have been documented in research conducted by Northwestern University Memorial Hospital.[64] The problem is compounded by the fact that pregnant addicts often receive little or no prenatal care and, themselves, may be malnourished. Under such circumstances, the chances for such children to have anything approaching a successful life are severly diminished; the likelihood that they will become wards of the state significantly enhanced.

Criminal Law Issues

The Argument is Joined: Defining the Problem

Threatened by the social implications, a number of legal scholars in the area of family law are suggesting that state legislative bodies revise state criminal codes to include criminal sanctions against prenatal substance abusers.[65] Such a recommendation is a serious and far-reaching issue of public policy which is still not fully understood. While admitting that important Constitutional and legal issues abound, their concerns are driven by the many ramifications which surround this growing problem.

At the recent national conventions of the National District Attorneys Association and the American Bar Association this issue was on the agenda. Many believe that the threat of criminal sanctions should be used to force drug-addicted pregnant women toward treatment. Michael Barber, the Sacramento attorney who was chair of the ABA's family-law section favors discretionary criminal sanctions, such as supervised probation, as well as ''threatened incarceration if, when she's pregnant, she's still taking drugs.''[66]

Others see it as more basic: Children have the right to be born free of drugs or malformed. If concerns exist about the rights of mothers, they at least equally exist for the rights of the fetus—not to mention society.

The argument for criminal-legal involvement centers around several propositions. In addition to the obvious concern over the damage done to the child as a fetus, there is also concern that cocaine abuse will risk the child's safety under the mother's care. Cocaine-effected babies suffer withdrawal symptoms which include extreme irritability, hyperactivity, and tenseness which makes bonding very difficult and interrupts the normal attachment vital to early maternal-fetal relationships.[67] Given the instability of the cocaine using mother, she may feel acute anger, rejection, guilt or depression. This could lead to increasing instances of child abuse in which these babies are subjected to physical violence. The mother, under the influence of narcotics, may also neglect providing the child with proper care as many social assistance agencies working with severe crack-addicted mothers can attest.

There is also the concern about AIDS. In connection with maternal drug abuse is the threatening possibility of the mother contracting the deadly Acquired Immune Deficiency virus and passing it on to her fetus as a result of intravenous drug use. The tragedy of fetuses being exposed to drugs is compounded by their possible exposure to AIDS. The AIDS virus is passed to fetuses from the mother by a similar process by which they become exposed to drugs.[68] Public health officials have estimated that 50 percent of the mothers infected with the AIDS virus will transmit the infection to the fetus and approximately half of those infected fetuses will die within the first 15 months of birth.[69]

Aside from the immense suffering involved, prenatal drug abuse has generated an enormous financial burden for society. Medical treatment costs for distressed, disabled, and/or withdrawing newborns are very high and growing at an alarming rate. In some areas, neonatal intensive care costs run over $1,700 per day for severly affected infants. Drug-addicted neonates—so-called hospital ''boarder babies''—require stabilization and nursing through withdrawal. While the hospital stay for a healthy newborn is three days, cocaine babies have required hospital stays as long as 42 days just for withdrawal. Average medical bills range from $7,500 to $31,000.[70] Since Medicaid pays for only a portion of this, the additional cost is imposed on private, insured patients and taxpayers.

The explosion of drug-affected infants has also taken its toll on our nation's child welfare system. Under child protection laws, some states have provided for postnatal state custody of infants born with illegal drugs or metabolites in their system. This is proving to be unworkable. Already facing a severe foster-care shortage, child welfare systems are unable to cope with the onslaught of drug-exposed babies. Caseworkers are already overburdened with heavy caseloads and specialists are saying that these children will need extensive follow-up and their mothers will need special training in parenting and special handling of drug-affected offspring. Already this immense burden on states has caused at least one state to reverse its policy of taking custody over drug-exposed infants.[71]

Of an equally grave nature, the financial and institutional stress that drug-affected children will place on America's educational system is incalculable. Educators are already being warned to begin to prepare for a new class of children who will require a specially structured educational environment. [72] Perhaps the single most devastating effect of maternal drug abuse is the "drug cycle" and its intangible cost to the public welfare. Among many prenatal substance abusers, researchers note a cycle of parental drug abuse and violence that spans generations.[73] Unless this cycle is broken, these children, like their mothers before them, run a high risk of being exposed to a childhood bound in the self-destructive and chaotic nature of the drug environment.

Developing Criminal-Legal Efforts

Like the AIDS situation, the authorities in some areas of the country have begun to slowly and cautiously respond to these fears. Courts have long held that states have a legitimate interest in preventing child abuse and neglect. However, such statutes are very cautious in their language and procedures. State actions to remove children from the home, criminally prosecute the parents, or undertake other conflicting family and privacy rights require protecting the parent's due process and privacy rights. There must be the assurance of a thorough investigation before the removal and the parents must be provided with an opportunity to respond before a long-term remedy is ordered. The statutes also limit state intervention to circumstances where there is no alternative to protect the child.

In spite of these constraints, there is some evidence of change occurring. Although in most states, courts do not consider a fetus a child, at least eight states now include drug exposure in utero in their definition of child abuse and neglect—some of these requiring nothing more than a positive drug test to instigate charges or remove a child from the mother. Slowly we are seeing an expansion of the authority of the courts and the public assistance agencies under dependency and neglect hearings to remove infants from mothers based on the mother's addiction or because of in utero exposure to the child.

Still, removing a child from its mother under existing neglect or dependency rulings is one thing; instigating criminal prosecution against mothers for exposing their infants to drug dependency is yet another. Nevertheless, some state legislators prompted by a growing public concern over the problem are beginning to consider introducing laws to make this possible. This places the criminal justice system squarely in the fray. But the criminal justice system has not always been merely a passive observer of this growing problem. Criminal justice officials, in the person of judges, prosecutors, and the police seeing the social consequences, are increasingly supporting such efforts and are stepping-up their encouragement for criminal prosecutions. Since 1987, 19 states and the District of Columbia have instigated criminal charges against mothers who victimize their newborns through perinatal drug addiction. More than 50 criminal cases have been tried in these states.

The advocates for criminal prosecution of mothers who give birth to crack-affected babies base their argument on the evidence that existing efforts to deal with the problem are not working. Non-coercive government programs such as public education, prevention efforts, and voluntary treatment programs are not stemming the tide. And even if states passed laws which permitted extending the concept of neglect to include drug-exposed neonates, the problem is not solved. While such laws would permit the state to take custody over the infant and either remove the child at birth, obtain court-ordered treatment and education for the mother, and initiate contempt or permanent custody proceedings if she failed to comply, the damage has already been done. Under these circumstances, court intervention comes too late. There is also the associated cost of such public care for infants. And policies of court-ordered rehabilitation of mothers under the threat of loss of their children is too often ineffective. As a noted legal scholar on the subject, Kathryn Schierl says, [the result is] ''the state simply has one more foster child, no rehabilitated mother, and most likely, more drug-exposed offspring in the future.''[74]

Although a few prosecutors have brought criminal charges against women for prenatal substance abuse, these efforts have been largely unsuccessful. At this time, there are no state laws which specifically make this act a crime. As a consequence, a prosecutor must attempt to use unsatisfactory existing laws such as criminal child abuse, delivery of a controlled substance to a minor, and involuntary manslaughter of an unborn.[75] There is some evidence that this is proving unworkable and juries and grand juries are unwilling to convict or indict under such contrived efforts.[76] It is also argued that the development of statutes which permit merely charging a crack mother with criminal abuse guarantees little beyond the removal of the child and costly taxpayer-borne foster care placement. Such laws also provide little in the way of meaningful penalties which might deter. In many cases, judges end up merely imposing a probation sanction on the mother under such statutes. Again, as Schierl points out:

> Like the other remedies available to address prenatal substance abuse, ad hoc prosecutorial attempts are inadequate for several reasons. The underlying problem concerning prosecutorial attempts is the lack of a criminal statute directly addressing this prenatal misconduct. Because prosecutors are applying existing laws that were not meant to apply to prenatal conduct, there is an issue involving notice to the women that there conduct is subject to criminal sanctions. Further, if it is not clear that delivery of [a] drug-affected newborn will subject the mother to criminal sanction, there can be no deterrence factor. Third, without clear legislative provision, a court or grand jury may find that the statute does not apply, and the mother will not receive compulsory drug treatment. Finally, and most importantly, ad hoc, innovative prosecutions will not aid in the establishment of a comprehensive, effective policy guided by the goals of deterrence and rehabilitation.[77]

The state has a compelling interest in providing more reasonable assurances than now exist that a child has the right to be born drug free. The state also has an interest in seeing that the cycle of drugs is broken, and with it, the ravages to society and the public health and welfare now associated with this problem. It is no historical accident that the courts have always taken a protective posture in the case of children who must be protected because of their special vulnerability. Although Constitutional issues of rights of privacy and maternal protection are important and fundamental concerns, many believe these rights as they apply to this issue are muted by the compelling and far-reaching consequences of failure to take steps—no matter how imperfect—to try to remedy the problem.

Initial Criminal Prosecutions

In July 1989, the attention of the legal community and special interest groups was focused on Judge O. E. Eatons, Jr's Florida courtroom. What came out of that courtroom was to be a landmark decision in criminal law. It was to be the first criminal conviction of a mother for exposing her baby to drugs while she was pregnant. Jennifer Clarice Johnson, a 23-year old crack addict, had given birth in 1987 to a son. Two years later, she gave birth to a daughter. Both babies tested positive for crack. In 1988, the Florida State Attorney's office decided to take criminal prosecution action in such cases and Johnson became the first woman in the country to be found guilty of making a drug delivery to her baby. The state charged Johnson with delivering a controlled substance to both children and one count of felonious child abuse involving her daughter.

Because Florida law did not provide a penalty for delivering a controlled substance to a fetus, the prosecution came up with a novel strategy: It based its case on the 60-second period that a cocaine metabolite may have passed through the infants' umbilical cords after they were delivered. The mother was found guilty and sentenced to 14 years on probation and one year in a rehabilitation program. During her period of probation, she must report any pregnancies to law enforcement officials and receive court approval for her prenatal care program.[78] The effect of the precedent rippled out. In Kentucky, a mother who gave birth to three children during her 17-year addiction to pills and intravenous drugs was sentenced to five years in prison for criminal child abuse. In 1990, a North Carolina prosecutor charged an addicted mother, whose newborn had a positive toxicology test, with a more pernicious crime—assault with a deadly weapon.[79]

Arguments Against Criminal Justice Involvement

Just as with AIDS, there are forces arrayed against the law enforcement approach to this problem. Feminist groups, some social workers, civil rights groups, the defense bar, and some members of the drug treatment establishment are opposed to such measures. Feminist and civil rights groups such as the American Civil Liberties Union argue that prosecuting women for their conduct during pregnancy violates Constitutional rights to privacy and turns users into second-class citizens bereft of the guarantees of equal protection and due process. They also point out the dangers of the extension of such thinking into other areas. If it is not stopped, they argue, it is conceivable that future actions involving prosecution will target pregnant women who are alcoholics or even smokers.

Civil rights groups also argue that jailing women because of their conduct while pregnant impinges fundamental guarantees of reproductive choice and bodily autonomy. There is also the equal protection concerns that punishment on the basis of pregnancy affects only women. It imposes controls on women's lives that are not placed on men and thus limits women's ability to function equally in society. Some militant feminists go so far as to contend that the ''attack'' on crack-using mothers is yet another abuse of impoverished teenage females and is also a blatant attempt to restore male hegemony. They

Prosecuting Mothers for Neonatal Drug Abuse

About 200 miles west of Detroit, along the I-96 corridor, lies Muskegon, Michigan. It is indistinct from many similar Midwest industrial cities: a tired, predominantly blue collar factory town, grimy around the edges and concerned about its own "drug problem." In some ways, it is a small caricature of the City of Detroit. Many of its residents feel that Muskegon's "drug and crime problem" is directly related to similar problems found in the Motor City. Other large cities in Michigan, such as Flint and Grand Rapids, also come in for criticism. The local police are quick to blame the drug dealers in these cities for much of what's happened: Spiraling increases in both property and violent crime, drugs in the local schools, deterioration of neighborhoods, increased welfare and public assistance costs. Perhaps this is too facile an explanation but it does provides such cities as Muskegon with a convenient excuse—something they are quick to grasp. Detective Al Van Hemert, a veteran narcotics cop, expresses what many community residents feel, "You can blame a lot of our problems on Detroit. The Detroit drug dealers told us that Muskegon is such a welfare town that its guaranteed income for them when the welfare checks come in."*

Whatever the cause, there can be no argument that changes have come to Muskegon in recent years. Crime is but one manifestation. Murders, break-ins, and muggings have shown a drastic increase. At one time, local judges were spending only one day a week on drug cases. Today, they are finding that drug or drug-related cases require three days of courtwork per week to clear their dockets. Blaming drugs, the local police chief and the county prosecutor instituted a high visibility anti-narcotics program involving a combination of educational programs aimed at deterrence. Along with this came stepped-up arrests of drug dealers and users. As a result, the county jail has been overwhelmed with defendants charged with drug crimes. A special narcotics hotline has been installed to provide social service or law enforcement help. A year after crack hit the area, county social workers removed 27 children in just one month from homes in which crack was being used.

Three of the children belonged to a 23-year-old black, single mother named Kimberly Ann Hardy. Hardy came to the attention of the county's Department of Social Services because she was the first woman reported by Muskegon General Hospital to bear a child who tested positive for crack cocaine. Tony Tague, the county prosecutor thought it was time to send a message. Tague, himself the son of a retired local police chief, had since assuming office been struggling with the contagion of narcotics in the local area. His campaign had been built around the idea of harsher treatment of those involved in drug and drug-related crimes. Borrowing a controversial new legal tactic which had been employed by prosecutors in Florida, Georgia, Massachusetts, and South Carolina, Tague ordered Kimberly Hardy arrested on the same charge prosecutors routinely used against drug dealers: delivering drugs in the amount of less than 50 grams. The charge is a felony in Michigan carrying a mandatory minimum jail term of one year and a maximum of 20 years.**

For Hardy, the problem began in 1988. Shortly after the birth of her second child, Nyeassa, she started smoking crack after a friend from New York had introduced her to the drug. In Muskegon, crack comes in miniature Ziplock plastic bags and sells for an inflated $20 a rock. "It was the 'in' thing to do in Muskegon Heights," says Hardy. "I had no sense of the danger."*** Soon, she was stealing money from her current live-in boyfriend and prowling the low-rise public housing projects in the Heights area of the city where young dealers gathered to peddle dope. Hardy related a tale of coming to Muskegon from Newton, Mississippi. Her parents were zealous Jehovah's Witnesses and when she became pregnant her senior year in high school—the last of her circle to do so—she knew she had to get away from Newton. Having relatives in Muskegon, she came north shortly after the birth of her young son, Darius.

Although Muskegon is not the "promised land" with its high unemployment from the auto-parts factories (which have never recovered from the automobile industry downturn brought about by the OPEC gas crisis of the early 1970s and foreign automobile competition), she managed to find work. But it was work interspersed with longer periods of welfare assistance. When Nyeassa was born, Hardy was again on welfare. When she first became pregnant she had quit her most recent job on the assembly line at a metal products plant where the burning oil used in the manufacturing process made her nauseous.

The father of her child is Ronald Brown, her 35-year-old boyfriend. Brown is less than an exemplary model of fatherhood. He already had four children by another woman when he first met Hardy. Himself an alcohol and drug abuser, his own children had been exposed to a life of drugs, alcohol, and violence. His children are now scattered throughout foster-care homes and prison. One, according to the Department of Social Services, which has worked with Brown and his family for 14 years, was born severely disabled because of the mother's drug and alcohol abuse.

Shortly after the sensationalism of the Hardy arrest, another arrest occurred in Muskegon which would prove to be even more thought-provoking. This time it was a 36-year-old single white woman, Lynn Ellen Bremer, who became the second woman to be brought to trial by Tague on charges of drug delivery to an infant. Bremer admitted to police that 40 hours before her daughter, Brittany, was born she snorted a gram of cocaine at a birthday party with some friends. The *Bremer* case was very unusual in that it involved an upper-middle class, well-educated professsional woman, having it would seem, all of life's advantages. Bremer, herself a practicing attorney, was well-versed in the dangers. Bremer's excuse: She simply couldn't control her need for cocaine.

The prosecution developed its case against each woman in similar fashion. It began with drug tests performed during labor. Hardy's urine had been screened for drugs shortly after she showed up at Muskegon General. According to a policy adopted by many public hospitals, Hardy qualified as a "high-risk" pregnancy—she had no prenatal care and was six to eight weeks early. At Bremer's hospital, her own obstetrician ordered her tested because he knew about her cocaine addiction for nearly five months. He had even threatened to drop her as a patient when he first became aware that she was using the drug. His threats made no difference, she still continued using cocaine refusing both residential and outpatient treatment.

In the *Hardy* case, a preliminary examination was held on a two-count felony complaint alleging one count of delivery of cocaine and another count of second-degree child abuse. The presiding judge at the preliminary examination listened to testimony concerning the birth of the infant and the cocaine-positive test results and the defendants admission of cocaine abuse. The defense and the prosecution argued constitutional and statutory issues pertaining to the prosecution at which time the defense made a motion to have the case dismissed. The motion was denied and the case was transferred to the felony court for trial. The felony trial judge, after hearing oral arguments on a defense motion to dismiss, dismissed the child abuse charge because of insufficient evidence of actual harm to the infant, but upheld the the cocaine delivery charge which is now in the process of being appealed to the Michigan Court of Appeals.***

An appeal is also pending in the *Bremer* case. Extensive arguments were held before the court conducting the preliminary hearing where Bremer was charged with a single count of delivery of cocaine. She was bound over to stand trial in felony court on this charge. Bremer's defense attorney then made a motion to quash this count before this court which was upheld. The Muskegon County Prosecutor's Office is appealing this ruling to the Court of Appeals.****

*Hoffman, Jan. "Pregnant, Addicted and Guilty?" *The New York Times Magazine* (August 19, 1990), p. 34.

**Ibid.

***Letter dated March 18, 1991 to the author from the Muskegon County Prosecutor's Office.

****Ibid.

link the recent efforts at the state and federal levels to reverse *Rowe v. Wade* (the 1973 decision permitting abortions) with efforts to prosecute pregnant mothers. Both actions are seen as efforts to control women and what they may do with their bodies.[80] Legal scholars have argued that courts should carefully scrutinize laws that restrict pregnant women because reproductive capacity has historically served as the primary justification for denying women equal treatment under the law.[81]

Anti-criminalization advocates argue that women have been the only targets for prosecution of fetal abuse, even though certain conduct by men can harm the fetus. Conduct that causes genetic damage to sperm can result in miscarriage, birth defects, neonatal death, and early childhood illnesses.[82] In 1987, a California woman who gave birth to a brain dead child who died six weeks later was charged with criminal neglect in part because she failed to follow her doctor's orders to refrain from the use of amphetamines or engage in sexual intercourse while she was pregnant.[83] While her husband was aware of the instructions and he initiated the sexual intercourse, he was not prosecuted. Although charges filed by the prosecutor were dismissed by the judge, it was the first criminal case that attempted to charge a mother for prenatal abuse.

Anti-criminalization advocates also contend that prosecution efforts will target a group of mothers which is primarily madeup of poor, minority women. Perhaps recognizing the fact that these are the most "at-risk" segment of mothers likely to be drug addicted has fueled the fires. Ira J. Chasnoff, the Founder and President of NAPARE, says that such penalties against addicted mothers is already showing this trend. He points to Florida's Pinellas County, where pregnant black users are nearly 10 times more likely to be reported for substance abuse than pregnant white users.[84]

Defense lawyers and some social workers are of the opinion that law enforcement officials are driving a wedge between mother and child. Lawyers are arguing that the maternal relationship is being turned into an adversarial one—"fetal rights" versus "maternal rights"—rather than being more appropriately joined. They also point to the fact that addiction should not be viewed as a criminal problem; it is a health problem which illustrates the severity of the disease suffered by addicted mothers. To buttress their argument, they point out that in a case some years ago, the Supreme Court held a statute that criminalized the status of being a drug addict violated the Eighth Amendment's prohibition against cruel and unusual punishment.[85]

Perhaps the most compelling argument is that attempts to prosecute the problem out of existence simply will not work. "Get tough" law enforcement efforts have not generally solved the problem of drug abuse in our nation and will not solve it among pregnant women. Like our nation's attempts to deal with drug abuse on the streets, there are consequences to law enforcement efforts which must be considered. For example, social workers are concerned that enforcement efforts will turn away addicted mothers who might otherwise seek treatment. Under such circumstances, basic prenatal care will not be sought out of fear that those seeking it will come to the attention of the authorities and run the risk of arrest and prosecution. More women will seek abortions or merely abandon their babies rather than risk going to jail.

This point is refuted by some prosecutors. In Charleston, South Carolina the County Solicitor has used a child neglect statute to prosecute a number of women in that jurisdiction. He reports that the hospitals in the area are seeing fewer cocaine babies and arrests have almost stopped since the fact became known that mothers would be prosecuted and face the risk of jail. He also indicated that there is no evidence that addicted women are avoiding prenatal care or having their babies out in the woods to avoid arrest.[86]

There are additional complexities surround the issue. The nation's drug treatment programs are not set up in many areas to help pregnant mothers. Residential treatment programs are very reluctant to accept pregnant addicts largely because of liability problems posed by high-risk pregnancies. Medicaid covers only 17 days of a typical 28-day treatment program and even the full 28-day program is acknowledged as not very successful as measured by those who complete the program and shortly thereafter slip back into renewed drug use. And most drug programs were set up to treat male heroin addicts and have no obstetrician on duty. A recent study of the Columbia University School of

Public Health and Beth Israel Medical Center found that 87 percent of New York City's drug abuse programs turn away pregnant crack addicts, even though the women were eligible for Medicaid. The rare clinics that did admit them almost never have child-care facilities—a critical shortcoming for most mothers.[87]

Like other issues of family crime discussed in Chapter 8, the problem is also complicated by the involvement of various agencies including criminal justice agencies in these cases. Prosecution of the mother occurs in criminal court. There is also the juvenile or family court involved in the removal hearing required for placing the child in a foster care facility for an extended period should the child's mother be sentenced to serve time for a criminal conviction or placed in a treatment facility undergoing mandatory court-imposed drug rehabilitation efforts.

Conclusion

As the reader can see from both the discussion of the special AIDS issue and perinatal drug abuse, both these issues are highly charged and emotional. It is still unclear at this time what the role of the criminal law should be. And with such a lack of a clear legal focus, the responsibilities of the criminal justice system itself. The chapter also points out the significant problems in trying to rely on conventional criminal laws as a means of dealing with these new problems. At the present time, the issue is primarily a legal one which must be resolved by state legislative bodies by means of appropriate statutory guidelines. It cannot be overlooked that these are critical issues to society which show no evidence of disappearing or being merely short-term social aberrations that will in a few years lose their saliency as public policy concerns. Although the effects of these two thought-provoking issues would seem to warrant the intervention of the criminal justice system—along with corresponding social efforts to deal with the problems of AIDS and neonatal drug transmission—the question of how is yet to be satisfactorily answered.

Still, it can be suggested with some confidence that change is coming. The seriousness of these two social problems demands a better national response than what has so far occurred. And yes, this will also necessarily involve the criminal-legal system. There seems to be a growing consensus that innocent sex partners have a right of protection as do neonates; a system of rights that overrides an AIDS carrier's or drug abusing mother's right to the often ephermeral legal doctrine of privacy. It is hoped that we are slowly but inexorably moving to a legal system with an underlying philosophy that affords rights of protection for the innocent; one that considers the goal of protecting vulnerable victims as socially appropriate and important.

When the response comes—and it surely must—the new "crime problem" it creates promises to pose additional challenges for the administration of justice. It will propel these issues into important crime efforts in those parts of our nation where these two problems are most serious. One thing is certain: It will prove to be another of a growing list of difficult challenges that our crime control efforts in the years ahead will face. These are indeed crime issues of the future.

NOTES

[1]Reed, Ralph R. "The Government War on AIDS," in Abt, Clark C., and Hardy, Kathleen M. (eds.) *AIDS and the Courts* (Cambridge, MA: Abt Books, Inc., 1990), p. xi.

[2]Findlay, Steven and Silberner, Joanne, "The Worsening Spread of the AIDS Crisis," *U.S. News and World Report,* (January 29, 1990), p. 28.

[3]Reed, *op cit.,* p. xii.

[4]Findlay and Silberner, *op cit.*

[5]Ibid.

[6]Fumento, Michael. *The Myth of Heterosexual AIDS* (New York: Basic Books, 1990).

[7]*Author's note:* Azidophinadine (or AZT) is an experimental drug developed to treat AIDS. In 1987, AZT was approved by the Food and Drug Administration, the quickest such approval in the long history of the Public Health Service.

[8]*Executive Summary, The Record of the Association of the Bar of the City of New York,* (January/ February 1989), p. 614.

[9]*Report of the Presidential Commission on the Human Immunodeficiency Virus Epidemic* (Washington, D.C.: U.S. Government Printing Office), June 24, 1988. p. 131.

[10]Gostin, Larry D. "Public Health Strategies for Confronting AIDS: Legislative and Regulatory Policy in the United States," *Journal of the American Medical Association,* Vol. 261 (1989), pp. 1621–630.

[11]See *Intergovernmental Health Policy Project, A Synopsis of AIDS-Related Legislation* (Washington, D.C.: George Washington University), July 1987.

[12]For example, some states such as California, Illinois, and New Jersey have laws imposing criminal penalties on persons who donate blood knowing that they have AIDS or have tested positive for the AIDS virus. States such as California, Connecticut, Hawaii, Michigan, Nevada, North Carolina, and Oklahoma have laws imposing enhanced penalties on persons who commit a sex offense or engage in prostitution knowing they have AIDS or have tested positive for the AIDS virus. Sexual conduct laws exist in states such as Florida, Louisiana, New Jersey, New York, and Rhode Island which impose criminal penalties on persons who engage in sexual intercourse or penetration knowing they have AIDS or have tested positive for the AIDS virus. Some of these laws make such conduct a crime only if the actor's sexual partner has not been notified of the actor's condition. Several states also have transmission or exposure laws such as Alabama, Idaho, Illinois, and South Carolina. These laws impose criminal penalties on persons who have AIDS and who knowingly commit any act likely to expose another to the AIDS virus or cause transmission of the virus to another. The state of Rhode Island has proposed a law which would make it a crime for a physician to fail to indicate on a death certificate that the person died from a contagious disease.

[13]Field, Martha A. and Sullivan, Kathleen M. "AIDS and the Criminal Law," *Law, Medicine and Health Care,* Vol. 15 (Summer 1987), pp. 46–60.

[14]American Bar Association. *AIDS: The Legal Issues* (Washington, D.C.: American Bar Association, 1988, p. 27.

[15]Ibid.

[16]"Spreading AIDS on Purpose," *Washington Post Health*, April 19, 1988. p. 6.

[17]Ibid., p. 6.

[18]Fitting, Thomas. "Criminal Liability for Transmission of AIDS: Some Evidentiary Problems," *Criminal Justice Journal*, Vol. 10 (Fall 1987), p. 73.

[19]*United States v. Moore*, 846 F.2d 1163 (8th Cir. 1988).

[20]Stansburg, Carlton D. "AIDS As a Weapon," IOWA LAW REVIEW, Vol. 74 (1989), pp. 951–67.

[21]Stauter, Robert L. "*United States v. Moore:* AIDS and the Criminal Law—The Witch Hunt Begins," AKRON LAW REVIEW, Vol. 22 (1989), pp. 503–24.

[22]THE NATIONAL LAW JOURNAL (July 20, 1987), p. 32.

[23]Field and Sullivan, *op cit.*, p. 55.

[24]Ibid.

[25]Ibid.

[26]Blumberg, Mark. "Transmission of the AIDS Virus Through Criminal Activity," CRIMINAL LAW BULLETIN, Vol. 25 (1989), p. 465.

[27]See Aiken, Robert. "Education as Prevention," in Dalton, H. and Burris, S. (eds.) *AIDS and the Law: A Guide for the Public* (New Haven, CN: Yale University Press, 1987), ch. 7.

[28]Field and Sullivan, *op. cit.*, p. 51. See also Blumberg, Mark. "The Limits of Quarantine as a Measure for Controlling the Spread of AIDS," in Blumberg, Mark. (ed) *AIDS: The Impact on the Criminal Justice System* (Columbus, Ohio: Merrill Publishing Co., 1990), pp. 137–46.

[29]American Bar Association, *op. cit.*, pp. 21–22.

[30]Ibid., p. 22.

[31]See Comment, "AIDS: A Legal Epidemic," AKRON LAW REVIEW, Vol. 17 (Spring 1984); Comment, "Tort Liability for AIDS," HOUSTON LAW REVIEW, Vol. 24 (October 1987); and Baruch, "AIDS in the Courts: Tort Liability for the Sexual Transmission of Acquired Immune Deficiency Syndrome," TORT AND INSURANCE LAW JOURNAL, Vol. 24 (Fall 1988).

[32]American Bar Association, *op cit.*, p. 23.

[33]Ibid.

[34]Discussion of these two approaches borrows heavily from the article by Field and Sullivan, *op cit.*, pp. 54–58. See also Gostin, L. and Curran, W.J. (eds) "AIDS: Law an Policy," LAW MEDICINE AND HEALTH CARE, Vol. 15 (Summer 1987). Entire issue provides an overview of legislative and regulatory policy pertaining to AIDS.

[35]Besharov, D.J. "AIDS and the Criminal Law: Needed Reform," American Legislative Exchange Council (Washington, D.C.: ALEC), 1987. p. 4–5.

[36]Field and Sullivan, p. 56.

[37]Ibid.

[38]Ibid.

[39]Ibid.

[40]Collier, R.M. and Taylor, J. "AIDS: Issues and the Law," AMERICAN JOURNAL OF TRIAL ADVOCACY, Vol. 10 (Spring 1987), pp. 527–43.

[41]Field and Sullivan, p. 57.

[42]For example, see Robinson, "AIDS and the Criminal Law: Traditional Approaches and a New Statutory Proposal," HOFSTRA LAW REVIEW, Vol. 14 (1985), pp. 97–98.

[43]Field and Sullivan, p. 58.

[44]For example, see Shapiro, Emily. *AIDS and the Criminal Justice System: An Assessment of Legal and Policy Issues* (St. Paul, MN: Research Department, Minnesota House of Representatives (January 1988); and Grady, John C. "AIDS Challenges the Criminal Justice System," NEW JERSEY LAWYER (January/February 1989), pp. 36–39 and p. 77.

[45]Fitting, *op cit.*, p. 75.

[46]Shapiro, *op cit.*, p. 6.

[47]Robinson, *op cit.*, pp. 91, 97.

[48]"New Findings on Heterosexual Transmission of AIDS," *The New York Times*, (June 19, 1987), p. 10.

[49]For example, the charge under the Model Penal Code is that an assault becomes aggravated if the attempt is to cause serious physical injury, or if the victim suffers that injury when the actor behaves purposely, knowingly, or recklessly and with extreme indifference to the value of human life. See Model Penal Code, sec. 211.1(2).

[50]Shapiro, *op cit.*, p. 9.

[51]Grady, *op cit.*, p. 9.

[52]Shapiro, pp. 9–10.

[53]The prosecutor in the *Moore* case was apparently able to prove these facts to the satisfaction of the jury, even though there are no known cases involving transmission of the virus through biting. Interestingly, several members of the jury in the *Moore* case stated that they would have convicted Moore of assault with a deadly weapon even if he had not been an AIDS carrier. See NATIONAL LAW JOURNAL (July 20, 1987), p. 32. It is, however, hard to believe that Moore's status as an AIDS carrier was irrelevant to the jury's decision, given the amount of testimony presented regarding Moore's infection with the AIDS virus, and given that people who bite other people are not usually charged with or convicted of this type of assault.

[54]Robinson, *op cit.*, p. 97.

[55]See Model Penal Code, sec. 211.2.

[56]American Bar Association, *op cit.*, pp. 26–27.

[57]*Bowers v. Hardwick,* 106 S.Ct. 2841 (1986).

[58]Schneider, Jane W. and Chasnoff, Ira J. ''Cocaine Abuse During Pregnancy: Its Effects on Infant Motor Development,'' *Topics in Acute Care and Trauma Rehabilitation,* Vol. 2, No. 1 (1987) p. 58.

[59]Gomez-Ibariez, Jose A. ''Cocaine Mothers'' (Cambridge, MA: Harvard University—Kennedy School of Government Case Program paper) 1990. pp. 3–4.

[60]Sherman, Rorie. ''Keeping Baby Safe from Mom,'' THE NATIONAL LAW JOURNAL, Vol. 11 (October 3, 1988), pp. 1 and 24.

[61]Roberts, Dorothy E. ''Drug Addicted Women Who Have Babies,'' *Trial,* Vol. 26 (April 1990), p. 58.

[62]Hoffman, Jan. ''Pregnant, Addicted and Guilty?'' *The New York Times Magazine* (August 19, 1990), p. 34.

[63]Burns, T., Chasnoff, I., and Scholl, J. ''Prenatal Drug Exposure: Effects on Neonatal and Infant Growth and Development,'' *Neurobehavioral Toxicology and Teratology,* Vol. 8 (1986) pp. 351–87.

[64]Schneider and Chasnoff, *op cit.*, p. 60.

[65]For example, see Schierl, Kathryn. ''A Proposal to Illinois Legislators: Revise the Illinois Criminal Code to Include Criminal Sanctions Against Prenatal Substance Abusers,'' JOHN MARSHALL LAW REVIEW, Vol. 23 (Spring 1990), pp. 393–423; Bailsy, Sam S. ''Maternal Substance Abuse: The Need to Provide Legal Protection for the Fetus,'' SOUTHERN CALIFORNIA LAW REVIEW (May 1987), pp. 1209–238; and Shelley, Barbara. ''Maternal Substance Abuse: The Next Step in the Protection of Fetal Rights?'' DICKINSON LAW REVIEW Vol. 92 (Spring 1988), pp. 691–715.

[66]Ibid.

[67]Chesnoff, Ira. ''Perinatal Effects of Cocaine,'' *Journal of Contemporary Obstetrics and Gynecology,* Vol. 10 (1987), p. 163.

[68]Shelley, Barbara. ibid., p. 708.

[69]Steinbrook, William. ''Steps to Reduce Rise of AIDS in Babies Urged,'' *The Los Angeles Times,* (February 21, 1987), sec. 2, p. 1.

[70]Hundley, Robert. ''Infants a Growing Casualty of the Drug Epidemic,'' *The Chicago Tribune,* (October 16, 1989), sec. 1, p. 1.

[71]Schierl, *op cit.*, pp. 400–01.

[72]Press release from National Association for Perinatal Addiction Research and Education, National Training Forum on Drugs, Alcohol, Pregnancy and Parenting (Chicago, IL: September 17, 1989).

[73]Regan, Thomas R. et al., ''Infants of Drug Addicts: At Risk for Child Abuse, Neglect, and Placement in Foster Care,'' *Nerotoxicology and Teratology,* Vol. 9 (1987), p. 315.

[74]Schierl, p. 404.

[75]Ibid., pp. 405–06.

[76]See Logli, Paul A. "Drugs in the Womb: The Newest Battlefield in the War on Drugs," CRIMINAL JUSTICE ETHICS, Vol. 9 (Winter/Spring 1990), pp. 23–39.

[77]Schierl, *op cit.*, pp. 406–07.

[78]Sherman, Rorie. "Keeping Babies Free of Drugs," NATIONAL LAW JOURNAL, Vol. 12 (October 16, 1989), pp. 1 and 28.

[79]Hoffman, p. 35.

[80]Monk, Richard C. (ed). *Taking Sides: Clashing Views on Controversial Issues in Crime and Criminology* (Guilford, CN.: The Dushkin Publishing Group, Inc., 1991), p. 283.

[81]Roberts, "Drug Addicted Women," *op cit.*, p. 58.

[82]Ibid.

[83]*People v. Stewart No. M508097* (Cal. San Diego Mun. Ct., February 23, 1987). In this case the defendant was arrested and charged with a state statute that requires parents to furnish food, clothing, shelter, and medical care for their child or fetus. The court dismissed the charges because the statute used to charge her was not applicable to the situation, but was intended to apply to fathers who are delinquent in paying child support.

[84]Hoffman, *op cit.*, p. 35.

[85]*Robinson v. California,* 370 U.S. 660 (1962).

[86]Lewin, Tamar. "Drug Use in Pregnancy: New Issue for the Courts," *The New York Times* (February 15, 1990), p. A-14.

[87]Hoffman, p. 57.

SECTION III

ISSUES AFFECTING THE SOCIAL ORDER

This final section of the book examines four criminal events (or developing social issues that are beginning to be dealt with as criminal events) that particularly affect the social order. While nearly all forms of crime have a direct or indirect economic consequence and all have a political component, all crimes also have a social component. Crime always affects the social order and society in its consequences.

Still, certain crimes have the potential for affecting society in ways not associated with more conventional criminal acts. Not only are there important direct consequences to victims from these criminal events, but broad-ranging indirect consequences to society itself. In this way, they cast a wide-net of cause and effect, asserting a wide ripple-effect of consequences: A unique form of victim transference that either encompasses or threatens to encompass large segments of society while posing an undermining influence to the existence of social order. All the crimes discussed in this section are well-recognized as major social problems in America today and have become major crime issues. The two possible exceptions to this is the growing involvement of the criminal law in the area of family offenses and environmental regulation.

While family violence and environmental concerns rank as major social concerns of the day, they have only recently become a growing subject for criminal law involvement. Singled-out for examination are violent youth gangs, crimes involving the family, the consequences of illegal narcotics, and the expanding area of criminal prosecutions for environmental offenses.

Chapter 7 examines the resurgence of youth gangs in America. The growth of violent youth gangs and the ''franchising'' of violence, drug dealing, and criminality that is being spawned in sections of our nation wracked by this problem prompted Louis Sullivan, Secretary of Health and Human Services to lament, ''during every 100 hours on our streets, we lose more young men than were killed in 100 hours of ground war in the Persian Gulf.'' And it isn't only young gang members in central cities who are falling prey to this violence. Increasingly, innocent third parties are being victimized by the random violence sweeping the streets of some major cities. Behind the crime and violence, a chilling statistic came out of a survey in Baltimore which indicated that 59 percent of young public school males in that city who came from one-parent or no-parent homes had carried a handgun. At the root of the problem is family dissolution, drugs, an open hostility toward and contempt for society, a growing willingness to use unrestrained violence, and an insensitvity characterized by a ''what the hell'' attitude toward its consequences.

This chapter examines the makeup of youth gangs, their history and current trends. A typology of gangs is developed including such recent phenomena as gang ''franchising'' and wanton gang-related violence. Racial and ethnic gang composition is also examined as is female gangs and youth gang communication and rituals. The causes of gang formation are evaluated using as a basis, existing research contributions in this area. Attention is then turned to strategies of gang control including those adopted by the criminal justice system as well as the community. It is argued that the criminal justice system can play only a limited role in dealing with gang formation and violence; if changes are to occur, they must involve involve important social change and community involvement.

Crimes among family members are also growing at an alarming rate as America's family structure unravels. The social illnesses afflicting our nation have found expression in the home and within the family. While the criminal justice and social assistance systems struggle to find ways to counteract this growing trend and define their roles, the problem continues unabated. This is the focus of Chapter 8. Three forms of ''family crime'' are examined: spousal or marital abuse, child abuse, and the growing awareness of the problem of elder abuse. Among the topics covered in this chapter are the problems of measurement, the criminal justice system's role and evolving strategies to deal with these issues, particular problems these forms of criminal acts pose, and the necessity to develop an appropriate jurisprudence of family crime, juridical attention, and criminal justice system response.

Chapter 9 looks at the illegal narcotics issue. In ways not fully known, the scourge of illegal drugs contributes much to our nation's crime problem. One thing is certain: It is a problem which has devastated the social fabric of at least portions of our nation like no other single event in our history. The present and future social consequences are still not understood. As a nation, we have begun slowly to turn away from a quarter century of drug experimentation, but the consequences of this legacy linger among certain segments of our population where it continues its destructiveness. Perhaps prophetically, the future consequences can be foretold by what has already occurred during the last 25 years. It remains a social (and crime) problem of paramount importance.

The chapter examines the history of our nation's efforts to control illegal drugs, the relationship between drugs and crime, changes in drug use, the direct and indirect consequences of our ''war on drugs,'' the arguments for and against legalizing narcotics and the transnational character of illegal drugs and what this realistically means for containment and effective enforcement efforts. It concludes by offering a somber postscript to the changing character of drug abuse and those most effected by its ravages.

Chapter 10 examines the growing issue of environmental crime. Increasingly, government is turning away from a policy of inaction or civil penalties to a policy of criminal prosecution for acts of environmental destruction and associated public health risks. The reader will be introduced to the evolving nature of environmental regulation, major criminal legislation governing enforcement efforts, problems of prosecution and deterrence, unanticipated consequences of increased regulation, and the federal and state enforcement structure. Also discussed is transnational environmental pollution and the inherent difficulties in trying to regulate this threat. Like many other crimes discussed in this book, environmental crime is a rapidly evolving area of the criminal law and its enforcement; an area which presents extraordinary difficulties while imposing an important future challenge for the agencies of criminal justice.

CHAPTER 7

The Rebirth of Youth Gangs

CONTENTS

A ''night of wilding'' in Central Park, ''murder zones'' in America's large cities, ''kids who kill,'' and ''gangs and supergangs'' read the covers of leading magazines and newspapers across the nation. Wanton violence, committed by young people in groups, appears to have become both more serious and more common in many parts of North America and around the world. Speculation abounds in attempting to explain these violent acts: Is it a result of the drug problem, a more hedonistic society, lack of adequate parental supervision, youth with no hope or connection to legitimate society, ''proving'' oneself to peers, or simply cheap thrills for a ''bored'' generation?

In order to understand the phenomenon of violent youth gangs in systematic fashion, five contemporary aspects of the gang problem will be addressed here:

1. What are violent youth gangs, their history, and how can they be distinguished from other types of youth crime?
2. What are the trends in youth gang activity?
3. What are the various types of youth gangs and what are their attributes?
4. What are the identified causes or correlates of gang delinquency as identified by researchers and government officials?
5. What control and prevention strategies have been tried and how effective have they been?

Three specific trends that have received comparatively little attention thus far will also be highlighted:

1. franchising of youth gangs among cities;
2. the growth of female gangs; and
3. how the current ''gang control cycle'' is destined for failure without a change in strategy.

Each of these issues poses unique challenges for the future that are described in the following discussion.

What Constitutes a Youth Gang?

Virtually all juveniles engage in criminal behavior at some point in their lives. This point is uncontested in the delinquency research literature.[1] In addition, many of these acts of delinquency occur in small groups.[2] Although group participation in delinquency has been found to vary by offense,[3] it is relatively rare for acts of delinquency to be committed alone or without the knowledge of peers. At what point, then, does the common experience of delinquency in groups become a ''violent youth gang?''

Researchers and law enforcement officials do not have a common definition of what constitutes a ''gang,'' but most use the notion of a gang to distinguish larger, more organized, and more visible groups of young people from those that are smaller, loosely organized, and casual groups of youth that occasionally commit crimes. A federal study of ''collective youth crime'' in 24 major U.S. cities attempted to distinguish ''gangs'' from ''groups'' in committing serious youth crime. In interviews conducted with police, judges, educators, gang members, and ex-prisoners, respondents identified the following elements as most important in distinguishing gangs from less organized forms of youth crime:

- Organization;
- Identifiable leadership;
- Territorial identification;
- Continuous association; and
- Specific purpose.

Half the 24 cities surveyed believed gangs contributed to their violent crime problem, but smaller cities were less likely to call their youth-crime problem gang-related.[4]

In a national survey, police identified two more gang characteristics to add to those above:

- Dress or body decoration; and
- Use of identifying graffiti.[5]

A large number of investigations of youth gangs have been conducted in specific cities to obtain a better picture of their nature and organization.

The pioneering study of gangs in the United States was conducted by Frederick Thrasher in 1927. He studied 1,313 gangs totalling more than 25,000 members in Chicago. Most gangs had six to 20 members, although a few had more than 100 members. He found that gangs are formed "spontaneously" in *interstitial* areas where there exist "cracks" in the normal social fabric of society, resulting from poverty, poor family supervision, and disorganized neighborhoods. According to Thrasher, the gangs are formed to fulfill the youthful need for play and adventure, which sometimes leads to delinquent acts, a finding that has been supported in subsequent studies.[6] In fact, it is not always the case that "street-corner" groups are necessarily delinquent.[7] The gangs become solidified, however, when there is continued conflict between them and authority figures.[8]

Interest in youth gangs flourished during the 1950s and 1960s, a trend that corresponded with the baby-boom generation, media portrayals of gang activity, and the infiltration of television into most American households to transmit these images across the nation. Sociologists Richard Cloward and Lloyd Ohlin published an influential study of delinquency in 1960 entitled *Delinquency and Opportunity: A Theory of Delinquent Gangs.* In that book, they argued that gangs arise from "blocked opportunity" for legitimate success, resulting in one of three outcomes:

1. Criminal subculture—where youths become part of adult career criminal groups, due to close bonds between offenders of different ages.
2. Conflict subculture—where youths turn to violence in search of status, due to frustration and discontent with their social position and lack of opportunities.

3. Retreatist subculture—where youths actively engage in substance abuse, due to lack of opportunities to join criminal or conflict groups.[9]

It is interesting that Cloward and Ohlin's typology has been substantially confirmed by studies of gangs in a variety of cities in recent years.

Jeffrey Fagan examined gang behavior in Chicago, Los Angeles, and San Diego in 1989 and found four major types: social, party, serious delinquent, and organized gangs.[10] The social and party gangs correspond with the "retreatist" subculture identified by Cloward and Ohlin, whereas the serious delinquent and organized gangs match the conflict and criminal subcultures, respectively. In a recent study of gangs in Columbus, Ohio, C. Ronald Huff also identified a similar typology to that of Cloward and Ohlin, calling them instead: hedonistic, predatory, and instrumental gangs.[11] Carl Taylor classifies gangs as scavenger, territorial, or corporate, depending on the motivation and organization of gang members.[12]

It should be noted that a survey of gangs in 24 U.S. cities found that violence appears to be more associated with contemporary gangs than was the case years ago.[13] This apparent increase in "conflict" gang activity is a cause for concern, and the proportion of gang activity that is criminal, retreatist, or violent is a trend to be watched in the future.

After initial interest in the study of youth gangs, however, interest in them virtually disappeared by the late 1960s. There exists little documented evidence of serious scholarly or law enforcement concern about gangs from the mid-1960s to the mid-1970s. Some argue this was the result of greater adherence to the "labeling" perspective toward delinquency which holds that identification and adjudication of juveniles as delinquents or "gang members" serves to stigmatize them further and alienate them from conventional society, possibly changing their self-image to encourage a criminal lifestyle.[14] Another explanation is that gang activities may have been channeled into more political activities, such as anti-Vietnam War, civil rights, or other social action groups.[15] In fact, the National Advisory Committee on Criminal Justice Standards and Goals reported in 1976 that "youth gang violence is not a major crime problem in the United States."[16] Concern about criminal gang activity rose once again in the mid-1970s, however, and it continues today at a high level. Immigration patterns and economic conditions since the 1970s have been identified as contributing factors in the reemergence of gangs.[17]

Trends in Youth Gangs

It is important to have an accurate understanding of the true extent of youth and gang violence, so that one is not mislead by a few sensational crimes and can bring a sense of history to the issue. In Racine, Wisconsin, for example, interviews with both adults and youth there found remarkably divergent perspectives regarding delinquent youth gangs in that city. Adults perceived these gangs to be a larger problem, more structured, and more dangerous than the youths did. The study found "stereotypical images" to influence perceptions, as well as media reporting.[18]

The dramatic increase in crack sales in Los Angeles during the mid-1980s was thought to be associated with similar changes in gang involvement. The Crips gang in Los Angeles, for example, was formed in 1969 and 1970 and has been primarily engaged in crack cocaine trafficking and linked to establishment of drug distribution in other cities.[19] Using law enforcement sources, a study at the University of Southern California found no relationship between the growing crack sales and gangs, however. Although cocaine sales arrests increased by 375 percent in two years, the analysis shows a ''diminishing gang effect'' over time and that those sales involving gangs differed little from those that did not.[20]

Nevertheless, more than 750 youth gangs with an estimated membership of over 50,000 have been identified by the California Attorney General's Youth Gang Task Force.[21] The Los Angeles Police Department believes the number of gangs there increased by 71 percent between 1985 and 1988 alone.[22] A study of youth crime in Chicago, Los Angeles, and San Diego found young people in gangs to engage in generally more serious delinquency more often, compared to non-gang youth.[23]

A Chicago Police Department report claims there are 100 gangs in that city, ranging in size from 10 to more than 4,000 members.[24] An independent survey of Chicago gangs found substantially similar results.[25] In Cleveland, there are 15 to 20 active gangs, and another 15 active gangs in Columbus, Ohio.[26] A 1990 review of officially identified gangs reported 31 in Phoenix, 66 in New York City, 80 in Dade County, Florida, and 35 in San Diego. Although gangs are increasing in some cities while decreasing in others, they represent significant social problems wherever they exist.[27] A teenage gang from Toronto, for example, was recently arrested with $150,000 worth of stolen property and weapons that included an Uzi submachine gun, which was to be sold to other high school students.[28] It should be noted, however, that the proportion of youths involved in gangs has not changed dramatically. Depending on the city and neighborhood, gang membership comprises between one and 14 percent of all youth, a fact that has been substantiated in a large number of studies encompassing many different types of youth.[29]

Police arrests also show a remarkable trend in recent years. Since 1970, the proportion of juveniles under 18 who have been arrested (compared to adults) has dropped for every one of the 25 crimes counted by the FBI except criminal homicide, embezzlement, weapons offenses, gambling, and offenses against the family.[30] Although this trend is likely the result of a shrinking number of young people in the U.S. population, it is noteworthy that both homicide and weapons offenses have increased, two crimes linked closely to gang activity in recent years.[31] It has been argued by some investigators that the increase in gang violence in recent years is attributable to some extent to possession of weapons by more gang members.[32]

Only when police classification of ''gang-related'' crimes becomes uniform will a more precise national estimate of gang activity be possible. Some police agencies define a ''gang crime'' as any offense committed by a youth identified as a gang member or associate, while other departments classify gang crimes as those arising from gang-related activity. Other departments count only certain types of serious crimes as possibly gang related.[33] A study of gang-related homicides in Los Angeles found the number dropped in half, if the homicides were classified in terms of the motive, rather than whether known members were involved.[34] Clearly, some standardization in definition is needed, if reliable estimates of trends in gang- related crime are to be made.

Typology of Gangs

There is no single type of gang. A book based on 47 interviews with gang members from 19 Milwaukee gangs found them to be ''unique and variable,'' depending on local factors that the gang reacts to and that require a flexible response.[35] Youth gangs vary in nature by organization, by age of members, gender, race and ethnicity, and in communications and rituals. Similarities and differences will be summarized here, as uncovered through numerous investigations of the problem.

Franchising of Gangs

As Cloward and Ohlin recognized, the three types of gangs they identified specialized in either violence, crimes for profit, or substance abuse. The organization of these gangs have become a growing concern, however. There is evidence that smaller cities, historically without gang problems, are now experiencing an influx of gang activity. Some of it is ''home grown,'' but many of these gangs appear to be ''franchises'' of existing gangs in larger cities.

Mid-sized metropolitan areas, such as Albuquerque, now have a gang problem attributed largely to pressure from police and rival gangs in other cities to move into new territories.[36] Readers of *The Seattle Times,* for example, rated the migration of the Bloods and the Crips gangs from Los Angeles to be the number one newsstory there in 1988.[37] According to the Drug Enforcement Administration, members of Los Angeles gangs have been identified in virtually every state, although the analogy to organized crime does not appear to hold. According to Eddie Hill of the DEA's cocaine desk, the formation of gang ''franchises'' in other cities does not imply an organized conspiracy. ''There is no organization,'' according to Hill. ''There is no head person in Los Angeles or San Diego or San Francisco telling a gang member to go from Los Angeles to your town, U.S.A.''[38] Instead, the spread of the Los Angeles gangs is due, at least in part, to ''aggressive law enforcement efforts'' and the large amount of cocaine available there, resulting in lower prices. The prospect of less police harassment and higher drug profits lures gang members elsewhere.[39]

In Denver, local youths have been found recruiting members from the Los Angeles area to obtain narcotics. Omaha has been found to have members from Los Angeles and Kansas City gangs.[40] Vancouver has reported that Los Angeles gangs have established operations there. Atlanta and Savannah, Georgia and Montgomery, Alabama have reported similar migration from a Miami-based gang.[41] A former member of the Los Angeles Crips gang was placed on probation and sent to live with relatives in Tyler, Texas where he joined a local gang and armed it. Gang graffiti began to appear and assaults rose markedly.[42] Outside Buffalo, six members of the Crips gang in Los Angeles were arrested on a possible connection to several drug-related shootings in Buffalo.[43] What may

"They said we disappeared during the 1970s, but they overlooked what was happening in our cities, neighborhoods, schools, and families. Guess what? We're back stronger than ever!"

loosely be called gang ''franchising'' appears to be an especially threatening trend for the future, as the neighborhood conditions that give rise to gangs, described so well by Cloward and Ohlin more than 30 years ago, are present in virtually every American city.

Age

The age of gang members covers a wide range, but the average age has been estimated to be 17 to 18-years old.[44] In Thrasher's pioneering study of Chicago gangs, he found 455 gangs comprised of juveniles between 11 and 17, and 305 gangs with members aged 16 to 25. He found very few gang members older than this.[45] Irving Spergel found the average age of gang offenders in Chicago during the mid-1980s to be nearly 18 years old.[46] Walter Miller's national survey of gangs in 24 cities found remarkably similar results: Most are adolescents and young adults in the 17 to 18 year range. Miller found only slightly fewer juveniles involved in gangs who were very young or older than earlier studies discovered.[47]

It is likely that the average age of gang members will *increase* in the future as the economy suffers. Legitimate job opportunities for unskilled workers will be fewer and, therefore, gang-related crimes for profit might become attractive for those with diminished legitimate opportunity.[48]

In addition, it has been suggested that some youth gang members "graduate" to become part of organized crime. As Cloward and Ohlin suggest, youth members of the "criminal subculture" pursue careers in crime when links to adult criminals exist. The successful prosecutions of a large number of organized crime figures in recent years will undoubtedly increase the opportunity for former youth gang members to fill the vacancies left by incarcerated members of organized crime.[49]

Female Gangs

Youth gangs historically have been overwhelmingly male, but this may be changing. Thrasher's pioneering study of more than 1,000 gangs found only about one percent were female gangs. Walter Miller found two female gangs of seven gangs he investigated in Boston.[50] Irving Spergel found only one female gang homicide offender in 345 gang-related killings in Chicago.[51] A national survey estimated that gang membership is more than 90 percent male,[52] although an evaluation of alternative education programs in 50 schools reported that 13 percent of males and 5.2 percent of females admitted involvement in a gang fight.[53]

Females are involved in gang activity in one of three ways: their own gangs, "branches" of male gangs, or sexually mixed gangs. It has been most common in the past for females to be involved in "branches" or "affiliated" gangs, and the females generally were excluded from the planning and action of criminal activities in sexually mixed gangs.[54] There is evidence that female-only gangs are on the rise, however. A survey of institutionalized girls found more than half belong to a gang.[55] In an important participant-observation study, Anne Campbell spent six months with each of three different female gangs in New York City: a street gang, a biker gang, and an Islamic gang. She found these gangs to be run independently by females. The reasons for female gang participation are strikingly similar to those identified for males. The gang members are "often from backgrounds of poverty, are unemployed, undereducated, and of minority status. Many have criminal records and most have little to look forward to in terms of economic success."[56]

It appears that females join gangs earlier and leave earlier than do males. Many enter gangs when they are 12 to 14 years old, but they often leave before they reach the age of majority. A study of four female gangs in Milwaukee found nearly all members had left the gang by the time they turned 18.[57]

It also has been reported that juvenile delinquent gangs in China have increased significantly since the 1970s, their crimes have become more serious, and they involve more women, and sophisticated technology.[58] It has been observed that one-third of all female gang members ultimately will be arrested, 84 percent will raise children without spouses, and most will be on welfare. As Anne Campbell concludes, "the attraction of the gang is no mystery in the context of the isolation and poverty that is awaiting them.''[59] Therefore, independent female gang activity is a trend to watch in the future.

Race and Ethnicity

Most gangs appear to be racially homogenous. In the United States, most investigators have found gangs to be either all white, all black, all Hispanic, or all Asian. The proportion of gangs of different racial and ethnic backgrounds corresponds to the city of origin. On the West Coast, there are more Asians so there are many more Asian gangs, while in cities with more blacks, there are more black gangs, and so on. Interestingly, gangs remain primarily a lower-class phenomenon located in interstitial neighborhoods, reacting to blocked opportunity or status, regardless of race or ethnic background.[60]

The reasons for the racial exclusivity of gangs is a function of neighborhood and cohesion. Most gangs exist in poor neighborhoods which often are dominated by a particular ethnic group. The rise of Italian organized crime in the United States can be traced back to similar interstitial neighborhood roots.[61] Second, there is little to hold gangs together. They share few constructive interests and often lack positive family tradition or supervision. Therefore, they are held together most effectively by shared frustration, often expressed as hatred toward other groups. This serves as a common purpose for holding the gang together. The frustration and hatred are often directed toward other racial groups, economic groups, and rival gangs who live in the same area. Evidence of this phenomenon is provided by studies of gangs in several different locations. A study of Hispanic gangs found ''fierce loyalty'' to their home turf.[62] Chinese, Samoan, and Vietnamese gangs have been found to battle members of their own ethnic group without regard for territory to battle rival gangs, although these gangs are more ''deeply enmeshed'' in legal and illegal enterprises than are most of their American counterparts.[63] The ''punk,'' ''skinhead,'' and ''white supremacy'' movements among whites have been found to engage in drug use, satanic rituals, and racially motivated acts of violence, illustrating how their cohesion lies in hatred and blame directed toward others for their own situation, rather than in any real purpose of their own.[64] The patterns of gang behavior that develop among the youth of newly arrived immigrants to the United States deserves serious attention from scholars and policymakers in the future.[65]

Communications and Rituals

Gangs often seek to distinguish themselves from other youth, and from society at large, through distinct forms of communication and rituals. These generally involve:

- Unique speech patterns;
- Tattoos and graffiti; and
- Common dress

Unique speech patterns include "passwords" and responses needed to traverse through hostile neighborhoods controlled by rival gangs, or verbal responses that have a secret meaning in conversation to conceal criminal activity or associations. Hand signals are also common among youth gangs. Some gangs have their own "secret" hand salute for recognition or to insult others.

Tattoos and graffiti are used to different degrees by youth gangs. Many Asian gangs have been known to have elaborate tattoos for purposes of recognition and subservience to the gang's common purpose.[66] Motorcycle gangs in North America also have an established history of tattoos for membership and loyalty purposes. Likewise, graffiti is often used by inner-city gangs to mark "turf," display dominance or control of an area to others, and to challenge rival gangs.

Uniform dress is employed by many gangs to increase cohesion. Jackets with gang names embroidered on the back, common hats, belts, sneakers, or colors are all used to one degree or another by youth gangs as a symbol of comraderie.[67]

Causes of Gang Delinquency

The causes of gang delinquency are many, but investigations in various cities show some common elements. Interviews with gang members in Detroit found them to be "obsessively materialistic." These materialistic goals were pursued through organized drug trafficking because it was easier than legitimate work, and law-abiding individuals are considered either "hypocrites or fools." This illegal drug trafficking was rationalized as no more harmful than the legitimate market in alcoholic beverages and cigarettes. The risk of violence, police apprehension, and imprisonment are considered a necessary part of the drug business. The study found that, overall, the 1980's youth gangs in Detroit attracted those interested in making a lot of money, personal protection, status or belonging, camaraderie, and adventure.[68]

Interviews with gang members, peers, relatives, and government personnel in southern California provides some insight into gang membership in urban, suburban, and rural barrios there. Hispanic youth found peer group identification in gangs when it was otherwise unavailable in families or schools. They also found self-protection, belonging, and roles for asserting "hyper-masculine" behavior. The urban gang, therefore, "helps their adolescent passage to adulthood."[69]

Interviews with five female gang members in Paris, France found them to occupy subordinate positions and are the "objects" of relationships among male gang members. It was found that the lives of gang members reflected the values of the working class from which the members came.[70]

As these interviews with gang members and affected community members suggest, there is no single explanation of gang formation or participation. The theories that have gained the most general acceptance are those that focus on either blocked opportunity or subcultures. Sociologists Cloward and Ohlin argue that gang crime is the result of frustration resulting blocked opportunity to obtain success in society through legitimate means. Therefore, youths turn to gangs and crime to achieve social acceptance and some form of "success".[71] Subcultural theories of delinquency, such as that of Albert Cohen, claim that deviant and illegal behavior are seen as acceptable and desirable behaviors within the delinquent subculture.[72]

Herbert Block and Arthur Niederhoffer suggest that gangs provide a means to bridge the gap between childhood and adulthood common in most societies. They compare gang characteristics to the puberty rites of primitive cultures. According to this anthropological perspective, tattooing and common dress provide common attachment for young people not prepared for the responsibilities of adulthood, but who are beyond the innocent freedom of childhood.[73] The existence of youth gangs in a number of countries around the world lends support to this notion that gang identification evolves naturally when adolescents are in a state of suspension between childhood and adulthood.[74]

A study of gang homicides and delinquency in Chicago found "social disorganization (the settlement of new immigrant groups) and poverty rather than criminal organization and conspiracy" best explain the growth and spread of youth gangs in the United States.[75] Chris Baca, executive director of Youth Development, Inc. in Albuquerque observes, "We do not see drug gangs proliferating in the more affluent areas of the Nation, nor do we see extensive recruitment of middle-class people to deal drugs in the streets."[76] A review of studies of criminal careers found that the "concentration of young males who lack firm controls of parental authority," in certain neighborhoods leads them to be controlled by their peers and supports criminal activities.[77] In addition, a long line of studies have found that gang members are usually poor students or school dropouts.[78]

Controlling Youth Gangs

There are three possible responses to the problems presented by youth gangs:

1. Police sweeps and crackdowns;
2. Intelligence gathering and development of informants; and
3. Community reforms.

Each of these responses has been relied upon to some extent in various cities around the world. A review of these strategies, and their success or failure, reveals how the overall strategy toward youth gangs must be changed to avoid a continuing cycle of gang involvement.

Sweeps and Crackdowns

Law enforcement "sweeps" are essentially mass arrests of gang members on minor charges. These sweeps are similar to an enforced curfew in that they take young people off the streets at night, most of whom are released by the next day. In Los Angeles, these sweeps have resulted in as many as 1,100 arrests on a single weekend.[79] The charges often resulting from these tactics are minor drug and weapons possession, and disorderly conduct, but it has been argued that such activities serve to disrupt gang activity, keep their gatherings out of public view, and enables police to develop information about the size and purpose of various gangs. As the Los Angeles Sheriff's Office has remarked, ''Law enforcement must make gang membership very uncomfortable . . . so we can again create a deterrent effect in gang activity.''[80] In Boston, police adopted a ''stop-and-frisk'' policy to search for drugs and weapons after gang violence occurred there in 1989. The policy was found to be unconstitutional because frisks were conducted without any evidence of illegal activity.[81]

The overriding problem with sweeps, of course, is that they have only a temporary effect and do nothing about the incidence of entrenched gang violence. Frank Radke, commanding officer of the Gang Crime Section of the Chicago Police Department, concluded,

> Today, we are arresting more gang members than ever before; we are getting more convictions than ever before; and we are getting longer sentences than ever before. But ironically, we have more gangs than ever before. Arrest and prosecution are not the deterrent we expected them to be.[82]

A review of 18 case studies of police crackdowns of varying types found the effects ''began to decay after a short period, sometimes despite continued dosage of police presence or even increased dosage of police sanctions.''[83]

Perhaps the most ambitious police effort of this kind was ''Operation Clean Sweep'' conducted in Washington, D.C. in the late 1980s. This crackdown involved more than 100 officers who conducted roadblocks, surveillance, undercover ''buys,'' and seizures in 59 street-corner ''drug markets'' in the nation's capital. This effort resulted in 30,000 arrests (at a rate of nearly 60 per day) in its first 18 months. An evaluation concluded that the operation was ''well-executed,'' and that fewer drug markets operated openly, however, drug use was found to increase substantially, drug markets were displaced to other areas nearby, and there was a dramatic rise in homicides. This led the evaluators to conclude that perhaps the intensified enforcement ''raised the violence of the drug trade, simply because the participants feel more threatened.''[84]

A similar police crackdown in Philadelphia, called ''Cold Turkey,'' targeted 56 corner drug markets. In only four days, 1,000 people were stopped and searched by a force of 450 officers. Less than 20 percent were arrested on narcotics charges, and a third were arrested for disorderly conduct. The operation provoked significant public protest and hostility, however, which effectively ended the operation.[85] In addition to increasing neighborhood hostilities, police crackdowns, such as one in Los Angeles in 1988, can aggravate racial tensions as well. A mass arrest of more than 1,000 people on a single weekend there resulted in less than a third being charged with any offense at all, and not a single white person was arrested.[86] The inability of the criminal justice response to put an end to gang crimes is only to be expected, as long as gang membership is seen as desirable to large numbers of youth. Police sweeps and crackdowns do nothing to alter this underlying problem and, in some cases, have aggravated it by increasing police-community tensions.

Intelligence and Informants

Intelligence strategies for combatting serious gang violence include: coordination of police gang units, identification of gang members, use of informants, controlled drug purchases, and surveillance of known gang hangouts.[87] These methods are used to gather information, disrupt serious gang activity, and to anticipate planned acts of violence by gangs. Los Angeles has created an interagency gang task force that developed a "Gang Reporting, Evaluation, and Tracking System" to assist police agencies in tracking gang members.[88] The California Youth Authority (CYA) operates 11 institutions that incarcerate serious young offenders aged 12 to 24. Each institution now has a "gang coordinator" to gather intelligence about gangs both inside and outside the facility for law enforcement use. The CYA also operates a "safe house" for parolees who do not wish to return to the gang culture and live in another community.[89]

Robert Martin, director of the Chicago Intervention Network, believes that police do a good job apprehending "hardcore" gang members, but "there are 10 other youngsters . . . just waiting to take their place."[90] A forum of police chiefs, scholars, and government officials concluded that the proper approach is to "view the drug gangs as organized criminal enterprises" and to use the enforcement techniques currently used against organized crime:

1. Development of informants through criminal prosecutions, payments, and witness protection programs;
2. Heavy reliance on electronic surveillance and long-term undercover investigations; and
3. Use of conspiracy, extortion, and racketeering statutes to prosecute the operation of gangs as "criminal enterprises."[91]

This forum recognized, however, that efforts such as these are also "time-consuming and expensive," and that they may not be required in dealing with "the relatively unsophisticated street-level drug gangs." The lack of a high degree of organization in street gangs, unlike organized crime, has made them vulnerable to "relatively superficial undercover approaches" in the past.[92] This is supported by the comments of a commander in the Los Angeles Police Department who indicates, "it is a myth that street gangs are well organized, with meeting halls, presidents, and boards of directors." Instead, he argues, most gang activity is analogous to pick-up basketball games where whoever is available participates in the action. They simply "don't sit down and develop a tactical plan."[93]

Nevertheless, courts are increasingly allowing evidence in court regarding gang membership, even though it often serves to prejudice juries through "guilt by association." In a Florida case, testimony about a defendant's membership in a motorcycle gang was held to be admissible by the U.S. Court of Appeals, enabling the prosecution to establish that club members depended on drug sales for a living and needed new members to maintain their trafficking operations.[94] As an Illinois court summarized, "Proof of gang membership is relevant and admissible when there is sufficient proof of relationship between such affiliation and the crime charged,'' in order to show motive or common purpose. In addition, it ''need not be excluded merely because of its tendency to prejudice'' the judge or jury.[95] This appears to be the rule in a growing number of cases across the country, where evidence of gang membership can be used when necessary to prove an element of the crime alleged.[96]

In addition, laws have been changed to enhance prosecution effectiveness. In California, a 1989 law increased the penalties for drug dealing and allows the state to freeze the assets of suspected ''gang drug lords'' prior to trial.[97] This was the first law of its kind, and it also made it a crime to belong to a gang that commits crimes. Such a membership-prohibition law has questionable validity under the Constitution, as the principles of criminal liability permit punishment only for those actually *participating* in a crime in some way. In any event, Los Angeles police began serving written notices on 3,700 gang members, who could face up to three years in prison if convicted.[98]

Community Reform

Efforts at community reform strive to accomplish one of two objectives: either to change the delinquent reponses of young people to unfortunate social circumstances, or else to change the social circumstances themselves to provide greater opportunities for legitimate success in society. A large-scale attempt to reduce gang delinquency in Chicago grew out of Thrasher's original work on the subject. Recreation opportunities, physical improvement of the community, and mediation efforts to help juveniles find non-delinquent solutions in dealing with problems were attempted simultaneously. The impact of this ''Chicago Area Project'' or CAP on delinquency was unclear, however. Decreases in delinquency in CAP neighborhoods was offset by increases in surrounding areas. Also, project evaluations were not able to assess the effect on gang membership.[99]

A similar project aimed at changing both the potential delinquent and his or her environment was Mobilization for Youth (MFY) in New York City. This project was directed at an entire neighborhood on the lower East Side of Manhattan during the 1960s. Through a large number of services to improve work skills, school performance, counseling, and community organization, an attempt was made to change a neighborhood of more than 20,000 people. Like the Chicago Area Project, MFY was only partially evaluated and the results were similarly disappointing. It may have been overly optimistic to expect to change an entire neighborhood in just a few years and lasting social change may be more complex and unwieldy than this program had anticipated.[100]

A component of both programs above was the use of ''Street Corner Workers'' or ''Detached Workers'' who would work out in the streets with the gangs and attempt to divert the gang's energies into more productive channels, such as sports, service projects, and self-help programs. Ironically, it was found that these workers did, indeed, increase gang cohesiveness, but they were unsuccessful in diverting them from crime. The result was that these groups became more organized and they committed more crimes, suggesting the workers did more harm than good.[101] The same outcome was experienced in

Boston's MidCity Project, using detached workers with members of 21 gangs.[102] An evaluation of a similar New York City effort concluded that directing "the gang's energies into constructive channels such as baseball . . . resulted mainly in bringing some additional 'baseball players' into the gang."[103]

Nevertheless, a number of community reform programs continue to try to prevent and disrupt gang activity. A Crisis Intervention Network (CIN) was developed in Philadelphia to deal with the rising number of gang-related injuries and deaths in and around schools. This community-based project works to increase reporting of gang crime through daily school and teacher visits. It also works with community agencies and sponsors a "conflict-resolution team" to address problems that may lead to gang violence.[104] In Los Angeles, Community Youth Gang Services (CYGS) was established in 1981 to reduce gang membership and violence. CYGS has 14 teams comprised of a total of 60 counselors that work in the street to mediate gang disputes, re-direct gang activity, and share information with police.[105] A similar program in Chicago, called the "Chicago Intervention Network," attempts to reduce juvenile gang crime through similar methods, as well as job training and services to institutionalized delinquents.[106]

The conclusion of a book-length study and interviews with juvenile drug-gang members in Detroit was that this "urban gang subculture" can be countered only through a community effort involving families, schools, churches, businesses, and criminal justice agencies. Such a "team" community effort would fulfill three conditions necessary to eliminate the gangs:

- Alternative values that emphasize constructive service to others;
- Development of satisfying careers independent of material rewards; and
- Negative consequences of pursuing a criminal lifestyle.[107]

The National School Safety Center has joined with several professional athletes to talk with inner-city youth about values and goals to steer them away from gangs and drugs.[108] This adoption of role models is used in response to findings that athletes, regardless of background, are less likely to be involved in serious crimes than non-athletes. They also have a better self-image, peer status, and interest in school and studying. Adult role models for youth have been found generally to substitute for the lack of a male father figure in the homes of many gang members.[109]

Every public school student in Boston caught with a weapon in school is now sent to a center for five to 10 days for a psychological and educational assessment. A plan is then developed for working with the youth once they are placed back in school or in an alternative setting. In its first few years, the program has shown a great deal of success in preventing future violations.[110] The "Teens on Target" program in Oakland offers another approach to the school violence problem. Student volunteers are trained as violence-prevention advocates, and then work in schools to teach methods of mediation and violence prevention.[111]

Contemporary responses to the youth gang problem can be summarized as follows: community organization, youth outreach, school/job opportunities, and law enforcement.

An identified problem has been that social programs for youth have often clashed with law enforcement suppression strategies, although the CYGS program in Los Angeles has been an exception.[112]

Interviews with 47 members of 19 gangs in Milwaukee found them to evolve from "the development of an urban minority underclass in the last decades" that began in large cities and has spread to smaller ones. The researchers found the entrenchment of gangs cannot be solved "by policies of more police and more prisons."[113]

There have been few efforts to evaluate the effectiveness of the prevention programs now in progress, so their future potential and viability are unknown. One evaluation attempt targeted two groups of 8th grade students in Chicago who were identified by teachers and a non-profit youth service agency as "at risk" for gang membership. Gang informants also reported that these students were not currently gang members. One group received classroom and/or after school sessions regarding the dangers, consequences, and alternatives to gang involvement, while another participated in organized athletic activities after school. The other group received no treatment (control group). To ascertain subsequent gang membership at the end of the school year "informants" were again used. It was found that only one member of the treatment group and four members of the control group became gang members. As the evaluators noted, despite "methodological difficulties" in their approach, their findings "tended to support" the prediction that youth who participated in the program would be less likely to join street gangs.[114] Better "accuracy in the identification of youth who are at risk" for gang membership would enable greater certainty in pre- and post-evaluations of the success of prevention programs.[115]

Another promising approach is the "House of Umoja" which opened in Philadelphia more than 20 years ago. It employs the African extended family model, where the mother and father are a parent to all the juveniles placed there. There are strict house rules, enforced with a signed contract. The extended family values are designed to promote self-esteem and work against anti-social pressures. Replications of this model are underway, and their success will depend on staffs who can work with youth in hostile street settings.[116] Several other independent efforts to ameliorate the conditions that breed gang activity have also shown some success: a small construction company in California, founded by Baxter Sinclair, has 150 employees, all of whom are current or former gang members. Sinclair says, "I'm the father they never had."[117] Bill Lindsey, director of the Fort Lauderdale Housing Authority, obtained his job after moving into a privately owned tenement slum, hiring some ex-cons to help him evict dealers, organizing a rent strike, and cleaning up the building. Since then, he has cleaned up 10 other projects in other bad neighborhoods throughout the city.[118]

Breaking the Gang Delinquency Cycle

It is clear that something more is needed than police work and neighborhood outreach programs. A study of the causes of gang crimes in Chicago concluded, "community organization and social opportunity in conjunction with suppression, rather than simply suppression and incapacitation," may be a more effective policy in dealing with the gang

"Hey ladies, is this female gang stuff a new version of women's liberation?" "No it's just that you guys can't seem to get into trouble without killing each other!"

problem than either is by itself.[119] A similar ''communitywide reponse'' has been recommended by the U.S. Office of Juvenile Justice and Delinquency Prevention.[120] Rallies in Los Angeles, where the community protested the epidemic of gang-related crimes there, and the closing of a store in Boston, where the community protested its sale of gang paraphernalia, are early signs that some neighborhoods are ready to participate in needed social change.[121] There remain too many communities in which gang violence is tolerated, as long as gang members victimize each other and do not bother the rest of us.[122]

Without such a community-wide approach, the contemporary cycle of criminal youth gang activity will continue: police will continue to arrest gang members, and courts are more willing to incarcerate them than ever before (as shown in government reports of increasing trends in youth incarceration).[123] Those who go to prison have been found to join "branches" of their gang that have formed behind prison bars, while new "recruits" are quickly found to take their place on the street.[124] When those incarcerated are released, the street gang welcomes them back to "active" membership in the "dead zones" (i.e., interstitial areas) that continue to exist in many American cities.[125] Continued pressure from police and rival gangs results in expansion to even more cities.[126]

Clearly, the law enforcement response is a short-term solution at best. In New York City, for example, police officers were assigned to ride with students in certain subway cars to protect them from robberies en route after groups of youths had committed more than 150 robberies and assaults against students on the subway in less than four months.[127] Longer-term solutions, as opposed to these stop-gap measures, are sorely needed. Gangs must cease to become an attractive alternative to youth from poor city neighborhoods where most gangs reside. It has been reported that some Hispanic gangs in California have members who are sons of former gang members, resulting in a perverted sense of "family identity."[128]

Ray Gott of the Los Angeles County Sheriff's Department believes that juvenile and family courts should have the "power to order parental training . . . and to hold parents accountable," a strategy that could work only if families in gang neighborhoods are intact.[129] The evidence suggests that for many families in these areas, parental absence and lack of supervision is typical. As C. Ronald Huff concludes, "if families, schools, and churches don't socialize children to act responsibly, and if the national and local economies don't provide adequate *legal* opportunity structures, then we as a society are in deep trouble."[130]

Breaking this cycle of gang membership will not occur until more is done to change families and communities, so that such large numbers of young people do not live under conditions that offer so little hope or that provide little connection to conventional society and its goals and values.

NOTES

[1]Hood, Roger and Sparks, Richard. *Key Issues in Criminology,* McGraw-Hill, 1970; for a review, see Albanese, Jay S. *Dealing with Delinquency: The Future of Juvenile Justice,* 2nd ed. (Chicago: Nelson-Hall, 1993), ch. 2.

[2]Zimring, Frankling E. "Kids, Groups, and Crime: Some Implications of a Well-Known Secret," JOURNAL OF CRIMINAL LAW AND CRIMINOLOGY, Vol. 72, No. 3 (1981), pp. 867–85; Aultman, M.G. "Group Involvement in Delinquent Acts: A Study of Offense Types and Male–Female Participation," CRIMINAL JUSTICE AND BEHAVIOR, Vol. 7, No. 2 (June, 1980), pp. 185–92.

[3]Erickson, M. L. and Jensen, G. "Delinquency Is Still Group Behavior: Toward Revitalizing the Group Premise in the Sociology of Deviance," JOURNAL OF CRIMINAL LAW AND CRIMINOLOGY, Vol. 68 (1977), pp. 262–73 and Erickson, M. L. "The Group Context of Delinquent Behavior," SOCIAL PROBLEMS, Vol. 19 (1971), pp. 114–29.

[4]Miller, Walter B. "Gangs, Groups, and Serious Youth Crime," in Shichor, D. and Kelly, D. H. (eds.) *Critical Issues in Juvenile Delinquency,* (Lexington, MA: Lexington Books, 1980).

[5]Lyman, M. D. "Street Youth Gangs," in Lyman, Michael D. *Gangland: Drug Trafficking by Organized Criminals,* (Newbury Park, CA: Sage Publications, 1989), pp. 95–111.

[6]Kornhauser, Ruth R. *Social Sources of Delinquency* (Chicago: University of Chicago Press, 1978).

[7]Whyte, William F. *Street Corner Society* (Chicago: University of Chicago Press, 1943).

[8]Thrasher, Frederick. *The Gang* (Chicago: University of Chicago Press, 1927).

[9]Cloward, Richard A. and Ohlin, Lloyd E. *Delinquency and Opportunity: A Theory of Delinquent Gangs* (New York: The Free Press, 1960).

[10]Fagan, Jeffrey. "The Social Organization of Drug Use and Drug Dealing Among Urban Gangs," CRIMINOLOGY, Vol. 27 (1989), pp. 633–69.

[11]Huff, C. Ronald. "Youth Gangs and Public Policy," CRIME & DELINQUENCY, Vol. 35 (1989), pp. 524–37.

[12]Taylor, Carl S. "Gang Imperialism," in Huff, C. R. (ed.) *Gangs in America,* (Newbury Park, CA: Sage Publications, 1990), pp. 103–15.

[13]Miller, Walter B. *Violence by Youth Gangs as a Crime Problem in Major America Cities,* Washington, D.C.: U.S. Government Printing Office, 1975; Miller, "Gangs, Groups and Serious Youth Crime"; Klein, Malcolm W. and Maxson, Cheryl L. "Street Gang Violence," in Weiner, N. and Wolfgang, M. E. (eds.) *Violent Crime, Violent Criminals* (Newbury Park, CA: Sage Publications, 1989), p. 218.

[14] The definitive explanation of the labelling perspective was put forth by Lemert, Edwin M. *Social Pathology: A Systematic Approach to the Theory of Sociopathic Behavior* (New York: McGraw-Hall, 1951) and Becker, Howard. *The Outsiders: Studies in the Sociology of Deviance* (New York: Free Press, 1963).

[15] See Bookin-Weiner, H. and Horowitz, R. "End of the Youth Gang: Fad or Fact?" CRIMINOLOGY, Vol. 21, No. 4 (November, 1983), pp. 585–602 and Zatz, Marjorie. "Los Cholos: Legal Processing of Chicano Gang Members," SOCIAL PROBLEMS, Vol. 33 (1985), pp. 13–30.

[16]National Advisory Committee on Criminal Justice Standards and Goals, *Report of the Task Force on Juvenile Justice and Delinquency Prevention* (Washington, D.C.: U.S. Government Printing Office, 1976).

[17]Diego Vigil, James. "Cholos and Gangs: Culture Change and Street Youth in Los Angeles," in Huff, C. R. (ed.) *Gangs in America* (Newbury Park, CA: Sage Publications, 1990), pp. 116–28.

[18]Takata, S. R. and Zevitz, R. G. "Divergent Perceptions of Group Delinquency in a Midwestern Community: Racine's Gang Problem," YOUTH AND SOCIETY, Vol. 21, No. 3 (March, 1990), pp. 282–305.

[19]Ibid.

[20]Klein, M. W., Maxson, C. L., Cunningham, L. C., *Gang Involvement in Cocaine 'Rock' Trafficking,* (Washington, D.C.: National Institute of Justice, 1988).

[21]California Office of the Attorney General, *Report on Youth Gang Violence in California* (Washington, D.C.: National Institute of Justice, 1981).

[22]Bryant, Dan. "Communitywide Responses Crucial for Dealing with Youth Gangs," *Juvenile Justice Bulletin* (September, 1989), p. 2; Squitieri, Tom. "Just Another Night in Gangland USA," *USA Today* (December 8, 1989), p. 6.

[23]Fagan, Jeffrey. "Social Processes of Delinquency and Drug Use Among Urban Gangs," in Huff, C. R. (ed.) *Gangs in America* (Newbury Park, CA: Sage Publications, 1990), pp. 183–219.

[24]Simandl, Robert J. *Identification of Chicago Street Gangs,* Chicago Police Department Internal Report, 1983.

[25]Bensinger, G. J. "Chicago Youth Gangs: A New Old Problem," JOURNAL OF CRIME AND JUSTICE, Vol. 7 (1984), pp. 1–16.

[26]Bryant, "Communitywide Responses Crucial," p. 2.

[27]Price, Richard. "Crisis Has 'Destroyed All the Youth'," *USA Today* (December 7, 1989), p. 1; Spergel, Irving A. "Youth Gangs: Continuity and Change," CRIME AND JUSTICE, Vol. 12 (Chicago: University of Chicago Press, 1990), pp. 182–84.

[28]Brown, Barry. "Teen Gang Found with Guns for Sale," *Buffalo News* (January 13, 1991), p. 5.

[29]Sampson, Robert J. "Effects of Socioeconomic Context on Official Reaction to Juvenile Delinquency," *American Sociological Review,* Vol. 51 (1986), pp. 876–85; Johnstone, John W. "Youth Gangs and Black Suburbs," *Pacific Sociological Review,* Vol. 24, No. 3 (1981), pp. 355–75; Savitz, Leonard D., Rosen, Lawrence and Lalli, Michael. "Delinquency and Gang Membership as Related to Victimization," *Victimology,* Vol. 5 (1980), pp. 152–60; Diego Vigil, James and Long, John M. "Emic and Etic Perspectives on Gang Culture: The Chicano Case," in Huff, C. R. (ed.) *Gangs in America* (Newbury Park, CA: Sage Publications, 1990), pp. 55–68.

[30]For an analysis, see Albanese, Jay S. *Dealing with Delinquency,* ch. 2.

[31]Maxson, C. L., Gordon, M. A. and Klein, M. W. "Differences Between Gang and Non-Gang Homicides," CRIMINOLOGY, Vol. 23 (1985), pp. 209–22; Miller, *Violence By Youth Gangs and Youth Groups.*

[32]Miller, *Violence by Youth Gangs;* Spergel, "Youth Gangs: Continuity and Change," p. 190; Gordon Witkin, "Kids Who Kill," *U.S. News & World Report,* April 8, 1991, pp. 26–28.

[33]Needle, Jerome A. and Stapleton, William V. *Police Handling of Youth Gangs* (Washington, D.C.: National Institute of Justice, 1983); Miller, *Violence by Youth Gangs.*

[34]Maxson, Cheryl L. and Klein, Malcolm W. "Street Gang Violence: Twice as Great, or Half as Great?" in Huff, C. R. (ed.), *Gangs in America,* (Newbury Park, CA: Sage Publications, 1990), pp. 71–100.

[35]Hagedorn, J. and Macon, P. *People and Folks: Gangs, Crime, and the Underclass in a Rustbelt City,* (Chicago: Lake View Press, 1988).

[36]McKinney, Kay C. "Juvenile Gangs: Crime and Drug Trafficking," JUVENILE JUSTICE BULLETIN (September, 1988).

[37]Kupelian, David and Masters, Mark. "Gangs, Drugs, and Single-Parent Families," *New Dimensions* (May, 1990), p. 22.

[38]Bryant, Dan. "Communitywide Responses Crucial for Dealing with Youth Gangs," JUVENILE JUSTICE BULLETIN (September, 1989), p. 3.

[39]Ibid.

[40]Adams, Laurel. "Pattern is Repeating Itself Across the USA," *USA Today* (December 7, 1989), p. 6.

[41]Morganthau, Tom. "The Drug Gangs," *Newsweek* (March 28, 1988), p. 25.

[42]Squitieri, Tom. "East Texas City Takes 'Non-Tolerance' Stand Against Gangs," *USA Today* (December 8, 1989), p. 6.

[43]Forero, Juan. "6 Seized Here Linked to Violent L.A. Gang," *Buffalo News,* (February 9, 1990), p. 1; Lieberman, Paul. "Gangs Impact Spreads Far Beyond California," *Buffalo News* (February 11, 1990), p. 3.

[44]National School Safety Center, *Gangs in Schools: Breaking Up is Hard To Do* (Malibu, CA: Pepperdine University, 1988).

[45]Thrasher, *The Gang.*

[46]Spergel, Irving A. "The Violent Gang in Chicago: A Local Community Approach," *Social Service Review,* Vol. 60 (1986), pp. 94–131.

[47]Miller, "Gangs, Groups and Serious Youth Crime."

[48]Sullivan, Mercer L. *"Getting Paid": Youth Crime and Work in the Inner City* (Ithaca, NY: Cornell University Press, 1990); James F. Short, "Gangs, Neighborhoods, and Youth Crime," CRIMINAL JUSTICE RESEARCH BULLETIN, Vol. 5, No. 4 (1990), pp. 4–5.

[49]Albanese, Jay S. *Organized Crime in America,* 2nd. ed. (Cincinnati: Anderson Publishing, 1989).

[50]Miller, Walter. "The Impact of a 'Total Community' Delinquency Contrl Project," *Social Problems,* Vol. 10 (1962), pp. 168–69.

[51]Cited in Spergel, "Youth Gangs: Continuity and Change," p. 219.

[52]Miller, Walter. *Violence By Youth Gangs and Youth Groups as a Crime Problem in Major American Cities* (Washington, D.C.: U.S. Government Printing Office, 1975).

[53]Gottfredson, Gary D. and Gottfredson, Denise C. *Victimization in Schools* (New York: Plenum, 1985).

[54]Weisfeld, Glenn and Feldman, Roger. "A Former Street Gang Leader Re-Interviewed Eight Yeras Later," CRIME & DELINQUENCY, Vol. 28 (1982), pp. 567–81; Bowker, L. H., Gross, H. S. and Klein, M. W. "Female Participation in Delinquent Gang Activities," *Adolescence,* Vol. 15, No. 59 (Fall, 1980) pp. 509–19.

[55]Giordano, P. C. "Girls, Guys and Gangs: The Changing Social Context of Female Delinquency," JOURNAL OF CRIMINAL LAW AND CRIMINOLOGY, Vol. 69 (1978), pp. 126–32.

[56]Campbell, Anne. *The Girls in the Gang* (New York: Basil-Blackwell, 1984), pp. 236–37; see also Bowker, L. H. and Klein, M. W. "The Etiology of Female Juvenile Delinquency and Gang Membership: A Test of Psychological and Social Structural Explanations," *Adolescence,* Vol. 18 (1983), pp. 739–51.

[57]Hagedorn, John. *People and Folks: Gangs, Crime and the Underclass in a Rust Belt City* (Chicago: Lake View Press, 1988).

[58]Xu, J. "Brief Discussion of New Trends in the Development of Juvenile Delinquent Gangs," *Chinese Education,* Vol. 19, No. 2 (Summer, 1986), pp. 92–102.

[59]Campbell, Anne. "Female Participation in Gangs," in Huff, C. R. (ed.) *Gangs in America* (Newbury Park, CA: Sage Publications, 1990), pp. 163–82; Hagedorn, J. M. *People and Folks,* 1988.

[60]Joe, D. and Robinson, N. "Chinatown's Immigrant Gangs: The New Young Warrior Class," CRIMINOLOGY, Vol. 18 (1980), pp. 337–45; Brown, W. K. "Black Gangs as Family Extensions," *International Journal of Offender Therapy and Comparative Criminology,* Vol. 22 (1978), pp. 39–45; California Office of the Attorney General, *Report on Youth Gang Violence.*

[61]Bell, Daniel. "Crime As an American Way of Life," *The Antioch Review,* Vol. 13 (June, 1953), pp. 131–54.

[62]Virgil, James. *Barrio Gangs* (Austin: University of Texas Press, 1988).

[63]Chin, Ko-lin. *Chinese Subculture and Criminality: Non-Traditional Crime Groups in America* (Westport, CT: Greenwood Press, 1990); Diego Vigil, James and Chong Yun, Steve. "Vietnamese Youth Gangs in Southern California," in Huff, C. R. (ed.) *Gangs in America* (Newbury Park, CA: Sage Publications, 1990), pp. 146–62.

[64]Stewart, Sally Ann. "Drugs, Violence, Rituals, Slaves," *USA Today* (December 7, 1989), p. 6; "Beaten Teenager Tells of 'Death Penalty'," *Buffalo News* (March 25, 1990); Campbell, A., Munce, S. and Galea, J. "American Gangs and British Subcultures: A Comparison," *International Journal of Offender Therapy and Comparative Criminology,* Vol. 26, No. 1 (1982), pp. 76–92; Dolan, Edward F., Jr. and Finney, Shawn. *Youth Gangs* (New York: Julian Messner, 1984).

[65]Jackson, Patrick G. "Theories and Findings About Youth Gangs," *Criminal Justice Abstracts* (June, 1989), pp. 313–29; Jackson, Robert K. and McBride, Wesley D. *Understanding Street Gangs* (Cosa Mesa, CA: Custom Publishing, 1985).

[66]See Siegel, Larry J. and Senna, Joseph J. *Juvenile Delinquency: Theory, law, Practice* (St. Paul: West Publishing, 1991), pp. 290–91.

[67]Lyman, "Street Youth Gangs," pp. 95–111.

[68]Taylor, C. S. *Dangerous Society,* (East Lansing, MI: Michigan State University Press, 1989).

[69]Vigil, J. D. "Group Processes and Street Identity: Adolescent Chicano Gang Members," *Ethos,* Vol. 16, No. 4 (December, 1988), pp. 421–45.

[70]Lagree, J. and Fai, P. L. "Girls in Street Gangs in the Suburbs of Paris," in Cain, Maureen (ed.) *Growing Up Good: Policing the Behavior of Girls in Europe,* (Newbury Park, CA: Sage Publications, 1989), pp. 80–95.

[71]Cloward, Richard A. and Ohlin, Lloyd E. *Delinquency and Opportunity,* Glencoe, IL: The Free Press, 1960.

[72]Cohen, Albert K. *Delinquent Boys,* Glencoe, IL: The Free Press, 1955.

[73]Block, Herbert and Niederhoffer, Arthur. *The Gang: A Study in Adolescent Behavior* (New York: Philosophical Library, 1958).

[74]Sarnecki, J. *Criminal Juvenile Gangs* (Stockholm: Brottsforebyggande Radet, 1983); Spergel, "Youth Gangs: Continuity and Change," pp. 172–73.

[75]Curry, G. David and Spergel, Irving A. "Gang Homicide, Delinquency, and Community," CRIMINOLOGY, Vol. 26, No. 3 (August, 1988), p. 401.

[76]McKinney, "Juvenile Gangs," p. 6.

[77]Reiss, Albert J. "Co-Offending and Criminal Careers," in Tonry, M. and Morris, N. (eds.) *Crime and Justice: A Review of Research,* Vol. 10 (Chicago: University of Chicago Press, 1988).

[78]For a review, see Spergel, "Youth Gangs: Continuity and Change," pp. 239–40.

[79]Bradley, Tom. "The New Los Angeles is Hard to Believe," *USA Today* (July 23, 1990), p. 11.

[80]McKinney, Kay C. "Juvenile Gangs: Crime and Drug Trafficking," *Juvenile Justice Bulletin* (September, 1988), p. 3.

[81]Squitieri, Tom. "Boston Braces for Summer Gang Wars," *USA Today* (May 22, 1990), p. 3.

[82]Bryant, Dan. "Communitywide Responses Crucial for Dealing with Youth Gangs," JUVENILE JUSTICE BULLETIN (September, 1989), p. 1.

[83]Sherman, Lawrence W. "Police Crackdowns: Initial and Residual Deterrence," in Tonry, M. and Morris, N. (eds.) *Crime and Justice: A Review of Research,* Vol. 12 (Chicago: University of Chicago Press, 1990), pp. 1–48.

[84]Reuter, Peter, Haaga, John, Murphy, Patrick and Praskac, Amy. *Drug Use and Drug Programs in the Washington Metropolitan Area* (Santa Monica, CA: Rand Corporation, 1988).

[85]Kleiman, Mark A. R. "Crackdowns: The Effects of Intensive Enforcement on Retail Heroin Dealing," in Chaiken, M. (ed.) *Street Level Drug Enforcement: Examing the Issues* (Washington, D.C.: National Institute of Justice, 1988).

[86]Cockburn, Alexander. "Los Angeles Can't Win Drug War by Cracking the Whip," *The Wall Street Journal* (May 5, 1988).

[87]Lyman, M. D. "Secret Youth Gangs," pp. 95–111.

[88]McKinney, "Juvenile Gangs," p. 4.

[89]Ibid.

[90]McKinney, Kay C. "Juvenile Gangs," p. 5.

[91]Moore, Mark H. and Kleiman, Mark A. R. "The Police and Drugs," *Perspectives on Policing*, No. 11 (September, 1989), p. 8.

[92]Ibid.

[93]Bryant, "Communitywide Responses Crucial," p. 2.

[94]*United States v. Harrell*, 737 F.2d 971 (1984).

[95]*People v. Anderson*, 153 Ill. App. 3d. 542, 505 N.E.2d. 1303 (1987).

[96]See *People v. Deacon*, 473 N.E.2d. 1354, *cert. denied* 106 S.Ct. 253 (1985); *People v. Connally*, 481 N.Y.S.2d 432 (1984); *Commonwealth v. Mason*, 358 Pa. Super. Ct. 562, 518 A.2d 282 (1986); For an analysis, see Theuman, John E. "Admissibility of Evidence of Accused's Membership in Gang," AMERICAN LAW REPORTS, Vol. 39 (1985), pp. 775–85.

[97]Stewart, Sally Ann. "Critics Doubt New L.A. Laws Will Curb Gangs," *USA Today* (September 28, 1988), p. 3.

[98]"New Weapons Against Gangs," *USA Today* (April 21, 1989), p. 3.

[99]Schlossman, S. L. and Sedlak, M. *The Chicago Area Project Revisited* (Santa Monica, CA: Rand Corporation, 1983).

[100]Weissman, Harold H. (ed.) *Justice and the Law in the Mobilization for Youth Experience* (New York: Association Press, 1969).

[101]Klein, Malcolm W. "Gang Cohesiveness, Delinquency, and a Street-Work Program," *Journal of Research in Crime & Delinquency*, Vol. 6 (1969), pp. 135–66.

[102]Miller, Walter B. "The Impact of a 'Total-Community' Delinquency Control Project," *Social Problems*, Vol. 10 (Fall, 1962), pp. 168–91.

[103]Yablonsky, Lewis. *The Violent Gang* (New York: Macmillan, 1962), p. 53.

[104]Swans, B. J. Jr. "Gangbusters: Crisis Intervention Network," *School Safety*, (Winter, 1985), pp. 12–15.

[105]"Confessions of a Homegirl," *New Dimensions* (May, 1990), pp. 36–39; McKinney, "Juvenile Gangs," pp. 5–6.

[106]McKinney, "Juvenile Gangs," pp. 5–6; Martin, Robert. "Effective Juvenile Delinquency Prevention Model," Statement before the Federal Coordinating Council on Juvenile Justice and Delinquency Prevention, June 22, 1988.

[107]Taylor, C. S. Dangerous Society, pp. 120ff.

[108]National School Safety Center, *Role Models, Sports and Youth: NSSC Resource Paper*, (Washington, D.C.: Office of Juvenile Justice and Delinquency Prevention, 1989).

[109]Santoli, Al. "What Can Be Done About Teen Gangs?" *Parade Magazine*, March 24, 1991, pp. 16–19.

[110]Witkin, "Kids Who Kill," p. 32.

[111]Ibid.

[112]Spergel, I. A. *Youth Gangs: Problem and Response,* (Washington, D.C.: Office of Juvenile Justice and Delinquency Prevention, 1989).

[113]Hagedorn, J. and Macon, P. *People and Folks,* p. 200ff.

[114]Thompson, David W. and Jason, Leonard A. "Street Gangs and Preventive Interventions," *Criminal Justice and Behavior: An International Journal,* Vol. 15, No. 3 (September, 1988), pp. 323–33.

[115]Thompson, D. and Jason, L. "Street Gangs and Preventive Interventions," p. 331.

[116]Fattah, David. "The House of Umoja as a Case Study for Social Change," *The Annals,* Vol. 494 (November, 1987), pp. 37–41.

[117]Stewart, Sally Ann. "Employer is 'Father' to Hard-Case Crew," *USA Today* (March 23, 1990), p. 6.

[118]Moore, Thomas. "Dead Zones," *U.S. News & World Report* (April 10, 1989), p. 30.

[119]Curry, G. and Spergel, I. "Gang Homicide, Delinquency, and Community," p. 401.

[120]Spergel, Irving A. and Chance, Ronald L. "National Youth Gang Suppression and Intervention Program," *National Institute of Justice Reports* (June, 1991), pp. 21–24; Bryant, "Communitywide Responses Crucial," pp. 4–5.

[121]El Nasser, Haya. "L.A. Rally Theme is Gangs Hurt Everyone," *USA Today* (March 30, 1990), p. 2; Squitieri, Tom. "Boston Braces for Summer Gang Wars," *US Today* (May 22, 1990), p. 3.

[122]Horowitz, Ruth. "Community Tolerance of Gang Violence," *Social Problems,* Vol. 34, No. 5 (December, 1987), pp. 437–50.

[123]Kline, Sue. *Children in Custody* (Washington, D.C.: Bureau of Justice Statistics, 1989).

[124]Jacobs, James B. *New Perspectives on Prisons and Imprisonment* (Ithaca, NY: Cornell University Press, 1983); Moore, Joan W., Garcia, Robert, Garcia, Carolos, Cerda, Luis and Valencia, Frank. *Homeboys: Gangs, Drugs, and Prison in the Barrios of Los Angeles* (Philadelphia: Temple University Press, 1978); Bryant, "Communitywide Responses Crucial," pp. 3–4.

[125]Moore, Thomas. "Dead Zones," pp. 20–32.

[126]McKinney, "Juvenile Gangs," p. 6; Bryant, "Communitywide Responses Crucial," p. 3.

[127]"Subway Police Protect N.Y. Students," *USA Today* (May 15, 1990), p. 3.

[128]Jackson, Robert K. and McBride, Wesley D. *Understanding Street Gangs* (Cosa Mesa, CA: Custom Publishing, 1985), p. 42.

[129]Santoli, "What Can be Done About Teen Gangs?," p. 18.

[130]Huff, C. Ronald. "Denial, Overreaction, and Misidentification: A Postscript on Public Policy," in Huff, C. R. (ed.) *Gangs in America* (Newbury Park, CA: Sage Publications, 1990), p. 316.

CHAPTER 8

Crimes Involving the Family

CONTENTS

In this chapter, we will be examining what have come to be called ''family crimes''—crimes committed among family members in which the victim is another member of the family. It is included in a book on contemporary crime issues because it is another of those crime topics which is both significant and gaining in interest. And like other new and evolving forms of crime, it has been ''discovered'' as an important problem—one that until a few short years ago was largely ignored or unrecognized. Attention will focus on what these offenses are, what we know and don't know about this form of criminal behavior, policies adopted by some agencies of criminal justice to deal with these offenses, important legal issues, and existing and future concerns.

Traditionally, family offenses have included crimes of domestic or spousal violence, abusive violence, and sexual offenses involving children. Some states have also added the category of ''criminal neglect'' as an offense against children. Recently, a new concern, criminal abuse by family members of the elderly, has also been added to the list of family crimes. This does not, however, include the growing concern over crime and violence to elderly victims by non-family care providers. As we have become more aware of the seriousness and the widespread prevalence of these particular offenses, increased interest has grown in these forms of criminal behavior. This has contributed to a general growing awareness of family crime by special interest and citizen groups, social scientists, the media, public policymakers, and the criminal justice system. Today, these groups are increasingly involved in reporting the problem, analyzing its many forms, and looking for strategies to deal with family offenses.

Crimes of violence committed by family members upon other family members is only one part of the family crime picture. Another form of family crime is non-violent offenses. The theft or illegal conversion of the property of an elder family member by his or her children is also a form of ''family crime.'' In some cases, the existence of a ''family'' relationship is inconsequential to what has been loosely lumped into family crime. For instance, the violent injury of a cohabitee by a live-in partner has tended to be lumped into the broad term ''family crime.'' While these types of actions may be more clearly understood as criminal events, much of what passes for ''family crime'' is also included in the catch-all term of ''family abuse.''

For example, psychologists may consider and lump such abusive behaviors as psychological or verbal abuse of spouses and elderly family members as forms of ''family violence.'' For our purposes, these latter forms of abuse will not be considered forms of ''family crime'' nor the subject of this chapter.* Such abusive behaviors are inappropriate to our examination of crimes against family members because they exceed the boundaries of both warranted and practical intervention by the criminal law and the administration of justice.

*For purposes of discussion in this chapter ''family crime'' will be those acts in which violence in the form of physical or sexual abuse is imposed by one family member on another or acts which constitute conventional crimes is intrafamilial in nature.

An Initial Problem: Measuring Family Crime

Using violence as a defining characteristic of what constitutes family crime leads us into another problem area. We simply have no reliable measure of how often family violence, which can be considered criminal in nature, occurs. In spite of the attention family violence has received, the actual extent of the problem remains largely hidden. Although students of crime have learned a great deal about conventional offenses during the last 20 years, we still have very little in the way of a meaningful understanding of criminal family violence. Unfortunately, this has not prevented a certain amount of sensationalism and exploitation of the subject. The host of a popular television talkshow recently spoke of "millions of cases annually in which victims of family violence suffered in silence and fear." While such pronouncements may generate viewer interest, concern must be expressed about such sweeping generalizations in view of what little is known about reliable estimates of its incidence.

Various studies have produced widespread estimates of the magnitude of the problem of criminal violence in the family. Official statistics of the extent of the problem rely on our nation's two major crime recording systems: The Uniform Crime Reports (UCR) and the National Crime Survey (NCS). These provide only incomplete estimates on the overall incidence of the problem. At best, they only highlight the possible extent of these crimes. Some data are also available from professionals who work with victims of family violence at the local level. Still, such local agency-generated data do not contribute to our understanding of the extent of the problem on a national level. These are typically small studies and their samples are likely unrepresentative. They are more prone to capture the incidence of violence primarily among lower class families. These data also suffer from the fact that any such available administrative statistics show a wide variation in the way they are collected and compiled. There are, for instance, wide difference among state and local jurisdictions not only in reporting requirements, but in how scrupulously such data are gathered. Administrative statistics on spousal or child-directed criminal violence and other forms of family problems are strongly affected by such things as the extent to which programs are available to cope with the problem, the number of social workers and other professionals employed to deal with family violence issues, the extent of attention given to developing careful statistical records, and the ways in which various abusive behaviors are defined and classified.[1] Those jurisdictions which record the highest incidence of criminal family violence are those who address the largest resources to the problem.[2]

There are also such governmental and private organizations as the National Clearinghouse on Child Abuse, the National Children's Advocacy Center, and the National Coalition Against Domestic Violence which compile data and provide information in their areas of interest. However, such organizations for the most part are not in the busines of compiling original data. They rely on published statistical reports such as the UCR and the NCS for their information. They are as captive to the statistical incompleteness of these sources as anyone. There have also been some noteworthy efforts by individual researchers to examine the problem. The Family Violence Research Program at the University of New Hampshire has done some extensive work in interviewing family members about intra-family conflict and violence. Based upon their interviews of more than 2,000 couples they, too, have made some projected national estimates.[3]

Uniform Crime Reports

Since one often-quoted source for statistics on certain aspects of family crime is the UCR, let's look at this crime measurement program for purposes of illustration. The Federal Bureau of Investigation compiles data supplied by reporting police agencies throughout the country. To appear in the UCR, the crime must have been reported to the police or the police must have discovered the crime. It is widely recognized that this leads to underreporting of criminal events in the UCR. Many crimes are simply not reported or otherwise come to the attention of law enforcement authorities. This is especially true in the case with family crimes.

In the UCR, these reported crimes are then broken down into eight serious "Index crimes" and a miscellany of less serious "Part II" offenses. Although one of the Part II crimes contained in the UCR deals with the category of offenses against the family and children, nobody would suggest that this crime category accurately captures the incidence of family violence or family-generated property crime victimization. While such offenses as homicide, rape, aggravated assault, robbery and larceny are included in the Index crimes, and simple assault is categorized under Part II offenses, as presently compiled, there is no way of telling whether these are committed by strangers, acquaintances, or family members.

The FBI recognizes the problem and has discussed the need for more complete statistics on family violence. This agency is also trying to move to an incident-based UCR reporting format which would capture more information about criminal events including aspects of victim-perpetrator relationships and the characteristics of arrested offenders. A more comprehensive and illuminating system, however, still seems some years away.

There is one exception to this limitation of the UCR. In recent years, the FBI has made some notable efforts to examine at least one particular offense more closely—the crime of homicide. In this single crime category, attention has focused on the relationship of the victim to the perpetrator. Since this new form of analysis has begun, it has been shown that of all known homicides committed in the United States which come to the attention of the police and subsequently find their way into the UCR, between 15 to 17 percent are committed by family members.

Still, this only ripples the surface. Less serious offenses like simple assault, which undoubtedly makeup many family violence cases, are likely prime candidates for under reporting especially if they involve a family member assault. Since these simple assaults are not analyzed as homicide cases, as to the relationships between the perpetrator and the victim, the incidence of family violence-related simple assault cases is unknown. From such omissions we cannot use crime statistics from police departments as represented by the UCR to develop anything approaching reliable family violence estimates on a national basis.

The National Crime Survey

There is a second national crime reporting system which may provide us with a little better estimate of family violence crimes. The National Crime Survey, sponsored by the Bureau of Justice Statistics, annually collects information on criminal victimization. It seems to capture some of the crimes which are not reported to the police and, thus, do not find their way into the UCR. Interviews are conducted in 49,000 households throughout the United States. Each person in the household (a total of about 100,000 individuals) is asked about certain target crimes which they may have been a victim of in the past six months. These same sample households are included in the survey for a period of three years so repeated acts of criminal victimization are recorded. If a person answers affirmatively to any of the screening questions, a detailed questionnaire is administered. In this way, the survey offers the potential for providing statistical information about various aspects of family violence, but only those events that a victim is willing to report in a survey of this nature.

Like the UCR, however, the NCS underestimates the prevalence of crimes by family members. There are a number of well-recognized problems with this technique. Although interviewers are encouraged to interview each respondent privately if possible, there may be other family members present during the interview. The victims may not feel free to discuss an incident if the offender is present. Victims may simply be too intimidated to tell the interviewer about the problem. Members of minority groups may not trust the official nature of such a government-sponsored interview or the interviewer. Middle-class respondents may be too embarrassed to admit their family-related victimization to a stranger. It has also been found that some victims regard victimization by non-strangers—especially family members—as a private matter and, therefore, do not define it as a crime. There is also evidence that the NCS doesn't adequately measure ''serial victimization'' where a victim experiences a number of similar crimes over a relatively short period of time.[4]

A final problem with the NCS and its attempts to uncover family crimes is that the survey measures crimes against people 12 years and older. Children under that age, who are victimized by relatives, will not be included in the estimates.[5] Undoubtedly, the most difficult information to obtain from such survey methodology is information on child abuse. Of all the family crimes, abusive acts of violence—both sexual and non-sexual involving children remain the most deeply hidden. During the early 1980s, additional research was conducted to determine if improved survey methodology could be used in the NCS to get information from younger children.

Efforts to develop such a strategy proved unsuccessful. The problem was not unexpected. Professionals working with abused children have found that a high level of trust is necessary for the child to feel free to describe what has happened to him or her. A survey interviewer who spends only a few minutes in the home asking general screening questions is unlikely to be able to establish the required trust in the brief time available. These problems are further compounded when a parent or another relative is the offender. Even if interviewers from the NCS could possibly interview children privately (which of course is unworkable), there would also be the problem of understanding on the part of the child and, of course, the reliability of any information obtained. This doesn't even take into consideration the "sensitive" nature and the legally questionable intrusiveness of any such survey technique where children are questioned.

Although the NCS has important limitations and shortcomings in capturing the incidence of family violence, it exists as the best national source we have. Perhaps it can then provide us with some general insights into the prevalence of intrafamilial violence. For this reason alone, it deserves more than passing attention. A few years ago, the NCS tried to assess through its surveys this question of the occurrence of family violence incidents on a national basis. The findings for this nine-year analysis are seen in Table 8.1.

While these family-based crimes only accounted for 7.2 percent of all violent crimes reported in the survey during these years, they show some interesting facts. Not unexpectedly, nearly 57 percent of NCS-based family crimes involving violence were committed by spouses or ex-spouses. As to the nature of the violent crimes committed by relatives, 88 percent were assaults, 10 percent were robberies, and 2 percent were rapes. Of the assaults, about a third were aggravated, indicating the use of a weapon and/or serious injury. The remaining two-thirds were simple assaults, indicating either a minor injury or a threat of harm.[6]

In nearly a third of all family violence incidents, the violator used some type of weapon. A gun or knife was used in about 20 percent of the cases in which there was an assault with a weapon. Where weapons were involved, these were used to either harm or threaten the victim. In all cases involving family violence, victims suffered an injury rate of about 50 percent. Fortunately, most of the attacks found the family victim incurring only such injuries as bruises, black eyes, cuts, or scratches. Apparently, family violence, when it does occur, is more likely to involve the use of fists and kicking or striking the victim. When a weapon is used, it typically is a weapon less lethal than a gun or knife.

Although it has been suggested that family violence—especially spousal or ex-spousal violence—strikes all socio-economic categories equally, this was not demonstrated from incidents reported to interviewers. The evidence indicated that all forms of family violence (spousal or ex-spousal violence, violence toward children, and attacks by relatives) were more likely to occur among black respondents.[7] It was clear from the data

TABLE 8.1 ESTIMATED FAMILY VIOLENCE REPORTED TO THE NATIONAL CRIME SURVEY BY RELATIONSHIP OF OFFENDER TO VICTIM (1973–1981)*

Relationship	*Total Incidents (%)*	*Annual Average*
Total by all relatives	4,108,000 (100.0)	456,000
Spouses or ex-spouses	2,333,000 (56.8)	259,000
Parents	263,000 (6.4)	29,000
Children	173,000 (4.2)	19,000
Brothers or sisters	351,000 (8.5)	39,000
Other relatives	988,000 (24.1)	110,000

*All estimates are rounded to nearest thousand.

Source: Bureau of Justice Statistics, *Family Violence* (Washington, D.C.: U.S. Department of Justice, April 1984), p. 3.

reported that lower-income persons and those in the 20 to 34 age range were more likely than other ages or income groups to be victims of family violence. As income levels increased, reported incidents of family violence fell off sharply. Women were also much more likely to suffer a violent assault at the hands of a family member than men. In fact, the reported incidence levels were in the order of almost 14 to 1. Victims reported resisting about three-fourths of the attacks by their relatives, but this resistance usually was a form of passive resistance such as trying to reason with the offender or trying to get away or obtain help. This occurred not only in acts involving spousal violence, but in all family violence incidents.[8]

Finally, the NCS interviewers tried to determine, in those cases of family violence which were not reported to the police, why the victim chose not to involve the authorities. The vast majority of respondents felt that the matter was personal or private and did not warrant reporting. This was by far the most frequent answer given. Less important as a reason for non-reporting was the fear of reprisal. Although some of the interviewed victims listed fear of reprisal as the major reason for not bringing the matter to the attention of the authorities, it did not seem to figure into their decision as strongly as might be thought. There was also the expressed feeling by the family crime victims interviewed that little could be accomplished by reporting their victimization to the police. Victims felt that they lacked any proof upon which law enforcement authorities could act or it wasn't important enough to justify calling the police or to involve police time.

These incidence estimates tell us certain things: First, family violence is a widespread problem and many acts of violence appear criminal in nature. Where physical harm has occurred, the offense of assault exists. There are also the crimes of threatening and reckless endangerment involved. Still, however, the "legal" extent of the "criminality" of these acts goes unanswered from such data. For example, acts of assault must determine who is the aggressor (or if there was co-aggression) in determining if an act of assault is prosecutable under the criminal law and/or existing prosecution practices. Of course, there also is always the question of the veracity of the respondents in any such survey. These are questions which will never be answered. Unfortunately, however, it is knowledge of these kinds of facts which are required for a better understanding of the problem and the role the criminal justice system can play.

Although the reader may get the impression from the preceeding discussion that the NCS is a far better indicator of at least family violence than the UCR, there is another issue. While it is true that the NCS may do this, the UCR, in fact, may be more beneficial for our use in another way. If we want to study the response of the criminal justice system to family crime, the UCR, since it deals better with the disposition of crimes reported to or discovered by the police, may be more useful for our understanding of how the criminal justice system responds when dealing with such criminal events.

At this point, we want to examine individually the crimes of domestic violence, abusive acts of violence against children and crimes against elderly family members. The discussion of each of these offenses should show the reader that they share common problems for understanding. They often raise similar issues as to what needs to be done to cope more effectively with the problems they pose. On the other hand, one should recognize that while they share some remarkable similarities, they also demonstrate some important differences. These differences mainly revolve around the characteristics of the class of victims.

Crimes of Domestic Violence

The National Crime Survey conservatively estimates that over 500,000 women annually are victims of a form of domestic violence which is criminal in nature. These victimizations occurred at least once during an average 12-month period. A significant characteristic of these victims is that they faced relatively high risks of exposure to recurring violence. During the six months after they experienced an act of violence, it was estimated that nearly one-third of the women were again victimized. Many of these crimes are not isolated instances; they are crimes which tend to victimize the same women repeatedly and generally by the same assailant. Many of the women in the NCS survey seemed unable to breakout from this cycle of repetitive violence. In fact, many of these women were victimized an average of three times. Domestic violence victimization seems to be much more likely to occur and, once it has occurred, to be repeated than crimes committed by strangers. Once a woman has been exposed to an act of domestic violence, she is much more apt to experience another such experience—and in a relatively short period of time—than is a victim of a stranger-to-stranger crime likely to experience another such form of victimization.

Domestic violence or spousal assault, especially when women are victims, became an important issue in the 1970s. Much of the impetus for this increased attention came from women's groups and victims' rights advocates. As these groups became a growing political force with local, state, and national political organizations, they were instrumental in the development of the shelter movement as an outgrowth of the domestic violence issue. Feminist groups were also successful in fostering other changes in the criminal law that women felt were particularly discriminatory. Two such notable changes are the modification of rape laws to include "marital rape" and to curtail sharply the use by the defense of the sexual history of a rape victim as an issue in rape trials.

In terms of domestic violence issues, one important statutory change is the adoption by many states of warrantless misdemeanor arrest powers for the police in such cases. Perhaps the most radical and controversial occurrence has been the recognition, primarily in certain case law holdings, of the "abused spouse syndrome." This has been established in a few well-publicized trials as a defense in cases where a woman murders her husband or lover and the killing is viewed as a justifiable homicide based on the batterer's past violent and abusive behavior.

These changes have injected themselves into the operations of the criminal justice system. The terms "domestic violence" and "domestic assault" are often used interchangeably. Generally, the use of these terms in their relationship to criminal offenses include any aggravated or simple assault, rape, or robbery committed against a married, divorced, or separated woman by a relative or other person well known to the victim.[9]

Although most instances of domestic violence would fall into the less serious legal category of a simple assault, such a legal category tends to mask the fact that, even in these cases, there is often some form of injury associated with the act. Many of these simple assaults are, in fact, relatively serious. As Langan and Innes say of this "masking problem" of domestic violence:

> Victim injury is at least as common among domestic crimes that would be classified as simple assaults as it is among felonies that would be classified as rape, robbery and aggravated assault. Moreover, in terms of actual bodily injury, as many as half of all incidents of domestic violence that police would classify as misdemeanors are as serious as or more serious than 90 percent of all the violent crimes that police would classify as felonies. The reason is that the presence or absence of victim injury is not critical [to the authorities] when deciding to classify a crime as a felony or misdemeanor. What is critical, however, is the presence or absence of a weapon. . . . This suggests that traditional ways of distinguishing felonies from misdemeanors may have the unintended effect of masking the seriousness of domestic violence.[10]

Domestic Violence Crimes and the Criminal Justice System

Police Response to Domestic Violence

Among criminal justice agencies, the primary role in dealing with domestic violence has been given to the police. America's local law enforcement agencies handle thousands of calls annually to "domestic disturbance" situations. Certainly not all of these are instances of spousal abuse. What these calls reveal is a wide range of domestic problems, including disturbing the peace, missing persons, drunk and disorderly conduct, property damage, trespassing, verbal arguments, threats of violence, minor assaults, aggravated assaults, and even homicides. Still, many of these incidents do not involve any criminal offense and some of those that do, involve non-violence between family members.[11]

Prior to the 1970s, the police generally followed a "hands-off" policy which eschewed making arrests in most domestic disturbance situations. Even such professional police organizations as the International Association of Chiefs of Police (IACP) suggested, in their training manuals, that the police would be better advised not to make arrests in responding to domestic violence situations.[12] It was felt that such "family problems" were more properly the province of social service and family assistance agencies. These agencies had the training and resources more appropriate to the task of dealing with these problems than did the criminal justice system.

Beginning in the 1970s, however, this idea began to change. In its place, a "strict enforcement" view began to take shape. This was the idea that arrest and stricter application of criminal sanctions would better protect victims and reduce the risk of subsequent violence.[13] A timeworn and traditional police practice of trying to merely mediate the violence or referring the case to a social service agency began to be called into question. This change seemed to come about not so much as a result of the idea that arrest policies were a better strategy (although this would supposedly be later demonstrated) as was the growing recognition that existing police policies in handling these types of cases did not seem to be working. This, in turn, was brought about by the public's growing interest in dealing more effectively with domestic and family violence.

The Police Begin to Examine New Ways to Deal with Domestic Violence

Buzawa and Buzawa have done an excellent analysis of tracing the factors which have caused many police agencies to change past practices of how they deal with crimes of domestic violence.[14] The reader is encouraged to look at this source. Among other things, change has been brought about by pressures from feminist groups, legal liability issues, funding priorities of certain federal agencies and their family crisis intervention demonstration project efforts.

Also important were the 1982 Report by the U.S. Civil Rights Commission, the 1984 recommendations of the Attorney General's Report on Family Violence, and the findings by some research efforts first conducted in the late 1970s. Together, a number of things were happening. These research efforts seem to be especially important. Research which examined domestic violence and police response to "domestic disturbance" calls began to call into question the traditional police methods of handling such calls.

The research undertaken by the Police Foundation into domestic violence in Kansas City, Missouri was especially important. It provided a framework for rethinking the traditional responses of the police to such acts of violence.[15] Using police records, the study examined domestic assaults and domestic homicides which occurred in that city over a period of two years. It was found that in the two years preceeding a serious domestic assault or homicide, in half of the cases, the police had been called to the address at least five times to handle a domestic distubance call.[16]

This raised both disturbing and thought-provoking questions. Obviously, the police have early recognition of possible problems of domestic violence. Could some of these serious resulting acts of violence have been prevented had the police taken a different course of action from those they typically employed in handling domestic disturbance calls? These findings also called into question the developing proactive response of police—something which was gaining greater emphasis in professional police circles. Rather than typically responding in a reactive nature to the need for police services, the police should devote more attention and resources to identifying proactive strategies which might prevent crimes.

One such proactive strategy was the question of what the police could do to prevent crimes of domestic violence—or at least their recurrence. It wasn't clear what the police might do at the time to try to prevent such crimes, but it did focus attention on an issue which sought a more effective police response.

It was within this framework that the issue of police effectiveness was addressed. In 1981, the National Institute of Justice in conjunction with the Minneapolis, Minnesota Police Department agreed to participate in an effort to see what specific strategy the

The Legal Impetus for Changing Traditional Police Handling of Domestic Violence

In recent years, a major reason our nation's police have been more willing to exercise their newly created arrest powers in cases involving domestic violence was the result of a civil suit against the police department and the city of Torrington, Connecticut.* Undoubtedly, this got the attention of police administrators and their employing communities.

In the *Thurman* case, Ms. Thurman and other relatives had repeatedly called the police pleading for help and protection for Ms. Thurman, who's estranged husband had threatened to shoot her and her son. In spite of these pleas, the police virtually ignored the situation. These threats to Ms. Thurman and her son occurred during a time when her estranged husband was already on probation as a result of a conviction for damaging her property. When she called the police they told her to return three weeks later and to get a restraining order in the meantime. This occurred even though they had the legal authority to take action.

Ms. Thurman then obtained the restraining order. Her estranged husband again threatened her after she had the court order. She again called the police. Again, they refused to arrest him giving the excuse that it was a holiday weekend and they were shorthanded. Some days later, she again called the police and insisted that he be arrested for his continuing threats. The Torrington police gave her the excuse that the only officer that could arrest him was on vacation. It was obvious that the police discounted her pleas for help and were probably irritated by this bothersome woman. The situation culminated when her estranged husband, in a rage, attacked her. She suffered multiple stab wounds to the chest and throat, resulting in permanent paralysis and disfigurement. She filed for civil damages for the lack of police assistance.

Her attorneys argued that the police had been negligent in performing their duties and in not protecting Ms. Thurman after repeated calls for help. The police, it was argued, have a sworn duty to protect citizens and, when requested, have a responsibility to take reasonable action to prevent subsequent victim injury from a known offender. The lawyers also argued that the police by ignoring her requests violated her Fourteenth Amendment rights of "due process" and "equal protection." The claim was based upon the differential treatment accorded to a man who batters his spouse as compared to an assault by a stranger. Since most victims of spousal violence are women, there was also the clear element of sex discrimination in the handling of the case.

**Thurman v. City of Torrington,* 595 F. Supp. 1521 (D. Conn. 1984).

Author's note: The federal courts following the *Thurman* case have generally held that the police, absent special circumstances, generally have no duty to protect citizens against domestic violence at least as far as this failure to protect constitutes a violation of the victim's constitutional rights. See

DeShaney v. Winnebago County Department of Social Services, 109 S.Ct. 998 (1989); *Balistreri v. Pacifica Police Department*, 901 F.2d 696 (9th Cir. 1990); and *McKee v. City of Rockwall, Texas*, 877 F.2d 409 (5th Cir. 1989), *cert. denied*, 110 S.Ct. 727 (1990). However, this does not preclude the possibility for successful lawsuits in state courts under a state-created duty to protect.

police might employ to better deal with the problem of domestic violence. In that city, three separate strategies were to guide police actions:

1. advise the parties involved;
2. order the suspected assailant to leave the premises for at least eight hours in an effort to "cool-down" the situation; or
3. arrest the suspect.

The first two strategies were, of course, the time-worn practices the police usually employed in dealing with these type cases. The arrest option was a new and novel way for the police to respond. These options were employed at random to the domestic disturbance calls handled by the Minneapolis police. To test the effectiveness of each of these responses, the victims were interviewed for six months following the police intervention. The follow-up interviews were for the purpose of determining whether the victim experienced another assault during the analysis period. From these interviews and from police records, the idea was to determine which of these three actions would better assure that no more violence occurred.

The findings indicated that when the police made an arrest, as compared to merely giving advice or ordering the batterer off the premises, subsequent assaults dropped. A third or more of the victims whose assailant was merely advised or ordered off the premises reported or were found to have suffered another incident of domestic violence during the six-month follow up period. In the case of arrested suspects, only 19 percent of the women in this group reported that the arrestee assaulted them again during the six-month period following the arrest. The evidence seemed to suggest that the best possible response of the police would be to arrest assailants in domestic disturbance calls where violence was indicated.[17]

The results of the Minneapolis study were given wide circulation in the criminal justice and police communities. It also received wide discussion in legislative circles. As a result of this study and as a consequence of threatened liability issues, states began reforming their arrest laws to permit the police to arrest for acts of domestic violence even though the violence only constituted a simple assault. This was an important change in the law. Under the statutes in force at that time, the police could only arrest for a misdemeanor offense such as a simple assault if the crime was committed in their presence. In most cases, they were powerless to arrest since they had not witnessed the crime occurring. The police could merely refer the victim to contact the prosecutor's office to obtain a warrant if she sought arrest and prosecution.

Still, there were issues surrounding the conclusions of the Minneapolis research which raised some questions.[18] In addition to the usual questions about methodology lapses in any type of "field experimentation" of this type, there were questions raised that arrests of offenders may have intimidated the battered women into not reporting further violence. The women may not have reported further acts of violence because they were threatened with significant harm from the men who had experienced arrest if they called the police again and subjected them to arrest a second time. The research also indicated that few of the suspects arrested served any jail time for their offenses. Although all arrested defendants spent the night in jail, there was no attempt to follow-up the deterrent effect of more than a night's exposure to jail. Since so few had such a penalty imposed by the court, the sample would have been too small to draw any conclusions anyway.

It has also been argued that many women may not call the police initially because they are so intimidated about possible reprisals from their assailants that they are effectively deterred from even making the initial call and reporting their victimization.[19] In such a latter situation, police practice would seem to have no effect. There have also been important concerns raised that the results of the Minneapolis research were incautiously publicized by the researchers themselves more than was warranted given the problems with how the study was conducted.[20] Interestingly, more recent research conducted in Omaha, Nebraska to confirm the appropriateness of the Minneapolis arrest policy, found that police arrests seem to have no effect on reducing subsequent acts of violence.[21]

This issue of police and on-scene warrantless arrests is further confounded by research done into police practices in Marion County, Indiana.[22] In this study, although the batterer was more angry when the police made an on-scene arrest (as compared to a summons to appear in court following a victim complaint or arrest on a warrant following victim complaint), this anger did not result in a higher likelihood of future violence directed toward the victim. In the view of the researcher conducting this study, the findings would seem to lend support to advocacy for rigorous criminal intervention against spousal batterers, if only to support the notion that seemingly harsher sanctions (on-scene warrantless arrest, prosecution, probation, mandatory counseling, or incarceration) do not place victims at greater risk of new violence.

Although it still remains unclear what is the best policy for the police to follow in both preventing acts of domestic violence and responding to such crimes when they occur, there has been a significant change in police policies in many communities in the past several years. One result of the new arrest laws is that arrests for domestic violence have significantly increased in many jurisdictions following the adoption of the new laws and their use by the police.[23] Sherman and Cohn estimate that nearly half of all police departments in cities of over 100,000 population now encourage arrest as the preferred response to domestic violence.[24] The criminal justice system now plays an increasing role in domestic violence situations.

But changes in police strategies to employ their arrest powers has been only one response from the law enforcement community. Although it has been the most dramatic and more common response of the police (at least judging by what is occurring), there have been some other imaginative and integrative responses begun by a few police agencies. A number of police departments, in addition to adopting the arrest strategy, have developed rather sophisticated programs of "tracking" domestic violence cases and working in conjunction with victims' rights groups, social service agencies, and the prosecutor's office to develop a more comprehensive effort to deal with the problem.

Although there are several noted models of police domestic violence intervention efforts, one such publicized undertaking is the Domestic Violence Prevention Program (DVPP) in New York City. Although this program cannot be considered representative of the various types of strategies that police agencies throughout the country have developed, it does serve as an example of how police agencies have moved to deal with domestic violence. It also shows how the criminal justice system has responded in a role of leadership to coordinate resources to deal with the problem.

The DVPP operates in three of New York City's police precincts. Not unlike similar programs developed in other cities, it operates on a team concept, consisting of a police officer and a victim services agency counselor. In this way the police share responsibility with other appropriate social service or victim assistance agencies. The purpose of this joint approach is to identify and to track violent households. Recognizing that the prosecutor's office must play an important role if the criminal justice system is to deal with family violence, meetings were initially held with the District Attorney's office to acquaint them with the project and to familiarize this office with the problems associated with these types of crimes. It was pointed out to the prosecutor's office that the experience of the police in that city, when dealing with domestic violence, showed that most often the victim didn't want to testify. The prosecutors agreed to pursue further prosecutions of cases even though the victim was not entirely cooperative.

The prosecutors asked the police to help them build stronger cases in prosecuting these offenses. The police were instructed in how to present an independently supportable case. This included evidence that a victim had been injured, supported by medical records or photographs of the victims and statements made to the police or other reliable witness. The DVPP program members also developed a case enhancement sheet that could be used by the district attorney in preparing the case for trial. This sheet includes references to the evidence and it provides the prosecutor with a history of police responses to the household. This proved to be an important factual item as it conveys to the court that this is not the first time the police have responded to the household.

Each day, project staff members review reports of domestic violence from the previous day's police incident reports and family disturbance calls. Reports of such calls are then filed and indexed by complainant's name and address. This allows the "tracking system" so crucial to handling such calls and referring them for prosecution. In this way, a pattern of domestic violence in a particular household is determined to be a first-time occurrence or whether a pattern of problems have developed. Intervention begins with a telephone call by the domestic violence prevention officer (DVPO), who explains that the household came to the project's attention as a result of a report of domestic violence. The officer explains to either the victim or the batterer that domestic violence is a crime and that the police department will be monitoring the situation in their household. If the victim is at home, the police officer requests to speak to her and discusses with her the forms of relief that may be available from both the police and the courts. The officer also informs her that arrests have been shown to have been a successful deterrent in reducing violence in the home.

The Role of the Prosecutor

The role of the prosecutor in domestic violence crimes is every bit as important as the police. In some ways, it may be even more important. If the criminal justice system is to better deal with acts of domestic violence—or any other crimes of family violence for that matter—prosecutor's must be willing to take such cases to court. If such steps are not taken, the police will quickly lose interest in enforcing such offenses even if they have the authority to make arrests for acts of domestic assault. Prosecutors have traditionally dismissed the majority of domestic violence cases whether these cases have been referred directly by the police or they are direct victim-initiated complaints.[25]

There have been a number of research efforts to examine why prosecutors decide to prosecute or decline prosecution in criminal cases.[26] It has generally been shown that such decisions are based upon both legal and organizational considerations. Legal considerations involve such factors as the strength of the evidence, the prior relationship between the victim and the perpetrator, the credibility of the victim (to the extent that both these factors may affect the probability of conviction), and the characteristics of the offender and the offense. Organizational considerations include the workload of the prosecutor's office, the availability of alternative dispositions (e.g., the prosecutor might feel this case is better handled by a dispute resolution center or referred to a social agency for assistance), the existing priorities established in the prosecutor's office as to what cases to pursue and what cases are relatively unworthy of attention, the personal views of the prosecutor, and the attitude of the police and the courts toward the prosecution of certain crimes and/or defendants, and the general expectations of the community.[27]

The most common reason given for the lack of attention to the prosecution of domestic violence cases is that these cases are relatively unimportant.[28] With prosecutors struggling to manage their caseloads of ''serious'' crimes—narcotics offenses, robberies, rapes, burglaries, and the occasional homicide—domestic violence cases are not seen as particularly important or worth the time or the attention of the prosecutor's staff. This occurs in spite of the fact, as already pointed out, that acts of domestic violence may constitute felony-type crimes. Although prosecutors are cautious not to downplay acts of domestic violence lest they run the risk of unfavorable publicity, they often argue that they must devote their limited resources to other types of crimes. Prosecutors also express the idea that such domestic violence cases tend to run certain risks for successful prosecution. This automatically makes these cases less attractive to deal with initially—especially if the prosecutor's office is struggling with a heavy workload of cases to screen, preparations for trial, and cases to try.

Prosecutors will also point out that in many domestic violence complaints, the incident often boils down to allegations and counter-allegations by the defendant and the victim. Many times there are no objective witnesses to the act of violence; the only witnesses are the victim and the alleged assailant. The victim may not have even called. The police may have responded to a ''domestic disturbance'' call reported by an anonymous neighbor. Often, both the victim and assailant are intoxicated or have been drinking or using narcotics which further aggravates the question of the victim's credibility or complicity in the circumstances which led to the assault. There are important legal issues the prosecutor must address, not the least of which is the ability to substantiate the charges. Objective and supportable evidence must accompany the prosecutor's decision to file on the charges and to justify the intervention of the court and the imposition of sentence.

Prosecutors (and the police) often justify not taking any action either to arrest or prosecute domestic violence cases on the basis of the so-called "kiss and makeup" experience; the tendency for a female victim of domestic violence to refuse to press charges or to cooperate with the prosecution when the case comes to trial. Studies of misdemeanor domestic violence cases in Indianapolis and Washington, D.C. indicated that the majority of such cases were dismissed at the victim's request.[29] There is evidence that although some women who are subjected to domestic violence want to end the relationship, many victims of domestic violence only want the violence to end; they want to remain in the relationship as long as the violence can be controlled.

Interviews with victims of domestic violence in Chicago indicated overwhelmingly that the victims remained with the batterer because of needs for financial support, because they loved the man, or they didn't know what else to do. Many of these victims wanted to maintain the existing relationship without the violence and they had called the police or sought help from the criminal justice system in the hopes that this would cause the assailant to change his behavior out of fear of arrest or prosecution, force him to get counseling, or impose a court order against further acts of violence. Many did not want to be the complainant in a subsequent prosecution or see the man necessarily jailed.[30] Under such circumstances, some prosecutors become quite cynical about the motives of domestic violence victims and the appropriateness of the use of the criminal justice system to deal with the problem.

Also, there are other factors suggested which tend to figure prominently in the decision to prosecute domestic violence cases. Among these include such issues as the fact that where there is a lack of serious injury, the crime only amounts to a simple assault which is a misdemeanor, the assailant may have had limited encounters with the police or the criminal justice system or this may be his first encounter, and there was no use of a weapon or aggravating circumstances. The availability of acceptable social service alternatives may also figure heavily into the decision of whether to prosecute.[31] So, too, might dispositional alternatives if the accused goes to trial and is found guilty. For example, it may be the prosecutor's experience that judges in domestic violence cases rarely impose any penalty other than a fine or probation. The prosecutor may, under the circumstances, feel that this doesn't justify the time and effort to prepare for and take the case to trial.

Although these are some of the reasons often given for the lack of follow-up prosecutions in domestic violence cases, there has been little systematic research to determine if these reasons, in fact, do figure into the prosecutor's decisions in domestic violence cases. One notable exception to this has been some research which was conducted in the Milwaukee (Wisconsin) County District Attorney's Office.[32] Both charged and non-charged cases were examined. In examining legally relevant factors, it was found that degree of injury to the victim, the instrument of attack, defendant's failure to appear at the charging conference, and defendant's record are clearly related to the prosecutor's decision to charge the case. Victims who suffered relatively severe injuries or who were harmed or threatened with some object or weapon more menacing than an open hand were more likely than other victims to see their complaints proceed to court. In terms of the dispositions for these cases that went to trial, defendants were less likely to be given lenient sentences if they failed to show up at the charging conference or had a prior conviction.[33]

There were also extralegal factors which seemed to play a role. Screening decisions (the screening of cases to determine which cases the prosecutor's office would take to trial) seem to hinge on five factors:

1. sexual intimacy with the defendant;
2. cohabitation with the defendant;
3. the couple's history of domestic violence;
4. the defendant's source of support; and
5. the use of drugs or alcohol which were related to the incident.

Victims claiming to have no prior sexual intimacy with the defendant were more likely to have their complaint acted upon and charges filed by the prosecutor. Also, cases were more often charged when the complainant did not live with the accused. But as the researchers pointed out, this may have been due to the prosecutor feeling that the victim is more likely to cooperate in the prosecution of the case if she isn't exposed to the continued presence or pressure of the defendant. Prosecutors were also more lenient toward those defendants who were employed as opposed to those who were not. For example, prosecutors tended to either decline to prosecute these cases, hold them open for later prosecution if the victim complained of a future act of violence by the accused, or refer the defendants to a diversion alternative. Likewise, the absence of alcohol or drugs tended to bring about a more lenient handling of the case by the prosecutor's office.

In recent years, some prosecutor's offices have taken steps to better deal with domestic violence cases. Among the most common are such efforts as reviewing all police calls to see if there have been any domestic violence calls and then following-up with an investigation; showing greater willingness to file charges; refusing to drop charges even if the victim appears uncooperative; automatically requesting a civil protection order from the court when the defendant appears; working closely with outside victim advocacy programs or establishing such a service as part of the prosecutor's office; and vidotaping the initial interview.[34] Although there is little research evidence as to how successful such efforts are, they do show, among some prosecutor's offices at least, a growing interest in dealing with these offenses.

The Role of the Court

While the court cannot act to deal with domestic violence unless the victim signs a complaint and/or the police make an arrest and the prosecutor follows-up by deciding to take the case to trial, the court's role is also crucial. But, of course, the courts are also constrained by evidentiary considerations, existing laws as to the court's authority, and the availability of alternatives for disposition (and the perceived efficacy) of these alternatives. We have already alluded to some of the evidentiary problems that might be present in domestic violence cases when we examined the role of the prosecutor's office. In many communities today, dispositional alternatives for defendants convicted of an offense of domestic violence are becoming difficult for judges. In many cities, although the judge may feel justified in sentencing the offender to a period of time in jail, the judge knows that overcrowding in local jails is causing a serious problem for the community. When jails are already overcrowded with defendants awaiting trial and filled-up with narcotics pushers, robbers, rapists and burglars, judges may tend to hesitate sending run-of-the-mill domestic batterers to jail.

The judge is also aware that other typical alternatives such as probation might not be appropriate or even useful in many case of domestic violence. Especially today, probation authorities are also overworked and understaffed. A third commonly used alternative is an order of protection or a restraining order issued by the court. Under court order the assailant is ordered to cease and desist from further violence, to vacate the premise, and to have no further contact with the victim. Such an order is enforceable by law and seems to be a favorite method employed by judges to dispose of domestic violence cases.[35]

In the court's handling of these cases then, the issues often turn on the nature of the offense, the evidence, the characteristics of the defendant, the personal attitudes of the judge, and the perceived appropriateness or availability of dispositional alternatives. Perhaps, too, the attitude of the victim is considered. What specific combination of these factors play a role will be as varied as the number of courts and judges who handle these cases. No research has been able to sort all of these factors out. Nor is it likely that any such research findings from one judge or one particular court would be broadly generalizable to other courts, judges, and jurisdictions.

Some locales have in recent years, made important strides to devise court procedures particularly focused on handling domestic violence cases. Some of these have been quite innovative in terms of their approach. This can be the assignment of a particular judge to handle all such cases, or even the creation of a special court—more likely a special division of a lower-level court to specialize in domestic violence cases. One such court created to improve the handling of domestic violence cases has been developed in Charlotte, North Carolina. This city has created a special courtroom, the domestic relations courtroom, to handle such offenses. Although there was some initial fear that such an arrangement might convey the message that this type of case is less important than "real" assaults that were conducted in the conventional criminal courtrooms in that city, just the opposite seems to have occurred. One researcher who has examined this issue and the prosecution of domestic violence cases in Charlotte with similar prosecutions in several other cities is very complimentary of Charlotte's approach. She says of Charlotte's domestic relations courtroom: "Because these cases (domestic violence) are consolidated in one courtroom, legal officials are immediately "flagged" when the case is called that this involves a domestic assault, frequently with complexities that extend beyond the single incident. Consequently, they are immediately aware of the problem."[36]

Interestingly, follow-up research on victim attitudes by the researcher in the several cities studied pointed out that the system in Charlotte was seen more favorably by victims of family violence than in the other cities. The researcher relates what she found:

> These judges [domestic relations courtroom judges] specifically volunteered for this assignment and presided over the courtroom for periods of several months. From what we observed and what victims reported, these judges were especially careful, professional, and courteous in their treatment of victims and their cases. They also verbally warned or lectured defendants about the consequences of their actions and the possibility of harsher punishment if they were violent in the future. Even when victims stepped forward only to drop charges, the judges frequently expressed concern about the incident and counseled the victim. Therefore, it is little wonder that Charlotte victims reported the highest rates of satisfaction with the judge and believed that judicial concern was shown for their interests.[37]

Child Abuse

Changes in Defining Child Abuse and Protective Efforts

Just as with domestic violence, important changes have also occurred in this area in recent years. For one thing, unlike spousal abuse, the past twenty years has seen a steady decriminalization of child abuse and neglect. The criminal prosecution of these offenses—although never a typical way to deal with the problem—gave way to an expansion of social service efforts in the guise of child protective agencies to deal with this situation. The impetus for this was the adoption by the federal government of the Child Abuse Prevention and Treatment Act of 1974 which provided a finacial incentive to states to enact statutes designating a specific state agency to be responsible for identifying, treating, and preventing child abuse. Such agencies were naturally housed in a combined state social service or a special Department of Youth Services and was "social-work oriented." The purpose of these child protective agencies is to not only protect the child, but also to help parents adequately care for their children through a mixture of mental health and supportive services. Based on their investigation of the home situation, a child protective agency decides what kinds of supportive services a child and his or her family needs and then helps them to obtain these. This might be counseling and guidance, financial assistance, day care or crisis centers, and homemaker care. It can be the placement of the child in a foster home or "home supervision" where a social worker can monitor the child's welfare while trying to treat the parents. But the past several years has seen this change.

The reason is the social service approach seems to be failing. With the shifting of responsibility to social service agencies has come a ten-fold increase in the number of cases of suspected child abuse or neglect reported to the authorities. Part of this increase is the result of mandatory reporting requirements enacted by all the states, or it may also partly reflect that this problem is growing worse. For example, in 1987, there

In 1989, national attention centered on the trial of Joel Steinberg a successful New York City attorney who was charged with the beating death of his adopted daughter. The child's mother, Hedda Nussbaum, testifying for the prosecution related a sordid story of family violence: years of beatings and intimidation by the defendant which culminated in the beating which led to the child's death. As with other forms of family violence, such revelations are only the tip of the iceberg. More than any other form of family violence, child abuse remains largely hidden from the authorities. It is only when such violence receives the noteriety of the *Steinberg* case is the problem brought home to many Americans.

were 1.7 million suspected cases reported nationwide.[38] Still, fewer than five percent of all substantiated cases of child maltreatment result in criminal prosecutions.[39] Although upon investigation, about 65 percent of these reports are determined to be "unfounded" there are still about one-half million substantiated reports each year. Of these substantiated reports, about 2,000 children die each year under circumstances which suggest abuse or neglect. Over 100,000 children each year are sexually abused or so seriously injured from abusive treatment, they require hospitalization. This has raised the issue that social service agencies are not necessarily the most effective way to handle the problem—at least in some cases. It is now increasingly being suggested that the criminal justice system should play a larger role in dealing with certain forms of child abuse.[40]

Statutes dealing with the prosecution of child abuse cases have also been changing. For one thing, laws of evidence in the prosecution of these cases have become less restrictive. Efforts for example, to permit hearsay evidence for consideration, the videotaping of a child's testimony so that he or she will not have to take the stand and be cross-examined in a courtroom full of strangers and before the parent or guardian charged with the abusive conduct, and the waiver of the requirement for the child's direct testimony at the preliminary hearing are all changes being considered or adopted in whole or part by changing state laws dealing with child abuse.[41] All of these point the way for greater criminal justice system involvement. Protective rights for persons against subsequent civil law suits for reporting instances of suspected child abuse have also been adopted.

Likewise, the legal definition as reflected in state statutes of what constitutes child abuse has been significantly broadened. While early child protective laws focused only on physically abused and battered children, a review of modern statutes indicates that child abuse or maltreatment laws now generally fall into several categories. The first deals with acts of physical abuse. Although all states recognize the right of parents or guardians to use corporal punishment as a means of disciplining their children, it must be "reasonable" or "not excessive." It is when physical actions become excessive, either by the way they are imposed or by their consequences, that they become abusive. Admittedly, this has caused some problem in the law in determining when the corporal punishment imposed by parents becomes "abusive" or "excessive."

Modern laws also protect children against sexual abuse and exploitation. Sexual abuse would consist of such acts as vaginal, anal, or oral intercourse or other forms of sexually exploitive activities. Sexual exploitation laws prohibit the use of a child in prostitution, pornography, or other sexually explotive activities.

Physical neglect also falls under anti-child abuse laws. This can be generally defined as failure to provide needed care (such as food, clothing, shelter, or appropriate supervision) which exposes the child to harm or significant risk.

There is also abandonment as a form of abusive act which exposes the child to potential or actual risk under circumstances that demonstrate an intentional abdication of parental responsibility.[42] A number of states have also gotten into the murky area of psychological or emotional abuse as a form of abusive behavior.[43]

The mandatory child abuse reporting laws now adopted by all states designates the agency to receive these reports. Usually it is the child protective agency, such as a department of Youth Services. In some states, the law gives the reporter the choice between the criminal justice system (prosecutor or police) and the child protective agency.[44] Even in these states, although the child protective agency may receive the initial complaint of aggravated abuse or neglect and could always refer these to the police or prosecutor's office, this often does not occur. Protective agencies often cling to the feeling that referral to the criminal justice system, except in the most serious cases, is inappropriate.

Social workers in these agencies have the problem of seeing beyond the need for ''treatment'' and not ''punishment'' (the latter being their view of the criminal justice system) as the most appropriate response. Child protective agencies also hold the opinion that the fear of possible criminal prosecutions would also deter parents from taking their children for needed medical treatment which might uncover acts of abuse.

A Movement Toward Greater Criminal Justice System Involvement

Still, the social service approach is falling into disfavor as a means to deal with the problems of child abuse—at least, in more serious cases or where social assistance doesn't seem to be working. The first reason is that there is growing recognition that treatment of problem families or child abusers has a poor record of solving the problem. Existing treatment programs are successful only with those parents and families who accept help and can benefit from it.

Estimates are that about 40 percent of the parents in substantiated abuse cases have such deeply ingrained psychological and emotional problems that they are not amenable to treatment.[45] By the same token, even well-funded federal child abuse projects with significant resources have been able to prevent the recurrence of neglect or abuse in about only 50 percent of the cases.[46]

Fifteen years ago, prison rehabilitation and treatment came under the same criticism for its inability to rehabilitate inmates. The same concerns are now leveled at family and abuser assistance and ''child protection'' programs operating under the auspices of social service agencies.

The practices of these agencies are also being questioned. In a number of cases, the abused child is removed from the home and placed in foster care facilities. The benefits of this are increasingly questioned. This may be more disruptive to the child then permitting the child to remain at home and removing the offending parent by court order or incarceration. It is also recognized that although foster care placement is only supposed to be temporary while the parents are undergoing treatment, this "temporariness" too often stretches into years.[47] It is also a consequence that at least 25 percent of all fatalities attributed to child abuse and neglect occurred while the child was under the supposed protection of the child protective agencies.[48] It is becoming obvious that relying on foster care placement to protect the abused child may no longer be possible. Foster care facilities today are at the breaking point. According to a national survey of foster care facilities released in 1990, a crisis is occurring in our nation's foster care network as the system is swamped with children; such facilities simply no longer exist to handle the problem.[49]

A third reason is that child protective agencies have often failed to properly involve the criminal justice system. Massachusetts is a case in point. In 1983, that state passed a District Attorney Reporting Bill which was enacted in large part because of media attention to incidents involving serious injury and death resulting from physical child abuse. In these publicized cases, the state's Department of Social Services failed to coordinate with law enforcement agencies, despite prior identification that the parent(s) had caused severe injury to the child.[50]

Against such a background, the criminal justice system's role in dealing with child abuse is growing. One indication of the movement to greater involvement in child abuse cases by the criminal justice system is the change in the last couple of years of state laws that, like Massachusetts, require the child protective agencies to notify law enforcement officials (usually the local prosecutor) of any case investigation conducted by the agency which indicates abusive injury, serious physical abuse, sexual abuse, or death. The message of such legislation is quite clear: Legislative bodies are considering these serious offenses and they expect prosecuting attorneys to take appropriate steps to prosecute such offenders. They have lost faith in the ability of social service agencies to deal effectively with the problem.

However, expecting the criminal justice system to better deal with child abuse is also frought with difficulty. The major problem faced with the problem of child abuse—especially if the criminal justice system is to become involved—is the need for an effective working relationship between the children's service agency, the police and the prosecutor's office. Much more than in other forms of family crime, the investigation and prosecution of such offenses are going to require a cooperative and coordinated approach.

It also needs to be recognized that unlike spousal abuse and abuse of the elderly, the criminal justice system is going to have to rely, in many instances, on the reporting initiative taken by such diverse groups or agencies as schools and teachers who suspect instances of abuse or neglect, the health professions who treat children for injuries, the children's service agency, or possibly relatives and neighbors. Unlike adults, children are not likely to contact the authorities to report their victimization. In this way, the ultimate solution lies outside the criminal justice system.

The Police

The police play a critical role in attempts to involve the criminal justice system in anti-child abuse strategies. The truth of the matter, however, is that the police often avoid involvement in these types of cases. There are probably several reasons for this. First, is the ambiguity in many situations of what constitutes ''abuse.'' The police, under such circumstances, would prefer to refer the case to a social service agency for determination. Yet, the police also tend to not report such possible offenses to the child protective agency unless the circumstances are serious. Only about 12 percent of cases investigated by a child protective agency are the result of referrals from the police.[51] Yet, the police are in a unique position to identify neglect or abuse as they perform such functions as responding to domestic violence calls or handling juvenile delinquency matters.

It is also to be expected that many police operate without clear guidelines either by law or the operating policies of their departments as to what actions they can take and under what circumstances. Unlike the clarity of the law which permits the police in many states to arrest for ''probable cause'' in cases of spousal abuse, interceding formally through their powers of arrest in child abuse or neglect cases is a little more problematic unless the abuse is obviously serious and criminal. What little research has been done on police intervention in child abuse cases indicates that the seriousness of injury and the criminal nature of the abuse are the two most important determinants police follow in making an arrest or referring the abuse case to other authorities.[52] And like other types of family crime, the police often have little confidence in the criminal justice system to deal with many abuse or neglect offenses. The existence of child protective agencies also lets the police ''dump'' messy family matters that they do not like to handle.[53]

It is obvious that as child abuse and neglect become more of a ''crime problem'' to be addressed by the criminal justice system rather than a ''social problem'' to be dealt with by child protective agencies, the police are going to have to play an increasing role. It would seem that law enforcement must have clearer statutory authority to intervene in such situations if this is to be a preferred response. Clearer guidelines must also come from police officials themselves to guide police personnel in what actions to take and under what circumstances. It is also to be recognized that not all police personnel will want or be capable of dealing appropriately with discovered cases or reports of child abuse or neglect. This may require that a specialist investigator handle these cases especially since these type offenses require such a coordinative role with other agencies and the prosecutor's office together with special considerations and treatment for the victim, and similar concerns which are not found in most crimes where adults are victims.

The Prosecution of Child Abuse Cases

Child abuse cases present some unusally difficult problems from a prosecution viewpoint. It is not unusual, for example, for an intra-family child abuse case to involve three different state courts if the parent is the alleged abuser. The juvenile court will focus on the dependency hearing; the family court will concern itself with visitation and custody proceedings; and the criminal court will deal with the criminal issues involved. Add to this overlap, the participation in each such hearing/case of the social service worker assigned the case, the social service investigator, and the involvement of the police, at least, in the juvenile court and the criminal court proceedings.

However, the most difficult problem is a jurisprudential one. This is especially true if it involves sexual molestation. While criminal prosecution of child abuse generally is frought with difficulty, sexual abuse cases involving children may be the most difficult of all criminal cases to prosecute. Experience has shown that certain aspects of evidentiary and procedural law which guides the prosecution of other criminal offenses may have to be modified to deal with crimes when young children are victims. As mentioned, states have generally moved to allow certain changes in ways which which recognize these unique problems. Still, such changes remain controversial and not all together satisfactory.

One problem which has been discussed frequently is the testimonial credibility of the child and the child's susceptibility to suggestion. As one noted legal expert on the subject says, "the whole area of developmental psychology has been injected into the law in such cases."[54] Is the testimony of the child believable or is he or she confused, possibly fantasizing or perhaps even outright lying? The child's testimony regarding his or her victimization is an important probative element in convincing a jury of an accused's guilt beyond a reasonable doubt. One major study tends to indicate that adults often question children's credibility as witnesses.[55]

The traditional test for determining a child's competency is twofold: whether the child understands the obligation to tell the truth, and whether the child has sufficient capacity to observe, recollect and relate.[56] This is a difficult issue for the courts or a jury in a criminal case to deal with—not only because a young child is involved, but also because the trauma associated with the abuse may further complicate this issue by affecting the victim's memory and ability to relate what happened. It often becomes an issue when the defense tries to contend that the child suffered the injuries accidentally. Of course, the prosecution has the right to call expert witnesses such as examining physicians to testify that, in their opinion, the injuries were not self-induced by an accident or that the child suffered sexual abuse.

One prosecution strategy in recent years is what has been referred to as a coordinative investigation effort. Along with this has come the increased use of vertical prosecution in such cases. Local prosecutors in some jurisdictions are developing coordinative investigation efforts involving the police, a social service investigator and the prosecutor's office. Together representatives from these three agencies conduct the investigation and interview the child. Rather then having the child-victim interviewed separately by representatives of all three agencies, the child is interviewed or, at least, the child's testimony is viewed by specially trained representatives from all three agencies. In this way, the need to have the child interviewed repeatedly by separate authorities is minimized. A specially trained member of the prosecutor's office is also assigned the case from its initial inception through the trial if formal charges are brought. This is the idea of vertical prosecution: One member of the prosecutor's office is assigned the case rather than the more common practice in most criminal cases to have one assistant prosecutor

*McMartin Pre-school Child Abuse Case**

Our nation's prosecutors must have drawn a pause when the McMartin Pre-school case was finally concluded in the Summer of 1990. Although not a case of family child abuse, it posed similar problems for prosecutors. What has been desribed "as a walk through hell" ended after seven long years. The longest (three years), costliest ($14 million) and arguably the most acrimonious criminal case in the nation's history came to a close when the second jury to try the case ended up as hopelessly deadlocked as the first. The Los Angeles District Attorney then threw up his hands and refused to seek a third trial. During a total of seven years of criminal proceedings that focused on the defendant Ray Buckey, a teacher at the school and three members of his family, the case involved federal and county grand juries, a preliminary hearing, two trials, 36 trial jurors, 17 attorneys, six judges, and hundreds of witnesses and alleged victims. Unknown were the thousands of investigative man hours that went into the case by law enforcement, social services, and the District Attorney's office staff. For five years, Buckey, himself, had been in jail as the criminal proceedings and the trial unraveled. Many of the alleged victims of sodomy and other acts of child sexual molestation who, as children at the McMartin Pre-school when the allegations first came to the attention of the authorities, were, by the trial's conclusion, teenagers.

The "costs" of this case can be expressed in other ways. The Manhattan Beach mother who alleged that "Mr. Ray" had sodomized her son which led to the beginnings of the investigation was apparently driven mad by McMartin and drank herself to death during the Christmas holidays in 1986. Other lives were also lost. A defense investigator committed suicide the night before he was to testify. A young man, who was implicated early in the investigation by several children, died of an apparent drug overdose. A juror whose wife died during the first trial pressed on without interrupting the proceedings to mourn. Those who lived were pushed to their emotional limits. The stress of the case affected the health of the judge and his family. The defense attorney developed back problems. Relationships were forged, strained, and severed. Participants' private lives became open to the scrutiny of the public.

Even though this historic trial has ended, legal experts say a host of other civil lawsuits generated by the case conceivably could keep the issue alive in the courts for decades. Among them, civil rights suits filed by former suspects against their accusers, against the media, and against the school's insurance carrier. Under California law, children who allege abuse have until their 19th birthday to file lawsuits on their own. However, some courts have held that child abuse victims can file at anytime in their lives. In the so-called delayed discovery theory, a statute of limitations does not take effect until the victim actually becomes aware of molestation. In a not unexpected turn of events, Buckey, shortly after the dismissal, filed a multimillion-dollar wrongful prosecution lawsuit.

If anything good came out of this case it was the fact that police departments, day-care centers, and courts were rocked by the fallout. Authorities analyzed time-worn procedures and created guidelines that became models for the nation. The California Attorney General released recommendations for preventing and prosecuting child abuse, noting that young victims were "re-victimized by the system as a result of clumsiness and insensitivity." New laws permitted children to testify by closed circuit TV and afforded protection of child witnesses from harassment and repetitive cross-examination. Trials must be expedited so that fading memories are less of a problem. No longer should probers immediately hand anatomically correct dolls to suspected victims, a technique which is criticized for being too suggestive. It was also realized that efforts must be made to initially tape interviews from the outset so that charges of "coercion" or "coaching" of the child are limited. In California, police academies also revised their curricula and law enforcement manuals were changed.

*From "McMartin: Trial is Over but Case May Never End for Many," *The Los Angeles Times* (July 29, 1990) p. A-42. Adopted with permission.

screen the case, a second to gather information upon which a prosecution decision is based, and a third to try the case if it goes to trial.

There are other issues surrounding the somewhat unique aspects of prosecuting a child abuse case that cannot be discussed. The important point for the reader to understand is that child abuse and neglect cases are unique. They present problems not encountered with traditional crimes involving adults which in turn, often provide significant problems for the criminal justice system. At this point, we want to turn our attention to a brief discussion of the last category of family crime, elder abuse.

Elder Abuse

In the 1960s, the problem of child abuse was "discovered" and in the 1970s it was spouse abuse. The decade of the 1980s would see elder abuse added to the list of "family pathologies" that, in their more extreme cases, would be added to the list of "family crimes." This interest seems to have evolved naturally. As the hidden aspects of family crime—initially child abuse and later spousal abuse—became a social issue, it was only natural that attention would then focus on other aspects of family life. It was a short step to bring elderly abuse by family members into the expanding net of "family problems" and "family crime."

Yet, elder abuse is only one part of the growing interest in crime victimization among the elderly. Since the mid-1970s, policymakers and criminologists have turned increasing attention to examining the entire range of criminal victimization among America's elderly. For the most part, however, this attention has focused on crime victimization rates among the elderly by what can be called "conventional criminal acts" or, at least, crimes committed on the aged by conventional offenders. For example, such issues as the specific violent and property crime rates suffered (i.e., the incidence of homicide, robbery, rape, larceny and burglary) among the elderly.

It was not only that elderly abuse by family members would naturally evolve out of family crime interests, it was also inevitable that studies and concern over crime victimization would sooner or later focus on the elderly. As a public policy issue it was bound to take on new significance as the elderly become an ever-larger segment of the American population. The Bureau of the Census estimates that by the year 2000, 20 out of every 100 Americans will be age 65 or older.[57] This figure is expected to continue to increase well into the first part of the 21st century. This sent a message to public officials. This "greying of America" has translated itself into political power: the power to translate numbers. In this case, the percentage of the voting electorate into a significant force of recognition. Elected officials are only too aware of how strong and concerted a voice the elderly can have in the political process as witnessed by any attempt to legislate change in Medicare benefits or such entitlement programs as Social Security.

Although crimes against the elderly are included in this chapter on discussion of family crime it should be recognized that not all new aspects of crimes against the aged are focusing on crimes committed by family members against the elderly. Interest-generated legislation is also looking at crimes against the elderly by provider organizations such as nursing homes and extended care hospitals. This, too, is a growing area of concern: an issue that like family-based criminal acts, promises to affect the criminal justice system and health care provider regulatory agencies in the years ahead.[58]

Extent of the Problem

In 1979, the House Select Committee on Aging held the first-ever hearings on the abuse of the elderly by their families which it titled, "The Hidden Problem." What, up until this time, had been called by such terms as "grannyslamming" or "grannybashing" came out of the Committee hearings with a new title—"elder abuse." In 1985, the Aging Committee's Subcommittee on Health and Long-term Care issued a follow-up report titled "A National Disgrace." In this report, elder abuse was described as "a full-scale national problem which existed with a frequency few have dared to imagine possible. In fact, abuse of the elderly by their loved ones and caretakers existed with a frequency and rate only slightly less than child abuse.

The report also contended that elder abuse was far less likely to be reported than the abuse of children. While one out of three child abuse cases was reported, only one out of six elder abuse cases come to the attention of the authorities. There was no question that the problem was increasing drastically from year to year. The subcommittee's report asserted that four percent of the elderly—one million older Americans—are victims of such abuse each year and found that: "The horrifying conclusion was that elder abuse was everywhere."[59] In 1990, a third report was issued by the Select Committee which sharply criticized the federal and state governments for failing to effectively take the initiative to deal with this problem and to heed the warnings and conclusions of the earlier studies and Congressional hearings.[60]

The 1990 federal report drew some conclusions about the examples of elder abuse they studied. These are:

1. Physical violence, including negligence, and financial abuse appear to be the most common forms of abuse, followed by abrogation of basic constitutional rights and psychological abuse.
2. The victims of elder abuse are likely to be age 75 or older. Women are more likely to be abused than men. The victims are generally in a position of dependency in which they are relying on others, such as family members or an unrelated caregiver, for care and protection. The likely abuser will be suffering great stress such as alcoholism, drug addiction, marital problems, and long-term financial difficulties. The most likely abuser is a son followed by a daughter in frequency. Many of the abusers were themselves abused as children.
3. The abused elder is less likely to report the incident of abuse than abused persons in other age groups. Only about one in eight cases comes to the attention of protective services. Victims are often ashamed to admit their children or loved ones abuse them or they may fear reprisals if they complain.[61]

While acknowledging that elder abuse is a problem and the conclusions reached in the report may be reasonably accurate, like all other aspects of "family crime" the incidence of criminal abuse against the aged is difficult to sort out. One of the problems is that major studies on the specific incidence of the problem are non-existent. Although there have been a number of efforts to examine elderly abuse in a general way, these studies lump together a wide range of "abusive" practices. They look at issues of psychological abuse, neglect, threats, abandonment, and exploitation almost indiscrimately.

For example, the study that the 1979 House Select Subcommitte used to suggest that four percent of elderly Americans were abused is based on a community sample of residents in the Washington, D.C. area. A questionnaire was mailed to 433 elderly residents. Categories of abuse on the questionnaire included physical abuse (including such subcategories as "fear" and "isolation"); material abuse (including "misuse of money or property"); and medical abuse (including "no medication purchased when prescribed," "no false teeth when needed," and "no hearing aid when needed").

Of the 433 persons sampled, 73 people or 16 percent of those questioned responded. Of these 73, three people, or 4.1 percent, indicated that they had been the victim of one of the specified forms of abuse.[62] This is a totally unreliable measure and one that cannot be taken as a representative sample throughout the nation. One scholar has called the conclusion from this particular study a "factoid"—numbers that appear to be facts but are not.[63] And although some forms of these behavior can be considered "abusive," many do not constitute grounds for the involvement of the criminal justice system. Even the Select Committee on Aging has categorized "elder abuse" into six broad categories: physical abuse and neglect, financial abuse, psychological abuse, self-neglect, sexual abuse, and violation of rights.

Legislative Responses

Advocates of federal involvement in the area of protective services for elders suggest that one way to encourage states to make the statutory and administrative changes would be to make federal funding for elder-abuse related programs contingent on certain state level requirements. The reader will recall that the Child Abuse Prevention and Treatment Act uses this approach in distributing funds to states for child abuse-related programs and almost every state has come into compliance. Several attempts over the past ten years to get a similar law passed to help prevent elder abuse has met with mixed success. In 1987, The Older Americans Act Amendments was adopted.[64] It requires area Agencies on Aging to assess the need for elder abuse prevention programs and for the states to develop a ''State Plan on Aging.'' Under this provision, the state plan would have to assure that any area agency carrying out elder abuse prevention activities would conduct its program consistent with state law and be coordinated with existing state adult protective services activities. The program was to provide public education to identify and prevent abuse; receive reports on incidence of abuse; provide outreach, conferences and referrals to other sources of assistance; and refer complaints to law enforcement or public protective service agencies. While $5 million dollars was authorized to be spent each year since the adoption of the Act, as of 1992, no federal funds have been appropriated to carry-out the program.

The most common legislative response at the state level has been the creation of Adult Services units in existing Departments of Human Services and the requirement that agencies and physicians suspecting or having knowledge of elder abuse must report this to the authorities—usually the Adult Services Unit. As of 1990, 43 states have such statutes.[65] Like child protective services' reports in the case of an abused child, lawmakers thought that the problem could best be dealt with by this mandatory reporting requirement. Evidence tends to indicate that this is not working well. There are any number of problems associated with this approach. The first of course, as in the case of other forms of family crimes, is to get professionals to cooperate. A study indicated that while 60 percent of the physicians interviewed thought they could diagnosis elder mistreatment, most expressed doubt or uncertainty about the availability of clear-cut definitions either from the legislation or from the American Medical Association itself, as to what constituted elder abuse upon which they should act.[66] Even with clear guidelines, however, it is pointed out that physicians often resist reporting because of the possibility that a case might go to court and the physician would be required to testify and be interviewed for purposes of the case investigation and trial. Studies in other states showed that physicians were often not aware of the mandatory reporting requirement or what state agency was responsible for receiving abuse reports.[67]

Associated with the diagnosis and reporting problems of elder abuse is the larger realization that such anti-abuse laws are considered by many to be inherently flawed and unworkable. A criticism of efforts to deal with elder abuse center on the way anti-abuse statutes have developed. In adopting elder abuse laws, states simply copied existing child abuse statutes with their mandatory reporting requirements. This may make sense with children who cannot speak up for themselves, but it raises some basic issues when applied to adults. For one thing it strips the elderly of the confidentiality between doctor and patient and certainly undercuts the rights of elderly adults to make their own decisions. This creation of an extensive (and demonstrably ineffective) legal system of reporting, investigating and even sometimes the involuntary institutionalization of a threatened aged person is raising concern in the legal community and among those studying the problem.[68] Ample evidence is developing that reporting requirements are not being met or are confusing, that investigative resources are not available to ferret-out instances of possible abuse, and effective remedies to protect the rights of victims from both abusers and the "protective" social service system are non-existent.[69]

Are official records of the criminal justice system any more helpful in uncovering the extent of the problem? As in the case of domestic violence or abuse, if arrests and prosecutions for assault or theft occur, these are not classified by existing crime recording efforts into family crimes let alone into "crimes against the elderly." Nor are they distinguished as such by the vast majority of police offense records, by prosecution officials, or by the courts. Instead, they merely become another in a long list of assaults or thefts occuring without any reference as to the particular characteristics which would make it a "family" crime or one involving a commission of a crime against an elderly family member. Since police departments don't routinely classify offenses accordingly and since states don't routinely keep records on elderly abuse cases (at least in a systematic and uniform way), problems abound in trying to get a handle on what's going on.

In this situation much of the problem is identified by after-the-fact analysis. What this means is that when the situation is serious enough to come to the attention of the authorities, then examination is conducted of those specific cases reported. For instance, studies of elderly abuse often cite examples of the records of the Baltimore City Police Department which is one of only a handful of police departments which keeps track of the types of assaults. Still it does little good to know how serious the problem may be in Baltimore or any American community for that matter merely to know that of the recorded assaults against citizens age 60 and over that two-thirds were committed by relatives other than spouses.[70] It is supposed that one is to assume that this is the case in all such assault cases. Never mind that we don't know what goes on in those elderly assault cases which never come to the attention of the authorities or the criminal justice system.

An interesting survey conducted by the Police Executive Research Forum of nearly 200 police departments of all sizes throughout the country indicated that thirty-one percent of the departments reporting said they were unaware of specific statutes governing the police response to elderly abuse actually had such state laws.[71] Obviously the message isn't getting out to the nation's police. Eighty-two percent of the departments responding did not know how many cases of elder abuse were handled by their departments and many of these had no idea of how such cases are brought to their attention.[72]

There is still another factor operating which has an important consequence for dealing with elder abuse. Advanced years bring about a breakdown of the extended family which contributes to the isolation (and the sense of isolation) experienced by those involved in abusive relationships.[73] This level of isolation may have two important consequences. To the extent that abusers or victims are isolated from the community, they are unlikely to avail themselves of the formal and informal support systems that may assist in the prevention or resolution of the problems confronting family members. This isolation also decreases the likelihood that those who engage in abusive acts against an elderly family member will have these acts detected or deterred by formal or informal systems of social control.

Legal and Prosecutorial Problems

In many ways, the prosecution of family-related elderly abuse crimes poses the same problems as prosecutions directed at parents in child abuse cases. Victims are often reluctant and too frightened to inform the authorities. Just as children they are often vulnerable and they realize it. They may also be intimidated by the consequences. The alternative to an abusive family setting is often no more than a room in a publicly supported nursing home. The elderly are often very reluctant to exchange the familiarity of their home for the unknown of an aged-care facility prefering instead to endure their victimization.

It is also important to emphasize that many studies have shown that those who engage in elder mistreatment are themselves elderly or near elderly.[74] In addition to adult children engaging in this form of abuse, it may be an elderly spouse who is the abuser. This raises additional problems for prosecution especially in those cases where the abuser is an elderly spouse.

If an elderly victim does contact the authorities or his or her victimization is brought to the attention of the criminal justice system, the competency of the elderly family member is one issue the authorities must consider. Not unlike a child abuse victim, the question often raised is how competent is the elderly abuse victim to testify in court and with the required credibility? Even the supporting statement of physicians often needed to corroborate the testimony of the victim is far from a guarantee of success.

Many elderly suffer from diminished powers of retention which affects memory. They are often easily confused which is demonstrated by the cross-examination tactics of defense counsel. Unlike child abuse cases, state laws do not generally allow special provisions for testimony of aged victims of family abuse. And if physical abuse is an issue in the prosecution how can the state prove beyond a reasonable doubt that the victim didn't accidentally sustain the injury himself? Although in some cases, physicians are able to testify that the type of injury sustained could not have been self-induced, say through a fall, these are rare circumstances. In many injury cases of this nature there is enough doubt raised that juries are unwilling to convict. Without independent and strong corroborative evidence it is very difficult to convict a family member of abusive acts toward an elderly member of the family.

Conclusion: Charting A Thoughtful Future Response

By now, the reader should be aware that there are many issues facing the problems of dealing with family crime. Undoubtedly, the criminal justice system will face growing pressures to involve itself more meaningfully in these issues in the future. The general movement toward criminalization of many forms of family violence will itself require greater attention by the agencies of criminal justice. But, the mere criminalizing of these acts will not assure that the criminal justice system can deal effectively with many of the problems a greater enforcement effort will require.

Although it is widely recognized that family crime is an important crime problem which has not been dealt with under traditional social service efforts, a lingering concern is that the criminal justice system may not be able to accomplish such a mandate. In fact, it may be inappropriate for the system to involve itself as a primary mechanism to deal with many forms of family abuse. This is not to suggest that the criminal justice system does not have an important role to play in dealing with these offenses, it only recognizes the obvious: Existing and appropriate legal restraints serve to impose significant burdens on the effectiveness of the formal mechanism of the law and the administration of justice. Family violence, even though it may be criminal in nature, also requires the interlocking of law enforcemnt and social service efforts.

It is not only the operational strategies of the police, the prosecution element of the system, and the courts which pose issues. Although these are important. (For example, should the police become more involved directly by arrest policies in dealing with family violence or should the police play more of a coordinative role with social agencies which are at issue? Or should prosecutors be more willing to prosecute cases of domestic violence or criminal abuse of the elderly?) There is a more fundamental concern and one which needs to be addressed before we can even talk about the specific role of police, prosecutors, or courts. There is an important and fundamental public policy issue involved; one which the advocates of greater legal and criminal justice involvement never address: This is the threat of further intervention of the government in the guise of the agencies of criminal justice to involve themselves in still another area of "net widening." We must chart a course which recognizes that our criminal justice system cannot be the answer to all social problems. Experience has repeatedly taught us that we cannot legislate or "criminalize" a problem out of existence. In some cases, frustration has driven us to such an ill-conceived recourse—usually with disasterous results.

Perhaps, as Franklin Zimring suggests, we need a jurisprudence of family violence.[75] This means, among other things, we need to better define what specific forms of family violence require attention by criminal-legal action. Specific laws and procedural guidelines must then be adopted to permit the agencies of criminal justice to better deal with the problems these kinds of offenses pose. These guidelines must take into account several important considerations: The unique characteristics of these types of crimes, the particular circumstances of their victims (especially their vulnerability), and they must also afford assurance that we do not move away from the procedural due process rights fundamental to our system of law while still adequately protecting victims and assuring that prosecutions and convictions will occur where warranted. This is a daunting task and one that promises to be very difficult to attain.

Along this line, a recent bill proposed in the Senate to curb spousal abuse promises to present even more potential problems if adopted. A special "spousal violence" crime bill would make this particular offense a federal violation. As proposed, such acts would constitute a deprivation of civil rights and permit federal prosecutions. Although well-intentioned, it is inconceivable that this would prove to be a workable solution or an answer to the need for a jurisprudence of family violence.

There are also state problems. In 1989, Texas adopted a new elder abuse law that may be the toughest in the nation. In addition to the usual criminal prohibitions about physical abuse of an elderly person, an important provision of the new law is that anyone in Texas who accepts responsibility for a person over age 64 must provide appropriate care. If appropriate care is not provided, the caretaker can be criminally prosecuted.[76] A woman and her husband are now being prosecuted by Houston authorities for their failure to take proper care of the woman's 70-year-old grandmother. Critics are saying the law is too vague to encourage successful prosecution and will ultimately end-up further discouraging criminal justice system involvement.

It is obvious that the criminal justice system and all its personnel—the police, prosecutors, and the judiciary must improve the way they have too often handled such cases in the past. Acts of family violence too often ''fall between the cracks'' of law enforcement and social service involvement. Both tend to view the problem in somewhat different ways and to employ different strategies to deal with it (neither of which seem to be working well at this point), especially as they too often operate independently and harbor suspicions of the working ethos of the other. Although this is to be expected, it doesn't encourage any optimism that future efforts will be better than past experience—at least as long as this situation exists.

It must also be recognized that the drug scourge that has struck so deeply into America has also struck deeply into the American family. The insolvability of the narcotics dilemma poses serious concern for our ability to deal with crimes of family violence. The two are inextricably linked and are crime issues along the same broad continuum. Crimes of spousal abuse, child abuse and neglect, and the criminal abuse of the elderly by family members is being fueled by drug abuse. Today, family crimes and intrafamilial violence are reaching epidemic proportions in areas and among those segments of the population most ravaged by illegal drugs. This, too, must present serious concern for the future of our nation and the policies we adopt.

It is ironic and of concern that at a time when we are faced with increasing commitments on the part of the agencies of criminal justice to deal with our nation's drug problems and the attending increases in serious forms of conventional ''street crimes'' along with some looming challenges to develop workable strategies to deal with developing and still not completely understood new forms of crime, we find ourselves turning increasing attention to family violence. The threat is real: our already overextended criminal-legal system and the agencies of justice, themselves, will fail under such a policy. In some areas of our nation, our capacity is already strained nearly to the breaking point. Focusing more of our already limited resources on dealing with family crimes is going to strain our capacity even further. Yet, to ignore the problem is to ignore an important social (and criminal) concern that simply cannot continue to grow worse.

Although some might argue that the system of justice under such circumstances should not take on such an additional resposibility, this overlooks the obvious: As the primary mechanism to protect members of society, it has a role it cannot escape. Victims of family abuse and violence are entitled to the same protection as any victim or possible victim of a criminal event. Somehow, the criminal justice system must find the resources and the ability to cope with still another form of non-traditional crime; a form of crime with which it has little effective experience or a proven record of even reasonably satisfactory accomplishment.

NOTES

[1]Hattery, Mark R. "Problems Associated with Measuring Family Violence," *Social Work Practice,* Vol. 8 (January/February 1985), pp. 14–18.

[2]Ibid., p. 17.

[3]Interestingly, The National Family Violence Surveys conducted by the Family Violence Research Program in 1975 and in 1985 show that although family violence is widespread in American families, there was a substantial drop in severe assaults on wives and an even more pronounced drop in the incidence of child abuse from the 1975 to 1985 survey findings. See Strauss, Murray A. "Physical Violence in American Families: Incidence, Rates, Causes, and Trends," in Knudson, Dean D. and Miller, JoAnn L. (eds.) *Abused and Battered: Social and Legal Responses to Family Violence* (New York: Aldine De Gruyter Publishing, 1991), pp. 17–34.

[4]Skogan, Wesley. *Issues in the Measurement of Victimization* (Washington, D.C.: U.S. Government Printing Office, 1981), p. 32. and Dodge, R. W. "Series Victimization—What is to be Done?" In *The National Crime Survey Working Papers, Vol. II: Methodological Studies* (Washington, D.C. Bureau of Justice Statistics, 1984.)

[5]Rose, Kristina and Goss, Janet. "Domestic Violence Statistics" (Washington, D.C.: National Criminal Justice Reference Service—Criminal Justice Information Package, 1989), pp. 3–4.

[6]Ibid., p. 3.

[7]Dutton, D. Hart, D.S., Kennedy, L. and Williams, K. "Arrest and the Reduction of Repeat Wife Assault," in Eve Buzawa and Carl Buzawa (eds.) *Domestic Violence: The Criminal Justice Response* (Westwood, CT.: Auburn House, 1990).

[8]Ibid., p. 5.

[9]Langan, Patrick A. and Innes, Christopher A. *Preventing Domestic Violence Against Women* (Washington, D.C.: U.S. Department of Justice, 1986).

[10]Ibid., p. 3.

[11]Black, Donald. "The Social Organization of Arrest," STANFORD LAW REVIEW, Vol. 23, pp. 1087–111 (1971); and Emerson, Charles D. "Family Violence—A Study of the Los Angeles County Sheriff's Office," *Police Chief,* Vol. 46, pp. 46–50 (1979).

[12]Mentioned in Elliott, Delbert S. "Criminal Justice Procedures in Family Violence Crimes," in Ohlin, Lloyd and Tonry, Michael (eds.) *Family Violence* (Chicago: University of Chicago Press, 1989) p.435.

[13]Field, Martha H. and Field, Henry F. "Marital Violence and the Criminal Process: Neither Justice nor Peace," *Social Service Review,* Vol. 47 (1973), pp. 221–40.

[14]See Buzawa, Eve S. and Buzawa, Carl G. *Domestic Violence, op cit.*, esp. Chapter 6.

[15]*Domestic Violence and the Police: Studies in Detroit and Kansas City* (Washington, D.C.: Police Foundation, 1977).

[16]Ibid., p. iv.

[17]Sherman, Lawrence W. and Berk, Richard A. "The Minneapolis Domestic Violence Experiment" (Washington, D.C. The Police Foundation, 1984); and Sherman, Lawrence W. and Berk, Richard A., "The Specific Deterrent Effects of Arrest for Domestic Assault," *American Sociological Review,* Vol. 49, pp. 261–72.

[18]A critical attack on the methodology of the Minneapolis research and its conclusions were presented in a paper by Binder, Arnold and Meeker, James, "The Use of Arrest to Control Misdemeanor Spousal Abuse," (n.d.)

[19]Langan and Innes, *op. cit.*, p. 4.

[20]For an excellent discussion of this issue, see Buzawa, Eve S. and Buzawa, Carl G. *Domestic Violence and the Criminal Justice Response* (Beverly Hills, Ca.: Sage Publications, 1991).

[21]Dunford, Franklyn W., Huizinga, David and Elliott, Delbert S. "The Role of Arrest in Domestic Assault: The Omaha Police Experiment," CRIMINOLOGY, Vol. 28, No. 2 (1990), pp. 183–206.

[22]Ford, David A. "Preventing and Provoking Wife Battery Through Criminal Sanctioning: A Look at the Risks," in Knudsen and Miller, *op cit.*, pp. 191–209.

[23]See Ferguson, H. "Mandating Arrests for Domestic Violence," *FBI Law Enforcement Bulletin* (Washington, D.C.: April 1987), pp. 3–5; and Cahn, Naomi R. "Innovative Approaches to the Prosecution of Domestistic Violence Crimes," (paper n.d.)

[24]Sherman, Lawrence W. and Cohn, Ellen G. *Police Policy on Domestic Violence, 1986: A National Survey* (Washington, D.C.: Crime Control Institute, 1987).

[25]Martin, Del. *Battered Wives* (San Francisco, CA: Glide Publishing, 1976); and Lerman, Lisa G. "Prosecution of Wife Beaters: Institutional Obstacles and Innovations," in Lystad, Mary. (ed.) *Violence in the Home: Interdisciplinary Perspectives.* (New York: Brunner/Mazel, 1986).

[26]For example, see Brosi, Kathleen. *A Cross-City Comparison of Felony Case Processing* (Washington, D.C.: INSLAW, Inc., 1979; Boland, Barbara. *et. al., The Prosecution of Felony Arrests—1979* (Washington, D.C. INSLAW, Inc., 1983; and Cole, George F. "The Decision to Prosecute" in Cole, George F. (ed.) *Criminal Justice: Law and Politics, 5th Ed.* (Monterey, CA: Brooks-Cole, 1984).

[27]One of the most definitive and insightful studies of the prosecutor's office including what typically is considered in charging decisions is Jacoby, J.E. *The American Prosecutor: A Search for Identity* (Lexington, MA: D.C. Heath, 1980).

[28]Lerman, L. "A Model State Act: Remedies for Domestic Abuse," HARVARD JOURNAL ON LEGISLATION, Vol. 21. (1984), p. 14.

[29]Ford, David A. "Prosecution as a Victim Power Resource for Managing Conjugal Violence," Paper presented at the annual meeting of the Society for the Study of Social Problems, San

Antonio, Texas, August 1984.; and Field, Martha H. and Field, Henry F. "Marital Violence and the Criminal Process: Neither Justice nor Peace," *Social Service Review,* Vol. 47, 1973, pp. 221–40.

[30]Caputo, Richard K. "Managing Domestic Violence in Two Urban Police Districts," *Social Casework,* Vol. 69 (October, 1988), pp. 498–504.

[31]Interestingly, many of these same calculations enter into the decisions of the police to initially arrest in domestic violence cases. See Dolan, Ronald, Hendricks, James and Meagher, M. Stephen. "Police Practices and Attitudes Toward Domestic Violence," *Journal of Police Science and Administration,* Vol. 14 (September 1986), pp. 187–92.

[32]Schmidt, Janell and Hochstedler-Steury, Ellen. "Prosecution Discretion in Filing Charges in Domestic Vioplence Cases," CRIMINOLOGY, Vol. 27 (August 1989), pp. 487–510.

[33]Ibid., p. 499.

[34]See Cahn, *op cit.*

[35]Walker, Lenore H. *Terrifying Love: Why Battered Women Kill and How Society Responds,* (New York: Harper & Row, 1989), p. 49.

[36]Smith, Barbara E. "Victims Who Know Their Assailants: Their Satisfaction with the Criminal Court's Response," in Hotaling, Gerald T. *et al.* (eds.) *Coping With Family Violence—Research and Policy Perspectives* (Beverly Hills, CA: Sage Publications, 1988), p. 189.

[37]Ibid., pp. 189–90.

[38]The National Center on Child Abuse and Neglect, U.S. Department of Health and Human Services, 1988. As reported in Bureau of National Affairs, Legislative Developments in the States, April 14, 1989. p. 3.

[39]Besharov, Douglas J. "Child Abuse: Arrest and Prosecution Decision-Making," AMERICAN CRIMINAL LAW REVIEW, Vol. 24 (Fall 1986), p. 315.

[40]Ibid.

[41]For a good overview of suggested reform efforts on behalf of child abuse victims including legal reform recommendations, see Whitcomb, Debra. "Improving the Investigation of Child Sexual-Abuse Cases: Research Findings, Questions and Implications for Public Policy," in Knudsen and Miller, *op cit.*, pp. 181–90. esp. pp. 183–84.

[42]This list is generally adopted from Besharov, Douglas J. "Child Abuse and Neglect Reporting and Investigation: Policy Guidelines for Decision Making," FAMILY LAW QUARTERLY, Vol. 22 (Spring 1988), p. 8.

[43]Davis, Samuel M. "Child Abuse: A Pervasive Problem of the 80s," NORTH DAKOTA LAW REVIEW, Vol. 61 (1985) pp. 193–224.

[44]See Meyers, John E. B. "A Survey of Child Abuse and Neglect Reporting Statutes," JOURNAL OF JUVENILE LAW (Winter 1986), pp. 1–72; and Meriwether, Margaret H. "Child Abuse Reporting Laws: Time for a Change," FAMILY LAW QUARTERLY, Vol. 20 (Summer 1986), pp. 141–71.

[45]Polansky, Norman. *Damaged Parents: An Anatomy of Child Neglect* (New York: Little Brown, 1981), pp. 161–62.

[46]U.S. Department of Health, Education, and Welfare, *Evaluation of Child Abuse and Neglect Demonstration Projects, 1974–1977* (Washington, D.C.: USGPO), 1978.

[47]U.S. Children's Bureau, *National Study of Social Services to Children and Their Families* (Washington, D.C.: Department of Health Education and Welfare, 1979), pp. 109–17.

[48]Besharov, *op cit.*, p. 320.

[49]"Looming Crisis in Childcare Services," *The Washington Post* (July 21, 1990), p. A-3, col. 1.

[50]Wilber, N. "Dilemmas of Child Sexual Abuse Reform: The Implementation of Massachusetts Chapter 288," Master's thesis (Cambridge, MA: Harvard University, 1985; Blose, James. The Sexual Abuse of Children in Massachusetts: A Prliminary Study of System Response. (Boston: Commission on Criminal Justice Statistical Analysis Center, 1979).

[51]Russell, A. and Trainor, C. *Trends in Child Abuse and Neglect: A National Perspective* (Washington, D.C.: National Center on Child Abuse and Neglect, 1984), p. 15.

[52]Willis, Cecil L. and Wells, Richard H. "The Police and Child Abuse: An Analysis of Police Decisions to Report Illegal Behavior," CRIMINOLOGY, Vol. 26 (November 1988), pp. 695–716.

[53]Besharov, Douglas J. "The Legal Aspects of Reporting Known and Suspected Child Abuse and Neglect," VILLANOVA LAW REVIEW, Vol. 23 (1977–1978), pp. 458–546.

[54]Wright Dzeich, Billie and Schudson, Charles B. *On Trial—America's Courts and Their Treatment of Sexually Abused Children* (Boston: Beacon Press, 1989) p. 53.

[55]See Yarmey, A.D. and Jones, H.P. "Is the Psychology of Eyewitness Identification a Matter of Common Sense?" in Lloyd, S.M. and Clifford, B.R. (eds.) *Evaluating Witness Evidence* (New York: Wiley and Sons, 1983).

[56]Davis, Samuel M. "Child Abuse: A Pervasive Problem of the 80s," NORTH DAKOTA LAW REVIEW, Vol. 61 (1985) p. 204.

[57]United States Bureau of the Census, *Projection of Age Demographics* (Washington: U.S. Government Printing Office, 1985).

[58]See Steinmetz, Suzanne K. *Duty Bound: Elder Abuse and Family Care* (Beverly Hills, CA: Sage Publications, 1988); Pilllemer, Karl A. and Wolf, Rosalie S. *Elder Abuse: Conflict in the Family* (Dover, MA: Auburn House Publishing, 1986); and Breckman, Risa S. and Adelman, Ronald D. *Strategies for Helping Victims of Elder Mistreatment* (Beverly Hills, CA: Sage Publications, 1985).

[59]Crystal, Stephen. "Elder Abuse: The Latest Crisis," *The Public Interest,* Vol. 88 (Summer 1987), p. 56.

[60]U.S. House of Representatives, Select Committee on Aging. *Elder Abuse: A Decade of Shame and Inaction* (Washington: U.S. Government Printing Office, April 1990).

[61]Ibid., pp. xii–xiii.

[62]Crystal, *op cit.*, pp. 58–59.

[63]Ibid, p. 59.

[64]P.L. 98-459 (1987).

[65]Select Committee on Aging, *Elder Abuse, op cit.*, p. iii.

[66]Daniels, R. Stephen, Baumhover, Lorin A. and Clark—Daniels, Carolyn L. "Physicians Mandatory Reporting of Elder Abuse," *Gerontology,* Vol. 29, No. 3, June 1989, pp. 321–27.

[67]Ibid., p. 324.

[68]Shapiro, Joseph P. "The Elderly Are Not Children," *U.S. News and World Report* (January 13, 1992), pp. 26–28.

[69]Ibid.

[70]This is the often cited work of Block, M. "Elder Abuse: the Hidden Problem." Briefing by the Select Committee on Aging, U.S. House of Representatives (Washington, D.C.: U.S. Governmnet Printing Office, 1980).

[71]Plotkin, Martha R. *A Time for Dignity: Police and Domestic Abuse of the Elderly* (Washington, D.C.: Police Executive Research Forum, 1988), p. 28.

[72]Ibid., pp. 21–22.

[73]Kosberg, J.I. "Preventing Elder Abuse: Identification of High Risk Factors Prior to Placement Decisions," *The Gerontologist,* Vol. 28 (1988), pp. 43–50.

[74]Pillemer, Kenneth A. and Finkelor, D. "The Prevalence of Elder Abuse: A Random Sample Survey," *The Gerontologist,* Vol. 28 (1988), pp. 51–57; and Steinmetz, S.K. "Dependency, Stress and Violence Between Middle-Aged Caregivers and their Elderly Parents," in Kosberg, J.I. (ed.) *Abuse and Mistreatment of the Elderly: Causes and Interventions* (Littleton, Mass.: John Wright, 1983), pp. 134–49.

[75]Zimring, Franklin E. "Toward a Jurisprudence of Family Violence," in Ohlin and Tonry, *op cit.*, pp. 547–69.

[76]"Who's Caring for Grandma?" *Newsweek* (July 29, 1991), p. 47.

CHAPTER 9

The Scourge of Narcotics

CONTENTS

- America's War on Drugs: A Historical Perspective
  - The First Tentative Steps
  - The Harrison Act and Expanding Federal Anti-drug Efforts
  - Scandals and Reorganization Efforts
- Some Evolving Aspects of the Drug Problem
  - The Latin American Connection
  - Changing Patterns of Drug Abuse
- Drugs, Crime and the Criminal Justice System
  - Drug Use Among Arrestees
  - Developing a Typology of Drug Offenders
  - Drugs and the Price of Corruption
- The Economics of Money Laundering
- The Latest Strategy: Attacking the Roots of Demand
  - Growing Anger of Foreign Officials
  - Programs to Avert Demand
- The Legalization of Drugs
  - The Hidden Economics of Illegal Drugs
  - The Drug War and Civil Rights
  - Concerns Raised by the Pro-criminalization Advocates

- **Changes in Drug Use and Possible Implications**
- **Conclusion**

To most Americans, the single most significant problem our nation faces is illegal drugs.[1] It is estimated that the United States is the market for over 60 percent of the world's supply of illicit narcotics.[2] In the public's perception, such chilling pronouncements make drug abuse and associated drug problems our country's most important crime. No other crime issue in our nation's history has so captured the public and the media: Drug trafficking, the use of narcotics, associated crime and the host of problems it has spawned, has riveted American attention. The ubiquity of our nation's "drug problem" is found in accounts in our daily newspapers and on the evening news. It reaches into our neighborhoods, our schools, our workplaces. Although its menace is often focused on the inner-city, its tentacles reach across America into rural and small town communities, working class neighborhoods, and the suburbs of the affluent. The presence of illegal drugs is seen creating serious social and economic consequences for the well-being of our nation. It reads like an all too familiar litany: crime, violence, health-care costs, prenatal addiction, family problems, lowered national productivity, and official corruption.

As a study in crime, the issue of illegal narcotics is an interesting phenomenon. Although the problem of drug abuse is seen as most pernicious among lower class urban minorities, it has broken the long-standing class imperative. Wealth, education, neighborhood—those factors that have often served to insulate segments of society from the ravages of traditional crime—have been effectively breached. Illegal narcotics seemed to have touched every segment of our population. The "cost" of America's insatiable appetitite for drugs will not be known for years. The full implications of our existing "drug problem" will be unfolding well into the 21st century as social scientists of today and the future trace its impact.

As with some other major crime issues of recent years, it is also a situation that has transformed our crime control efforts beyond our nation's borders and thrust our efforts into a global undertaking. In the eyes of the public, this is how it is seen. When a sample of Americans were asked to rank the most important domestic and international concerns facing our nation, narcotics trafficking was at the top of both lists.[3] This is an extraordinary response. Except in wartime, no other single issue has been capable of capturing America's attention as both the nation's most pressing domestic and international concern. This raises it to a national public policy issue almost without precedent. The international aspects of illegal drugs also raises another insidious implication: It calls into question our nation's ability to deal with illegal narcotics. Since it seems unlikely that we will find any short-range solution to our nation's "drug problem" illegal drugs will remain high on our agenda of concerns well into the future.

The issue of the illegalization of narcotics is not without its critics. There are those who contend that narcotics have primarily become a problem because of the way our government has chosen to deal with drugs. Critics of American drug policy argue that our attempts to deal with narcotics through a process of criminalization have actually worsened the problem. This mistake is then compounded by our government's almost singular preoccupation with the supply side of the demand curve. Concentrating our efforts on law enforcement activities to interdict drug trafficking and to criminalize the use of drugs has actually abetted illegal drugs and especially its obvious spin-off: drug-related crime. While such claims are interesting and thought-provoking, they have as yet, not gone beyond the realm of theoretical discourse. Perhaps such contentions are on target, but no one can really say. We really have no idea of what the situation would be today had we chosen another way to deal with narcotics. At this point such arguments still remain largely, if not almost exclusively, academic. The official policy of the government, which seems largely supported by the vast majority of Americans, calls for a national effort to reduce the availability of illegal drugs. We shall return to this issue later.

America's War on Drugs: A Historical Perspective

The First Tentative Steps

For the last three-quarters of a century, America has tried to deal with many forms of non-prescription drugs by making them illegal.[4] It wasn't always this way. Cocaine is a good example. Up until the late 19th century there were no laws restricting the sale, advertising, or consumption of this drug. In this *laissez-faire* atmosphere, entrepreneurs quickly made cocaine an elixir for the masses. Alcoholic extracts from the coca leaf were readily available to Americans in drug and grocery stores, saloons, and from mail order vendors. By 1885, the pharmaceutical firm of Parke, Davis and Company was selling pure cocaine and coca in 15 forms. This included coca-leaf cigarettes, cocaine inhalant, a coca cordial, cocaine crystals, and cocaine solution for hypodermic injection. Even Coca-Cola contained traces of cocaine and it wasn't until 1903 that the firm was forced to substitute caffeine for the use of cocaine in its formula. Cocaine was even prized for its "therapeutic" effects. Its benefits were widely heralded by such noted contemporaries of the time as Sigmund Freud, Thomas Edison, Sarah Bernhardt, Emile Zola, Henrik Ibsen, and even Pope Leo XIII.[5] The availability of morphine was also unregulated. Many of the patent medicines of the day which could be readily purchased over the counter contained a morphine or opium base.

This was soon to change and with it a fundamental change in the role of government itself. The drug issue and its ultimate criminalization is an excellent example of the growing regulatory power of the government—particularly the federal government—under the expanding public welfare doctrine. Until the early 20th century, the federal government was less predisposed to become involved in the wide-ranging regulatory aspects so familiar to most of us today. In the area of narcotics, what nascent regulatory efforts existed were imposed by a few states in the last decade of the 19th century. Even these early state regulatory efforts focused only on morphine and cocaine. The public interest of the time—at least as it was applied to federal policy—was reflected in the attitude that states had the preeminent regulatory role. Our national government in its oversight effort should maintain a "hands-off" policy in many areas of social and economic intercourse. Since the regulatory authority of the federal government was seen as especially intrusive, its oversight authority was to be kept purposely weak and ineffective.

Beginning in the late 19th century, concern began to mount that opium and cocaine needed to be controlled. It was also increasingly suggested that the states alone could not do the job and the federal government must play a lead role in such regulatory efforts. The impetus for Congressional attention to the developing "drug problem" came initially from a small but active group of reformers. These crusading anti-drug advocates (many of whom were also part of the anti-alcohol reform movement) claimed that the relationship between drug availability and its use and the incidence of crime and potential social disorder was real and substantial. These reformers loudly assailed the federal government to adopt laws controlling drugs. Not unlike similar pronouncements today, it was argued that our national interests would be undermined if government didn't immediately take action to stamp-out the availability and use of drugs.

This led to efforts by the federal government to consider ways to regulate such substances. In 1906, Congress took the initial step to control narcotics. In that year, the first Pure Food and Drug Act became law. Among other things this legislation made illegal the sale of patent medicines containing morphine, heroin, or cocaine. This was to be a precursor to what was to follow. In 1909, the federal government prohibited the importation of smoking opium. This was the same year that the federal government held its first hearings on the "narcotics problem." At these hearings the government's leading narcotics expert provided testimony which would serve as the rallying cry for the growing anti-narcotics forces: "Cocaine and other forms of narcotics transforms safe and otherwise tractable individuals into dangerous characters, and in most instances, wrecks the individual and all dependent on him as well as jeopardizes the lives of many."[6]

Although there was no evidence that such dire pronouncements were based on any scientific facts—certainly given our rudimentary pharmacological knowledge at the time—this was of little consequence. The threat became the reality of the moment and Congress was galvanized to action. The federal government had several options in trying to control narcotics. Among such options were governmental control and regulation either through government dispensing of drugs, the licensing of approved and regulated dispensers, the use of its taxing authority as a regulatory mechanism, or it could also deal with the control of these substances by making them illegal and then enforcing these illegal drugs out of existence. Congress decided that the best policy would be to regulate and tax legal manufacture and distribution of drugs and to criminalize illegal manufacture, distribution, and use. This decision would point the nation down a long path.

The Harrison Act and Expanding Federal Anti-drug Efforts

In 1914, Congress took an important step: It adopted the first major legislation directed at controlling and regulating certain forms of drugs. In that year, the Harrison Narcotic Act became law. This precedent-setting act controlled the sale of opium and opium derivatives. It also ushered in our nation's anti-narcotics policies and supporting enforcement program. This important piece of legislation served to create a drug enforcement legacy that, when one examines the record, still proves to be very fragmented and, at best, inconclusive. Initially, the responsibility for policing drugs under the Harrison Act was given to the Treasury Department. Under this arrangement, certain forms of narcotics became a licensed and taxed commodity that brought the taxing power, and with it, the enforcement authority of this agency to bear. The Treasury Department was given the authority to regulate legal distribution sources such as pharmaceutical manufacturers and to enforce laws against illegal drug sources. In 1919, the National Prohibition or Volstead Act was passed which ushered in the nation's disasterous experiment with prohibition. A new prohibition unit was created to stamp out the illegal distribution and sale of liquor. The prohibition unit was given a secondary responsibility: the enforcement of the Harrison Act.

In the competitive in-fighting among government bureaucracies, the Treasury Department knew how to play the game. Resources follow "need"—either actual or contrived. In its quest for more authority and appropriations this agency wasn't above stretching the truth a bit. In the same year it received its prohibition enforcement authority, it issued an alarming report about the nation's "narcotics problem." The Treasury Department claimed that 1.5 million dangerous addicts were at large in the streets. This was an extraordinary statement given the fact that the nation's population at the time was slightly in excess of 100 million. It was also contended by the authorities that heavy addiction was epidemic among youths, and that smuggling and peddling rings of unprecedented cunning and power had emerged.[7]

Even though the 1920s were the heyday of prohibition arrests, more people were actually arrested by the Prohibition Unit for violation of the Harrison Act. In the late 1920s, some serious scandals occurred in this agency, resulting in the creation in 1930 of a separate Bureau of Narcotics largely consisting of former prohibition agents. Under the aggressive leadership and political skills of the director of the new Bureau of Narcotics, this agency convinced Congress that other forms of drugs were also menacing America. Marijuana came under special attention as did other forms of drugs that the Bureau categorized as "dangerous." (It is interesting to note that although the Bureau of Narcotics singled-out marijuana for special attention, in 1920 the U.S. Department of Agriculture had published a pamphlet urging Americans to grow cannabis (marijuana) as a profitable undertaking). With this expansion of what constituted illegal drugs, the resources of this agency grew dramatically.

Scandals and Reorganization Efforts

Over the ensuing years, all forms of narcotic substances including amphetimines, barbiturates, and hallucinogens were outlawed as controlled substances. There was a "cost" associated with such efforts however. Problems of ineffectiveness and corruption attended our "success" at criminalizing drugs. Serious scandals occurred in the Bureau of Narcotics among those given the responsibility to enforcement the government's anti-narcotics laws. This would prove to be a harbinger of the future. Although the Bureau of Narcotics went through several efforts at reorganization following scandals, it proved incapable of effectively enforcing the problem out of existence. There was a growing feeling that the federal government needed to restructure and reprioritize its anti-narcotics enforcement efforts. As a result, the agency was disbanded. In 1968, a new federal agency, The Bureau of Narcotics and Dangerous Drugs (BNDD) was created. This new agency now became the government's lead agency in narcotics enforcement efforts. The problems didn't end with the creation of the BNDD. It, too, found its task daunting while corruption also found its way into this agency. In the late 1960s, serious scandals occurred in the agency's New York City office resulting in almost every agent being transferred, forced to resign, or fired.[8] It was reported that collusion between BNDD agents in this office and drug traffickers was ''deeply ingrained.''[9] Again, the regulators were finding the drug problem difficult to control with any degree of success or effectiveness.

In 1973, President Nixon, who had been elected on a campaign platform promising ''law and order'' which included a strong anti-drug stance, again reorganized the federal drug enforcement agencies. Under the new policies, the government's primary enforcement agency became the Drug Enforcement Administration (DEA). This new agency located in the Department of Justice was given additional resources and the number of enforcement agents significantly increased. Similar problems of ineffectiveness soon plagued this agency and several efforts were made to restructure the DEA with little apparent success.[10] Frustration began to mount, and again, the federal government sought a better means to ensure the success of its enforcement efforts. In an effort to shore up and intensify federal efforts against narcotics, a significant step was taken in 1981. The Federal Bureau of Investigation (FBI) was given authority to oversee the efforts of the DEA and to share enforcement responsibilities with the DEA in the area of narcotics. This was a monumental escalation in the government's anti-drug efforts. Behind this latest reorganization effort was the idea that this would bring the resources, investigative expertise, and prestige of the FBI to bear on the problem. Drugs would now get the attention of the federal government's most prominent investigative agency.

Transferring joint authority to the FBI for illegal narcotics was just part of a major reorganization strategy to combat drugs. Along with this latest restructuring, a new wrinkle was added. A page from the federal government's organized crime efforts was adopted. This strategy which employs assigned federal ''task forces'' to areas of particularly active organized crime involvement would be used to target areas and individuals involved heavily in drug trafficking. This inter-agency task force called the Organized Crime Drug Enforcement Task Force Program was begun in 1982. The task force program was divided into 12 regions. It was to attack the problem of illegal drugs using a multi-agency approach involving special attorneys from the Department of Justice, local U.S. Attorneys, FBI, DEA, Customs and IRS agents, the Marshal Service, and the Coast Guard. Special legal assistance was also provided by the Department of Justice. The task force was also to be aided by participating state and local investigative personnel. Congress has also passed the National Drug Control Program and created the Office of National Drug Control Policy—the so-called ''drug czar'' position to which the first appointment was made in 1989. The director of the Office of National Drug Control Policy has been given the responsibility to develop an annual plan to be submitted to the

President and then to Congress. It has also been suggested that a cabinet-level position be created for the "drug-czar."

Recently, there has been talk of expanding the task force. It has been suggested that the United States go one step further: the United States government should create a multi-jurisdictional international task force of federal agents to work with law enforcement personnel from other nations to attack cocaine production sources in South America. This international task force as proposed, would not only involve the authorities of Latin American countries, but seek cooperation from European authorities as well. The hope was expressed by administration spokespersons that West European nations who are also experiencing increased problems with cocaine would agree to participate.[11] Although such a proposal is being studied by the National Drug Control Policy Board, important diplomatic questions and issues of international law and national security concerns are raised by this proposal. At this point, there has been little interest shown by either most Latin American countries or the nations of West Europe to seriously consider such a multi-national drug task force.

An even more risky and increasingly costly proposal has been to involve the Pentagon and U.S. military authorities in a plan to crush the Latin American narcotic cartels. The Bush administration had significantly increased military spending and presence in Central and South American and throughout the Carribean region. Military spending on drug eradication, control and interdiction efforts has increased from a Pentagon-budgeted \$439 million in 1989 to \$1.2 billion in 1992. Initially cool to the idea of any involvement in the anti-drug efforts, the military have become more eager participants since the Cold War appears over and the Gulf War has been successfully concluded. Worried about appropriations cutbacks unless it can find justification for major expenditures, the military has become more enthusiastically involved in a wide-range of programs and the adoption of military hardware to the effort.

Military anti-drug efforts are well underway. Military aircraft and aerostat balloons detect drug planes using radar while AWACS and reconnaissance planes track aircraft and ground radars spot border crossers on foot. Army National Guardsman inspect vehicles at southern border crossings while Green Berets and marines maintain secret border listening posts. Navy frigates, cruisers and hydrofoils search for drug boats while Navy Seals surreptitiously inspect the hulls of ships. Some of the most sensitive military activities are taking place deep in South America. The Army's Green Berets instruct counternarcotics forces in Peru and Bolivia and Navy Seals train river guards, while military tactical-analysis teams process intelligence on traffickers.[12]

The effort is being coordinated through the Army's Southern command in Panama City and the Navy's Atlantic Command. Efforts are focusing on three zones: The production zone consisting primarily of Bolivia, Peru and Colombia; the smuggling zone stretching from Northern Colombia thru Central America, the Caribbean, and into Mexico; and the border zone which rings the United States with special emphasis on the nation's borders stretching from southern California up through the coasts of the Carolinas. The Army's Southern Command has developed a Counternarcotics Operation Center which has been given the go-ahead to develop a plan for a hemispheric narcotics bust.[13]

It calls for the armed forces of Colombia, Bolivia and Peru to mount a simultaneous attack on the existing drug network in their countries. Although American troops would not be involved, the effort would be supported by equipment, training, logistics and intelligence supplied by the United States. This has raised some concerns that the nation may be dangerously embarking on another disastrous Vietnam-like involvement.

In late 1991, the General Accounting Office issued a very critical report of the military's anti-drug efforts. It reported that the nearly $2 billion dollars spent by the military's detection and monitoring efforts during the two years examined in the study have not had a significant impact. In 1990 alone, of the nearly 900 metric tons of cocaine produced, only a little over 300 tons were seized by the combined efforts of all military and law enforcement efforts in the United States and throughout the entire hemisphere region.[14] There is also growing evidence that serious problems are beginning to develop between law enforcement and military authorities over what steps need to be taken and how. Law enforcement authorities are critical of the unsubstantiated "body count" mentality of military efforts and the military's lack of appreciation for the arrest and prosecution issues of law enforcement for which the military seems fundamentally ill-suited. The military, for their part, criticize the DEA as a bunch of city cops with no real training for jungle operations and no appreciation for tactics which would ensure better success in conducting raids on drug-trafficking locations.[15]

Some Evolving Aspects of the Drug Problem

The Latin America Connection

In the last few years, certain aspects of the drug problem have been evolving. The illicit use of drugs and associated problems were for many years viewed primarily as a problem of industrialized nations. This has been changing. Drug abuse, associated crime increases, corruption, and, in many cases, violence, is now a major concern in many drug-producing, exporting, and transhipment nations. Some of these nations—many of which can be considered "third world" nations along with those nations bordering them—are also experiencing increased drug-associated problems.

Nowhere is this more apparent than in Latin America. Although such a situation would seem to give rise to the greater possibility of U.S. and host country cooperation in anti-drug efforts than was the case only a few years ago, meaningful cooperation still seems to be absent. Many of the major Latin American drug-involved countries (such as Peru and Bolivia) continue to resist any intrusion of American anti-drug efforts in their nations. With the possible exception of Colombia, the proposal for a multi-regional hemisphere-wide task force involving the United States and major drug-growing and transhipment countries in the region have received only passive interest by countries in the southern hemisphere.

Although a number of the nations in Latin America have offered token support by allowing U.S. agents to work with their military and police units—which is usually conditional upon the receipt of some type of American foreign aid—the fact remains that

Another Failure?

Again, there are serious questions being raised about the federal government's enforcement agencies charged with stopping the flow of illegal drugs. Particular criticism is focusing on the DEA as the nation's leading drug-war agency. Many observers and insiders are saying it is failing. In 1990, this was acknowleged by the administrator of the agency who admitted, "The DEA has been unable to keep pace with the major drug trafficking organizations in operation."* Much of the recent criticism has focused on this agency's operating strategy. Many critics blame the agency for emphasizing arrest and seizure statistics—a "bust and buy" mentality similar to the "body counts" during the Vietnam War—rather than systematically gathering the required intelligence and using this technique to attack the drug trafficking choke points. The agency is also being criticized for its inadequate training efforts. The DEA also admits that it is critically short of intelligence analysts and its computer system is badly in need of improvement.

The problems don't end here. During 1989 and 1990, five agents in charge of field divisions retired and many other senior agents are close to retirement. More than half of DEA's field agents have less than five years experience with the agency. Poor salaries and working conditions are blamed for the high turnover among agents at all levels. Tension within the agency has been increased by a divisive and morale-sapping, six-year-old discrimination suit filed by a group of Hispanic agents and the recent and alarming arrests and convictions of some agents on drug-related charges. There has also been criticism of the ineptness on the part of supervisory and executive-level agents by field investigators. Perhaps the major and fundamental problem, however, is that the agency is simply overwhelmed with its task.

* "The Drug Warriors' Blues," *U.S. News and World Report* (April 30, 1990), p. 25.

many of our southern neighbors are only lukewarm to America's anti-drug initiatives. This is most obvious by their lack of cooperation in rebuffing repeated extradition efforts to hand in-country traffickers over to American authorities to answer charges brought by American courts. The same also can be said about such countries as Burma which plays an important role in the so-called "Golden Triangle" area of heroin production as well as other opium producing nations and regions of Asia and the Middle East.

Still, it is possible that with the increased problems involving drugs more of the nations in Latin America will, as Colombia has, become more receptive to cooperative efforts. Yet, this remains highly problematic given the nature of the region. The instability of governments in Latin America and the Carribean coupled with the serious economic and social conditions these nations face and the power and corruptive influence exercised by the drug overlords, make serious efforts to support American anti-drug initiatives in the region questionable. There is also the question of economics involved.

Unless the United States can somehow convince these countries that their interests are the same as ours—a questionable proposition at best—meaningful (as compared to token cooperation) will continue to elude our efforts. This is an area of extreme importance. It would seem that the U.S. government must give this area increasing attention in future years. It is developing as one of the major foreign policy issues of the 1990s.

There is also growing awareness that drug trafficking cartels may have matured. This, too, may have implications for our anti-narcotics efforts. The operations and problems of initial organization and struggles for the control of markets, as in the case of cocaine so prevalent during the early 1980s, may have largely been overcome.[16] There is a growing operational sophistication and consolidation of the control of the production, manufacture, and transhipment network by major drug suppliers. Evidence of this transition can be seen from the fact that violence, at least among the upper-echelons of major trafficking organizations, seems to have subsided in the United States. Although serious violence still attends the trafficking of drugs on the streets of our central cities, the continued violence seems to be moving into a stage where it is primarily centered among low-level pushers and drug users. The full implications of this are just beginning to unfold. This may suggest, for example, that law enforcement efforts to successfully stop the flow of drugs may be even more difficult in the future. Although it can be hoped that our own anti-drug initiatives are also improving, this will be another area worth watching closely for the next several years.

Another area demanding close attention is the apparant receptiveness of certain nations to receive drug operations or, at least, not to overly interfere when the drug cartels are forced to relocate. We are now seeing this occur in certain Latin American countries. Drug growing and manufacturing operations are relocating to more "friendly" nations as increased pressure is placed upon them by their own national authorities with the assistance of the United States.

Changing Patterns of Drug Abuse

There is some tentative and preliminary evidence that drug use also seems to be changing. Still, we must be cautious and a little skeptical about drug use surveys and their purported conclusions. Findings from two federal studies on drug use in America show that since the late 1970s young Americans have generally been reducing their use of all drugs except cocaine, and that in the mid-1980s the popularity of cocaine too, apparently reached its peak.[17] According to the National Institute on Drug Abuse, marijuana use peaked in 1978, and by 1985, seven out of 10 high school seniors said they believed marijuana use to be harmful. Young people's use of hallcinogens such as LSD and PCP has fallen since 1979. By 1987, cocaine use had also sharply declined among this group.[18] There is also evidence that cocaine-related emergencies at U.S. hospitals, after reaching their peak in the last quarter of 1988, fell off sharply by the last quarter of 1989.[19] By mid-summer of 1990, there was also evidence that the wholesale price of a kilo of cocaine in a number of American cities had increased from around $25,000 a year earlier, to nearly $40,000 and that the purity of seized cocaine had dropped.

Law enforcement officials quickly seized this as a sign that interdiction and enforcement activities were beginning to have an impact. Other drug researchers are less optimistic. It may only be a situation where traffickers are holding back on their product and, in some cases, adulturating the cocaine to drive up profits. The diluting of the street-level cocaine may also explain the drop in hospital emergencies.[20] It is entirely coinceivable, however, that the message about the dangers of drug use are beginning to seep into the American consciousness—at least among certain segments of American society, notably the more affluent and better educated middle class who may be turning away from recreational drug use. Unfortunately, surveys of high school students as an indicator of drug use also do not take into consideration dropouts who we can expect to be a high "at-risk" category.

If the indications that drug use at least among the more affluent and educated Americans may be waning, can we be optimistic that the United States may be poised to begin to turn the corner on drugs? It would seem that such optimism is premature at this time. First, middle-class drug use is very hard to assess as to its extent. This makes it difficult to show relative trends of decreased use.

Drug use is changing in still another way. Until the late 1970s to early 1980s, heroin was considered our most serious illegal drug. Most experts contend that cocaine and its derivatives now pose the most serious drug problem for the United States. It is widely available, relatively cheap, seems to be highly addictive—at least among some users—and poses significant and still not completely understood health consequences. Cocaine, unlike heroin, has also made inroads into a much broader segment of Americans than other addictive drugs. In this way, it has not only broadened the so-called market, but poses additional problems of controlling, uncovering, and treating instances of abuse. The National Narcotics Intelligence Consumers Committee (NNICC) estimates that cocaine consumption in the United States increased from 31 metric tons in 1982 to over 70 million metric tons by the mid-1980s.[21] And there has been evidence that, until recently, consumption has continued to grow inexorably each year.[22]

And no definitive studies have been done on the impact of "crack," a form of cocaine, and "black tar," a form of pure heroin, which seem to be growing in use among urban minorities. There is some indication that this problem may well be the major "battleground" of the future both in terms of the drugs of choice and those who use them. Perhaps, as potentially threatening is the introduction of highly addictive smokeable "ice" (crystalized methamphetamine), which has been introduced in Hawaii and has begun to appear on the West Coast.[23] It is possible that this will spread to other metropolitan areas.

Drugs, Crime, and the Criminal Justice System

Whenever drugs are mentioned, they are associated with the problem of crime. Just what is this relationship and in what ways are crime and drugs related? John Kaplan, writing in a recent issue of *Public Interest,* implies that drug use is *ipso facto* associated with

A Ray of Hope on Cocaine Abuse?

In what Federal researchers called "a strong indication that the nation's cocaine epidemic may have peaked," government figures released in late 1990 showed that cocaine-related visits to hospital emergency rooms dropped four percent in the first quarter of 1990 as compared to similar figures from the last quarter of 1989. According to the National Institute on Drug Abuse, this was the third quarterly drop in a row and it came on the heels of a 24 percent drop for the last quarter of 1989. Optimistic government spokesmen are hailing the results of the data as "the turning point in our nation's drug war."

Still, important and ominous signs exist. The Institute reported that the number of deaths reported in the United States resulting from cocaine use are continuing to rise. The figures rose from 2,254 in 1988 to 2,496 in 1989. This was an 11 percent increase in one year. According to the experts and the medical personnel studying drug use, there are two possible explanations for this apparent contradiction. One conclusion which is supported by government-sponsored studies is that while cocaine use is dropping among casual or recreational users, there has been no corresponding drop among heavy users—those who are most likely to be flirting with death because of their use of cocaine. Some criminal justice officials are also of the opinion that the drop in hospital emergency room admissions may partly be a result of stepped-up enforcement action on the part of the authorities and the greater likelihood that such patients will end-up being prosecuted for drug use. This may discourage some users from seeking medical help.

crime.[24] He is not alone in his thinking. In the eyes of most Americans, the two are inextricably related. For example, a 1986 survey of inmates from state correctional facilities found that 43 percent of the surveyed inmates were using illegal drugs on a daily or near-daily basis in the month before their current incarceration.[25] Such studies also tend to convince the criminal justice system.

This can be seen by the efforts of courts, probation and parole authorities to demand abstinence from all illegal drug use as a condition of probation and/or parole. Any number of jurisdictions operating under the same assumption have started such testing programs. Under a program which has been operating in Washington, D.C. and is now widely copied elsewhere, defendants who test positive at arrest may be ordered as a condition of pretrial release to participate in a pretrial urine monitoring program that requires weekly testing.[26] Another effort is to treat offenders in the community through outpatient methadone, outpatient drug-free (i.e., counseling without methadone for offenders residing in the community), and residential or "therapeutic communities." There are also many in-prison treatment programs.[27] Such programs and efforts suggest that any further involvement in drugs—besides drug use itself being criminal—is almost certainly to be associated with crime.

Along with such efforts involving defendants accused of criminal acts and those found guilty of crimes, the federal government is pushing for involving more workers in mandatory urinalysis programs. While this might be argued as an attempt to lower "demand" as much as an accusation that drug use leads to crime, it is as equally concerned about the crime issue (with the user being the criminal) as it is the demand issue. Along this line, a less intrusive means of detection—the analysis of fibers of hair for trace elements of drug use is also growing in popularity. Although the Supreme Court has approved the mandatory testing of certain classes of employees, and the federal government wants to expand such programs, reservations are being raised about important civil rights issues being violated under the widening net of government or employer-testing programs.

It must be recognized that not all drug use results in criminal behavior aside from the fact that mere illegal drug use itself may be a crime. Simply stated, not all drug users engage in crime to support their dependence or are driven to crime by drugs. This should be obvious with a little thought. Recreational drug users, for instance, are not always driven to commit crime, although it may be said that they certainly contribute to the illegal drug enterprise. It must also be recognized that there are different forms of crime—some certainly more serious to society than others. There are consensual crimes (e.g., prostitution), property offenses such as theft and burglary, and more predatory violent crimes such as robbery, assault, forcible rape, and homicide. Each can generally be thought of as escalating the threat they pose to society.

What we have then are different types of crimes which have to be measured as to their relationship to drug use, and yes, their seriousness to society. This complicates the picture because among other things, criminals involved in consensual crimes are often not involved in violent predatory offenses. A prostitute is not necessarily going to be involved in robbery or homicide. We then deal with a twofold problem: What is the relationship between drug use and crime, generally, and, more specifically, what is the relationship between drug use and certain types of crime such as violent crime?

Given the complexities surrounding this issue, the fact of the matter is that we have no clear idea of how drug use and crime are interrelated.[28] This is especially true in so-called "predatory crimes" which are of such concern to Americans. As two noted researchers on the subject say:

> In short, no single sequential or causal relationship is now believed to relate drug use to predatory crime. When the behaviors of large groups of people are studied in the aggregate, no coherent general patterns emerge associating drug use per se with participation in predatory crime. (*Author's note:* when the researchers defined "predatory crime" they had in mind instrumental offenses committed for personal gain. This did not include aggressive crimes such as marital violence, homicide, or assault unrelated to robbery or burglary). But research does show that different patterns appear to apply to different drug users. The observed relationship of drugs to crime varies by populations and subgroups, including groups defined by age, race or sex.[29]

Much of the problem is that no research has been able to convincingly draw supportable conclusions that cannot be attacked on methodological grounds. Although we have all been exposed to media accounts of the violence surrounding efforts to control drug trafficking territories, these acts do not explain how drugs are associated with most criminal events.[30] Obviously, such information would be invaluable for our efforts to deal with the nation's drug (and crime) problem. Given this lack of knowledge, most objective observers are very cautious about drawing any hard and fast causal conclusions about the relationship between the two. Although no one would argue that drugs don't contribute to crime, much still has to be learned before we can be more definitive as to how the two are related.

Drug Use Among Arrestees

In the past couple of years, the issue of drug use and crime has gotten a big boost from some research which has been conducted by the National Institute of Justice. Although this research still doesn't answer what specific relationships exist between the two—it merely examines the use of drugs among arrestees—the authorities, as in the case of prior drug use among state prison inmates, are quick to imply (or at least the reader tends to infer) that this is evidence of a causal relationship. Merely being arrested does not always mean someone committed the crime let alone demonstrate convincingly a nexus between their drug use and the crime. Merely testing positive for the presence of drugs doesn't tell us a great deal about how drugs figured into any criminal behavior on the part of the accused.

Secondly, some important research tends to indicate that high-rate criminals who do not use drugs, or use them only sporadically, are far less likely to be arrested than are their counterparts who use drugs frequently.[31] This fact will affect any drug-use inferences drawn from a typical sample of arrestees.

Still, The Drug Use Forcasting program, which has been operating since 1987, has provided some useful insights. Beginning with the city of New York, the program by 1990 had been expanded to include 25 cities. Data are gathered in central booking facilities in these 25 locales. Periodically, trained local staff obtain urine specimens and conduct interviews of arrestees at these sites. An analysis is then made of the specimens for drug use including types of drugs and associated characteristics of the person arrested.

The evidence suggests that recent drug use is very high among the arrestees sampled at random. Ninety-one percent of those arrested and charged with drug offenses tested positive while about 67 percent of those arrested for non-drug related crimes were found to have recently used drugs. Recent drug use among the arrestees in the sample is more than 10 times higher than is reported in surveys of persons in households or senior high schools.[32]

The high prevalence of drug use among those arrested for drug-related crimes is not unexpected. They consisted of both those arrested for drug use as well as possession. Under the circumstances, drug use would be expected to be quite high among this group. Even for those not arrested for narcotics-related offenses, however, the incidence of drug use is disturbingly (although again, not surprisingly) high.

For those who tested positive for recent drug use, the most prevalent identifiable offenses for which males in the sample were arrested were drug sales/possession, burglary, and larceny.[33] In the area of violent crimes, they were most likely to have been arrested for assault and robbery.[34] Looking at the adult females in the sample, most were arrested for the crimes of drug sales/possession, larceny, and prostitution.[35] The studies also showed that half of all male and female arrestees were between the ages of 21 and 30 and blacks were alarmingly and disproportionately represented among those arrested. Interestingly, the drug analyses showed that drugs of choice may vary by region of the country. This may indicate the need for different prevention and enforcement approaches as well as different treatment programs. The highest rates of cocaine use among the arrestees—almost 70 percent—was found in the Northeast. Cocaine use was much lower, and surprisingly similar, in the Midwest, South, and West (43 to 48 percent). Opiate use is much more prevalent in the Northeast and West than elsewhere, while amphetamine use was predominantly a West Coast phenomenon.

Developing a Typology of Drug Offenders

Some extensive research has also developed a description of different types of offenders who use and sell drugs both among adolescents and their adult counterparts. It incorporates observations and interviews with young people across the nation, clients in drug treatment programs, offenders on the streets of major cities, and offenders incarcerated in jails and prisons in a number of states. Tables 9.1 and 9.2 summarize findings about different forms of drug use and their relationship to behaviors, using data drawn from in-depth studies of small groups of offenders as well as national surveys.

The data seem to indicate from this research effort that both the use of drugs and attendant crimes are highly variable. Just as with most criminal events, a small percentage of the drug users and traffickers would seem to be committing most of the drug-associated crimes—at least the more serious violent offenses. These are indicated by the term drug-involved violent predatory "losers." Although the "winners" are also involved in extensive criminal activity, much of their "criminal activity" it would seem is less randomly violent and consists of crimes involving the distribution of drugs (as compared to robberies and burglaries to get drug money). This can be inferred from their "successful" mid-level role in existing drug distribution heirarchies. The predatory "losers" have not been assimilated into this organizational structure for purposes of "gainful employment" to purchase drugs. Instead, they must turn to crimes outside the distribution network for their drug funds and to meet their other needs.

Drugs and the Price of Corruption

There is another insidious side to our nation's efforts to deal with the problem of illegal drugs. In its efforts, the criminal justice system runs real risks of being seriously compromised by corruption. According to experts, the system of justice has not experienced such widespread corruption since the era of Prohibition.[36] It is particularly pronounced

TABLE 9.1 **TYPES OF DEALERS WHO SELL DRUGS FREQUENTLY OR IN LARGE AMOUNTS**

Type of Dealer	*Typical Drug Use*	*Typical Problems*	*Contact with Justice System*
Top-level dealers			
Adults (only)	None to heavy use of multiple types of drugs.	Major distribution of drugs; some other white-collar crime such as money laundering.	Low to minimal.
Lesser predatory			
Adolescents	Moderate to heavy drug use; some addiction; heroin and cocaine use.	Assaults; range of property crimes; poor school performance.	Low to moderate contact with juvenile or adult justice system.
Adult men	Moderate to heavy drug use; some addiction; heroin and cocaine use.	Burglary and other property crimes; many drug sales; irregular employment; moderate to high social instability.	Low to high contact with criminal justice system.
Adult women	Moderate to heavy drug use; some addiction; heroin and cocaine use.	Prostitution; theft; many drug sales; addicted babies; AIDS babies; high-risk children.	Low to moderate contact with criminal justice system.
Adults	Frequent use of multiple drugs; less frequent addiction to heroin and cocaine.	Commit many crimes; major source of income from criminal activity; take midlevel role in drug distribution to both adolescents and adults.	Minimal; low incarceration record.
Smugglers	None to high.	Provide pipelines of small to large quantities of drugs and money.	Variable contact.
Drug-involved violent predatory offenders:			
The "losers"			
Adolescents	Heavy use of multiple drugs; often addiction to heroin or cocaine.	Commit many crimes in periods of heaviest drug use including robberies; high rates of school dropout; problems likely to continue as adults.	High contact with both juvenile and adult criminal justice system.
Adults	Heavy use of multiple drugs; often addiction to heroin or cocaine.	Commit many crimes in periods of heaviest drug use including robberies; major source of income from criminal activity; low-status roles in drug hierarchy.	High contact with criminal justice system; high incarceration.

TABLE 9.1 TYPES OF DEALERS WHO SELL DRUGS FREQUENTLY OR IN LARGE AMOUNTS (continued)

Type of Dealer	*Typical Drug Use*	*Typical Problems*	*Contact with Justice System*
The "winners"			
Adolescents	Frequent use of multiple drugs; less frequent addiction to heroin and cocaine.	Commit many crimes; major source of income from criminal activity; take midlevel role in drug distribution to both adolescents and adults.	Minimal; low incarceration record.
Adults	Frequent use of multiple drugs; less frequent addiction to heroin and cocaine.	Commit many crimes; major source of income from criminal activity; take midlevel role in drug distribution to both adolescents and adults.	Minimal; low incarceration record.
Smugglers	None to high.	Provide pipelines of small to large quantities of drugs and money.	Variable contact.

Source: Chaiken, Marcia R. and Johnson, Bruce D. *Characteristics of Different Types of Drug-Involved Offenders* (Washington, D.C.: U.S. Department of Justice), February 1988, pp. 6–8.

in the law enforcement community. Yet it is not only the police which are succumbing: corrections personnel, prosecutors and judges are also susceptible.

Although state and federal court cases involving law enforcement personnel charged with some form of complicity in drug trafficking have grown alarmingly in recent years, nowhere is the problem more serious or has it caused more of a senasation than in Miami. During the 1980s, dozens of officers in the Miami Police Department came under investigation for narcotics trafficking or collusion with dope dealers. The most significant federal investigation of the Miami Police Department occurred after 16 Miami narcotics officers raided a smuggler's boat on the Miami River and stole nearly 400 kilos of cocaine. During the raid, three lookouts working for the drug smugglers reportedly fell into the river and drowned. Indictments and convictions against the officers followed.

In New York City's most far-reaching police corruption scandal in nearly two decades, 13 existing or former officers assigned to that city's 77th Precinct in the crime-ridden Bedford-Stuyvesant neighborhood of Brooklyn were charged or convicted of offenses involving narcotics and narcotics-related coverups. In 1990, as a result of an ongoing FBI investigation, members of the Buffalo, New York Police Department were arrested by the federal authorities for dealing drugs—some even allegedly distributed from patrol cars while on duty. Other cities, both large and small, have also been hit by revelations of drug use and dealing by members of their police departments.

The most recent and large-scale police corruption scandal occurred in Los Angeles. Members of the Los Angeles County Sheriff's Department Special Narcotics Squad have been convicted of "skimming" hundreds of thousands of dollars from the huge amounts

TABLE 9.2 TYPES OF DRUG-INVOLVED OFFENDERS

Type of Offender	*Typical Drug Use*	*Typical Problems*	*Contact with Justice System*
Occasional users			
Adolescents	Light to moderate or single-substance, such as alcohol, marijuana, or combination use.	Driving under influence; truancy, early sexual activity; smoking.	None to little.
Adults	Light to moderate use of single substances such as hallucinogens, tranquilizers, alcohol, marijuana, cocaine, or combination use.	Driving under influence; lowered work productivity.	None to little.
Persons who sell small amounts of drugs			
Adolescents	Moderate use of alcohol and multiple types of drugs.	Same as adolescent occasional user; also, some poor school performance; some other minor illegal activity.	Minimal juvenile justice contact.
Adults	Moderate use of alcohol and multiple types of drugs including cocaine.	Same as adult occasional user.	None to little.
Type of Dealer	*Typical Drug Use*	*Typical Problems*	*Contact with Justice System*
Persons who sell drugs frequently or in large amounts			
Adolescents	Moderate to heavy use of multiple drugs including cocaine.	Many involved in range of illegal activities including violent crimes; depends on subtype (see Table 2).	Dependent on subtype (see Table 2).
Adults	Moderate to heavy use of multiple drugs including heroin and cocaine.	Depends on subtype (see Table 2).	Dependent on subtype (see Table 2).

Source: Chaiken, Marcia R. and Johnson, Bruce D. *Characteristics of Different Types of Drug-Involved Offenders* (Washington, D.C.: NIJ-U.S. Department of Justice), February 1988, pp. 4–5.

of cash confiscated during drug arrests. Authorities in Los Angeles are now focusing similar attention on the Los Angeles City Police Department. When police raids encounter major drug operations where hundreds of thousands or even millions of dollars are found, the temptation is proving too irresistible.

It isn't only police agencies in urban areas that are finding drug-related corruption among their own. South Georgia, for instance, has been particularly hard hit in recent years. When the federal government's efforts to seal off Florida landing sites made it too risky to fly into remote areas of that state, the traffickers switched their landing sites to neighboring Georgia. With this change came increased instances of police corruption. Other states such as Louisiana, Mississippi, Alabama, and Texas have also experienced increased drug trafficking in the many remote areas that can serve as landing sites in these states. With this has come increased corruption. A disturbing number of law enforcement officers in these states have been found guilty of trafficking, conspiracy, or aiding and abetting drug smugglers who have paid them to look the other way when shipments arrive.

The federal authorities are also concerned that drug money may be too tempting to some of their own people. The Customs Service has beefed up its anti-corruption efforts as has the DEA and the FBI. Even the federal Organized Crime Strike Force in Boston has had problems with personnel being bribed and corrupted. Police agencies in areas where narcotics trafficking is heavy have found the need to significantly increase their efforts at anti-corruption.[37]

The Economics of Money Laundering

There is still another aspect of drug-related corruption. When U.S. drug agents tallied up the amount of cocaine seized during fiscal 1989, their haul totaled 49 tons. The wholesale value of the coke, as much as $28 billion, is testimony to another dark genius:[38] Vast sums of money attend illegal drugs. It has been warned that the vast flow of cash threatens currency, banks, and economics—particularly among some Latin American countries. Even specially trained federal agents have had only limited success in tracing and understanding the complexities of currency exchange or money laundering associated with the huge drug profits.

Part of the problem is the ingenuity of drug traffickers and their financial consultants in devising new schemes to launder money and the willingness of the world's banking industry to look the other way. Although Congress has passed a number of laws that attempt to trace currency in the banking systems of the United States, it has not been very successful in the world banking community. In 1989, a special federal task force began taking shape. The Financial Crimes Enforcement Network (FINCEN) hopes to better zero-in on money launderers with computer programs capable of spotting suspicious movements of electronic money. This strategy recognizes that the major problem is that drug money is easily mingled with legal money. The financial transactions system involving banks operates on wire transfers, overnight interbank loans, and the unregulated Eurodollar market, which is beyond the direct regulatory power of the U.S. government.

Adding to the problem is the fact that special banking laws have been passed by some nations, such as the Netherlands Antilles which resist any attempt to disclose information to U.S. authorities. There are also any number of "investors" and international financiers only too eager to help conceal drug-tainted money by handling investments into legitimate businesses by establishing "dummy" corporations to make purchases and transactions for a reported seven to 10 percent of the investment proceeds.[39]

Since the late 1980s, major laundering activities have largely shifted to the Pacific Rim. Hong Kong has become the preeminent laundering center in the Pacific. In this city, which has become a mecca for unscrupulous entrepreneurs aided by strict bank secrecy laws and the absence of regulatory mechanisms, laundering flourishes. Even such remote islands as Nauru in the Western Pacific and Palau and Truk in Micronesia find drug profits flowing into their banks. Citizens of Vanuata, a volcanic archipelago of some 80 islands formerly known as the New Hebrides, have found that international finance, at least for some interests in these islands, beats coconut and taro farming. In Port Vila, the capital, it is not unusual for a $100 million transaction between major international banks to take place on any given day.[40]

Careless and unscrupulous American banks have also contributed to the problem. Such banking stalwarts as the Bank of America and the Bank of Boston have had to pay hefty fines for their involment in laundering schemes. These kinds of arrangements are sought after by major drug traffickers who would like to keep their money in the United States for investment purposes. The developing scandal involving the American and international bank holdings of the Bank of Credit and Commerce International (BCCI) include allegations that this banking network was extensively involved in the international laundering of drug money. In the United States, a money-laundering center can be spotted by the huge surplus of cash that flows into the Federal Reserve System. In 1985, the Miami branch posted a $6 billion excess. But after several years of intense federal probes of South Florida banks, Miami's cash glut dwindled. Much of the business is reported to have moved to the Los Angeles area where the cash surplus ballooned from $166 million in 1985 to nearly $4 billion in 1989.[41]

This focus on the money side of drugs is important for prosecution. It is impossible for federal authorities to link major drug traffickers with the sale of drugs except through such tracking. Major drug dealers are too well insulated from the sale of narcotics. Federal authorities must then conduct a currency trail that leads from the sale back to the kingpin. A second prosecutorial concern is to use the evidence of such resources to seize traffickers' assets gained through narcotics dealing and/or to prosecute for income tax violation. This policy attempts to cripple the cartels by seizing both assets and working capital.[42] Unless the government is successful in both tracing and linking the assets to narcotics profits, such seizure programs are ineffective. The simple fact remains, however, that many major traffickers have so far been successful in concealing their laundering operations and their assets from government.

The Latest Strategy: Attacking the Roots of Demand

It is becoming increasingly apparent that the federal government's programs to control drug abuse are failing because, among other things, they emphasize a futile crackdown on suppliers while neglecting the equally important task of weaning the American public from its habits. At least this is the growing consensus of many of the nation's experts on our country's drug problem. In spite of record levels of drug confiscations and a threefold increase in arrests of major drug traffickers, a government-sponsored study on the effects of our anti-narcotics efforts claims that only a small percentage of the cocaine, heroin and a somewhat larger percentage of the marijuana coming into our country in recent years has been seized.[43] It is also recognized among drug enforcement officials that in spite of highly publicized domestic marijuana eradication efforts, the problem of home-grown cultivation of marijuana seems to be as prevalent as ever.

Growing Anger of Foreign Officials

One of the unanticipated outcomes of our futile efforts to stop the flow of drugs has been to increase the bitterness foreign officials express about our drug efforts. They are angry because they feel the United States has not done enough to curb the demand for drugs and they are risking their enforcement agents' lives in the drug fight when the United States appears unable or unwilling to curb its domestic appetite for drugs. One such outspoken critic of America's efforts is the recent Attorney General of Mexico. He pointed out that 154 Mexican police officers were killed by traffickers between the years 1983 and 1988; a fact that he contends seems to go unrecognized by the American media and the officials in Washington. He also argued that the traditional separation between producer and consumer countries is no longer valid. His view, which is becoming widely shared, is that the United States has developed a black-and-white mentality in which the producing nations are the villains and the consuming nations the victims. He calls such a simple dichotomy false. It is not only a problem of the United States not being able to control its seemingly insatiable appetite for drugs, it is also the fact that interests in the United States provide unlimited opportunities for traffickers to launder drug monies, provide financial capital for drug smugglers, and all the while increases its own exports in certain illegal drugs.[44] For these reasons, America must share the burden of both creating and sustaining the drug problem.

Some foreign officials are also outraged by other indications of America's response to drugs. The Colombian government was seething over the fact that Washington, D.C. Mayor Marion Barry was convicted on only one minor count of cocaine possession. When informed of the trial verdict, the President of Colombia ordered a study of the extradition agreement under which two dozen Colombians have been handed over to the United States to face drug charges. Officials in this nation felt the Barry verdict was an example of U.S. hypocrisy; America expects tough treatment for Colombian drug traffickers while dealing lightly with high-profile drug users in the United States.[45]

Foreign officials are also concerned about another problem associated with America's drug scourge—one which has become closely linked with the growing violence in other drug-involved countries. The United States has become the arsenal that supplies a large share of the weapons used by the gangs trafficking in drugs. Either openly, through legitimate gun dealers, or, as is usually the case, more covertly through the available illicit market operating in the United States, automatic weapons, explosives, and other forms of weaponry and armaments are available for the price. There have been several notable attempts to purchase sophisticated weaponry from illicit sources in the United States by Colombian drug cartels which became public when the federal authorities learned about the pending sales.[46] Unknown is how many of these sales have been consumated without the knowledge of authorities.

Programs to Avert Demand

Although the Reagan, and now the Bush Administrations, have been calling for a drug-free society, and Nancy Reagan mounted a nationwide program to "just say no" to drugs, many question the motivation for such efforts. Although well-intentioned, it may have been more political hype than substance. It is interesting to note that the current administration appears less enthused about supporting such efforts than the Reagan Administration. There is also substantial criticism that such poltically visible programs have not been effectively followed through. In spite of growing concern over the demand problem, the bulk of federal dollars still go to enforcement efforts.

Although the federal and state governments have been increasing expenditures for drug treatment and awareness programs in the past couple of years, it is still the supply side of the drug equation which continues to receive the vast majority of monies spent for the "war on drugs." The charts in Figures 9.1–9.5 depict such facts as drug interception costs, criminal justice expenditures, seized assets, and drug seizures. Also included are facts on state spending for alcohol and drug-abuse services and the growing numbers of Americans seeking help in drug-abuse programs. While Congress and the states increased appropriations for "user-targeted" programs, there is a great deal of skepticism that abatement or anti-demand programs are "cost-effective" as measured by both success rates and who they reach. Treatment programs, in spite of a some supposedly successful efforts, still seem to have a poor record of keeping drug abusers off drugs.[47] Even Nancy Reagan's "just say no" program came under sharp criticism. A report on drug abuse prevention by the General Accounting Office concluded that the program has not been effectively evaluated and there are uncertainties about its applicability to all segments of the population and its long-term benefits.[48] This is a major problem with such programs. They may not reach many of the urban high-risk users and school dropouts: Those who contribute overwhelmingly to the nation's drug problem.[49]

There is also skepticism of what educational abatement programs can hope to accomplish. Most of the monies spent to abate demand through prevention programs have been given to the Department of Education to develop and support drug education programs in the nation's schools. Even the former Secretary of Education (who later became the first so-called federal "drug czar"), speaking in 1988 before the House Select Committee on Narcotics Abuse and Control, expressed skepticism that much of what passes for drug education has any value. He is not alone in questioning the value of such programs. The Rand Corporation in its analysis of the school-based educational efforts, and the General Accounting Office have also expressed strong reservations about such programs, given the fact that so little evidence supports the benefits of such undertakings.[50]

Still, such educational programs cannot be effectively evaluated until future years. Although we may never know what specific role our educational efforts may have contributed to future decreased drug abuse among our young people, it may be safe to as-

Figure 9.1. Federal spending on the drug war. (The amounts, in millions of dollars, represent only drug-related expenditures for the departments and programs listed.)

Drug interception programs	*Amount spent in 1989*	*Estimated spending in 1990*	*Amount requested for 1991*
Coast Guard	$ 629.5	$ 670.2	$ 727.0
Customs	427.0	512.9	455.3
Department of Defense	354.5	783.1	1,111.5
Immigration and Naturalization Service	52.0	52.3	59.4
Office of Territorial and International Affairs	0.4	0.9	1.3
Federal Aviation Administration	3.2	9.8	18.2
Total	1,466.6	2,029.2	2,372.7
Criminal justice			
	$ 542.9	$ 548.7	$ 700.0
Federal Bureau of Investigation	209.9	140.6	172.1
Organized Crime Drug Enforcement Task Forces	0.0	214.9	330.0
Criminal Division	13.3	11.5	18.3
Tax Division	2.2	1.4	1.5
U.S. Attorneys	134.0	137.1	182.2
U.S. Marshalls	124.4	154.2	201.0
Prisons	787.5	1,502.8	1,044.8
Support of prisoners	72.1	111.0	135.0
Immigration and Naturalization Service	126.4	128.0	140.9
Office of Justice Programs	185.6	481.0	525.6
Forfeiture Fund*	271.6	356.8	372.0
INTERPOL	0.7	1.1	1.4
U.S. Courts**	39.2	59.0	81.7
Total	2,509.8	3,848.1	3,906.5

*The proceeds from assets seized that go to antidrug programs.

**For drug prosecution, pretrial drug treatment and corrections.

Source: Office of National Drug Control Policy

sume that should future drug use decrease, it may at least be partly attributable to our early and unremitting efforts to educate the young against the dangers.

Several things are obvious from the discussion of the "demand side" of the nation's efforts to stem the drug problem. First, it must receive more attention than it has

Figure 9.2. **Seized assets. (Value of houses, vehicles and other property confiscated from drug suspects by Federal authorities, in millions of dollars.)**

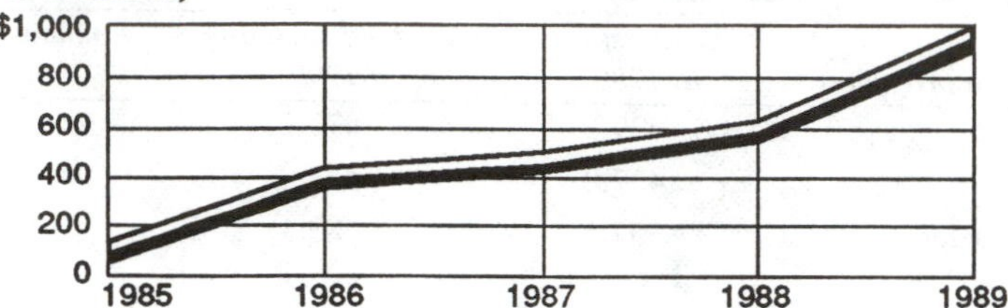

Source: Drug Enforcement Administration (Adapted with permission from *The New York Times* (April 22, 1990), p. E-6.

in the past. Efforts must be made to concentrate simultaneously our nation's efforts on both law enforcement and, at the same time, reduce consumption. Second, until consumption patterns are changed, continuing efforts to deal with the situation through interdiction and law enforcement will continue to be an abysmal failure. Third, if we are to spend public funds for such programs as education and treatment to lower market demand, we must devote more attention to finding out what types of programs are successful and with whom. This is no easy task—in fact, it may be the single most difficult objective to achieve. If educational programs and other abatement efforts are to be effective, they must begin early and be unremitting in their message.

We must accept the fact that with many users and potential users such programs will not be effective. The goal then, is to drive down the use of drugs to an acceptable threshold. It will never be possible to totally eliminate the use of illegal drugs. But it must be shrunk to a level of drug usage and associated problems that we can live with and accept as a nation. This seems to be the only practical and workable strategy.

The Legalization of Drugs

Amid the many problems with our anti-drug efforts, the unspeakable is being spoken. A small but growing number of voices are suggesting that the United States consider legalizing drugs. Generally, such suggestions in the past were those coming from radical libertarians who held the view that people have an inherent right to use drugs. Or they were the product of radical and obscure academics or drug culture advocates whose motives were dismissed as uninformed or couched in hedonistic self-interest. It was easy to dismiss these sources. It may not be as easy to disregard these latest and more responsible and objective voices. These voices emenate from notable public officials, reputable scholars, and even a few members of the criminal justice community. Although certainly a distinct minority, they raise important issues. While such suggestions are not new, the source of these comments add a more thoughful dimension than past pro-legalization arguments.

This is a far-reaching recommendation and one with extremely thought-provoking implications. It mirrors how seriously the narcotics situation has become and, to some at

Figure 9.3. Burden on the states. (The rise in expenditures for some state-supported alcohol- and drug-abuse services, caused overwhelmingly by the impact of drugs.)

	1985	*1988*	*Percent Increase*
New York	$309,368,481	$504,208,790	63.0%
California	201,933,720	261,474,670	29.5
Pennsylvania	65,712,000	86,250,353	31.3
Florida	42,891,735	75,132,664	75.2
Illinois	47,356,816	68,056,900	43.7
Oregon	10,915,230	60,600,918	455.2
Connecticut	27,087,735	57,951,823	113.9
Minnesota	5,009,800	46,052,625	819.3
New Jersey	22,307,000	45,311,570	103.1
District of Columbia	18,897,677	30,771,287	62.8

Source: National Association of State Alcohol and Drug Abuse Directors

least, the futility of continuing our present policies. Fundamental to the decriminalization argument is the realization that asking the criminal justice system to put an end to the tragedy of drugs is asking the impossible.[51] It is time to consider getting the criminal justice system out of the business of trying to control a health problem and putting that responsibility where it belongs—in the hands of the public health system. Much of the substance abuse problem, it is argued, is impervious to any punishment that the criminal justice system could reasonably mete out. While we continue to unsuccessfully struggle to control drugs which results in the arrests of hundreds of thousands of Americans annually for violating drug laws (most of which are for possession charges) our police and the criminal justice system finds itself unable to concentrate sufficient attention on predatory crimes. As a result, many serious crimes receive insufficient investigation and go unprosecuted and unpunished as we drain resources of the police, prosecutors, the courts, and our prison systems to combat a losing effort.

In light of the growing debate over the issue of legalization, there is a broad range of issues underlying the proponents' position on this topic. Americans need to consider these arguments along with those who say that continued criminalization and stepped-up enforcement activities and efforts at lowering demand for legal drugs is the only logical policy for the United States to follow. This is not to say that legalization is the answer; it merely suggests that alternative policies and these thought-provoking arguments should become part of the public dialogue on our nation's policies to deal with illegal narcotics.

The "Hidden Economics" of Illegal Drugs

This argument over legalization or the continued criminalization of drugs is pushing the drug issue to the forefront among public policy questions of the 1990s. And this is how Ethan Nadelman, writing in the *Journal of Foreign Policy* sees the issues.[52] He

Figure 9.4. **Seeking help. (Numbers of people in the U.S. entering drug-abuse treatment programs, in thousands.)**

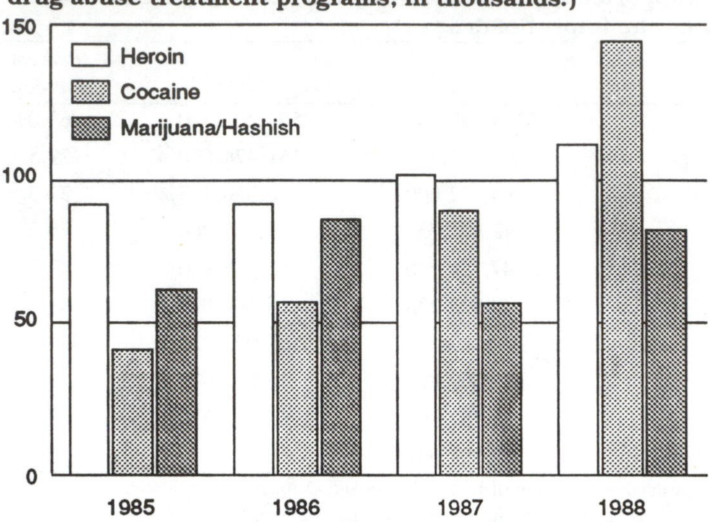

Source: National Association of State Alcohol and Drug Abuse Directors

recognizes, as do all students of government, that government policies have beneficiaries and victims—"winners" and "losers." By making drugs illegal, the idea is that the "winners" are those who would become drug abusers if narcotics were legal. The "losers" are those people who traffic drugs. This is the underlying assumption behind current anti-drug efforts. Yet, Nadelman contends, this has not happened. Instead we have created a network of unintended winners and losers. The winners are, of course, the drug manufacturers and traffickers who have managed to grow rich, provided they avoid arrest and the seizure of their assets by the authorities or violence from other drug criminals. The losers are the American people, who must pay extraordinary sums to try to control what appears to be the uncontrollable. There are also other losers including the exporting countries and, ultimately, the larger national interests of the United States.

This idea of "winners" and "losers," because it serves as one of the important cornerstones in the legalization of drugs, needs to be examined carefully. The first winner-loser argument deals with the question of international economics. In this case, the United States, the world's largest debtor nation hemmorhaging from its international monetary drain, finds itself a "loser" by subsidizing the economies of drug-producing and exporting nations. Yet, it is not a type of economic exchange that permits underdeveloped countries to benefit fully from its export commodities. Take the case of cocaine. Although recognized benefits "trickle down" to the individual native worker cultivating a few acres of coca plants or the Colombian workers involved in converting the raw coca into coca paste and then into coca hydrochloride, the vast profits go into the hands of the drug overlords and corrupt public and military officials. Although this has happened in the past with legal export commodities, such as the exploitive sugar

Figure 9.5 **Drug busts. (Federal drug seizures, in pounds.)**

	Heroin	*Cocaine*	*Marijuana*
1982	514.8	12,291.4	2,379,281.0
1983	690.4	18,554.8	1,953,053.3
1984	779.2	24,167.4	2,836,694.9
1985	967.8	54,240.8	1,893,848.4
1986	858.9	60,009.2	1,564,307.1
1987	802.3	81,660.5	1,429,006.0
1988	1,824.7	125,649.5	1,324,831.6
1989	1,705.0	181,362.5	739,332.9

Source: Drug Enforcement Administration

empires and the well-known excesses of the American Fruit Company (the profits of which were controlled by rich landowners or absentee corporations), there are some important differences.

A major difference is the violence and corruption that controls the drug network. In parts of Latin America, it has become open season on police, prosecutors, and judges. In the Summer of 1989, a bloody week of assasinations attributed to the Medellin and Cali cocaine cartels marked a new era of violence. Judges in Colombia went on a national strike demanding greater protection from the government after 11 of their colleagues were assassinated in a single day. The Attorney General of Colombia—the fifth such official in six years and the only one who would accept the position—fled to the United States for protection. A direct consequence of this violence has been the undermining of both the government and the legal framework in that country and the resources from drug profits which make this possible. Similar threats and destabilization exists among other drug-exporting nations in the region. The characteristic instability of Latin America has been further undermined by America's policy of making drugs illegal and then trying to enforce them out of existence. This instability affects America's long-range national interests in the region.

The huge drug profits are being used to destabilize the area in another way. Narcotraficantes-supported guerilla and terrorist groups are reaping important benefits. Funneling drug monies to these groups provide them the resources to buy weapons and support guerilla activities. This makes it that much more difficult for the government to function or to take steps to eradicate coca production even if they wanted to. It has also been reported that America's arch-enemy Castro's Cuba has not only been involved in the trafficking of cocaine destined for the United States, but has actually sponsored Cuban agents in the United States in establishing cocaine distribution networks.[53] It is not only in Latin America where our anti-narcotics strategy is giving assistance to our enemies. A 1988 report to the Congress by the General Accounting Office states that anti-American countries such as Iran, Afghanistan, Laos, and Burma produce much of the world's supply of opium used in the production of heroin, most of which finds its way into the United States.[54] These countries have no interest in cooperating with the American authorities.

Iran uses its drug-producing resources to continue its virulent anti-American policies and to support dangerous turmoil in the Middle East. And we provide the market and the capital for their efforts.

There is another insidious side to our policy of criminalizing drugs and its international implications. We were not fully aware of—nor could we reasonably forsee—the way our own agents of government would condone drug trafficking out of a sense of "national interest." Congress has investigated charges that the Central Intelligence Agency was in deep collusion with certain drug dealers in Southeast Asia and blocked a federal prosecution in Chicago of a drug smuggler from Thailand who was on the agency's payroll. Other allegations and charges have been leveled at the C.I.A.—often by law enforcement agencies—for the same behavior in Latin America and Mexico.[55] Members of Congress were aghast at U.S. government involvement in the use of drug monies and the support of traffickers to finance the Contras in Nicaragua.

We find ourselves in a perplexing situation. Today, in Latin America, it is said that our government, in the interests of containing communism or at least regimes antithetical to our interests, abets corruption. Furthermore, our policies contribute to the misery and violence of the drug trade. The situation is compounded when other nations and interests attempt to counter our efforts by using the same tactics. The results are the same: Real reform is thwarted.

Legalization advocates also contend that the policy of trying to enlist support for our eradication efforts in Latin America are doomed to failure. It is estimated that in Colombia alone drug organizations provide direct employment for nearly a million Colombians and indirect employment of another 5 million. The figures also run into the millions in Bolivia and Peru.[56] The governments, farmers, and workers benefitting from the cocaine enterprise in these regions have no meaningful incentive to support such efforts. In the case of farmers, crop substitution programs cannot hope to compensate for the loss of monies to those who rely on coca production for their livelihood. The substitution of legal crops would not guarantee them the same income and conventional crops are much more difficult and costly to cultivate then coca producing plants. A coca farmer in the late 1980s could net up to $2,600 per hectare per year, over four times what he could expect to earn from cultivating oranges and avocados, the next most profitable traditional crops.[57] Basic crop cultivation economics also play a role. In the most fertile coca producing regions, a coca crop can mature at least several times annuallly. A total of several thousand acres of coca plants can supply several tons of processed cocaine. Unlike conventional crops then, significant acreage does not need to be in cultivation to produce a crop to satisfy the existing market and these cultivation areas can be spread out and more easily hidden in a country of any size.[58]

American officials seem also to be blind to the economic-political-social infrastructure that exists in the drug-producing regions of Latin America. These have become, in many important ways, interlocked with the cocaine trade. Rensselaer Lee, in a penetrating article in the foreign policy journal, *Orbis,* discusses with unusal clarity the problems the United States faces in this region.[59] First, Andean governments worry about the impact of successful drug-control policies. The consequences of even partially successful eradication efforts would exacerbate rural poverty and create new legions of unemployed which would strengthen anti-democratic, or at least, anti-government forces in the region. Already precarious governments would crumble and the officials in these countries know and fear this. Coca-growing peasants would be drawn to insurgent groups. This has occurred in the Upper Huallaga Valley of Peru where it is estimated that 90 percent of the peasants in the region derive income from coca cultivation. As a result of U.S. pressure on the Peruvian government to "crackdown" on cultivation efforts, many peasants have already been driven into the ranks of the fanatical Maoist-inspired Sendero Luminoso ("Shining Path") guerillas operating in this area.

Many Latin Americans also see the economic benefit of drug trafficking. Drug-related business is an important economic safety valve which has cushioned the general economic downturn in the region during the 1980s. Income, jobs, and foreign exchange (the latter having the effect of stabilizing their currencies) are provided these countries.

Just as other countries have come to view American initiatives throughout the world, Latin Americans tend to see U.S.-imposed drug enforcement measures as infringements on their national sovereignty. This may be heightened by the fact that some of the cocaine cartels have provided support for charitable activities and used a portion of their financial resources to provide better housing, health care and recreational facilities for the poor. Increasingly, anti-American hostility is growing and U.S. policies are viewed as another extension of the historical long-standing American imperialism in the area.

It is also a problem that governments exercise little or no control over the remote territories where drug production flourishes. Such areas are relatively inaccesible mountainous or jungle terrains—many of which also are protected by anti-government guerilla groups. The problem is made worse by the fact that corruption is rampant in the area. The Colombians have a saying, "Plomo o plata" (lead or silver), meaning "a bullet or a bribe, the choice is yours." That saying very vividly describes the Colombian drug cartels' approach to ensuring their success in the drug business. The criminal justice system has been seriously compromised in these countries and there is little hope that reasonably effective administration of justice can be restored. While the governments draw up elaborate plans to eradicate coca and police make a few highly publicized token arrests and a few prosecutions of lower-level traffickers or growers occur, these are cosmetic.[60]

The economics of illegal narcotics play other other roles. One of the most obvious is the one that law enforcement people see existing. Given the amounts of money that can be made in dealing in narcotics, it is almost impossible to breakup dealer networks. Arrests are made of traffickers and their place is quickly taken by other dealers willing to chance arrest, prosecution, and imprisonment for the money that can be made. America's prisons are overflowing with people convicted for dealing in narcotics, yet the flow continues unabated. In this vein, a study by the Rand Corporation at the request of the Department of Justice, indicates that efforts to cut-off the supply of cocaine will not work given the profit margins that exist in the narcotics trade. Using mathematical models, the researchers confirmed the legalization advocates worst fears: Assuming an existing 20 percent seizure rate of narcotics and if the authorities could raise this to where

50 percent of the cocaine coming into the country is seized, the loss would add only three percent to the retail cost of cocaine.[61]

There is also the growing recognition that interdiction efforts can not hope to stem the tide. It is estimated, for instance, that the nation's annual cocaine consumption amounts to what could be transported in two large aircraft.[62] If this is the case, the efforts to seal our borders is a hopeless exercise in futility.

The Drug War and Civil Rights

There is another attendant "cost" to our "war on narcotics" which is disturbing to some Americans. There is growing concern that the government, in its attempts to curtail drugs, threatens civil liberties.[63] The issue hits home in two areas: the growing spread of drug testing requirements and whether drug-war tactics are eroding constitutional rights. Despite continued concern about the appropriateness of drug testing programs and the accuracy of urinalysis, the national trend toward pre-employment and on-the-job drug testing is spreading. The other concern is that aggressive law enforcement is undermining the rights of the individual.[64] SWAT team raids, questionable search tactics such as stop-and-frisk practices, and a wide variety of aggressive surveillance technniques such as drug-courier profiles and housing-project sweeps are the hallmarks of the police offensive against drug trafficking in cities from coast to coast.[65] An interview with a former administrator of The Drug Enforcement Administration resulted in the revelation that this agency's computerized index, known as the Narcotics and Dangerous Drug Information System, contained the names of many persons against whom there were "unsubstantiated allegations of illegal activity." He went on to admit "that less than five percent (of the total 1.5 million persons whose names were added to the computer since 1974) . . . are under investigation as suspected narcotics traffickers by DEA."[66] The Department of Housing and Urban Development's recent proposal to evict all public housing tenants from buildings in which drugs were being distributed raised important legal and civil rights issues.

Finally, the legalization advocates contend that our present anti-drug response can be compared in many ways to the nation's disasterous efforts to prohibit the sale of alcohol. They contend we are moving down the same path with the same results. Legalizing narcotics may be the only answer. With legalization would come diminished violence, corruption and drug-related crime. The government under a process of regulation could control the distribution, purity, and potency of drugs. Resources now lost to the illegal trafficker could be captured by the government and put to public use. The problem of AIDS would be reduced if heroin addicts could obtain sterilized needles under a legalization program. It is also said a great deal more money which is now being spent on criminal justice efforts could be diverted to treatment and educational programs and issues of civil rights could be protected.

Although the arguments of those who would legalize drugs are generally compelling, it is still, only one side of the issue. While it is true that some of the problems associated with our policy of criminalizing drugs and trying to enforce them out of existence would be reduced or eliminated, there are also other issues to consider.

Concerns Raised by the Pro-criminalization Advocates

Those who favor the continued policy of criminalizing drugs contend that the legalization of drugs will result in increased drug use and dependence. While this proposition has not been tested on a national basis, there is some evidence for concern that this might indeed occur. The experiences of a state like Alaska which had legalized marijuana as a result of a ruling by that state's Supreme Court (until recently, adult Alaskans could possess up to four ounces for personal use in the privacy of their home), is not encouraging.[67] Research has shown that 53.2 percent of Alaskan teens have used pot at least once, compared with a nationwide teenage use rate of 23.7 percent.[68] It is also argued that decriminalization, besides undermining and weakening our nation through increased experimentation with drugs, will not result in many of the outcomes suggested by the drug legalization proponents. One of the biggest myths is that legalization will reduce crime. Although legalizing will cut the crime having to do with the sale of drugs, it will not result in a decrease of violent crime. Since legalization will encourage drug use—and since they contend that drug use is associated with violent and irrational behavior just as is alcohol—increased levels of drug use will result in increased crimes of violence such as assaults, family crimes and homicides. It will certainly increase such offenses as driving under the influence.[69]

Along this line, some legalization advocates propose high taxes on legalized drugs so that the drug consumers will pay for the networks of regulation, education, and treatment required of administering the program as well as rehabilitation efforts for those who want to esacape their dependency.[70] This heavy taxation of drugs, however, may actually force drug users to commit crimes as they do now to support their habit.

There is also the problem of how the drugs would be handled and at what level of government. This is perhaps one of the major criticism of the legalization advocates' position. Those proposing such a policy have not begun to address how such a system would work. While they are adept at pointing out the failures of the existing efforts to deal with illegal narcotics, they have not developed a convincing alternative that is workable. Would it for example, be the responsibility of the federal government? If so, which parts of the drug-distribution system would the government take over and control? Will it grow the poppies, coca, and marijuana? Will it establish and control laboratories for the processing of these drugs as well as the production of amphetimines, barbiturates, LSD and all sorts of designer drugs? Will it relegate itself only to inspecting the drugs such as in the legal pharmaceutical industry and the "retailing" of the drugs through government outlets? What role will the states and local units of government play? Jocobs in a very insightful article on the problems associated with legalizing drugs contends that if the federal government controls legal drugs it may well take a Constitutional amendment guaranteeing the American people the right to ingest whatever substances they desire or banning all state prohibitions on the production, sale, possession, and use of psychoactive substances. Legalization under federal rather than state control would certainly be quicker and less complicated than waiting for all the states to develop political support for legalization and then to develop their own policies and institutions for drug production and/or retailing.[71]

When the Feds Turned Drug Dealer

Legal drugs came to America back in June of 1997. Speaking the now historic words, "O.K., let's give it a shot," an obviously reluctant President Quayle bowed to the will of Congress and signed the Prohibition Repeal bill into law. With the defeat of the Friedmanites, named for their spiritual leader Milton Friedman ("I would distribute drugs the way aspirin is distributed"), control of drug distribution was denied to private industry and placed in the hands of the federal government.

In the first year alone, the government opened 40,000 Reactive Chemical Dispensation Centers, or package stores, all of them frankly modeled on McDonald's hamburger shops. Clean and bright, with illuminated color-coded menus up high behind the smiling, nonjudgmental sales help. The gold menu (for "golden oldies") featured nostalgia drugs for older buyers—crack, heroin, angel dust, LSD and weak marijuana. Green was for more current and powerful forms of cocaine and marijuana. Red—an active, youthful color—signified designer drugs, most of them concocted by computer in college chemistry labs under government contract.

In Year Two, the drug program expanded to 120,000 outlets, mostly by taking over the shops of the bankrupt Roy Rogers chain. Despite this enormous capital outlay, government experts predicted that the drug program would be in the black within three years. Violent street crime fell 10 percent. Drug-related prosecutions dropped 80 percent. Since the government was buying most of the cocaine produced in Colombia and Peru, relations with Latin America brightened. Drug Czar Alan Dershowitz said, "Our long national nightmare is ending."

By the end of Year Two, the *New York Times* expressed editorial concern about the rise in drug use—up about 15 percent since repeal—but Dershowitz called it "a brief statistical spasm." More disconcertingly, the package stores were having trouble holding the line on drug prices. Back in 1989, a rock of crack sold for $3 in New York, or four for $10. A decade later, in terms of 1989 dollars, the price was $5.89 at a government store, and $4 on the street. There were jokes about $600 toilet seats and "normal government efficiency."

Hijackings and Lawsuits

Dershowitz told Congress that drug planners had underestimated the costs of the business. Ethan Nadelmann, a pro-legalization lobbyist of the 1980s, had predicted a $10-billion-a-year government profit from drug sales, but he hadn't counted on the costs of quality control, product development, insurance, theft and a sprawling civil-service drug bureaucracy. Because of the bombings at package stores, the department had to install foot-thick concrete walls and 24-hour guards. Hijackings were a constant problem. Four tons of cocaine and a shipment of European chemicals disappeared from Kennedy International Airport on a single day. Soon the department was paying the Army and Navy to escort cocaine shipments from Latin America.

To the amazement of most Americans, the dangerous drug gangs that ruled the streets in the 1980s were still thriving. Violence was down because the gangs had finally come to terms and divided America up into regional monopolies, a standard feature of mature capitalism. Business was booming because the gangs knew that the successors to the yuppies, the affluent TWITS (an acronym for Those With Income to Squander), did not wish to stand on line for drugs at a former Roy Rogers. They wanted a whiff of the romance and danger that come from buying a hot new drug from a slightly ominous contact in a dimly lit club.

When the product-liability suits against the Drug Department began to roll in (40,000 were filed in the month of September, 1999, alone), Congress mandated a sin-month testing period for all new drugs. Since most designer drugs faded from the market in less time than that, this gave the street gangs almost total control of the more fashionable drugs.

But the bulk of the gang business was kids. Since the Prohibition Repeal Act forbade sales to those under 21, the gangs had the high-school and college markets as monopolies. When Congress tried to cut into the gang profits by legalizing drugs for 18-year-olds, the gang aggressively preyed upon younger and younger children. Addiction rates for 10-to-12-year-olds rose tenfold.

Street crime rose sharply; more addicts meant more muggings. With sales slumping, and a 42 percent addiction rate among Drug Department employees, Dershowitz resigned. The new Drug Czar, Ira Glasser, said confidently that sales would reach the break-even point within six years. With drug victims filling 78 percent of hospital beds, Congress authorized $97 billion for hospital construction. New forms of brain damage and disease began to show up among users, so Congress mandated weaker doses, thus sending thousands of the more serious users to the black market for their heavier hits.

With the cocaine market glutted and a million hectares of Colombian soil under cultivation, the Medellin government started dumping excess coke on American streets at fire-sale prices. No one bought coke legally. That finished off the government stores, which, with only 17 percent of the U.S. drug market, were $4 billion in debt.

On Dec. 1, 2002, with 100 million Americans using drugs, with the economy a shambles and with child abuse at five times the level of 1989, Congress voted unanimously to make drugs illegal once again. Debate began on which civil liberties might be preserved during the cleanup. Former Czar Dershowitz said: "So I was wrong. What can I do about it now?" Former Czar Glasser said simply, "It was a noble experiment."

Source: Reprinted with permission from John Leo, "When the Feds Turned Drug Dealer," *U.S. News & World Report,* 13 November 1989, p. 75.

The idea that legalized drugs would drive out illegal drugs is unwarranted. There is a danger in this supposition that most people fail to grasp. It may, in fact, create a market for the development of illegal "designer" (chemically formulated) drugs that are more potent and, therefore, in greater demand than drugs that can be legally purchased. A whole new area of illegal narcotics enterprise will open up for the sale of these drugs. Users now in the illegal drug-trafficking market would also be deprived of their income and unless these traffickers are given a profitable role in the legalized distribution system, they cannot be expected simply to wither away. More than likely they will continue to compete fiercely with one another and with the legalized market.[72] In such a situation, a black market in illegal drugs will continue to exist in spite of the availability of legal narcotics.

And the health care costs of a nation which has legalized drugs could be astronomical as seen by the health care costs associated with tobacco and alcohol. This could more than compensate for the public funds now expended for efforts to enforce drug laws. There is also the recognized problem of pre-natal addiction. Encouraging drug use through legalization and availability would contribute to the transmission of intergenerational drug-related health problems from addicted mothers.

Although the arguments and counterarguments swirl about the questions of continued criminalization or the legalization of drugs, one conclusion is readily apparent: We are no nearer to a solution of the vexing problem of how we are to deal with illegal narcotics than we were before the turn of the century. Instead of the problem of illegal narcotics disappearing, it is now worse than ever before in our nation's history. To legalize drugs would be tantamount to admitting that that our government's anti-narcotics policies since the federal government first made drugs illegal over 75 years ago have been a failure. Along with this must come the realization that we have failed in trying to eradicate the "drug menace" despite the billions that have been spent. Perhaps it is too much to ask for a nation to admit to such a massive and futile mistake. Yet we must be cautionary. Had we chosen a different means to regulate drugs or had we initially embraced legalization and associated regulation the consequences may have been even more disasterous. Given this possible alternative, who can really say it has been a mistake?

Changes in Drug Use and Possible Implications

If there is some truth in the fact that drug use is changing, these changes are both promising and ominous. On the one hand, the information-acquiring segments of the population seem to be getting the message: Drugs are dangerous and dumb. Their cachet is gone. Drugs like cigarettes are declasse and adolescent status anxiety may prove to be our most potent weapon in the "war" on drugs. The changes are certainly important in terms of their implications and what they might suggest for future drug control issues and policy.

Still, changes in the characteristics of drug abuse could be potentially as explosive an issue for the country as the legalization debate and the concerns that surround existing drug use. While there is growing evidence that drug use is decreasing among white, middle, and upper-middle class America, this is not true for all Americans. And as is generally the case in all wars, the the casualties are disproportionately and increasingly among the poor—especially urban minorities. There is then, a social issue here which is related to drug abuse. If such present trends continue, these changing patterns of consumption will begin to be felt in the next several years. From our still inconclusive evidence, we can make some reasonable predictions about the future. Preliminary indications are that the following is already taking place or is likely to become a reality:

- With the exception of heroin and crack among the poor, the use of illegal drugs appears to have peaked, including snorting cocaine.
- Evidence tends to indicate that people turning away from drugs are the most educated and affluent. The poorest and least educated have continued to increase their drug use.
- ''Crack'' has largely remained a poor-people's drug. Its rise in the last few years has had devastating effects on poor inner-city neighborhoods, but it has failed to make the same inroads into more advantaged socio-economic groups.
- The most deadly impact of legal drugs may be yet to come as tens of thousands of intravenous drug users, their sexual partners, and their children contract AIDS. There is also the growing threat of prenatal addiction and the already escalating health and social service costs of these children abandoned by their mothers or placed in foster homes by the courts. This situation is fast approaching a crisis in this country. Many of these problems will also center on the urban poor.[73]

As the''drug problem'' becomes more focused among these groups, it may become less important as a national policy of concern. There is some historical precedent for this. As long as narcotics were generally relegated to groups outside the mainstream of American life such as opium use by the Chinese immigrants in the 19th century, blacks in urban ghettos, musicians or counter-culture people, little widespread public concern or outcries for anti-drug efforts surfaced. Heroin, for instance, has long been a problem in inner cities that never really crossed over into mainstream society. As long as the ''problem'' was relegated to these underclasses, it didn't have the required visibility to receive a great deal of attention from government. It was only when drug use spread to other segments of society and associated drug problems such as increased crime, violence, and welfare costs bled-over into the social mainstream and its victimizing nature rippled outward, did the nation really gear-up to attack illegal narcotics.

If present trends continue, we may have an emerging tale of two drug problems: one in which middle and upper-middle class Americans pass through a generation of experimentation with illegal drugs; the other in the America of the poor, where amid hopelessness, lack of education and opportunity, and the dissolution of basic social structure, this segment of society will suffer the worst consequences of drug abuse—addiction, crime and criminal victimization, violence, and AIDS. To the extent that this occurs and to the extent that future drug-related problems can be better contained than they presently are, our nation's ''drug problem'' may become less pressing as a national issue. But there is also the knowledge that the American underclass—those particularly vulnerable to drug abuse—is growing. This may have significant implications.

Under such circumstances, it is possible in the years ahead that the "war on drugs" will lose some of its saliency—and with this its urgency as a national priority. It then follows that the legalization versus criminalization debate will also lose its meaning and urgency.

The issue than is not merely illegal drug use. It is its extent and the "social" costs associated with it. A portion of society will always use drugs. It is when this segment of society becomes as large as it has in the United States in recent years and the "direct" and "indirect" costs (subsidization of criminal cartels, undermining of national economies and governments, violence, crime, corruption, drug addicted children, health care costs, welfare assistance, and the threat to civil liberties) become intolerable that we must take action. To the extent that the problem is reducible to an acceptable public threshold of tolerance may be the issue.

The question is one of threshold: At what point will we resign ourselves to an acceptable level of drug abuse and associated problems and then turn our attention to other issues that press upon our nation for attention? Although we certainly are not at the point of such acceptance now, changes in the public's perception of the "drug problem" in the years ahead may signal an important reduction in our willingness to continue such massive efforts to fight illegal drugs. And we must remember that thresholds of acceptability change under unremitting pressures. Tolerance levels have a tendency to be adjusted upward. What this emerging mixed message of hope and despair signals for our nation is still unclear.

Conclusion

The decade of the 1990s will be crucial for our nation's anti-drug efforts. Unless major efforts are successful in reducing illegal drug use, we can expect that Americans will become increasingly restive and frustrated with the scourge of illegal narcotics and the problems it poses for the nation. They will also become less patient with programs and efforts that show little sign of being effective. Yet, we cannot lose sight of the fact that it is a problem that cannot be solved overnight. It promises to be a long and costly struggle and thoughtful Americans must understand that.

It is also a situation which is certainly doomed to failure if we continue to concentrate so much of our efforts on the supply side of the problem. While we cannot afford to discontinue our efforts to choke off the supply of illegal drugs, it is imperative, at the same time, that the nation reduce its demand for drugs and significant resources must address that need. The decriminalization proponents are right when they clammor for greater recognition that our drug problem is at least as much a public health concern as it is a criminal justice concern. Our policy makers have yet to take this recognition seriously. We must begin to concentrate on both these fronts simultaneously. This means effective education programs, available treatment efforts—and yes, law enforcement and punitive responses for users as well as suppliers who contribute to the existing market for drugs. If our nation's anti-drug strategy is to be successful, there is one verity: Americans must be weaned from the illegal use of drugs. There is simply no other solution. Major efforts in our nation must move inexorably to lowering demand rather than merely placing so much effort on supply.

NOTES

[1]Associated Press Poll, June 22, 1990.

[2]Office of National Drug Abuse Policy, *Preliminary Drug Abuse Statistics—A Report* (Washington, D.C.: U.S. Government Printing Office, February 1988), p. 12.

[3]As reported in *The New York Times,* April 10, 1988, p. 10.

[4]For an excellent overview of the development of restrictive laws against narcotics, see Nahas, Gabriel G. *Cocaine: The Great White Plague,* (Middlebury, VT.: Paul S. Eriksson, Publisher) 1989, esp. pp. 30–83.

[5]Musto, David F. "America's Forgotten Drug War," *Reader's Digest* (April 1990), p. 148.

[6]King, Refus. "The American System: Legal Sanctions to Repress Drug Abuse," in Inciardi, James and Chambers, Carl D. (eds.) *Drugs and the Criminal Justice System* (Beverly Hills, Calif.: Sage, 1974), p. 21.

[7]Epstein, Edward J. *Agency of Fear* (New York: G.P. Putnam's Sons, 1977), p. 105.

[8]Ibid., p. 106.

[9]Ibid.

[10]See Wilson, James Q. *The Investigators* (New York: Basic Books, 1978).

[11]"U.S. Considering International Cops to Fight Cocaine," *The Los Angeles Times,* June 17, 1988, p. A-12.

[12]Lane, Charles. "The Newest War," *Newsweek* (January 6, 1992), pp. 18–23.

[13]"Risky Business," *Newsweek* (July 16, 1990), pp. 16–19.

[14]Lane, *op cit.,* p. 19.

[15]Ibid., p. 22.

[16]For example, see Reuter, Peter, Crawford, Gordon and Cave, Jonathan. *Sealing the Borders* (Santa Monica, CA: Rand Corporation, 1988).

[17]"The American Drug Problem Takes on Two Faces," *The New York Times* (July 10, 1988), p. E-5.

[18]Ibid.

[19]Drug Abuse Warning Network Bulletin, May 1990.

[20]Treaster, Joseph B. "Cocaine Epidemic has Peaked, Some Suggest," *The New York Times* (July 1, 1990), p. 14.

[21]National Narcotics Intelligence Consumers Committee, *Estimates of Cocaine Use in the United States, 1982–1985* (Washington: NNICC, 1987).

[22]As reported in Graham, Mary C. "Controlling Drug Abuse and Crime: A Reserach Update," in *NIJ Update—Drugs and Crime* (Washington, D.C.: U.S. Department of Justice, March/April 1987).

[23]See Pennell, Susan. "Ice: DUF Interviews Results from San Diego," *NIJ Reports No. 221* (Washington, D.C.: U.S. Department of Justice) Summer 1990, pp. 12–13.

[24]Kaplan, John. "Taking Drugs Seriously," *Public Interest* (Summer 1988), pp. 32–50.

[25]Bureau of Justice Statistics, *Profile of State Inmates* (Washington, D.C.: 1986).

[26]Visher, Christy A. "Incorporating Drug Treatment in Criminal Sanctions," *NIJ Research in Action*, No. 221 (Summer 1990), p. 3.

[27]See Wexler, H.D., Lipton, D. and Johnson, D. *A Criminal Justice System Strategy for Treating Cocaine-Heroin Abusing Offenders in Custody* (Washington, D.C.: National Institute of Justice, 1988).

[28]For an excellent discussion of the problems of showing this causal relationship and the complexities of the issue based upon a survey of empirical studies, see Chaiken, Jan M. and Chaiken, Marcia R. "Drugs and Predatory Crime," in Tonry, Michael and Wilson, James Q. (eds.) *Drugs and Crime* (Chicago: University of Chicago Press, 1990), pp. 203–39.

[29]Ibid., p. 205.

[30]United States General Accounting Office, *Drug Control—U.S. International Narcotics Control Activities* (Washington, D.C.: U.S. Government Printing Office), March 1988.

[31]Chaiken, Marcia R. and Chaiken, Jan M. "Who Gets Caught Doing Crime?" Discussion paper, Washington, D.C.: U.S. Department of Justice—Bureau of Justice Statistics, 1985.

[32]National Institute of Justice, *Cocaine Use: Arrestees in Washington, D.C.* (Washington, D.C.: NIJ), December 1989.

[33]We use the term "identifiable" because many of the arrests in the study were for "other" offenses which included family offenses, disturbing the peace, and for outstanding bench warrants.

[34]Ibid.

[35]National Institute of Justice, *1988 Drug Use Forcasting Annual Report*, "Drugs and Crime in America," (Washington, D.C.: NIJ) March, 1990. pp. 24–25.

[36]"The Enemy Within: Drug Money is Corrupting the Enforcers," *The New York Times*, April 11, 1988, p. A-12.

[37]Ibid.

[38]Beaty, Jonathan and Hornik, Richard. "A Torrent of Dirty Dollars," *Time* (December 18, 1989), p. 50.

[39]Ibid.

[40]Ibid., p. 55.

[41]Ibid.

[42]The states also have adopted similar drug-related forfeiture laws. See Stellwagon, Lindsey D. *Use of Forfeiture Sanctions in Drug Cases* (Washington, D.C.: National Institute of Justice) July 1985.

[43]Kaplan, *op cit.*, p. 34.

[44]Ibid., p. 35.

[45]"Barry Outrage" *Newsweek* (August 27, 1990), p. 6.

[46]See General Accounting Office, *Report on Drug Abuse Prevention* (Washington, D.C., U.S. Government Printing Office), December 1987, p. 12.

[47]One large multi-year study of drug abuse treatment programs says that positive results can occur if the treatment is of the right quality and duration. See Hubbard, Robert L., Marsden, Mary E., Valley Rachal, J., Harwood, Henrick J., Cavanaugh, Elizabeth R. and Ginzburg, Harold M. *Drug Abuse Treatment: A National Study of Effectiveness* (Chapel Hill, NC: University of North Carolina Press), 1989. Also contending that certain programs are workable are Angling, M. Douglas and Hser, Yih-Ing. "Treatment of Drug Abuse," in Tonry and Wilson, *op cit.*, pp. 393–460.

[48]*The New York Times,* April 12, 1988, p. A-10.

[49]For an excellent review of this issue, see Botvin, Gilbert J. "Substance Abuse Prevention: Theory, Practice and Effectiveness," in Tonry and Wilson, *op cit.*, pp. 461–519.

[50]Ibid.

[51]For a discussion of this general issue, see Schmoke, Kurt L. "Drug Laws Ignore Addicts While Helping Criminals," *Addiction Review,* Vol. 2, No. 1. (January 1990).

[52]Nadelman, Ethan A. "U.S. Drug Policy: A Bad Export," *Foreign Policy,* Vol. 70 (Spring 1988), pp. 83–108.

[53]U.S. Senate Committee on Internal Security Hearings (Washington, D.C.: U.S. Government Printing Office, 1983).

[54]United States General Accounting Office, U.S. International Narcotics Control Activities., *op cit.*, p. 19.

[55]Gerth, Jeff. "C.I.A. Shedding Its Reluctance to Aid in Fight Against Drugs," *The New York Times* (March 25, 1990) p. 1 and p. 22.

[56]Florez, Carl P. and Boyce, Bernadette. "Colombian Organized Crime," *Police Studies,* Vol. 13 (Summer 1990), p. 86.

[57]Owens, Gerald. "Costs of Production: Coca," *Report to the U.S. Agency for International Development,* December 31, 1986, p. 6.

[58]For an excellent article on the economics of growing coca and the problems of substituting other cash crops, see Massing, Michael. "In the Cocaine War the Jungle is Winning, *The New York Times Magazine,* (March 4, 1990), pp. 26 and 88–91.

[59]See Lee, Rensselaer W. "Why the U.S. Cannot Stop South American Cocaine," *Orbis,* Vol. 32 (Fall 1988), pp. 499–519.

[60]Ibid., pp. 513–14.

[61]See Reuter, Peter, Crawford, Gordon and Cave, Jonathan. *Sealing the Borders* (Sanata Monica, CA.: The Rand Corporation), 1988; and Reuter, Peter. "Can the Borders be Sealed?" *Public Interest* (Summer 1988), pp. 51–65.

[62]Sweitzer, James P. "The Economics of Cocaine Trafficking," *Policy Studies,* Vol. 29 (1989), pp. 31–44. Similar conclusions have also been reached by the Rand Corporation in their studies of the economics of cocaine.

[63]For example, see Sonrett, Neal R. "War on Drugs—or the Constitution?," *Trial,* Vol. 26 (April 1990), pp. 24–30.

[64]What is disturbing is that a Washington Post-ABC News poll taken after President Bush's announcement of the National Drug Control Strategy in 1989 indicated that 62 percent of those surveyed would be "willing to give up some of the freedoms we have in this country if it meant we could greatly reduce the amount of illegal drug use."

[65]"Uncivil Liberties," *Newsweek* (April 30, 1990), pp. 18–19.

[66]Christensen, Dan. "Drug Agents Keeping Tabs on Leaders, Stars, Clergy," *Ft. Lauderdale News and Sun Sentinel,* July 3, 1984. Sec. A.

[67]Personal correspondence from Nancy E. Schafer, University of Alaska at Anchorage. Professor Schafer provided the details about the legal background and history of Alaska's permissive marijuana possession law.

[68]"Goodbye Pot," *Newsweek* (October 29, 1990), p. 10. Author's note: Alaskans by a narrow margin voted in the 1990 general election to bring back marijuana criminalization.

[69]Evans, David G. "Legal Drugs: More Crime, Dramatic Increase in Use," in *Addiction Review, op cit.,* pp. 1 and 5.

[70]Grinspoon, Lester. "The Harmfulness Tax: A Proposal for Regulation and Taxation of Drugs," *Drug Policy 1989–1990: A Reformer's Catalog* (Washington, D.C.: Drug Policy Foundations, 1989).

[71]Jacobs, James B. "Imagining Drug Legalization," *The Public Interest,* Vol. 101 (Fall 1990), pp. 28–42.

[72]Ibid., p. 33.

[73]"Drugs' Impact is Seen Rising Among the Poor," *The New York Times* (August 30, 1987), p. 28.

CHAPTER 10

The Growth of Environmental Crime

CONTENTS

''Psst Bubba, you wanna buy a barge cheap? I'll give you a good price. Oh yeah, I forgot to mention one small thing: Its loaded with a 120 tons of New York's finest garbage. Why you ask? . . . Well, poor ole Tuffy the tugboat is getting a hernia. . . . You see he's been dragging this thing up and down the coast for two years now. No you say? . . . Let me think. I got it! Would you be interested in a long-term lease on a Pampers diaper landfill?''

These are just two examples of the growing environmental problems we Americans face. To many, the issue of environmental destruction is more than Tuffy the tugboat's plight or what to do with disposable diapers. And the problem is not only relegated to the United States any more than its focus is merely disposable waste concerns. Environmental destruction in all its forms is a broad global problem. It is argued that the continued emission of airborne toxic substances, the pollution of surface waters and underground acquifers, and the production and disposal of toxic chemical substances is causing growing alarm for the future of the planet earth and its people. It is becoming increasingly recognized that the world community of nations—industrialized as well as underdeveloped countries—must find ways to combat the insidious menace of toxic discharge and atmospheric deterioration: A task that must be done before we pass a point beyond which available remedies no longer exist.

Federal, state, and local governments have attempted to respond, producing much new and amended legislation: Laws that are proving very difficult to enforce even by multiple administrative bureaucracies. The initial challenge was to protect the environment and the population by ensuring that toxic wastes were not emitted into the environment and those solid toxic wastes which were produced were disposed of in tight containers and secure landfills.[1] Laws were passed; Federal technical standards were set by the Environmental Protection Agency (EPA); program implementation responsibilities were delegated to the states; permits were issued; and business continued pretty much as usual. These initial efforts to deal with toxic pollutants—especially hazardous solid wastes—would soon demonstrate that studies were more prevelant than engineering action; the laws created more ubiquitous than means to enforce them.

As it became evident that the environmental issue did not involve simply disposing of wastes, but also required efforts at lower emissions, waste treatment, and the management of hazardous pollutants and chemicals, attention began to shift to tougher questions about the fundamental nature of America's chemical-based industrial society and how to regulate it. While comparative economics and investment decisions were instrumental in the slow pace at which these laws were initially implemented—and still are a major reason corporate interests and the business community are often unreceptive to regulation—the result over the past 20 years has been an increase in the types of environmental hazards subject to legal regulation. But such regulatory efforts have often been hard to follow, with legislation and conceptual thinking racing to keep pace with growing political pressure.[2]

Along with this, there grew a second recognition: That willful and purposeful emission of toxic substances into the environment in violation of these developing laws and regulations requires effective enforcement actions beyond administrative sanctions. The system of criminal justice and the use of the criminal law including penal sanctions and criminal fines where warranted, must be part of the arsenal of environmental defense. Most Americans agree that the criminal law and the criminal justice system has a legitimate and necessary interest in combatting certain forms of hazardous environmental pollution.[3]

Less understood is both the appropriate and workable role of the criminal justice system and its criminal-legal machinery to deal effectively with the problem. Yet, the issue of ecological deterioration may be more basic. For example, there exists a continuing debate over the consequences and extent of environmental pollution. It is also argued that the impact of tighter enforcement measures may have a deleterious economic effect on capital investment and productive output; that stringent compliance and enforcement efforts may affect our nation's competitiveness in global and even domestic markets. The concern is also expressed that the costs of environmental toxic abatement and cleanup programs may prove to be a public expenditure that the federal and state governments are unable to assume.

As we can see, many issues surround the question of environmental pollution beyond those merely involving the criminal justice system. And although the literature on the environment is voluminous, little has been written about the role or effectiveness of the criminal law in this area. This chapter will serve as a primer on environmental crime and how the criminal justice system has begun to respond. It should provide a basic understanding of the issues, the legal framework, the efforts, and the problems of dealing with environmental pollution as a criminal event.

Corporate Crime: The Framework for Understanding Environmental Crime

Generally speaking, environmental crime can only be understood in the broader context of what can be referred to as corporate crime. Environmental crime shares with corporate crime many of the same characteristics in terms of regulatory efforts and how such offenses (and offenders) are classified and dealt with. Corporate crimes are a distinguishably large body of violations which are not normally associated with such ordinary crimes as burglary, robbery or assault. The unconventional nature of corporate crime explains many of the problems associated with dealing with these forms of criminal behavior. As we saw in chapter one, corporate crimes are themselves only one part of a larger miscellany of offenses which are referred to as white collar crime.[4] The reader will recall that such offenses are distinguished by the nature of the offender, the characteristics of the offense, and the situations in which they occur. Experience with this form of criminal activity has shown that they incorporate another specific characteristic: the penalties imposed are far more likely to be administrative and civil rather than criminal in nature, even where a criminal penalty is available.

Although corporate crimes generally involve illegal financial acts, it is also true that they may be associated with actual or potential injury—even death. In terms of environmental disasters, The Union Carbide toxic disaster in Bhopar, India comes immediately to mind. There are other examples of purposeful or negligent corporate environmental crime. Allied Chemical Company, knowing from its own laboratory research that its chemical pesticide, Kepone, could cause serious injuries including cancer, still produced and marketed this substance. The Chemical Control site in Elizabeth, New Jersey, the Hooker Chemical Company's toxic waste dumping in Love Canal, the so-called Vally of the Drums in Shepardsville, Kentucky, and the Stringfellow Acid Pits in California are examples of corporate environmental irresponsibility which produced explicit physical harm.[5]

A distinguishing characteristic of corporate crime is that a corporation cannot be jailed. While it can be fined and its officers imprisoned, the major penalty of imprisonment provided for ordinary offenders is not available for cases involving corporations. Another characteristic is that, for the most part, these offenses are handled by quasi-enforcement bodies, including government regulatory agencies such as the Food and Drug Administration or in the case of environmental offenses, the EPA or state environmental agencies. The law generally provides these agencies with alternative administrative, civil or criminal actions. In some cases, such agency regulations do not even provide for criminal penalties. Furthermore, the difficulties encountered, the lengthy procedures of most court actions, as well as the necessity to take prompt action, make it expedient to rely on administrative penalties even where criminal penalties are available. These take the form of such actions as the seizure or recall of commodities, consent decrees (voluntary agreements where the firm does not admit guilt but agrees to cease and desist or take corrective action), and monetary penalties.[6] And unlike most conventional crimes, it is generally impossible to determine the seriousness of a corporate offense by the nature of the action taken. A major study of violations of regulatory law by the *Fortune 500* corporations found that even serious violations generally received only administrative sanctions; in fact, two thirds of the serious cases and four-fifths of the moderately serious offenses were handled in this manner.[7]

This then, is the context in which we often find environmental regulations and criminal actions taken against offenders. The reader must approach the issue of environmental crimes with this in mind. Although it makes it no less a criminal event to violate the criminal provisions of existing environmental regulations, certain factors exist both in the eyes of the law as well as in the way the law is applied—without arguing the appropriateness or inappropriateness of this unique treatment—to render this form of crime somewhat different from other forms of more conventional crime.

History of Anti-pollution Laws

Early recorded evidence of anti-pollution laws are much older than most people imagine. Although 19th century industrialization would give rise to growing environmental pollution, there were concerns even before the Industrial Revolution. England is a case in point. In London, during the 14th century, the pall of smoke that hung over the city was so noxious that Edward I passed a proclamation on smoke abatement. To enforce this edict, the King prescribed the death penalty for Englishmen who defied it.[8] History does not tell us how or if the Crown enforced this proclamation nor is there any recorded evidence that such drastic steps as the death penalty were ever imposed for its violation, but it does point out that the problem was apparently serious enough to warrant such a drastic step.

In America, little attention was focused on environmental concerns. The states largely ignored the problem including (not surprisingly) those industrialized states where the problem could be expected to be found at its worst. But there were some initial stirrings. A recognizable problem was developing as early as the late 19th century over the dumping of industrial and human sewage into those rivers in our nation's largest and most industrialized urban centers. In response to this concern, Congress, in 1899, passed the first federal law addressing the control and discharge of toxic pollutants. This was the Rivers and Harbors Act. Although primarily adopted to govern construction upon or the obstruction of navigable waters, it did have a clause that prohibited the dumping of ''refuse matter'' into the navigable waters of the United States.

This law, however, was for the most part feckless. First, it made the violation of this act only a misdemeanor and provided for a maximum fine of $500. More importantly, it was a law that was simply ignored by both polluters and enforcers. The time had yet to come for any serious concern or effort to deal with environmental pollution. It would not be until after World War II that even the most minimal enforcement of the act would occur. In the state arena, even less was being done. Generally the states continued to ignore the problem either out of expediency to industrial interests or simply because they were ignorant of the existence and consequences of pollution.[9]

The 1960s saw the problem of pollution becoming more acute. Citizen environmentalist groups began to grow and began to agitate for more governmental involvement in the regulation of environmental contaminants. Spurred-on by such bizarre occurrences as the fire which ignited Cleveland, Ohio's Cuyahoga River, concerns were expressed about the deteriorating quality of the air and the nation's water. The growing problem of toxic waste disposal was also recognized as a situation which had to be dealt with. In 1970, Congress authorized and President Nixon signed into law an act creating a federal agency to oversee federal anti-pollution efforts and administer most of the federal government's regulatory and environmental protection statutes. This agency was also given the responsibility to provide technical assistance to state governments in their own antipollution efforts. In this way, the Environmental Protection Agency (EPA) was born.

In the past 20 years, a number of additional laws have been passed and amendments to existing laws have broadened the scope of regulation. Agencies given the authority to exercise regualatory oversight have also grown. And, as we shall see, there has been a progression in the penalties that can be imposed. While the metamorphosis of law in this area can be attributed to the growing awareness of the danger and the growing impact of special interest groups such as environmentalists, it is also a reaction to growing scientific knowledge of what substances have toxic or potentially toxic effects. It has been these conbining factors which have become the major motive force behind the growth of environmental law.

An Overview of Environmental Law

An examination of both federal and state laws pertaining to criminal enforcement show a common pattern of development. For the most part, such laws initially specified most acts of criminal pollution as misdemeanors, or at most, as minor felonies.[10] It was not, for example, until 1980 with the amendments to the Resource Conservation and Recovery Act (RCRA) that the first felony sanctions for any federal environmental crime were established.[11] Interestingly, these RCRA amendments were important for another reason: the enactment of the first "endangerment" offense in federal law (see RCRA Table 10-1).

Although this view of environmental offenses as relatively "non-serious" is changing, especially at the federal level, the pattern of change is uneven. This is especially true among the states. While some states have taken an aggressive regulatory and enforcement stance, many states still appear hesitant to define criminal acts in this area as serious criminal violations—or at least to aggressively pursue criminal enforcement. The one possible exception to this is in the area of toxic waste disposal. States, like the federal government, generally have moved to provide the most severe penalties in terms of both fines and imprisonment for this type of willful pollution.

An example of this can be found in a recent case in Pennsylvania. In 1989, a criminal court in that state sentenced the accused to a mandatory two to five years for the illegal disposal of chemical wastes in violation of state hazardous waste laws. It was the first time a corporate officer had been sentenced to a period of imprisonment under the provisions of the state's Solid Waste Management Act.[12]

The criminal-legal remedies to the states (and to the federal government) for these acts of pollution can be found in several possible sources. One of course, is the specific environmental statutes which carry criminal penalties. Other legal sources include criminal laws dealing with the public health and welfare, criminal statutes that deal with data disclosure (e.g., failure to maintain adequate records of toxic waste generation or disposal), conventional criminal laws that deal with fraud and public corruption, criminal conspiracy, solicitation and aiding and abetting statutes, and state laws modeled after the federal government's Racketeer Influenced and Corrupt Organization (RICO) statute which can be used when violators tend to show a continuing pattern of purposeful (or negligent) environmental contamination.[13] Government attorneys involved in the prosecution of environmental crimes recommend that, whenever possible, these be used jointly in the prosecution of such cases.[14]

This raises another issue. Experience in the investigation and prosecution of these offenses has shown that there is generally no thing as a pure "environmental crime." Violation of environmental laws often lead to evidence of more widespread violation of general criminal laws by a violating firm. More often than not, cases include such offenses as fraudulent practices, conspiracy, false statements and claims, perjury, obstruction of justice, tax evasion and mail and wire fraud.[15] Nor are many offenders just environmental polluters. Judson Starr, Director of the Environmental Crimes Section of the Department of Justice discusses the typical defendant prosecuted by his agency. He certainly does not paint the picture of someone who "innocently" or only "negligently"

TABLE 10.1 MAJOR FEDERAL ENVIRONMENTAL LAWS AND THEIR CRIMINAL PROVISIONS

CLEAN AIR ACT.[18] Governs emission of hazardous air pollutants. Prohibits operation of emissions source in violation of applicable standards; release of designated hazardous air pollutants in violation of emission standards; removal of asbestos or demolition of asbestos-covered structure in violation of asbestos work practice standards; false statement or tampering with monitoring device.

Penalties: Before 1990—misdemeanor; as amended in 1990 a midemeanor if negligent emission or endangerment; a felony if it involves "knowing release or endangerment." Punishable by imprisonment up to 15 years and if an "organization" is involved a fine up to $1 million. Penalties double on second conviction.

Author's note: Each of these laws provide for a series of fines as well as possible imprisonment. Since these fines vary so widely according to the provisions of the acts violated, the interested reader should check the appropriate statute in the Alternative Fines Act (18 U.S.C. sec. 3571) or 33 U.S.C. Sec. 1319 for clarification.

CLEAN WATER ACT (Federal Water Pollution Control Act).[19] Governs discharge of pollutants into the waters of the U.S. Unpermitted discharge (of certain specified pollutants) into U.S. waters; discharge of any pollutant into publicly owned treatment works (POTW) in violation of pretreatment standards; introduction into sewer system any pollutant which could cause personal injury/property damage or cause POTW to lose its treatment permit; knowing endangement (i.e., placing another in danger of death or serious bodily injury during knowing discharge of pollutants); false statement or tampering with monitoring device; failure to notify U.S. agency of oil or hazardous substance discharge into navigable waters of United States.

Penalties: Before 1987—misdemeanor offense for either negligent or willful violation with maximum of one year imprisonment. After 1987—maximum one year imprisonment for negligent violations; felony (three to 15 years imprisonment) for knowing violations. Fines doubled upon second conviction.

RESOURCE CONSERVATION AND RECOVERY ACT (Solid Waste Disposal Act).[20] Governs transportation, storage, treatment, and disposal of hazardous waste; transportation of hazardous waste to an unpermitted facility; treatment/storage/disposal of hazardous waste without or in violation of a permit; omission of information or false statement; destruction or alteration of or failure to keep required records; transportation of hazardous waste without a manifest; exportation of hazardous waste to another country without its consent; storage/treatment/transportation of used oil in violation of permit; knowing endangerment (i.e., showing reckless disregard for human life by placing another in imminent danger of death or serious bodily injury during transportation, storage, treatment or disposal of hazardous waste.)

Penalties: Felony offense with maximum two to 15 years imprisonment. Penalties double on second conviction.

FEDERAL INSECTICIDE, FUNGICIDE, AND RODENTCIDE ACT.[21] Governs the use of pesticides. prohibits distribution, sale, or shipment of any unregistered pesticide; removal, alteration, or destruction of any required labelling; refusal to keep required records; improper use of a restricted pesticide; using a pesticide in a way inconsistent with its labelling.

Penalties: Commercial-type violators—maximum one year imprisonment; private-type violators—30 days imprisonment.

RIVERS AND HARBORS ACT (Refuse Act).[22] Regulates any construction near or obstruction of U.S. navigable waters. Unauthorized construction of any dam or dike in any navigable U.S. water; unauthorized building of any pier, breakwater or jetty in any navigable river or water of the U.S.; unauthorized evacuation, fill, or alteration of any navigable U.S. waters; unpermitted discharge or depositing of any refuse into any navigable U.S. waters.

Penalties: Misdemeanor offense with maximum one year imprisonment and minimum fine of $500.

COMPREHENSIVE ENVIRONMENTAL RESPONSE, COMPENSATION AND LIABILITY ACT (Also known as Superfund).[23] Governs the notification and clean up of spills or releases of hazardous substances

TABLE 10.1 MAJOR FEDERAL ENVIRONMENTAL LAWS AND THEIR CRIMINAL PROVISIONS (continued)

into the environment. Failure to notify immediately the National Environmental Response Center upon learning of the release of a hazardous substance into the environment; submission of false or misleading information in any notification of release into the environment.

Penalties: Before 1986—misdemeanor with one year maximum imprisonment; after 1986—felony with three years maximum imprisonment; five years on second conviction.

TOXIC SUBSTANCES CONTROL ACT.[24] Regulates storage and disposal of poly-chlorinated biphenyls (PCBs) and chemical substances and mixtures which present a risk of injury to health or the environment. Also sets forth recordkeeping, reporting, removal, storage, inspection and disposal requirements.

Penalties: Misdemeanor with one year maximum penalty.

MARINE PROTECTION, RESEARCH, AND SANCTUARIES ACT (Also known as Ocean Dumping Act). Unpermitted transportation of any material for the purposes of dumping it into the ocean waters.

Penalties: Misdemeanor with one year maximum imprisonment.

violates our nation's environmental laws. Of course, it should be pointed out that this agency has the track record of criminally prosecuting only the most egregious violations and violators. He says:

> Our experience has shown that the conduct of the typical defendant in our cases is no different and no less serious than the conduct of one who has been convicted of the more traditional felonies—whether committed by a "white-collar" or "street-crime" offender. The acts are generally willful, deliberate, rational, premeditated and committed with some forethought over a period of time. There are seldom mitigating circumstances . . . in fact, no perceptible defense is generally offered—except that compliance was too expensive. Individuals who commit environmental crimes—particularly those involving hazardous wastes—commonly demonstrate a complete disrespect for the law and disregard for the safety of others, and are motivated by a desire to enjoy the substantial profits that can be derived from such illegal activities.[16]

The federal government relies primarily upon eight major laws in its enforcement efforts.[17] These laws and their basic criminal provisions are shown in Table 10-1. These statutes deal with such concerns as the emission of hazardous pollutants into the air and waters, the treatment, storage and disposal of solid hazardous waste, the regulation on development and use of toxic chemicals, insecticides and pesticides, and the authority for the EPA to respond to releases or threatened releases of hazardous waste into the environment. This latter law also creates a mechanism to deal with such occurrences and is commonly referred to as the highly publicized so-called "Superfund."

Environmentalists and legal observers of the federal government's efforts in anti-pollution are unanimous in their feelings that the federal government and the EPA have until recent years not really been serious about the problem.[25] For example, although the EPA agency was created in 1970, it wasn't until 1981 that an Office of Criminal Enforcement was created within the agency. It wasn't until late 1982 that the first criminal investigator was hired. Similarly, it was 1987 before the small Environmental Crimes Unit in the U.S. Department of Justice was upgraded to a section in this agency. Even members of government agencies responsible for enforcing these laws admit that they have been slow in getting started. In a recent article, the head of the Environmental Crimes Section of the U.S. Department of Justice candidly admits this fact. He tries to convince the reader that this is no longer the case. He says:

> Criminal enforcement at EPA has come of age. Until the mid 1980s very few criminal cases were referred to the Department of Justice. (*Author's note:* i.e., referred for prosecution.) When cases were brought, defendants were frequently acquitted or sentenced to perform community service during relatively short periods of probation. Juries were often unwilling to convict corporate officers for environmental violations and courts were generally unwilling to send first-time white-collar offenders to prison. However, with heightened public sensitivity to the serious and often irreversible effects of pollution, criminal indictments, successful prosecutions, and lengthy prison terms for corporate offenders have become more common. From 1983 through May, 1989 the Department of Justice obtained more than 520 indictments for violation of federal environmental law resulting in more than 400 convictions, $22.5 million dollars in criminal fines and more than 248 years of imprisonment were imposed.[26]

State Anti-pollution Enforcement Efforts: Fragmentation and Overlap

Although most of the publicity about anti-pollution efforts and the major cases largely focus on the efforts of the federal government, all states have laws which regulate environmental pollutants and toxic sources. Like the federal authorities, the states also became more active in their regulatory efforts during the 1980s. In fact, a handful of states appear to be more aggressive in their criminal enforcement efforts than the federal government.[27] Part of state response was attributable to "the stick" of new federal laws which required state compliance together with "the carrot" of available federal funds and technical assistance efforts. Much of it is also simply the result of increased public attention which focused on environmental concerns. In response, state (and even local) legislative bodies created laws and either vested existing regulatory agencies with additional authority and responsibilities or created new agencies specifically for this purpose. Along with the creation or strengthening of this regulatory structure, states also gave additional authority and jurisdiction to existing enforcement agencies.

Of the many regulatory aspects of government, few, if any, are as fragmented or is there such overlapping of authority as one finds in the area of environmental regulation. A common pattern has prevailed. States seem to have generally fragmented the responsibility among various agencies and actors charged with either enforcement authority of a civil or criminal nature. This has and continues to pose serious problems. It certainly impedes effective law enforcement efforts to play an important role in curtailing present and future efforts directed at illegal pollution. Part of the problem is a result of how states have approached the issue of environmental regulation over the years. When the environment first became a public issue, states generally assigned some regulatory authority to a major state agency such as a Department of Conservation or Natural Resources. These large agencies generally relegated this responsibility to a minor one within the department. They also had little expertise to deal with the problem and often their statutory authority although ostensibly clear, was vague in actual application.

Today, the states approach their environmental enforcement efforts in a number of ways. While 29 states have some form of environmental crime enforcement unit at the state level, their approach is varied.[28] Some rely almost extensively on their state Department of Conservation or Natural Resources to deal with the problem. Within this agency may be an environmental resources division which has primary responsibility for environmental regulations, compliance inspections, and civil and criminal enforcement. Some states have created specialist investigative units in their state police organizations. One may also find designated legal specialists within the state attorney general's office to assist in the civil or criminal prosecutions brought by the state's regulatory agency. The EPA, realizing the important role that state Attorneys General play in the prosecution of state cases, has established a liaison office operating out of its Washington, D.C. office and sends out a periodic newsletter on environmental crimes prosecution to assist state Attorneys General in their efforts.

Some larger and more industrialized states rather than relying on a specific unit within a larger Conservation or Natural Resources Department have chosen to create special Departments of Environmental Conservation to deal with environmental issues. Others have created a specific enforcement unit in the Attorney General's office. Still others have taken a mixed approach. Pennsylvania, for example, has a Department of Environmental Resources which carries out regulatory, enforcement, and land and resource management responsibilities in the Commonwealth. In that state's Attorney General's office there is an Environmental Prosecution Unit which has law enforcement agents, prosecutors and regulation inspectors which are involved in the prosecution of criminal violations of Pennsylvania's environmental statutes.[29]

The investigation and prosecution of environmental crimes by the states has indicated that these types of offenses require coordinative efforts. Environmental offenses are proving much more complex to deal with than conventional crimes. They often require, for example, a joint undertaking involving scientists and technicians who provide the analysis of toxic substances and the expert testimony required at hearings or trials, investigators specially trained in the uncovering and gathering of evidence and the particular elements associated with the offense, and specialist-attorneys who have experience in the laws and the prosecution of such cases.[30]

Under state laws regulating environmental toxins, local prosecutors also generally have the authority to enforce these laws at the local level. Generally, however, with some notable exceptions such as in California, local prosecutors have not played much of a role in such cases. The reason is obvious: Local prosecutors have neither the resources nor the skills to deal with these type offenses—especially when they involve anything more than minor cases where a small time offender is caught violating the laws with such impunity

Regulatory Fragmentation and Non-coordination: The Case of New York

There have been several examinations of state enforcement efforts to deal with criminal aspects of environmental pollution.* The State of New York is an excellent example of the problems which can result when states attempt to gear-up to meet a major social problem in a short period of time and with little legislative or existing operational experience. In that state, as public pressure mounted for more effective anti-pollution efforts and the state legislature responded, additional laws were created. As we have seen, a state can initially assign the responsibility to an existing agency with related responsibilities on the theory that its operational experience can then be transferred to meet the new challenge. On the other hand, it can create a new specialist agency. Either way, experience has shown that such new laws designed to deal with environmental pollutants and polluters are sufficiently broad in scope to permit jurisdiction to ''bleed-over'' into other agencies such as state Attorneys General. This happened in New York. Although New York State is being singled-out as an excellent example of this kind of ''patchwork,'' similar experiences have taken place in other states. As already mentioned, it is not unusual, for example, for states to experience shared jurisdiction between a special environmental regulatory agency, a state conservation agency, a special unit in the Attorney General's office, and local prosecutors who have the authority to prosecute criminal (and in a few cases civil) environmental lawbreakers.

New York State's efforts are organized into a Department of Environmental Conservation (DEC). This agency administers not only the air, water, solid waste, hazardous waste, and other pollution-type environmental laws under the State Environmental Conservation Law, but also the fish and game, marine resources, lands and forests, and mineral resource laws. The pollution statutes are administered through the DEC's Office of Environmental Quality which is further divided into separate Divisions for Air, Water, Construction Management, and Solid and Hazardous Waste. The Division of Solid and Hazardous Waste alone has a Bureau of Municipal Waste, a Bureau of Resource Recovery, A Bureau of Hazardous Site Control, and two bureaus organized geographically for taking remedial action. Formal investigation is carried out by two independent units, the Division of Environmental Enforcement (DEE) which is itself a division of the DEC's General Counsel's Office and the Bureau of Environmental Conservation Investigations (BECI). These two groups operate largely autonomously of each other. There is also the Division of Law Enforcement which is the uniformed police of the DEC. These bureaus and divisions operate through and are superimposed on a structure of Regional Directors and Regional Attorneys.**

In addition to the hazardous waste regulation and enforcement structure of the DEC, the New York Attorney General also plays a significant role in hazardous waste enforcement. This office includes its own Bureau of Environmental Protection (BEP), which has its own staff of attorneys, scientists, and investigators to develop and prosecute both civil and criminal environmental cases. In 1985, it created an Environmental Crimes Unit (ECU), consisting of assistant attorneys general and investigative personnel. The ECU develops its own cases—interestingly, few seem to be referred from DEE or BECI—and seeks indictment by use of the state's grand jury system.*** There is some feeling that the various environmental law enforcement and investigative groups do not cooperate. One report which examined the state's anti-pollution enforcement efforts concludes, "there is some perception that BECI institutionally seeks to maintain control of its "own" cases and resolves most of them by issuing "tickets" charging only misdemeanors, or by referring them to the local DAs for prosecution."**** Obviously, different enforcement strategies and priorities exist among the enforcers.

The various county and local District Attorneys also have a significant role in at least one aspect of environmental crimes—hazardous waste enforcement. They may enforce county or local ordinances not preempted by state hazardous waste laws and may accept cases from the DEC to prosecute. Some prosecutors in the New York City area have established units for prosecuting hazardous waste crimes. The New York State Police has a unit focusing on hazardous waste/hazardous materials enforcement. In addition, the City of New York has its own hazardous waste enforcement system. It is pointed out that at a hazardous waste scene in New York City, one may find the city's Department of Environmental Protection, Sanitation Department, Fire Department, New York City Police Department, Department of Health, BECI, and the Attorney General's Environmental Crimes Unit all poking around.*****

New York is perhaps only unique by virtue of the fact that it is a populous state with a large, cumbersome, and complex state bureaucracy and a state that is both highly industrialized and has experienced some severe problems with pollution.

*For example, see Decicco, John and Bonnanno, Edward. "A Comparative Analysis of the Criminal Environmental Laws of the Fifty States: The Need for Statutory Uniformity as a Catalyst for Effective Enforcement of Existing and Proposed Laws," THE CRIMINAL JUSTICE QUARTERLY, Vol. 9, No. 4 (Summer 1988), pp. 216–307 ; Rebovich, Don. *Understanding Hazardous Waste Crime: A Multistate Examination of the Offense and Offender Characteristics in the Northeast,* Trenton, N.J.: New Jersey Division of Criminal Justice, 1986.

***Author's note:* The following discussion of New York State's environmental regulatory effort is provided by an anonymous draft of the Environmental Law Institute Report on New York Hazardous Waste Enforcement (March 31, 1987) which was obtained by the author.

***Ibid., p. 4.

****Ibid.

*****Ibid., p. 7.

that the burden of proof is overwhelmingly obvious and proveable. It must also be recognized that local prosecutors often do not have the time nor are they particularly motivated to involve themselves with the prosecution of these offenses. They often contend they are too overwhelmed by traditional forms of crime to become involved in efforts at prosecuting environmental polluters. If such efforts are undertaken, they often involve the local prosecutor's office in coordinative efforts with state officials such as the Attorney General's office or the state environmental regulatory authorities who provide the specialized guidance and assistance required.

Uneven Enforcement and Non-uniformity of State Laws

Like all areas of crime, there is a great deal of unevenness in the enforcement of environmental laws—both civil and criminal. This unevenness is seen both within the states as well as from state to state.[31] To the extent that this exists, it hampers our nation's efforts to use existing remedies especially the remedy of the criminal law and its sanctions as a means to deal with illegal pollution. Perhaps, not surprisingly, the states have yet to develop a uniform approach to criminal prosecutions for the disposal of hazardous wastes or pollutants. While all states have developed existing programs of compliance and inspection—some obviously better than others—they show little common regard for employing the criminal law to prosecute offenders. Some states have virtually no experience with prosecuting illegal polluters. A few states have developed extensive investigative and prosecutorial track records, and a third category which although they have "experimented" with the use of criminal prosecutions, still almost exclusively rely upon civil law provisions to punish offenders and to exact compliance.

In spite of new compliance laws, financial encouragement and technical assistance efforts, the federal government has generally played a limited role in trying to get states to deal more effectively with the problem. When Congress passed the Resource Conservation and Recovery Act in 1976, it created minimum requirements with respect to treatment and disposal of hazardous substances as well as minimum requirements for criminal penalties. States were required to conform to these guidelines although the states were free and even encouraged to develop more stringent guidelines and penalties if they so desired. Congress felt that states should have the primary responsibility for dealing with toxic substances entirely generated and disposed of within the state. Looking back, there are now some second thoughts about the wisdom of such an approach.[32]

Table 10-2 is a general summary of state environmental laws which carry criminal provisions. The reader will note that these laws are very similar in terms of their provisions to the major federal crimes already shown in Table 10-1. Both the federal government and the states regulate and prohibit similar forms of toxic emissions and disposal of toxic substances.

Problems in Prosecution

One of the legal hurdles in bringing the criminal law to bear on those who criminally pollute—especially corporate officers is the requirement that the illegal act must have been done knowingly. And following the requirement for the burden of proof in criminal cases, this knowledge in and intent to violate the law must be shown by the government

TABLE 10.2 SUMMARY OF MAJOR CRIMINAL PROVISIONS ENACTED BY STATES

Hazardous Waste: Criminal sanctions are imposed on individuals who dispose, treat, store, and transport hazardous waste without authorization.

Providing False Information and Concealment: It is illegal to give false information, make false statements, conceal evidence of toxic production or disposal, or render inaccurate monitoring devices pertaining to hazardous waste, water or air pollutants.

Water Pollutants: Criminal penalties can be imposed on individuals who discharge water pollutants without a permit or who do not meet toxic or effluent standards.

Clean Air: Individuals can be criminally prosecuted who discharge contaminants into the air in excess of permit limitations, or without a permit.

to have existed beyond a reasonable doubt. These requirements can provide a significant obstacle to successful prosecution. There is certainly no problem where a corporate officer is caught ''red-handed'' actually committing a violation of environmental laws. For example, the somewhat unlikely occurrence where a corporate officer is caught actually dumping in a river what is clearly hazardous waste. But what about the situation in a large firm where employees are caught dumping a toxic pollutant? The workers claim that they were only following their superior's instructions. The corporate officer of course, denies this and denies any knowlege or culpability in the criminal act.

Fortunately, in theory at least, neither the corporation or the corporate officer can escape responsibility. This was not always the case. Under the common law and the law which existed for many years in the United States, corporations were considered incapable of commiting crimes. This is no longer true.[33] The Supreme Court has held that the corporate officer cannot escape liability so easily. The Court held in a landmark case that the President of a supermarket chain was responsible for violations committed by his firm because it was his duty to prevent them.[34] Still, if the particular law being violated requires the government to demonstrate criminal intent on the part of the corporate officer, problems for the prosecution are presented. In such a situation one noted legal expert suggests that, if possible, another statute which doesn't impose this burden on the government be used.[35]

This alternative is referred to in the law as the ''strict liability'' doctrine which is applicable to certain offenses. Under this doctrine the government can charge someone with a crime without the burden of proving the degree of knowledge and intent required in most crimes. Unfortunately, such ''strict liability'' crimes also generally carry diminished penalties. But the law in this area is still shadowy. As a result, the vast majority of criminal prosecutions which employ this doctrine are directed toward the offending business firm and criminal fines are imposed on the business itself using the ''strict liability'' doctrine rather than the officers of the firm whose successful prosecution is more closely tied to the requirement of showing knowledge and intent.[36] Even though corporate officers could theoretically also be prosecuted as individuals under the strict liability doctrine, the government has been less apt to use this legal tool against offending individuals.

This explanation for why the federal government by use of the ''strict liability'' doctrine has not sought to have more corporate officers charged and imprisoned for such offenses as illegal toxic waste disposal was explained to the author by a prosecution specialist from the U.S Department of Justice. Juries seem unwilling to convict under the doctrine if possible imprisonment of a corporate official is a likelihood. It would seem, that juries are hesitant to merely impute knowledge of the crime. Unless the government can show that the corporate officer actually knew of the crime and was therfore complicit in its commission—often a very difficult thing for the government to ''prove''—jurors feel uncomfortable, especially where a prison sentence could be imposed. Juries have less reservations, under the circumstances, levying a criminal or civil fine on the firm. Federal prosecutors realize the problem this poses for a successful prosecution.

There have been other associated problems with the legal enforcement of environmental laws. One is the situation where a landfill or solid waste disposal center is used by a number of firms. Toxic wastes in violation of the law are found at the site. What about the problem of determining which of the site users is responsible? How does the government pinpoint the guilty party? Without being able to determine responsibility the government has no case—at least no criminal case.

The Issue of Fines as Punishment

Many legal scholars, criminologists, and environmentalists have been critical of the efforts and effects of civil or criminal fines to prevent illegal environmental damage.[37] Studies by the General Accounting Office (GAO) and Congressional hearings on environmental pollution come to one conclusion: The problem [of illegal environmental contamination] is widespread. The few highly publicized cases such as the Exxon oil spill off the coast of Alaska, are just the tip of the iceberg. For every instance of detected criminal (or accidental) pollution, hundreds go undetected.[38] The conclusion is that the imposition of economic sanctions such as civil fines or criminal fines directed against a firm (as opposed to officers and employees of the firm) seem not to be working as a deterrent.[39] Criminal pollution is an economic crime. It is done to escape the costs of dealing with hazardous materials properly. Fines imposed by regulators are merely seen as a ''cost of doing business.'' This is especially true in non-owner operated corporations where even fines are payed by the shareholders rather than the corporation's officers. The liability of corporate officers is generally limited only to the extent that they are also stockholders and how costs of the fine and any attendant bad publicity hurts the business and the equity position of the firm as reflected by its stock value.

The problem is not only with these corporate non-owner managers. The same calculated risks are also borne by entrepreneurs who are owners of firms. They are going to consider the risks and the associated ''costs.'' If compliance expenses are costly, and the chances of being caught are minimal, a strong incentive to pollute exists. Especially, if they can be reasonably assured that the only penalty which will be imposed will be a monetary one in the way of a fine.

If deterrence is to work in theory—which underlies any aspect of criminal law—the penalties must appear to be greater than the benefits received from participation in a criminal act. Punishment must be seen as both meaningful and likely. Remove either of

The Complications of Environmental Law

The complications of environmental law are providing a costly learning lesson to firms in the Buffalo, New York area. Already a center of environmental attention brought about by the infamous Love Canal issue in nearby Niagara Falls, the area finds itself the focus of another hazardous waste issue. Roughly 200 firms—from small manufacturing companies to the large Harrison Radiator Division of General Motors and including firms that make everything from lithium batteries to parts for outdoor power equipment—are involved in a joint venture that brings anything but smiles to the companies involved.

It began when the firms contracted with Envirotek Ltd. to dispose of their hazardous waste material. Licensed by the state of New York and the Environmental Protection Agency as a hazardous waste disposal company, Envirotek was paid by the firms to dispose of their toxic substances. This would prove to be an unfortunate choice of a waste disposal company. In 1989, investigators from the State of New York's Department of Environmental Conservation, the EPA and the FBI raided raided Envirotech's office. They were looking for proof that Envirotek violated its permits by dumping and burying hazardous material at the waste-disposal facility. They found what they came for. The firm was accused by the state and federal governments of improperly disposing of the materials it had been paid by these firms to dispose. Shortly after the raid, Envirotech filed for bankruptcy. Rather than being the end of the story, this was just the beginning.

''We did it by the book. We followed every rule that we were aware of. We used a licensed facility that had all of the proper permits, and still this happened. Its just not fair,'' said James McLean, chief executive officer of the Herr Manufacturing Company which is one of the over 200 firms who contracted with and paid Evirotech to dispose of their waste.

What is not fair to McLean and other spokespersons for the involved firms is that they now find themselves in the waste cleanup business. Since Envirotech is now a defunct company and not in a position to pay for the cleanup of the improperly disposed of hazardous waste, under federal law the responsibility to clean up the mess now belongs to its former customers. Preliminary estimates are the cleanup costs of the 1,200 drums of hazardous waste which have gathered at the Envirotech site is nearly $2 million. And as one attorney for the firms says, ''the meter is still running.'' In the eyes of the law the firms have become what is called a ''Potentially Responsible Party'' or a PRP for short. Jean McCreary, a lawyer for the group says that ''when EPA invites you to a party, that's what they call you, a PRP.''*

''The law imposes strict liability, as well as joint and several liability,'' McCreary said. ''Strict liability means it doesn't matter whose fault the problem is. The job must be paid for.''** The law in question is the Superfund Amendment

Reauthorization Act of 1988. It includes a provision that places ''cradle-to-grave'' liability on companies that produce hazardous materials. What this translates to is that every single company who contracted with Envirotech can be held responsible for the cleanup costs, or it can be apportioned among the firms. The problem in the latter case is identifying and apportioning cost among the companies based on the amount of hazardous waste material at the site which has not been properly disposed. What hazardous waste belongs to whom? This is proving to be a daunting task. Investigators and members of the contracting firms are trying to sort out the waste material and apportioning costs. What is compounding the problem is that investigators are not sure that some of the hazardous waste on the site doesn't actually belong to companies who are not among the 200 or so identified as doing business with Envirotech.

The federal government's position has been that somebody is going to pay for this situation. The message given to the companies is straightforward: Either they work out a voluntary cleanup plan with the government, or the EPA would take care of the job and send them a bill. Either way they are going to pay. According to a spokesman for the EPA's regional office in New York City, ''Companies are considered responsible for the materials they generate. Part of that responsibility extends to making sure that the disposal company is operating on the up and up.''*** This is not the first instance of companies being caught in a similar situation. The EPA has acknowledged that other firms in the past have had to pay under similar circumstances. There will certainly be additional future cases where this also occurs.

While the efforts go on to sort-out respective areas of liability which is causing acrimonious squabbling between the firms and the hunt for additional parties who can be brought into the cleanup costs goes on, the issue may drag out for years. The worry is that Envirotech has illegally disposed of waste in landfills which have yet to be discovered. In ten years or so, these landfill burials may be found and the companies may then find themselves liable for cleaning up these additional sites and disposing of the hazardous waste they contain.

Right now the U.S. Attorney's Office in Buffalo and The EPA is busy trying to sort all this out. In addition, a criminal investigation of Envirotek is proceeding parallel to the cleanup operation. Former employees have given the government a 73-page affidavit that the firm repeatedly and routinely engaged in the illegal dumping of hazardous waste. Not surprisingly, these allegations are denied by the former president of Envirotek. A federal grand jury will be given the opportunity to decide who is telling the truth.

*Thomas, G. Scott. ''Envirotek Mess Tangles 220 firms,'' *Business First,* Vol. 7, No. 2 (October 29, 1990), p. 2.

**Ibid.

***Ibid.

these conditions from our equation and deterrence theory will certainly fail. It has been suggested that the threat of punishment in the form of public censure and the likelihood of imprisonment will have its greatest effect on white collar criminals. A criminal as opposed to a civil action and an action which threatens imprisonment for company officials rather than a criminal fine directed at the offending firm will be more threatening. Even with little in the way of an increased likelihood that enforcement actions will occur, the fact that a businessman or a corporate officer would likely be charged with a crime and if convicted would be sent to jail or prison, must figure into the "costs" of polluting. It would raise the cost significantly.

One of the problems of employing corporate (or individual) fines is that too often the statutory structure of fines for criminal offenses is not adequately sensitive to the wealth of the offender. This is also true of environmental crimes statutes. It has been argued that that penalty levels are too high for smaller offenders and too low for super-rich multi-national corporations.[40] Of course, one might argue that it then becomes upon conviction, the responsibility of the court to take this into consideration and adjust the fine imposed accordingly. Although this is of course possible since environmental offenses like most white collar crimes only impose a maximum penalty, the judge can then impose a fine somewhere within the range as prescribed by law against the convicted offender. But this is easier said then done. Although there are exceptions such as the federal judge's overturning of the $100 million criminal penalty imposed on Exxon because he thought it wasn't enough given the high profitability of the firm, fines like other forms of criminal sanctions are offense-regarding more than they are offender-regarding—they are related to the offense much more than the offender.

If corporate fines are going to be employed, one novel suggestion is that offending firms be forced to pay a "day-fine" for illegal pollution.[41] Under this system, the fine is set at the amount of profit earned by the firm for each day it is not in compliance with environmental standards. Of course, this runs into the problem of trying to determine the firm's specific profit for the period in question. Accountants will tell you that this may not be that easy. It also might possibly run into a problem like this. Suppose a small chemical firm finds it self with an excess of a toxic waste substance. It contacts several disposal firms all of whom tell the firm that because of the nature of the chemical, disposal will be expensive. The hazardous waste disposers quote figures which vastly exceeds the firm's profits for the period. If the company was only concerned about profit maximization (and not the moral issue), it would be economically rational for the firm to illegally bury the substance and pay the price if caught. To make it economically non-rational, the fine would have to exceed the disposal costs. But, of course,this also assumes that there is the absolute certainty the firm will get caught if it buries the substance and knows this.

Economists also talk about the "shifting" phenomenon. A corporate fine as imposed will fall on either customers in terms of increased product price or owners depending upon the firm's market control. The offending firm can pass it on in the form of production costs to consumers if it has market power. If it doesn't have this market control, the argument says that fine and consequent increase in price will reduce total profit and the firm will suffer directly through the loss of profit or indirectly through the protest of shareholders. While a possibility, this argument isn't totally correct. The firm, if it has a strong market, will still be making the maximum profit under the altered conditions of the fine. Once the fine is amortized, the firm will be able to return to its original profit-maximizing position. For many firms, the temporary move away from the maximizing position will be a mere blip in a history of high profitability.

If it can't shift the costs of the imposed fine to the consumer, it will fall unto the owners by diminishing its assets and reducing its stockholder's equity. It is suggested in the latter instance that stockholder's could force the firm into compliance with the law or remove the head of the corporation. Neither is likely to happen. The interests of individual stockholders are often so diffuse that the fines imposed would not provoke them into action and many stockholders in large corporations at least, are typically apathetic. As long as dividends are paid and there is a reasonable expectation that their stock will increase in value, the shareholders will be satisfied even if there are a few fines imposed.

The Argument Regarding Incarceration

Even the idea of jail or imprisonment for offending parties is not always that foolproof. The problem with jail is that only individuals may be jailed, but corporations are common offenders in environmental cases. It thus becomes necessary to to find the responsible party within the corporation. Yet even if that person is found, and this may be difficult, the fact that he suffers the penalty may mean that the corporate entity itself is not punished and therefore not deterred. The responsibility of finding a responsible party to affix blame is a real one.[42] The prosecution of the case (in the absence of a "strict liability" doctrine and its discussed pitfalls) requires both a finding of *actus reus* and *mens rea*. In most crimes, this is not a problem, in others it is. The height of complexity is reached in in cases involving corporate defendants.

To see what we mean, consider this situation: During the construction of a petrochemical plant, it is discovered that shifting and sinkage is highly probable. This could lead to the rupture of holding tanks and the pipe system resulting in the discharge of toxic chemicals into the environment. The project engineer contacts the vice-president for engineering who kicks it "upstairs" to the firm's executive vice-president. The executive VP is concerned about the "sunk-costs" already into the project which makes it financially impossible to suddenly stop construction and build elsewhere. He tells the engineering vice-president, "I'm too damn busy to deal with this now, do what you can to make sure no spillage occurs, but get the thing built within budget." The vice-president tells the project engineer what the executuve VP said. "I can't do that and remain within the budget," the project engineer claims. "Yes, you can, just do it," is the vice-president's reply.

The project engineer afraid of losing any chance for future promotion in the firm—or worse—realizes that correcting the underground problem would be too costly and unacceptable to his superiors, leaves the design as is. One of the tanks erupts several years later. Who would you prosecute and possibly send to jail if the latter was your intention?

Some might say all three of the individuals, but what if you must prove the concept of criminal responsibility? Analysis of this case can support the punishment of the project engineer since both *mens rea* and *actus reus* are arguably present, but given the directive he received, can it truly be said he was responsible? The vice-president for engineering might also be considered culpable, yet his defense counsel will argue that the statements of the Executive Vice-President relieve him of responsibility. That leaves the Executive Vice-President whose defense is obvious.[43] It has been suggested that cases like these might call for some innovative recommendations. One interesting recommendation is for divestiture for persistent offenders (i.e., forcing the sale of all or part of an offender's business). This approach may be criticized that it would also affect the employees and shareholders. Still, it is little different than the ''ripple-effect'' of other forms of sentencing as when a convicted defendant's family suffers when he is convicted. It may also be a case where a firm which has an excellent record of protecting the environment would want to buy the firm. Delicensing has also been a suggestion. This means not only the license to operate, but someone who is a ''night hauler'' would also lose license to his truck.[44]

So why don't we use these strategies and let our laws reflect the imposition of such penalties and with this, our serious concern about the problem? In addition to the legal problems already discussed, the answer is to be found unfortunately, too often in the traditional reponse of government law making to the interests of business. Business interests and capital have always enjoyed a favored position and treatment in the United States. Szasz in looking at the adoption of federal legislation to control the disposal of toxic waste concluded that one of the major reasons that laws are less than effective in this area is because those who would be regulated were successful in getting Congress to waterdown any controlling legislation in this area.[45] Business interests simply successfully lobbied against laws which would impose more severe penalties.

A good example of the kinds of consideration go into the passage (and enforcement) of environmental laws and the ''tradeoffs'' that might accompany such legislation is seen when Congress set about to enact the first ''reckless and knowing endangerment'' offense in federal environmental law.[46] The reader will recall that this provision in the RCRA provided someone could be found guilty of a criminal offense to knowingly place another person in imminent danger of death or serious bodily injury while committing an act forbidden by the RCRA that demonstrated a lack of concern for the individual or individuals being endangered.[47]

Although the reckless endangerment provision was adopted by Congress without member opposition, its implications quickly became the subject of intense concern in the business community. This concern was expressed by the Business Roundtable—a group of lobbyists representing among others, a number of the *Fortune 500* companies. Under the circumstances, Congress decided to reconsider this amendment. Following several weeks of negotiation, an agreement was reached between attorneys for the Business Roundtable and the Justice Department. A compromise was hammered-out at the insistence of the business community. The essence of the compromise was straightforward: In exchange for keeping the endangerment provision and dramatically increasing the maximum penalties, the burden of proof on the government to prove a violation was made more difficult. In addition to the requirement that the government prove the defendant's knowledge concerning the illegal activity (e.g., transporting hazardous waste to a facility without a permit; the placement of another person in imminent danger of death or serious bodily injury), conviction would now require proof that the defendant's conduct manifested either ''unjustified and inexcusable disregard for human life'' or ''extreme indifference to human life.'' The change in this language would now make it more difficult to prosecute such cases.

It seemed to accomplish just that. It was obvious that government prosecutors were reluctant to initiate criminal prosecutions under these difficult to prove guidelines. Three years after these compromised guidelines went into effect, not a single indictment (let alone a prosecution) occurred. Congress realizing that it had gone too far—and under attack by environmentalists and criticized by enforcement agencies who also felt the heat of environmental criticism—repealed the''unjustified disregard'' and ''extreme indifference'' part of the law in 1984. Since then, the federal prosecutors have been less reluctant to use the act and indictments and convictions have taken place.[48]

Still, it wasn't until 1987 that the federal government obtained its first criminal conviction under these new requirements. The first corporation found guilty of the ''reckless'' and ''knowing endangerment'' provisions of the RCRA was a Colorado firm, Protex Industries. The firm was found guilty of fifteen felony counts for ''knowingly'' exposing three of its employees to toxic pesticides and solvents. Government prosecutors ironically argued that this action showed the firm's reckless, indifferent and inexcusable disregard for human life although this amending requirement had been struck from the statute.''[49]

In 1988, Albert S. Tumin became the first individual to be convicted of the knowing endangerment provision of RCRA.[50] Tumin was originally targeted as an illicit drug manufacturer when a chemical supplier notified the federal Drug Enforcement Administration of Tumin's purchase of three 55 gallon drums of ethyl ether which is commonly used in cocaine production. Tumin eventually abandoned the three drums in a residential area in Rockaway, New York. This led to Tumin's conviction for two violations of the RCRA, knowing endangerment, and knowing transportation of hazardous waste to an unpermitted facility. [51]

The problem isn't only with business interests who generate pollutants, other interests are represented too. Kentucky is a good example. Large industrial and chemical corporations are located in several small towns in Western Kentucky. These firms over the years routinely dump toxic materials into surrounding rivers. Environmentalists want this practice stopped. They have marshaled their forces against these firms. Arrayed against the environmentalists are employees of these factories and local town businessmen who see the environmentalists as a threat to their livelihood. Should these plants be successfully shutdown, employees and local merchants will pay the economic consequences. Similar problems exist in any international or transnational discussion of pollution abatement as we shall later see.

Illegal Pollution: Unanticipated Consequences and Organized Crime

There is yet another dark side to the problem of criminal pollution of our environment. It has fostered criminal activity and in certain areas of the country organized crime has gotten into the act. The generation of hazardous waste is a necessary by-product of modern industrial production. Once such toxic substances have been produced, federal and state environmental laws require that such waste matter be processed and disposed of in accordance with what are supposed to be strictly promulgated laws. Until a few years ago this was not the case. Industrial hazardous waste was legally indistinguishable from other solid wastes. Toxic waste was disposed of with ordinary garbage at landfills and in coastal waters at low cost to the firms generating such waste.

In the 1970s, it was recognized that such practices were creating intolerable environmental and public health concerns. In 1976, Congress enacted the Resource Conservation and Recovery Act (RCRA) which issued a minimum set of federal compliance standards to govern the generation and disposal of toxic waste all of which was to be regulated by the EPA. There were provisions, however, that state authorities could become primary regulators if the state enacted similar legislation at least as strict as the RCRA. The EPA and the states were required to register firms who created hazardous waste and issue waste generator permits to inspected and approved firms. This was only one part of the new requirements. Special permits were also required for those in the business of transporting and disposing of hazardous waste. Hazardous waste hauling firms, storage sites, treatment facilities and hazardous waste disposal sites all came under the requirements. In this way, a "cradle-to-grave" regulatory scheme would govern hazardous waste from production to disposal.

Although the RCRA and similar state laws considered both toxic waste generation and waste disposal, it was the issue of disposal that became the most difficult to regulate. The disposal requirements created a new system of permits, licenses, manifests, inspections, and, ultimately, merely "good faith" compliance by waste disposers.[52] These new laws which distinguished hazardous waste from other waste and by directing that such wastes be treated differently from conventional solid or liquid wastes, created almost overnight a new industry: hazardous waste transporters and disposal systems.[53] It also significantly increased the cost of waste disposal to firms generating hazardous substances who now had to comply with the new regulations. This would prove to cause problems as hazardous waste generating firms sought to circumvent the cost of the new requirements by engaging non-regulated (illegal) "midnight haulers" and "midnight dumpers."

What quickly developed was a situation where the passage of legislation which sought to curtail illegal dumping through regulation and control, actually abetted the problem. Since it soon became apparent in the industry (e.g., among chemical producers and industrial chemical users) that neither the EPA or the state enforcement agencies were up to the task of regulating the industry, some toxic waste producers saw the opportunity to get a leg up on their competition by getting around the high costs of disposal by having unlicensed firms and storage sites dispose of their toxic wastes. Although they had to pay a "premium" to have illegal transporters and disposal sites do this, it was far less expensive then contracting with approved and regulated transporters and disposers who had to pass-on the more costly requirements imposed on them.[54] Apparently, waste producers found little in the way of a problem of locating unscrupulous hauling firms who were only to eager for their business.

There is still another twist to this. In those parts of the country where garbage hauling and landfill operations have been historically controlled by organized crime, their movement into the newly created hazardous waste market was an immediate extension of their businesses. This occurred most notably in the states of New York and New Jersey. In New Jersey, for example, organized crime had for decades controlled the garbage industry through ownership of garbage hauling firms, by their ownership of landfill sites, and through practices of labor racketeering.[55] The problem is not merely confined to the Northeast. There are indications that organized crime has made inroads into the toxic waste business in various parts of the country. This was pointed out in a survey by the U.S. Senate Permanent Subcommittee on Investigations which suggests that about one-third of the states, especially the largest and most industrialized, have had their toxic waste disposal industry infiltrated by organized crime.[56] Many states are not aware of this occurrence nor have they had enough experience with the investigation and prosecution of organized crime to recognize this danger or to ferret it out.

Testimony before a Congressional Committee investigating organized crime's involvement in the garbage and toxic waste disposal industry of New Jersey shows how the system operated. Years ago, organized crime developed a monopoly on garbage hauling in many areas of that state. Once associates of organized crime owned a number of hauling firms in any geographical area, they established an organizational structure that governed their relationships and ensured high profits. The cornerstone of the system was one of "property rights." Municipal solid waste hauling contracts were illegally divided among haulers. Having a property right meant that the hauler held rights to continue picking up the contract at sites he currently serviced without competition from others. Other mob-controlled hauling firms would submit artificially high bids or not bid at all when a contract came up for renewal. This would assure that the contractor kept his site. Of course, in such a non-competitive situation the organized crime associates could also establish a pricing structure for their services which proved to be very lucrative. These property rights were recognized and enforced by means of threats or violence. Even hauling firms which were not owned outright by organized crime in these areas abided by the rules or they were forced to sell and get out.

When the new regulations were passed, mob-connected garbage haulers found it easy to obtain state permits and set themselves up as hazardous waste transporters and disposers. Of course, they brought with them their same form of organization and operation. Individual haulers holding established property rights assumed that they would transfer these property rights to the new type of waste.[57] They did exactly that.

It was in the area of organized crime controlled disposal operations where the problem really became serious. Under the law, the hazardous waste material had to have someone from a registered and approved disposal site sign that the toxic substances had been properly disposed of. Mob control of hauling is not enough. Organized crime figures had to also have ownership of, or at least influence over, final disposal sites to make the system complete and to maximize profits. Since organized crime already controlled and nearly monopolized landfill sites, these sites readily accepted shipments of hazardous waste disguised as ordinary municipal waste.[58] Landfill owners of approved disposal sites not directly associated with organized crime were bribed to sign for shipments never received (the mob haulers would dump it along roadways, down municipal sewers or into the ocean or other waterways) or accept hazardous waste that was designated on the manifest as assigned elsewhere.[59] Known organized crime figures also started to seize control of a network of phony disposal and "treatment" facilities such as Chemical Control Corporation in Elizabeth, New Jersey and in other cities.[60] Licensed by the state, these facilities could legally receive hazardous waste and sign the required manifest. Rather than disposing of the toxic waste, they would merely stockpile it on the site where it would stay until it exploded, burned or in some way came to the attention of the authorities or they merely "disposed" of it by illegally dumping it somewhere.

New Jersey's experience is too typical in yet another way. When the major federal law regulating the transportation and particularly the disposal of hazardous waste was passed, there simply weren't enough qualified transporters and landfill sites in the state (or the nation) which could accommodate the waste that industry generated. There still isn't today. Concessions had to be made on industry would have strangled on its own toxic effluent. To deal with the need to dispose of toxic waste while imposing some regulatory controls, temporary licenses were issued to what would later prove to be bogus carriers and to firms who had no proper disposal sites. Incredibly, the supervision by New Jersey authorities was also non-existent. It was four years after the federal law was passed before New Jersey even had a single person in the state capital to monitor the manifests filed by the transporters and the disposers with the state.[61] And as we have seen, the EPA certainly wasn't up to the task in the early 1980s. In a report issued in the mid-1980s, a federal government study found that the existing manifest system designed to control the transportation and disposal of hazardous waste was simply not working because of the lack of effective monitoring of the system by the states and the federal government.[62]

The inepitude of the enforcement of anti-pollution laws by the state of New Jersey was graphically pointed out in the Congressional hearings when it was disclosed that the state's agencies charged with this responsibility—the Interagency Hazardous Waste Strike Force, the Division of Criminal Justice, and the Division of Environmental Protection—were incapable of producing effective enforcement even when tipped off to specific instances of illegal hazardous waste dumping.[63]

Although testimony during the investigation of organized crime's inroads into hazardous waste disposal tended to absolve the firms who generated the toxic wastes from any complicity in these crimes by painting a picture in which the firms in good-faith turned their waste over to what they thought were licensed and therefore comptent haulers and disposers, this "innocence" is not shared by all observers. For one thing, it was pointed out that generating firms have no interest in turning-in the hauler or disposer in spite of any suspicions. The reason was simple: These firms didn't want to "turn-in" their low bidders.

This discussion is meant to do two things: First, it points out that well-intentioned and required social legislation (anti-polllution laws just being one example), can lead to some unanticipated consequences. These laws may not only foster the breaking of the law, they may actually encourage law breaking if we are not careful. They may, for example, create an opportunity for the intent of the law to be thwarted on a scale even greater in scope and, perhaps with more serious future consequences, than what existed before the passage of the legislation. In New Jersey, for example, not only was the law violated while serving to strengthen the tentacles of organized crime, it also did one other important thing: It seems to have encouraged at least tacit lawbreaking by ostensibly non-criminal elements (the industrial generators of toxic waste) in order to avoid the costs imposed by the new requirements.

The Federal Government's Increase in Criminal Prosecution and Penalties

Although it has been slow to begin a concerted effort to apply criminal prosecutions and sanctions in the area of environmental pollution, the federal government now seems to be entering a new stage of willingness to use the criminal as opposed to civil and administrative remedies to attack willful environmental destruction. For example, during fiscal year 1989 the EPA's enforcement activity surpassed 1988's efforts in almost every category. New records for both criminal prosecutions and criminal fines were established. During the 1989 fiscal year the number of cases referred to the U.S. Department of Justice rose to 60. This is a 50 percent increase in criminal referrals from just a few years earlier.[64] The Justice Department indicted 101 corporations and individuals in fiscal year 1989, and 107 guilty pleas and convictions were obtained. These prosecutions yielded $12.7 million in fines and more than 53 years of imprisonment in contrast to 1985, when fines totalled only $565,000 and a mere five years of prison were imposed for all defendants convicted of these offenses.[65] Indications are that the 1990 figures will be even higher.

There are a number of reasons for these changes. Environmental laws are being strengthened with tough new criminal penalties. Congress and state legislative bodies are passing new laws each year and amending old laws—a number of which lower standards of proof which inhibited criminal prosecution in the past. Congress, for example, created new felony sanctions in 1986 under the Comprehensive Environmental Response Compensation and Liability Act and again in 1987 under the Clean Water Act. New York was one of several states to increase criminal penalties for the violation of environmental laws when it passed its new environmental crimes act in 1986. Undoubtedly, this has encouraged federal and state prosecutors to move on these cases. There has also been some change in the attitudes of enforcement officials. Perhaps spurred-on by the recognition of the problem and increased public sensitivity to environmental concerns, more officials are opting for criminal prosecution. Our legal system including judges and prosecutors are becoming more well-versed in the intricacies of environmental offenses. Two things seem to be operating simulataneously: Growing awareness of the problem and growing refinement and familiarity with investigative and prosecutorial techniques. There is also evidence that prosecution and law enforcement officials so armed are stepping up their use of these criminal sanctions as a means of deterring environmental offenders.[66] The increase in imprisonment and fines has been brought about by the growing number of environmental laws that prescribe incarceration for conviction and stiff fines.

One major development is the change in environmental statutes which provide that criminal sanctions can be imposed for merely negligent, as opposed to intentional, violations. Prosecutors are beginning to move on this front and such a standard has the potential for bringing industry officials into the courtroom as defendants. The Clean Water Act and New York State's Environmental Crimes Act are examples of statutes that make corporate officers criminally liable for negligence. Under such statutes, officers may be found guilty based solely on their position of responsibility, without reference to any participation in or knowledge of the violation.[67] A few environmental statutes go even further and do away altogether with scienter. Here we are speaking about imposing the "strict liability" doctrine which we discussed earlier. The reader will recall that these crimes require no proof of criminal intent whatsoever. Examples of such "strict liability" laws include violations of the RCRA and certain hazardous waste crimes which have been adopted in such states as California, New Jersey, Pennsylvania, and New York.[68]

But there have been set-backs, too. In 1989, the proposed Environmental Crimes Act failed to be adopted by Congress. This ill-fated Act proposed significant increases in penalties for violating a number of federal environmental statutes. It also proposed adding the "knowing" and "reckless endangerment" provisions which are already part of the RCRA and the Clean Water Act to a broad range of federal environmental crimes. As a backlash to the Exxon Valdez oil spill, it would also have provided enhanced penalties for "negligently endangering life" or "causing environmental catastrophe." This would have further widened the opportunity for criminal and civil prosecutions. While environmental and conservation groups supported the bill, regulated industries such as the American Petroleum Institute and the Chemical Manufacturers Association called it "overkill" and argued against its adoption.[69]

Tougher laws are just part of the reason for the increase in criminal prosecutions. The federal government and some states are also developing new investigative and prosecution strategies. For example, some states are routinely evaluating nearly every civil enforcement proceeding for possible criminal violation and prosecution. Other efforts include developing prosecution specialists in environmental crimes to concentrate their attention on such violations and violators. These specialists are responsible for not only preparing the government's case when it goes to trial, they are also coordinating investigations, collecting evidence, and training invstigators in the legal intricacies of environmental cases. We have also seen that the Department of Justice has created a special Environmental Crimes Section to deal with these crimes. This Section now operates with 20 attorneys who are specialists in the legal intricacies of prosecuting environmental crimes. The EPA has increased the number of investigative personnel and created a National Enforcement Investigations Center with a special Office of Criminal Investigation.[70] The FBI has also agreed to investigate at least 30 cases each year upon the EPA's request.[71] This has generated investigations by the FBI in dozens of environmental cases each year and has made available this agency's investigative expertise, and technical and forensic laboratory resources. In New Jersey, a suggestion has been made by the governor to create a ''chronic environmental offender program'' which would be the target of the recently created special environmental prosecutor in that state.

There is also a growing willingness on the part of traditional enforcement agencies to get involved with investigating environmental crimes. In 1990, Congress passed new legislation which requires greater enforcement efforts and authorizes the creation of a National Enforcement Training Institute to provide comprehensive civil and criminal environmental enforcement training for federal, state, and local police and prosecution authorities. Increasingly, local police departments are also providing basic training to their personnel in recognizing certain forms of environmental crimes and what agencies to notify in case of suspected violations. Environmental crimes are also receiving the application of methods typically used to investigate and prosecute traditional crimes such as grand juries, electronic surveillance, undercover operatives and the use of informants.[72]

In several areas of the country, Environmental Crimes Coordinating Units have been established on a metropolitan or regional level. These have begun as a result of the recognition that federal, state, and, in a few cases, local governments must cooperate in the investigation, enforcement, and prosecution of environmental crime cases. It is being recognized that there is a particular need for better working arrangements between the federal authorities (e.g., the EPA, the FBI, and local U.S. Attorney's offices) and their counterpart agencies at the state levels such as environmental investigative units, local prosecutors and offices of State Attorneys General. The EPA is even enlisting public support for their efforts to locate criminal polluters by recently establishing a system of awards for people who report illegal pollution.

There has also been a refinement in the case processing decision-making process. For instance, the EPA in deciding whether to seek criminal prosecution considers such things as the existence of proof of the required criminal intent where necessary; the nature and seriousness of the offense; the deterrent effect of prosecution; the subject's history of compliance; and the relative efficacy of other available remedies.[73] Another consideration is the effect of the violation on the government's ability to regulate. The government's enforcement efforts depend to a large extent on voluntary reporting from the regulated industry. Violations that involve destruction or falsification of documents, or that otherwise threaten the integrity of the reporting system, provides the government with special incentives to prosecute.[74] Each year, the EPA publishes specific enforcement priorities. Bad faith reporting ranks high on these lists. Another priority category is the prosecution of those who attempt to dispose of hazardous substances without notifying the government or obtaining a permit. These are offenders who try to save the expense of compliance by not reporting at all. Both bad faith reporters and those who completely fail to report are being targeted by enforcement authorities, and are likely candidates for criminal prosecution.[75]

Of all the considerations involved in the decision to prosecute, the primary goal is one of deterrence. By imposing the threat of imprisonment it is anticipated that those contemplating the violation of environmental laws will think twice. Corporate officials may no longer view environmental compliance merely as a cost of doing business. Instead they must contend with the possibility of potential prison terms and substantial public relations considerations of a society growing increasingly restive about environmental pollution and those who pollute. F. Henry Habicht, former Assistant Attorney General in charge of the Justice Department's Lands and Natural Resources Division, notes that

> [the] Justice Department and the EPA strongly believe that members of the regulated community will be less likely to consider willful or calculated evasion of governmental standards when they know that discovery may lead to a prison term. It is no accident, therefore, that three times as many individuals have been prosecuted by the Environmental Crimes Section as corporate defendants. . . . It has been, and will continue to be, Justice Department policy to conduct environmental criminal investigations with an eye toward identifying, prosecuting and convicting the highest-ranking responsible corporate officials.[76]

Once a criminal proceeding is brought, however, the defendant is not immune from other types of enforcement activity. Under appropriate circumstances, parallel civil or administrative proceedings can be brought against the the same defendant. According to EPA procedural guidelines published in 1989, parallel proceedings may be brought in several different situations, but are used primarily when "there is an immediate risk to human life or health or a significant environmnetal hazard, [or] there exists a need for immediate action to stabilize a physical structure to prevent imminent deterioration which, unless addressed will result in immediate environmental harm."[77]

Changes in Federal Sentencing Law

Criminal prosecution has also been significantly bolstered and encouraged by some important changes in federal sentencing laws. At one time, federal prosecutors might have been discouraged to bring environmental cases before the federal courts only to see such defendants once convicted receive nothing more than probation or a suspended sentence by judges. The new Federal Sentencing Guidelines has changed old sentencing practices dramatically. Judges are now required to deal more harshly with offenders who are convicted of environmental offenses. The new guidelines which contain a separate category for environmental crimes replace the subjectivity of judges in the past with greater uniformity and removes the discretion judges have to mete out a slap on the wrist for environmental offenders.[78] A "scoring system" has been added based on such factors as "repetitive release of hazard substances" and the defendant's criminal history to arrive at a sentencing decision.[79]

Fines for violation of environmental laws have also increased. In addition to jail sentences, convicted defendants may also be required to pay substantial fines. The guidelines provide that the court "shall impose a fine in all cases as determined by the offense level." If, however, the judge finds that the offense involved financial gain to the defendant or financial loss to someone else, the judge under these circumstances may set the fine at twice the gain or loss, whichever is greater.

It should be noted that the Sentencing Guidelines were supplemented in 1989 with proposed guidelines which would apply specifically to organizations. A firm's penalty could increase if certain factors were present. Among other things, this would also take into account the role of upper-level management in the offense. If an officer or director aids and abets an offense, this is considered an aggravating circumstance which could increase the firm's liability.[80]

Transnational Criminality and the Environment

Discussion of environmental pollution and crime would be complete without a discussion of what may prove to be even a more serious problem and one which promises even greater difficulty to regulate. We can look at the problems we are having in the United States in developing effective laws to deal with controlling harmful environmental pollutants and magnify the problem at least a hundredfold when we apply it to the international scene.

What we have seen is that effective environmental efforts must incorporate at least several workable components:

1. required laws must be adopted;
2. effective compliance must be monitored to ensure that the intent of the laws are carried out; and
3. sufficient penalties must be imposed to make the laws work.

Although our batting average is improving, it is instructive that this has as yet to be accomplished in the United States let alone among the world community.

The first requirement is for effective laws to regulate the discharge of environmental pollutants. Transanational efforts in this area take the form of treaties and accords among nations. These may be bi-lateral agreements between two counties such as the United States and Canada, or they may be resolutions and accords between a number of nations sponsored by some world agency such as the United Nations.

Experience in this area has been a mixed-bag. On the one hand there have been a few successful efforts such as the Nordic Convention on the Protection of the Environment which operates among cooperating Scandinavian countries.[81] There have also been some limited successes among certain West European countries. For the most part, however, although industrialized nations are especially quick to subscribe to the idea that something must be done, translating this into effective action lags. Even the best of neighbors have found it difficult to cooperate. The United States and Canada are prime examples. Although these two countries have made important bi-lateral strides to deal with the pollution of the Great Lakes, their efforts in such other areas as U.S.-generated acid rain and the chemical toxicity of the lower Niagara River have stalled among swirling recriminations.

Self-interest plays an important role in any effort to deal with environmental problems—whether this be among industrialized nations or the Third World. Such an unlikely source as the novelist, Charles Dickens, points out the problem. In the 1800s, Dickens vainly attempted to arouse his fellow Englishmen to the evils of industrial growth uninhibited by governmental regulation. In his satirical novel, *Hard Times,* Dickens has his leading spokesman to the benefits of the industrial revolution explain to a visitor to industrial Coketown:

> First of all, you see our smoke. That's meat and drink to us. It's the healthiest thing in the world in all respects, and particularly for the lungs.[82]

Even industrialized nations contain social and regional groups that have not shared in the fruits of economic affluence. These groups and the elected officials depending on their support are especially wary of environmental controls which threaten to halt regional or local economic growth just at the time when they are about to share in its rewards.[83] Even in nations such as the United States and Canada regionalism in the presence of states and provinces—and the diversity of industrial and economic interests they contain—make the problem that much more difficult in terms of *effective* national and state policies let alone international accords.

The problem is even more pronounced in Third World countries. They correctly see that industrialization and economic development is the means to general economic improvement. Such nations are also without the resources to attract large and more technologically sophisticated pollution-free enterprise. They must fall back on what they can get. Efforts to impede this develoment are viewed as further efforts to keep them backward and to continue the polarization of the world into have and have-not nations. This is only one part of the problem of dealing with underdeveloped nations in a transnational policy of pollution control. Even if they wanted to cooperate, underdeveloped nations do not have the government structure that could effectively control environmental pollution.

For example, policy analysts studying environmental regulation efforts point out that long-range policy of environmental control require among other things: systems which are equipped with technical experts who can translate conditions of nature into comprehendable societal dangers; systems where such experts have political access; where economists are able and willing to convert physical data of pollution into economic costs; and where literacy and the media exist so that ordinary citizens can understand the hazards and mobilize around these newly defined dangers.[84] In underdeveloped countries, such conditions are often non-existent.

There is still another problem. National stability is recognized as a condition for foreign investment. If underdeveloped or third-world nations want capital to flow into their country, they must be seen as a stable haven for investors. This stability can be imposed by a ruling clique or dictator who are not receptive to the "costs" of pollution control. Such individuals or groups may well view this as an impediment to industrial development, or worse, make their country's growing industrialization and the opportunity it provides, less potentially lucrative to them personally.

Finally, in dealing with the development of effective policies of world-wide pollution abatement which must necessarily involve the underdeveloped nations, there is another hurdle. Capital investment often flows into these countries from trans-global corporations in industrialized nations who expressly seek out investment opportunities in locales where regulations are lax or non-existent. This affords them the opportunity to escape the environmental controls and the associated costs in their parent countries. San Paulo, Brazil and Mexico City are prime examples. Although this is beginning to change, these countries have adopted a laissez-faire approach to industrial regulation in an attempt to attract industry. They have become havens for foreign investment and transglobal firms seeking to escape stringent regulations and production cost advantages. A by-product of this has been a dangerous increase in levels of industrial pollution and associated health problems in these cities. World health groups point out that levels of pollution in these two cities have reached a crisis stage.[85]

Prosecuting International Polluters

Without effective and cooperative regulations how can the problem be policed through monitoring and enforcement efforts? The answer is it simply cannot. Even with treaties and agreements among nations an effective tribunal does not exist to enforce international law. Although the International Court of Justice exists in the Hague to settle disputes of international law, it has no jurisdiction over criminal matters and its effectiveness depends upon mutual agreement . So much so in fact, that governments must agree to even submit a case to this body for adjudication. And for this tribunal to act in the first place, it must have an established body of international law to apply. Although it can theoretically enforce treaties and accords among nations, the legal underpinnings of an effective international or transnational body of laws is simply non-existent at this time.

Such questions as criminal versus civil sanctions, penalties, burden of proof, prosecuting authority and other such basic legal questions must be resolved. This does not even take into consideration such mundane matters as place of incarceration should criminal sanctions and imprisonment be an alternative or who pays for such adjudication and incarcerative costs. If, as the General Accounting Office and the Office of Technology Assessment estimate, in the United States alone only a tiny fraction of one type of polluting activity (toxic waste dumps) is known, what does this say about the magnitude of the problem and how it can be dealt with on a national let alone international basis?

Conclusion

As the issue of environmental pollution and the consequences of toxic poisoning continue to be of prime concern in the years ahead, the criminal law and the criminal justice system will increasing be called upon to play an ever larger role in this problem. We are just beginning to understand the complexities of involving our criminal-legal system in this effort. Experience is demonstrating that it is proving to be a very complicated area of criminal law that is fast becoming the province of legal specialists both for the prosecution and the defense. Still, we cannot escape the recognition that the criminal justice system has a role of growing importance in dealing with environmental pollution. The years that lie before us may well see the issue of environmental pollution as important a criminal issue as traditional forms of criminal activity are today.

But we must approach the problem cautiously and with a degree of flexibility. We are beginning to realize that conventional anti-crime efforts when directed at environmental polluters may require different forms of response. America's policymakers need to experiment with different forms of regulatory controls, examine the effects of various sanctions as means of deterrence, and tailor regulatory mechanisms and statutes so that prosecution is possible while at the same time observing and applying fundamental rights of due process and equal protection. Our statutory and enforcement efforts must carefully balance these considerations. Like other unconventional crimes discussed in this book, there is a critical and immediate need to re-think carefully many aspects of these type offenses and offenders. It promises to be an interesting and complicated challenge for our lawmakers, the criminal justice system, and those given the responsibility to enforce our growing environmental laws.

NOTES

[1]Mazmanian, Daniel and Morell, David. "The Elusive Pursuit of Toxics Management," *The Public Interest,* Vol. 90 (Winter 1988), p. 82.

[2]Ibid.

[3]"Americans Favor Tough Environmental Laws," *The Los Angeles Times* (November 12, 1989), p. 3, col. 1.

[4]For example, see Clinard, Marshall B. *Corporate Ethics and Crime* (Beverly Hills, Ca.: Sage Publications 1983).

[5]Harris, Christoper, Cavanaugh, Patrick O. and Zisk, Robert. "Criminal Liability for Violations of Federal Hazardous Waste Law: The Knowledge of Corporations and their Executives," WAKE FOREST LAW REVIEW, Vol. 23 (1988), pp. 203–36.

[6]Clinard, *Corporate Ethics, op cit.,* p. 10.

[7]Clinard, Marshall B. and Yeager, Paul C. *Corporate Crime* (New York: Free Press, 1980), p. 124.

[8]McMurry, Robert and Ramsey, Stephen D. "Environmental Crime: The Use of Criminal Sanctions in Enforcing Environmental Laws," LOYOLA (LOS ANGELES) LAW REVIEW, Vol. 19 (June 1986), pp. 1133–169.

[9]Chestman, Daniel M. "The Turmoil Among Environmental Regulators," *Environmental Reporter Newsletter,* Vol. 3, No. 4 (June, 1981), p. 3.

[10]See Allan, Richard H. "Criminal Sanctions Under Federal and State Environmental Statutes," ECOLOGY LAW QUARTERLY, Vol. 14, No. 1 (1987), pp. 117–79.

[11]Harris, C., Cavanaugh, P. O. and Zisk, R. L. "Criminal Liability for Violation of Federal Hazardous Waste Law: The Knowledge of Corporations and their Executives," WAKE FOREST LAW REVIEW, Vol. 23, 1988, p. 207.

[12]*Environmental Reported,* Vol. 20, No. 10 (July 7, 1989), p. 522.

[13]Mustokoff, Michael M. *Hazardous Waste Violations: A Guide to Their Detection, Investigation, and Prosecution* (Washington, D.C.: U.S. Department of Justice, February 1981), p. 6.

[14]Ibid., p. 6.

[15]Starr, Judson W. "Countering Environmental Crimes," BOSTON COLLEGE ENVIRONMENTAL AFFAIRS LAW REVIEW, Vol. 13, No. 3 (1986), pp. 379–96.

[16]Ibid., p. 382.

[17]These are Clean Air Act, Federal Water Pollution Control Act, Rivers and Harbors Act of 1899, Resource Conservation and Recovery Act, Toxic Substances Control Act, Federal Insecticide, Fungicide, and Rodentcide Act, and the Comprehensive Environmental Response Compensation and Liability Act (i.e., the so-called "Superfund").

[18]For the complexities of this law and subsequent amendments see 42 U.S.C. secs. 7401–7642.

[19]Pub. L. 92-500, 86 Stat: 816.

[20]42 U.S.C. 6901 *et seq.*

[21]7 U.S.C. sec. 136–136y.

[22]33 U.S.C. sec. 401 et seq.

[23]42 U.S.C. 9601 et seq.

[24]15 U.S.C. sec. 2601–2629.

[25]For example, see Kuruc, Michael. "Putting Polluters in Jail: Imposing Criminal Sanctions on Corporate Defendants Under Environmental Statutes," LAND AND WATER REVIEW, Vol. 20, No. 1 (1985), pp. 93–108; Doerr, Barbara H. "Prosecuting Corporate Polluters: The Sparing Use of Criminal Sanctions," UNIVERSITY OF DETROIT LAW REVIEW, Vol. 62 (Summer 1985), pp. 659–76; and Milne, Robert A. "The Mens Rea Requirements for the Federal Environmental Statues: Strict Criminal Liability in Substance but Not Form," BUFFALO LAW REVIEW, Vol. 37, No. 1 (Winter 1988–1989).

[26]Seymour, John F. "Civil and Criminal Liability of Corporate Officers Under Federal Environmental Law," *Environmental Reporter,* Vol. 20, No. 6 (Washington, D.C.: BNA Inc., June 9, 1989), p. 337.

[27]Riesel, Daniel. "Criminal Prosecution and the Regulation of the Environment," paper presented at the American Law Institute—American Bar Association special symposium on environmental law (Washington, D.C.: February 14–16, 1991) at pp. 411–12.

[28]National Association of Attorneys General, State Attorneys General Guide to Environmental Law (Washington, D.C.: 1990), p. 174.

[29]This description is adopted from the testimony of Keith Welks, Chief Counsel, Pennsylvania Department of Environmental Resources. Hearing before the Subcommittee on Criminal Justice of the Committee on the Judiciary, U.S. House of Representatives on the Environmental Crimes Act of 1989, December 12, 1989.

[30]Radimore, James P. "The Investigative Requirements of Environmental Offenses," *Water Resources Management Newsletter,* No. 6 (June 1988), p. 3.

[31]It should be noted that some states have taken a very aggressive posture toward enforcing the criminal provisions of their state environmental laws. New York, for example, reviews every civil infraction of environmental law for possible criminal involvement and subsequent prosecution. Many states however are not this aggressive.

[32]"Congress Looks with Concern at State Anti-Pollution Efforts," *The Washington Post* (November 25, 1989), p. A-5.

[33]At common law corporations could not commit crimes because the corporation was *incorporeal* (i.e., it could not possess criminal intent). These have been discarded in favor of more workable approaches, such as imputed or vicarious corporate liability for the actions of its agents, employees and officers. See *New York Central and Hudson River Railroad v. United States,* 212 U.S. 481 (1909); *United States v. Carter,* 311 F.2d 934 (6th Cir.); *Apex Oil Co. v. United States,* 530 F.2d 1291 (8th Cir.), 1976.

[34]*United States v. Park,* 421 U.S. 658 (1975).

[35]Mustokoff, *op cit.,* pp. 53–54.

[36]Milne, *op cit.,* pp. 312–13.

[37]For example, see Block, Alan A. "Crime in the Waste Oil Industry," *Deviant Behavior,* Vol. 9, No. 2 (1988) pp. 113–29; Allan, Richard H. "Criminal Sanctions Under Federal and State Environmental Statutes, ECOLOGY LAW QUARTERLY, Vol. 14, No. 1, 1987, pp. 117–79; and McMurry and Ramsey, *op cit.*

[38]U.S. House of Representatives, *Organized Crime and Hazardous Waste Disposal* (Washington, D.C.: U.S. Government Printing Office, 1983); United States General Accounting Office, Enforcement of Hazardous Waste and Toxic Substance Laws (Washington, D.C.: U.S. Government Printing Office, 1985).

[39]McMurry, Robert and Ramsey, Stephen D. "Environmental Crime: The Use of Criminal Sanctions in Enforcing Environmental Laws," LOYOLA (LOS ANGELES) LAW REVIEW, Vol. 19 (June 1986), pp. 1133–169; and Milne, *op cit.*

[40]Wilson, John D. "Re-thinking Penalties for Environmental Offenders: A View of the Law Reform Commission of Canada's Sentencing in Environmental Cases," MCGILL LAW JOURNAL, Vol. 31 (1986) p. 315–32.

[41]Wilmoth, Robert D. "Re-thinking the Imposition of Fines in Environmental Cases," HARVARD ENVIRONMENTAL LAW JOURNAL, Vol. 6, No. 2 (1987), pp. 57–81.

[42]Ibid., p. 321.

[43]This discussion is adopted with slight modification from Wilson, John D. "Re-thinking Penalties for Corporate Environmental Offenders: A View of the Reform Commission of Canada's Sentencing in Environmental Crimes," MCGILL LAW JOURNAL, Vol. 31 (1986), pp. 322–23.

[44]Ibid., pp. 325–30.

[45]Szasz, Andrew. "Corporations, Organized Crime and the Disposal of Hazardous Waste: An Ex-

amination of the Making of a Criminogenic Regulatory Sturcture,'' CRIMINOLOGY, Vol. 24, No. 1 (1986), pp. 1–26.

[46]Specifically, sec. 3008(d).

[47]The acts covered such forbidden things as: knowingly transporting hazardous waste to a facility which does not have a permit; knowingly treating, storing or disposing of hazardous waste without a required permit; or knowingly omitting material information from a permit application. See 42 USC sec. 6928 (f)(6).

[48]For a good discussion of this issue as it relates to the prosecution of cases, see Harris, C., Cavanaugh, P. O. and Zisk, R. L. ''Criminal Liability for Violations of Federal Hazardous Waste Law: The ''Knowledge'' of Corporations and their Executives,'' WAKE FOREST LAW REVIEW, Vol. 23, No. 2 (1988) pp. 203–36.

[49]*United States v. Protex Industries, Inc.*, No.87-CR-115 (D.C. Colo. Mar. 4, 1987).

[50]*United States v. Tumin* (East. Dist. of N.Y.) April 13, 1988.

[51]Nittoly, Paul G. ''Current Trends in the Prosecution of Environmental Offenses,'' TOXICS LAW REPORTER (Washington: Bureau of National Affairs, January 25, 1989), p. 1033.

[52]Scarpitti, Frank R. and Block, Alan A. ''America's Toxic Waste Racket: Dimensions of the Environmental Crisis,'' in Bynum, Timothy S. (ed.) *Organized Crime in America: Concepts and Controversies* (Monsey, NY: Criminal Justice Press, 1987), p. 118.

[53]Szasz, *op cit.*, p. 2.

[54]New York State Senate, *An Investigation into Illegal Hazardous Waste Disposal on Long Island: An Interim Report* (Albany: February 25, 1981); McKenna, J.B. ''Organized Crime in the Toxic Waste Disposal Industry,'' U.S. Senate Permanent Subcommittee on Investigations, (Washington: U.S. Government Printing Office, 1983).

[55]U.S. House of Representatives, *op cit.*, p. 21.

[56]U.S. Senate, Permanent Subcommittee on Investigations, ''Staff Summary, State Attorneys' General Hazardous Waste Survey,'' (Washington: U.S. Government Printing Office, 1984).

[57]Ibid., p. 22.

[58]Ibid., p. 22.

[59]Ibid., p. 70.

[60]Szasz, *op cit.*, p. 9.

[61]House of Representatives, *op cit.*, p. 124.

[62]General Accounting Office, pp. 25–31.

[63]House of Representatives, *op cit.*, pp. 144–46; Szasz, p. 11.

[64]Environmental Protection Agency—Office of Enforcement and Compliance Monitoring, *Environmental Protection Agency Enforcement Accomplishments Report—FY 1989* (Washington: U.S. Government Printing Office, 1990), p. 16.

[65]Memorandum titled, "Statistics FY-83 Through FY-90" from P. Hutchins to Joseph G. Block, Chief Environmental Crimes Section, U.S. Department of Justice (January 26, 1990).

[66]Kafin, Robert J. and Port, Gail. "Criminal Sanctions Lead to Higher Fines and Jail," THE NATIONAL LAW JOURNAL, Vol. 12, No. 46 (July 23, 1990), p. 20.

[67]For example, see *United States v. A.C. Lawrence Leather Co.*, Crim. No. 82-L-07-L (Dist. New Hampshire 1982) which found the firm's president and vice-president guilty under the Clean Water Act because they should have known of the violations.

[68]Kafin and Port, *op cit.*, p. 20.

[69]For an insight into this proposed legislation and the testimony which surrounded it, see Environmental Crimes Act-Hearing before the Subcommittee on Criminal Justice of the Committee on the Judiciary, House of Representatives, December 12, 1989. (Washington: USGPO) 1990.

[70]Matulewich, Vincent A. "Environmental Crimes Prosecution: A Law Enforcement Partnership," *FBI Law Enforcement Bulletin* (April 1991), p. 23.

[71]Memorandum of Understanding Between the EPA and the FBI, cited in Habicht, F. Henry. "The Federal Perspective on Environmental Criminal Enforcement: How to Remain on the Civil Side," ENVIRONMENTAL LAW REPORTER, Vol. 17 (December 1987) pp. 10478–479.

[72]See, for example, Maioli, Thomas M. and Staub, Michael A. "The Utilization of Traditional Investigative Methods in the Investigation of Hazard Waste Crimes," NATIONAL ENVIRONMENTAL ENFORCEMENT JOURNAL, Vol. 4 (October 1988).

[73]Memorandum from Robert A. Perry, Associate Administer of the EPA, to Regional Counsels, entitled "Criminal Enforcement Priorities for the Environmental Protection Agency," (April 12, 1982).

[74]Kafin and Port, p. 20.

[75]Ibid., pp. 20–21.

[76]Habicht, *The Federal Perspective, op cit.*, p. 10480.

[77]Environmental Protection Agency-Office of Criminal Enforcement Policy Compendium, *Guidelines on Investigative Procedures for Parallel Proceedings* (n.d.) at p. 11.

[78]U.S. Sentencing Commission Guidelines Manual, Sec. 2Q1.1 *et seq.* (November 1989). Also see Starr, Judson W. and Kelly, Thomas J. Jr. "Environmental Crimes and the Sentencing Guidelines: The Time has Come . . . and it is Hard Time," ENVIRONMENTAL LAW REPORTER, Vol. 20 (March 1990).

[79]Kafin and Port, *op cit.*, p. 21.

[80]54 Federal Register 8C2.1(d)(2)(D), at 47059 (November 8, 1989).

[81]These countries include Denmark, Finland, Iceland, Norway and Sweden. See Broms, Bengt. "The Nordic Convention on the Protection of the Environment," in Flinterman, C., Kwiatkowska, B. and Lammers, J.G. (eds.) *Transboundary Air Pollution* (Boston: Martinus Nijhoff Publishers, 1986), pp. 141–52.

[82]Charles Dickens, *Hard Times* (New York: E.P. Dutton, 1907), pp. 112–13.

[83]Enloe, Cynthia H. *The Politics of Pollution in a Comparative Perspective* (New York: David McKay, 1975), pp. 320–21.

[84]Ibid., p. 321.

[85]Ibid., p. 137.

Index

C

J

K

L

M

N

O

S

T

U

V

W

X

Y

Z